Gellerman's International
REED ORGAN ATLAS

Gellerman's International
REED ORGAN ATLAS

Second Edition

Robert R. Gellerman

Some account of the Various
Manufacturers of Reed Organs
of Divers Kinds including

SERAPHINES, MELODEONS, HARMONIUMS, CABINET ORGANS,
PARLOR ORGANS, COTTAGE ORGANS, ORGUES-EXPRESSIFS,
ORGUE-MELODIONS, ORGANETTES, and PLAYER ORGANS

With such information about them as shall convey a Fair idea of
their Nature and the period in which each was Active, and
including a Geographical Index.

Essex, Connecticut

VESTAL PRESS, Inc.
An imprint of The Globe Pequot Publishing Group, Inc.
64 South Main Street
Essex, CT 06426
www.globepequot.com

Copyright © 1998 by Vestal Press, Inc.

Cover credit: The Mason and Hamlin Parlor Model organ, 1895.

All rights reserved. No part of this book may be reproduced in any form or by any electronic or mechanical means, including information storage and retrieval systems, without written permission from the publisher, except by a reviewer who may quote passages in a review.

British Library Cataloguing in Publication Information Available

Library of Congress Cataloging-in-Publication Data

Gellerman, Robert F., 1928–
   [International reed organ atlas]
   Gellerman's international reed organ atlas/ Robert R. [I.e. F.] Gellerman. —2nd ed.
     p.   cm.
   Includes bibliographical references and index.
   ISBN 1-879511-34-7
   1. Reed organ builders. I. Title.
ML597.G46   1998
786.5'519—dc21   97-51267

ISBN 978-1-879511-34-7 (cloth)

This is for David, Eileen,
Matthew, Michael,
Daniel and Mary Kate.

CONTENTS

List of Abbreviations ix

Preface xi

Alphabetical Listing 1

Doubtful Listings 279

Geographical Index 283

Contributors 307

Bibliography 309

Photographic Credits 315

ABBREVIATIONS

In order to save space, the names of the states of the United States are abbreviated as follows:

AL	Alabama		MO	Missouri
AK	Alaska		MT	Montana
AZ	Arizona		NE	Nebraska
AR	Arkansas		NV	Nevada
CA	California		NH	New Hampshire
CO	Colorado		NJ	New Jersey
CT	Connecticut		NM	New Mexico
DE	Delaware		NY	New York
DC	District of Columbia		NC	North Carolina
FL	Florida		ND	North Dakota
GA	Georgia		OH	Ohio
HI	Hawaii		OK	Oklahoma
ID	Idaho		OR	Oregon
IL	Illinois		PA	Pennsylvania
IN	Indiana		RI	Rhode Island
IA	Iowa		SC	South Carolina
KS	Kansas		SD	South Dakota
KY	Kentucky		TN	Tennessee
LA	Louisiana		TX	Texas
ME	Maine		UT	Utah
MD	Maryland		VT	Vermont
MA	Massachusetts		VA	Virginia
MI	Michigan		WA	Washington
MN	Minnesota		WI	Wisconsin
MS	Mississippi		WY	Wyoming

PREFACE

This second edition of *Gellerman's International Reed Organ Atlas* continues the objective of the first edition in presenting a complete listing of all reed organ manufacturers in the world, from the beginnings of the instrument in the early nineteenth century to the present. A brief history of each maker is included wherever information is available, with particular emphasis on data that will help establish the identity and age of the instruments. The length of the entries bears no particular relationship to the importance of the makers, but rather reflects the amount of information available.

In addition to the actual manufacturers of instruments, suppliers of components and materials have been included to give a more complete view of the industry. In some cases manufacturers supplied complete instruments to dealers with the dealer's name or "stencil" applied to the instrument. These dealers frequently represented themselves as manufacturers, and it is often difficult to determine if they did in fact make their own instruments. Since many of these organs still exist, the names are included here to help in identification.

The first edition of the *Atlas* appeared in 1985, inspired by *Michel's Organ Atlas*, published in 1969 by the late N.E. Michel. Since then hundreds of additional names and thousands of historical facts have come to light. Researchers in many countries have have spent countless hours tracking down their domestic manufacturers and have generously given permission to publish their material. In particular I would like to acknowledge the work of Pam Fluke, who has regularly added new entries and additions to existing ones, and has reviewed each of the approximately twenty computer printouts of the *Atlas* since 1985. Arthur W.J.G. Ord-Hume's *Harmonium*, published in 1986 includes an index of hundreds of reed organ makers throughout the world. Nelson Lee in Norway, Rey Akai in Japan and Michel Dieterlen in France have provided the nearly definitive data on reed organ makers in those countries. (I say *nearly* in the hope that more information is yet to be found.) The recently published *Das Harmonium in Deutschland* is the work of a team of researchers headed by Christian Ahrens and Gregor Klinke, and including Sven Dierke, Sigrid Eul, Birgit Goede, Christiane Rieche, Ira Schulze-Ardey and Sandra Zydek. This scholarly work is the result of an exhaustive search of public and private archives throughout Germany. Christiane Rieche has been especially helpful in contributing to and reviewing the material in the *Atlas* relating to Germany.

To facilitate further research, the geographical index has been expanded to include the names of the cities where reed organ manufacturers were located. Hundreds of individuals have provided additional names and data for the *Atlas*. So much of this work is the result of these contributions that I have included a list of contributors as an appendix. Many of the original sources used in compiling this work contain errors and some have conflicting information. I have made every effort to minimize these problems, consulting as many sources as possible, but it is frequently a matter of judgement as to which version of a name or which date is correct. Continuing research has shown that a few of the names of reed organ makers in the first edition or in other publications were in error, or that their validity could not be independently established. These names are included in the "doubtful listings" to make it clear that they have not been overlooked.

This edition is the result of a continuous process over the years of adding and correcting. Readers who discover errors in this work or who find additional information are invited to send them to the author so that future editions may be more nearly complete and correct.

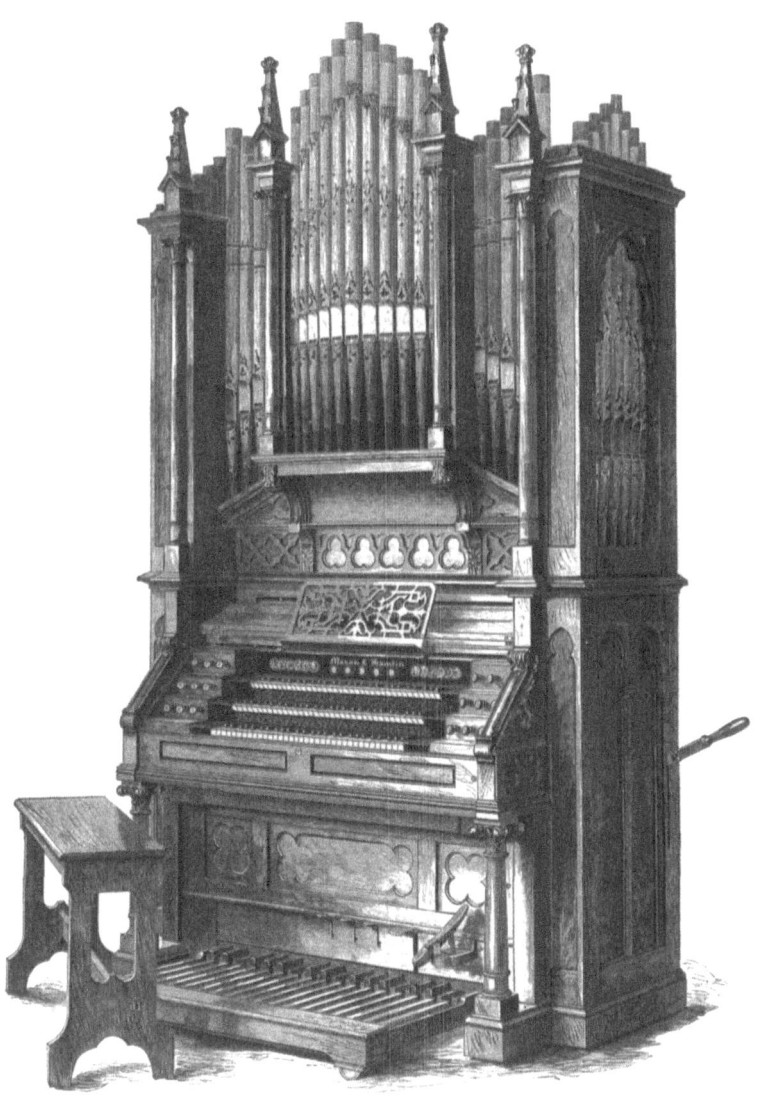

Mason & Hamlin Style 1202, three-manual and pedal Liszt organ, 1895.

A

AAGESEN, N.O.; Trondheim, Norway. Harmonium maker.

ABBEY FRÈRES, E. & J.; 79 boulevard du Montparnasse, Paris; factory at 12 rue de la Chancellerie, Versailles, France, 1896, 1903. Established 1828. Joseph and Eugène Abbey, proprietors. In 1909 shown as *J. Abbey*.

ABBOT & SMITH. (Name only, no further information available.)

ABEILLE, LÉON; (*Meritan & Cie.*), 125 rue Thomas, Marseille, France in 1903. Established 1888.

ABEL & SHERMAN; Milwaukee, WI. Established 1865. Melodeon maker.

ABLER, see *Odenbrett, Abler & Co.*

ACADIA ORGAN CO.; Bridgetown, Nova Scotia, 1881-1886. John Bath Reed, a furniture manufacturer, built a frame building and started an organ factory in 1881. By the next year it was run by J.P. Rice and Arthur E. Sulis, then by Sulis alone. The business later occupied the old St. James Church building, which was eventually demolished in 1973.

ACHARI, NALLATHANU, SONS; Panagudi 627109, Tirunelveli District, India. Currently manufacturing Indian table harmoniums.

ACME organ, see *Alleger & Sons*.

ADAMS, WM.; 4 Hockley Hill, Birmingham, England, 1878-1893. Organ and harmonium maker.

ADAMSON, A.; showed a harmonium teaching device at the Musical and Ecclesiastical Exhibition in London, 1892.

ADAMSON, G.F.; steam works at 1 Nisbet Place, High Street, Homerton, London. Established 1880, extant 1900. Made keyboards for harmoniums and organs.

ADLER ORGAN CO.; Chestnut & NW Corner 29th St., Louisville, KY. Established in 1903 by C.L. Adler, also shown as the *Adler Manufacturing Co., Adler Music Co.*, and the *Beckwith Organ Co.* Adler later acquired the *Geo. P. Bent Co., Inc.*, makers of the Crown organ. Adler was apparently controlled by *Sears, Roebuck & Co.*, (qv). Adler made the Adler, Loreto, Beckwith and Crown organs. Serial numbers: 1910—104666, 1911—121292, 1914—144773.

ÆOLIAN CO., THE; Meriden, CT., 18 W. 23rd St., New York, NY. Established 1891, later *Æolian Organ and Music Co.* See *Mechanical Orguinette Co.*

AEOLICON, melodeon with strings invented by Rufus Nutting and made by *Hovey & Bachelder.*

AEOLUS harmonium, see *Deutsch-Amerikanische Orgel Harmonium Fabrik R. Metzner.*

AGGIO, FRATELLI; Via Saccarelli, Turin, Italy, 1909. Harmonium makers. Probably the same as *Luigi & Cesare Aggio* listed in Rivoli, Italy in 1930.

AHLBORN & STEINBACH; Einsteinstr. 2, Heimerdingen b. Stuttgart, Germany. Active in the 1950s.

AHON, JUSSI, JA KUSTAA NIEMEN HARMOONITEHDAS; Lapua, Finland. Founded in 1879 by Jussi Aho and Kustaa Niemi.

AJELLO, GIULIANO, & SONS LTD.; in 1878 at 11 Park St., Camden Town, London NW; in 1885 at 104 Park St., Camden Town and 28 Bishop's Road, Bayswater, London. By 1906 there is no mention of the Bishop's Road address. Discontinued organ production before 1921.

ÅKERMANS & LUNDS ORGELFABRIK AKTIEBOLAGET; Sibyllegatan 10, Stockholm, Sweden, 1860. Harmonium maker.

AKTIEBOLAGET J.P. NYSTRÖM'S ORGEL- & PIANO FABRIK, see *J.P. Nyström.*

ALBAPHON, see *A.J. Spencer.*

ALBERDI; Paseo de Gracia 126, Barcelona, Spain. Active 1890-1950. Antonio Alberdi Aguirresabal, proprietor. Made numerous models from a four-octave folding organ to a five-octave instrument with 4½ sets of reeds and 15 stops, all with transposing keyboards.

ALBERTSEN, see *Hinners & Albertsen.*

ALBOUY; Vienna, Austria. Organized the *Schiedmayer* workshops in Stuttgart, Germany ca. 1853. Showed a harmonium at the Vienna Exhibition in 1873.

ALBRECHT, see *Harmoniumbau Albrecht.*

ALDEN, A.O.; Springfield, MA in 1889. Built four enharmonic instruments for *J.P. White* in the early 1880s. Later built reed organs under his own name.

ALEXANDER ORGAN CO.; Chicago, IL; *W.W. Kimball* was sole agent for Alexander in 1862. See *Waterloo Organ Co.*

ALEXANDRE ET FILS; later *Alexandre Père et Fils.* Offices and sales rooms at 10 boulevard de Bonne-Nouvelle, Paris 1829-1851; 39 rue Meslay, 106 rue Richelieu in 1883, rue Victor Hugo and 81 rue Lafayette, Paris 1903. Factory at rue Victor Hugo in Ivry-sur-Seine, France in 1860. The firm was still operated by its successors, G. Fortin, as late as 1939 at the 81 rue Lafayette address. Founder: Jacob Alexandre (1804-1876).

DEPOT
OF THE
ALEXANDRE ORGAN,
203 Broadway, New York.

SOLE MEDAL OF HONOR AT THE UNIVERSAL EXHIBITION OF 1855.

The excellence of the various instruments adapted to **Churches, Chapels, Schools,** and **Drawing-rooms,** has been vouched for by the Testimonials of all the great professors in Europe and America.

His son Édouard died in 1888. Listed as a Société in 1864. Introduced the Orgue-Mélodium in 1844, a copy of *Debain*'s Harmonium made under license, and received a bronze medal at the Paris Exposition. Made a wide variety of reed organ types including portable, one- two- and three-manual organs with and without pedal bass, a combination reed organ and piano, a combination reed and pipe organ, and the Orgue Américain with a suction bellows. Alexandre bought the rights to the percussion action invented by Martin de Provins. The factory had 300 employees in 1860, 400 in 1872. Factory capacity 1,000 organs per month in 1878. By 1901 Alexander had produced 131,123 instruments. The Alexandre name continued in use after 1907 by Fortin. Many of the other builders started with Alexandre such as *Trayser, Christophe & Etienne*. Serial numbers: 1851—855, 1857—15213, 1859—19391, 1866—50256, 1867—55488, 1875—77913, 1901—131123.

ALIBONSSY, P.; Verdun, France. Made harmoniums with transposers.
ALLEGER, H.W., & CO.; Washington, NJ. Hiram W. Alleger made reed organs under his own name 1870-1875 and also in partnership with Charles P. Bowlby and Ed Plotts under the names *Alleger, Bowlby & Plotts*, (Gold Medal Organ), and as *Alleger, Bowlby & Co.* 1876-1880; again as *Alleger & Sons*, (Acme Organ), beginning in 1880. H.W. Alleger also owned the *Star Parlor Organ Co.* Listed as *H.W. Alleger & Co.* 1885 and 1899, with a factory capacity of 2,000 organs per year, of which 60% were exported. See *Warren Organ Co.* Serial numbers: 1881—4100, 1883—5900, 1884—7640, 1885—7000.

ALLEN, THOMAS R.; 180 E. Washington St., Syracuse, NY in 1861. Melodeon manufacturer.
ALLEN, WM. J.; piano and harmonium manufacturer and dealer. In 1891 located at 8 Bread St., Wokingham, Berkshire, England; in 1895 at 6 Rose St., Wokingham.
ALLEN & JEWETT, see *Jewett & Co.*
ALLETTI, CARLO; Monza, Italy. Organ and harmonium maker, 1883.
ALLEY, JOSEPH (1804-1880); Newburyport, MA. Built at least one reed organ in addition to the "euharmonic" organ built for *H.W. Poole* (qv). Alley and Poole were awarded U.S. Patent No. 6565 on July 3, 1849.
ALLIN, OTTO B.; 65 Kobmagerg, Copenhagen, Denmark. Harmonium maker.
ALLISON, ARTHUR, & CO.; 108-110 Wardour St., London in 1873, also at Apollo Works, Leighton Road, Kentish Town. By 1878 located at 40 Great Marlborough St. The Apollo Works was then used exclusively as a piano factory, reed organs being built at the steam works at 10 Charlton Road, Kings Road, London. Established 1840. Piano, harmonium and American organ manufacturer. Discontinued organ production before 1921.
ALLMENDINGER PIANO & ORGAN CO.; Ann Arbor, MI. David Frederick Allmendinger (1851-1916) learned cabinet making starting in 1866 at Thomas Rauschenberger's shop, then began working for *G.F. Gaerttner & Co.* in 1868 where he learned pipe and reed organ building. He married Marie, daughter of G.F. Gaerttner, in 1871 and bought the Gaerttner business that same year. Incorporated in 1888 as *Ann Arbor Organ Co.* (qv). Manufactured reed organs, pianos and a few pipe organs. Serial numbers:

1874—1000	1888—2450	1901—3230
1877—1200	1890—2600	1904—3310
1880—1400	1894—2670	1907—3420
1884—2100	1897—2840	1913—3650
1886—2300	1900—3100	

ALM, N.O.; Boden, Sweden in 1903; established 1869. Harmoniums were made by others for sale under his name.
ALMQUIST, see *Östlind & Almquist*.
ALVAH; Instrument seen at auction, probably of U.S. origin.
AMELOTTI, CARLO; Alessandria, Italy in 1883.
AMERICAN AUTOMATIC ORGAN CO., THE; 100 Milk St. 1883, 1884; office and warerooms at 164 High St., Fort Hill Square, Boston, MA. G.W. Turner, gen. mgr.; Henry Sawyer, president; John V. Spalding,

sec.-treas.; O.H. Arno, supt. Later became *Automatic Organ Co.* Organette maker, see *Massachusetts Organ Co.*
AMERICAN ORGAN & PIANO CO.; 41-43 Maiden Lane, New York, NY, 1886. Sold direct to consumers.
AMERICAN ORGAN CO.; Garry-en-Zonen, Westhavn 45, Gouda, Netherlands. Made suction organs, exact copies of American organs.
AMES, GEORGE A.; Norway, ME; manufacturer of piano and melodeon keys, 1861.
ANDERSEN, VELJEKSET; (Andersen Brothers), also *Broder Anderssens Orgelfabrik*, Pännäinen, Finland.
ANDERSSONS, K.A., ORGELFABRIK; Kammakaregatan 27, Stockholm, Sweden 1903; Holländaregaten 11, Stockholm in 1911. Established in Linköping in 1875, moved to Stockholm in 1885.
ANDREASSEN, KARL; Torsken, Norway, (1871-1950). Made a total of twelve harmoniums ca. 1900-1950.
ANDRESEN, JOHANNES P., & CO.; Ringkøbing, Denmark established 1891, in business at least until 1924. Joh. P. Andresen, C. Gravesen & L.C. Tang, proprietors in 1903.
ANDRESEN, P., & CO.; Langesgade 10, Aalborg, Denmark 1913.
ANDREWS, A.H., & CO.; Chicago, IL.
ANDREWS, ALVINZA; Waterville, NY 1834, Utica, NY 1854. Made reed and pipe organs in partnership with John Gale Marklove.
ANDREWS, C.W. & F.M.; Picton, Ontario, 1857. Melodeon makers.
ANDREWS, W.F.; Biddeford, ME.
ANDRUS BROTHERS; 135 Dundas St., manufactory in King St., London, Ontario, 1859-1874, also in Bloomington, IL in 1871. Founded by E.B. Andrus, it was sold in 1874 to Copwell and Bradford, who retained the Andrus name. It continued in operation until at least 1881.
ANGELUS player, see *Wilcox & White*.
ANGSTER, JOSEF, & SOHN; Mariengasse 35, Pecs, Hungary in 1903; established 1867.
ANNAPOLIS ORGAN CO.; Annapolis Royal, Nova Scotia, 1880, 1882.
ANN ARBOR ORGAN CO.; Ann Arbor, MI; incorporated 1888, Frederick Schmidt, president; M. Seaboldt, vice-president, D.F. Allmendinger, superintendent. Also shown as *Ann Arbor Organ Works*. Successor to *Allmendinger Piano & Organ Co*. About 1902 purchased the trademark, business and patents of *The Story & Clark Organ Co.* In receivership in 1910, reorganized as the Ann Arbor Piano Co. in 1913 but finally went out of business in 1916. Discontinued reed organ production about 1913. See Allmendinger for serial numbers.

The Ann Arbor Organ Co. factory before 1888.

ANNEESSENS & FILS, CHARLES; rue du Nord, Halluin, Belgium; Menin, Belgium in 1903; pipe organ and harmonium maker. Established in 1865 by Charles Anneessens (1835-1903) and his sons Paul, Oscar and Jules in a large steam factory in Grammont, Belgium. In 1893 they moved the factory with its 100 workers to Halluin and Menin on the border of France. Oscar Anneesens married Mathilde Veranneman in 1899 and used the firm name of *Anneessens-Veranneman*. Mathilde died in 1910 and in 1912 Oscar married Laurentia Marinis, changing the firm name to *Anneessens-Marinis*, located at 10 boulevard Philippe-d'Alsace, Courtrai, Belgium. In 1883 P.H. Anneessens is listed as an organ builder in Ninove, Belgium.
ANNEESSENS, OSCAR; 29 rue Conscience, Courtrai, Belgium 1837. Harmonium maker. Father of *Charles Anneesens*.
ÅNSTRADD, GOTTFRIED; 19 Bafvernsgrand, Uppsala, Sweden.
APOLLO; an electrically blown harmonium, probably made in Italy.
APOLLO organ, an instrument of recent make by *Rushworth & Dreaper*, (qv). The Apollo is a two-manual and pedal practice organ built to RCO specifications and made to look like a pipe organ console. It usually has four sets of reeds on each manual and one or two sets on the pedals.
APOLLO CO., LTD.; 67 Berners St., London. Still working in 1906. Discontinued organ production before 1921.
ARBOR CITY; Ann Arbor, MI.
ARION; Cortland, NY.
ARISTON organette, see *Paul Ehrlich*.

ARMBRUSTER, R.H.; Springfield, IL. Folding organ, 1904. Probably made by others with the Armbruster stencil.
ARMSTRONG, ELMON, see *Collins & Armstrong*.
ARTCRAFT ORGAN CO.; Santa Monica, CA., 1915-1928. Incorporated 1922. Reed and pipe organ makers.
ASTRON, see *Eesti Klavierivabrik A/S 'Astron.'*
ATHENS organ, see *Southern Organ Co.*
ATLAS PIANO; Louisville, KY. Piano and reed organ maker.
ATLAS PIANO, see *Brother Musical Instrument Co. Ltd.*
AUGUST & CO.; Ritterstr. 76 SW, Berlin in 1903. J.S. August, proprietor; maker of the Kosmos harmonium.
AUSTIN, CHARLES; Concord, NH, 1844-1847, melodeon maker. David M. Dearborn became a partner in 1848, the firm was called *Austin & Dearborn*. In 1848 Austin & Dearborn was supplying reeds for Coleman's Patent Aeolian Attachment for pianos made by *T. Gilbert*. Dearborn left in 1852 and the firm was named *C. Austin & Co.*, operating under that name until 1875, part of the time in partnership with Charles E. Austin, son of Charles. From 1876 until 1915 the firm operated under the name *Charles E. Austin*. See *Abed Coleman, T. Gilbert*.
AUTOMATIC ORGAN CO., see *American Automatic Organ Co.*
AUTO-ORGAN CO.; 39 Blenheim Road, Upper Holloway, London. Player harmonium.

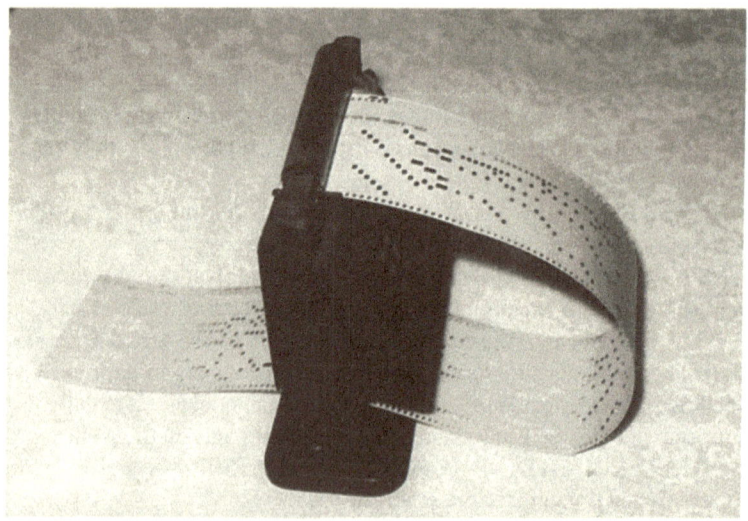

An Autophone hand-operated organette, Mike Perry collection.

AUTOPHONE organ; name used initially by *Prof. Merritt Gally* (qv) for a player organ of his invention in 1879. He later used the name Orchestrone, probably to avoid conflict with the products of *The Autophone Co.*

AUTOPHONE CO., THE; Ithaca, NY, 1879 until at least 1928. Organized by F.M. Finch, H.F. Hibbard & H.B. Horton; Horton sold out in 1883 and H.A. St. John came into company. Production in 1882 was 18,000 organettes. Made the Gem, Chautauqua, Concert & Grand Roller Organs.

AVILL & SMART; Apollo Works, Tabernacle St., Finsbury, London, EC. Piano, American organ and harmonium manufacturer. Proprietors: W. & F. Grover from 1878 to 1886. W. Luck took over in 1886 and reed organ production ceased.

B

BABCOCK, see *Chase & Babcock*.
BACCLIERI, G.; rue Vivienne 2, Paris. Portable organ.
BACH; Doubs, France. Maker of pianos and harmoniums. Maître de chapelle at Ornans, wrote a book on harmonium repair ca. 1930.
BACHELDER, see *Hovey & Bachelder*.
BACHER, EUGEN; Schulstrasse 15, Schorndorf, Würtemberg, Germany. Harmonium maker ca. 1940.
BACON, CHARLES E.; Buffalo, NY. A member of the firm of *George A. Prince & Co.* and a partner in its successor, *Prince & Bacon*, (qv). In 1874 he was operating under his own name as a manufacturer of organ stop knobs.

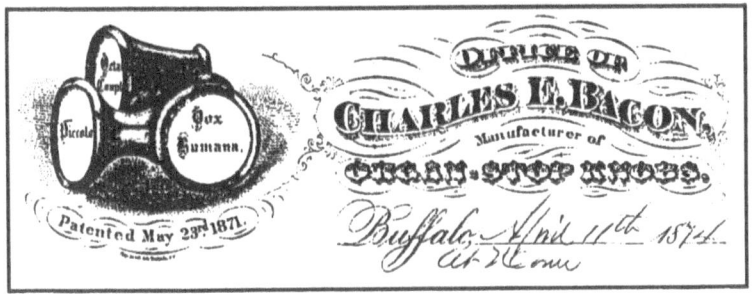

BACON, JAMES; London.
BAGNALL, JOHN, & CO.; Victoria, British Columbia, 1863-85.
BAILEY, CLAUDIUS R.; 1-3 Chalfont Road, Holloway, N. London, 1884-1888. Piano and harmonium maker. Made Sunday School Union organs, apparently using American-made actions with bellows and case made in England.
BAILLIE-HAMILTON, JAMES; British inventor of the Vocalion, U.S. patent 1884, first manufactured 1886 by *Hamilton-Vocalion Organ Mfg. Co.*, Worcester, MA. He was briefly connected with *S.R. Warren*. Baillie-Hamilton soon left the company and production was taken over by *The New York Church Organ Manufacturing Co.*; acquired in 1890 by *Mason and Risch* and in 1903 acquired by *Aeolian*. Vocalions were built at least until 1910, and are now highly prized by collectors for their solid construction and fine tone, attributed to the qualifying chambers. Serial number: 1906—4801.
BAKER, G.F., & CO., LTD.; Leeke Street Corner, King's Cross Road, London. Made components for reed organs, ca. 1914-1931.
BAKER, GEO., & CO.; Geneva, Switzerland, later *Baker-Troll*; made music boxes with reeds.
BAKER, HENRY, & SON; 70 Weybosset, Providence, RI, 1852 until at least 1883.
BAKER & RANDALL; Providence, RI; 1857-1875. Made folding melodeons.
BALBIANI, NATALE; Milan, Italy, (1836-1912). Harmonium and pipe organ builder. Still in business as a pipe organ maker under the name Balbiani-Vegezzi-Bossi. See *Vegezzi-Bossi*.
BALCH, H.M.; 843 Mission St., San Francisco, CA. Piano and reed organ maker, 1883.
BALDWIN, D.H.; 158 West Fourth St. in 1862; later 142-144 West Fourth St., Cincinnati, OH. Established in 1862 as a music dealer, eventually operating a chain of music stores. Reorganized as *D.H. Baldwin & Co.* in 1873, in 1889 acquired the *Hamilton Organ Co.* Incorporated 1892 with Lucien Wulsin, president; D.H. Baldwin, vice-president; G.W. Armstrong, secretary. Later also made the Monarch organs, Baldwin, Valley Gem and Ellington pianos. Bought out *Minshall-Estey* and produced that organ for a time. See *Hamilton Organ Co.*
BALDWIN, W.T.; 131 Stapleton Rd., Bristol, England 1903. Listed in 1883 and 1903.
BALDWIN, see *Whitaker & Frisbie*.
BALL, JACOBUS; Grosvenor Square, London. Melodeon maker.

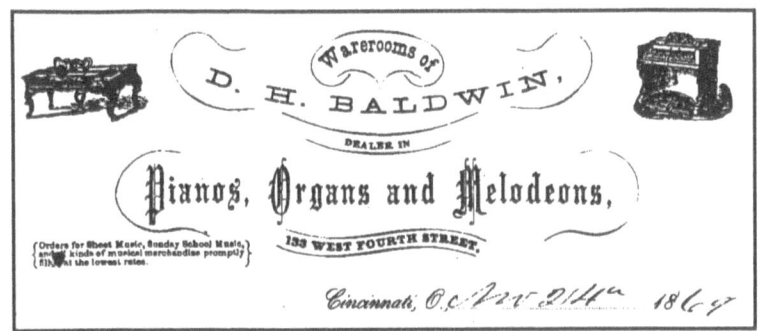

BALLARD, GEO.; 69 Tobago St., Glasgow, Scotland. Harmonium maker 1879-83.

BALLOU & CURTIS; Pleasant St., Concord, NH, 1870-1880; Oliver Ballou and George H. Curtis. Ballou first worked with *Austin*, then in 1870 joined up with Curtis and from 1881 to 1883 he worked at *Prescott Organ Co.* See *George H. Curtis*

BALTHASAR-FLORENCE; rue de Fer in 1869, rue de Collège in 1883; 12, 21-23 rue Dewez in 1903 and 1922, Namur, Belgium. Piano and harmonium maker, established 1869. Henri Balthasar (1844-1915) married Clemence Florence, a piano maker's daughter, and took his firm name from the two surnames. Gold medal at Anvers Exhibition, 1894; Grand Prix at Liege in 1904 for a three-manual and pedal harmonium; Grand Prix in 1910 for harmoniums d'Art including Celesta. His son Franz-Joseph took over the business in 1910, and about 1920 Henri's daughter Maria-Amelie took over, but the business closed in 1925.

BALTZER, ADOLPH; Zollverein, Nr. 82, Frankfurt on Oder, Germany. Exhibited the Aeolodion in 1851, a six-octave reed instrument in which the reeds can be tuned several notes higher or lower by turning a key fixed to a micrometer screw. Also a clockmaker.

BANCROFT, MARSHALL S.; Toronto, Ontario, Canada 1872. In 1873 he went with *Canada Organ Co.*

BANNICKE, MAX; Zeitzer Strasse 24a, Sidonienstr. 48 in 1935, Adolf-Hitler Str. 24 in 1940, Leipzig, Germany. Musical instrument dealer. Harmoniums with this name made by *Conrad, Martin & Törste*, by *Max Leonhardt & Co.* and by *Karl Stock*.

BARANOFF, J.S.; Dorf Alexandrowskoje, Schlusselburg-Prospect 1, St. Petersburg, Russia. Harmonium maker ca. 1906.

BARBATO, C.; Messina, Italy, 1883.

BARBIERI, ANGELO; 26 rue S. Vincenzo, Milan, Italy. Made suction reed organs and a combined piano and reed organ.

D.B. Bartlett lap organ label, 1846.

BARBU, J.P.; Paris. Established 1840. Received an honorable mention at the London Exhibition of 1862 for good work on reeds.

BARCKHOFF, CARL, (1849-1919); Pittsburg, PA 1865, Salem, OH 1882, Mendelssohn, PA 1895, Latrobe, PA 1897, Pomeroy, OH 1900, Basic, VA 1913. Pipe organ and melodeon maker. Son H.C. Barckhoff was a member of the firm and a partner in *Shipman Organ Co.*, (qv).

BARDELL organ. Possibly a stencil instrument.

BÄRMIG, JOHANN GOTTHILF; (1815-1899). Pipe organ and harmonium maker in Saxony, Germany.

BARNARD & PRIOR HARMONIUM WORKS; Sauquoit, NY.

BARNES, W.H.; 59 Walworth Road, SE London and 20 New Kent Road, London. Piano and harmonium maker, tuner and repairer 1891-1906. Discontinued organ production before 1921.

BARNETT, SAMUEL & SONS; 32 Worship St., Finsbury Sq., London, 1883. In 1879 Nelson Samuel became a partner and the firm name was changed to *Barnett, Samuel & Sons*. (In 1889) "Messrs. Barnett, Samuel & Sons have entirely recovered from the late fire on their premises in Worship Street and the rebuilding is proceeding, so that the firm may return to them before the Winter Season. The salvage having been taken by the Insurance Co. all their present stock is entirely new." In 1900 located at 32-38 Worship Street, Finsbury. Reed organ and piano maker established in 1832. Awarded a second prize at Sydney, Australia in 1878. Later became the Decca Record Co., and in 1921 advertised the Deccalian, a portable gramophone (phonograph).

BARNOVA, see Tusseling.

BARON; Belgium. Exhibited the Theorgue, a type of harmonium, in 1846.

BARROUIN, F.; 91 rue de Sèvres, Paris. Harmonium and piano maker. Won several medals and diplomas of honor at exhibitions.

BARTLETT, DANIEL B.; 180 Main St., Concord, NH 1847; Bartlett bought out David M. Dearborn's share of *Dearborn & Bartlett* in 1847. Serial Numbers: 1844—117, 1846—573, July 1847—904, Nov. 1847—973.

BARTLETT, JOSIAH; Concord, NH 1836.

BARTON, FR.; Hotzendorf, Austria-Hungary, 1903.

BARTUNEK, ADOLF; Tylgasse 496, Kutna Hora (Kuttenberg), Czechoslovakia 1930; established 1890.

BARTZ, R.; Bismarckstrasse 36, Kircheim, Teck, Germany. Founded 1938, closed 1969. Harmonium maker. Also *Otto Barz*, same address.

BATES ORGAN MANUFACTURING CO.; Boston, MA ca. 1895; organettes.

BATES, THEODORE CHARLES; Ludgate Hill, London, ca. 1845. Pipe organ maker; also made seraphines.

BATES, see *Ludden & Bates*.

BATT, THOMAS S., & CO.; 103 Cromer Street, London WC. Bellows maker 1880. In 1887 at 103 Cromer Road and 20 Hornsey Road, Holloway Station. In 1896-1900 only at Hornsey Road and then called *W.J. Batt*. Established 1854.

Automatic Melodista organette by Bates Organ Mfg. Co. ca. 1895. Mike Perry collection.

BAUDET, FLORENTIN; 11 rue Neuve Popincourt, 1860; 22 Rue de Lancry, 1883; Paris. Established 1853. Manufacturer of harmoniums for church and salon, won medals at the Exhibition in Besançon in 1860.

BAUER, GILBERT L., & CO.; 21 Kings Road, St. Pancras, London in 1883; 49 Tottenham St., Tottenham Court Rd.; 34 King's Rd. in 1897 and 1903, London; estab. 1865; made a variety of models, both pressure and suction, including a large three-manual and pedal model with forty stops and 1,365 reeds. Awarded a medallion at the Philadelphia Exposition of 1876.

BAUER, JULIUS, & CO.; 156-158 Wabash Avenue, Chicago, IL. Established in 1849 as a music dealer in New York and soon after began manufacturing pianos. Moved to Chicago in 1857 where he established a music store on the northeast corner of Clark and Washington Streets. In 1864 the business moved into the Crosby Opera House, and was burned out in the Chicago fire of 1871. He began again in the fall of 1872, locating in the Palmer House, then moved to 182-184 Wabash Ave. In 1883 he moved to 156-158 Wabash Ave. In addition to the retail store, Bauer manufactured the Bauer pianos and organs, although few if any of the organs have survived. Julius Bauer died in 1884. His son, William Max Bauer, born in 1870, was trained in the factory and in 1900 was elected vice-president and general manager.

BAUER, MATTHÄUS; Kaiserstr. 50 in 1883, Vienna, Austria 1930.
BAUGHM, see *Clark & Baughm.*
BAUM, see *Dickel & Baum.*
BAYNTON, J., & CO.; 23 Bayford St., Mare St., Hackney, E. London in 1883, manufactured American organs, Jordan's transposing harmonium and portable harmonium; made cases and soundboards 1878-1896.
BAY STATE ORGAN CO.; 101 Bristol St, Boston, MA 1885; see *C.B. Hunt.*
BAZIN, JAMES AMIRAUX; Canton, MA; made sliding brass reed pitch pipes 1821, mouth organ 1828, lap organ with reed pipes 1833, accordion 1835, reed lap organ 1836; later he was city clerk of Canton, MA. Bazin was given credit by many of the early leaders in the reed organ industry for being the source of the earliest instruments in the United States.
BEALE & CO. LTD.; factory and head offices, 41-47 Trafalgar St., Annandale, New South Wales, Australia, showrooms at 340 George St., Sydney. Piano manufacturer, established 1895, closed in 1970. Beale sold the Haydn organ, possibly made by *Peloubet* for Beale. A Haydn organ in the possession of George Nichols shows New York on the stop board and is marked "P & Co." on the keyboard.
BEASANT, THOMAS; 17 Portugal St., Lincoln's Inn, London about 1865; 11 Kirby St., Hatton Gardens in 1867; 32 Manchester St., King's Cross 1879-1882, 35 Orchard St., Ball's Pond in 1900. Harmonium maker.
BEAT-HOVEN organ, see *Beatty Organ Co.*
BEATTY ORGAN CO.; office Broad St. & Washington Ave., factory Railroad Ave. & Beatty St., Washington, NJ, later D.F. Beatty, established about 1879 by Daniel Fisher Beatty; bankrupt 1884; started again as *D.F. Beatty Piano & Organ Co.*, 1884-86; began manufacturing in 1880, previously bought organs from *Bridgeport Organ Co.* and from *Alleger & Bowlby*. Sold direct to consumers by mail order. Convicted of using the mails to defraud. Later sold a few organs made for him by *Lawrence Organ Co.*, Easton, PA. Serial number: 1881—85756.
BEATTY & PLOTTS; Washington, NJ. Daniel F. Beatty and Ed Plotts, proprietors. Predecessor of *Beatty Organ Co.*
BEAUCOURT, H.-C.; Monplaisir près Lyon, 4 place de la Reconnaissance, Lyon, France, 1903. Factory at Halluin (Nord). Extant 1862. Won a medal from the Academy at Lejous for improvements to his harmoniums.

BECKMANN, HEINRICH; Döhren, Germany. Established 1890, operated at least through 1930.
BECKWITH ORGAN CO.; Chestnut & NW Corner 29th St., Louisville, KY 1903 until at least 1922; also had a factory in St. Paul, MN; see *Sears Roebuck & Co., Adler Organ Co., R.S. Hill & Co.* Serial Numbers: 1910—F25561, 1913—136889. The Louisville factory building is no longer in existence.
BEDFORD, DAN.; 326 Goswell Road, London. Harmonium maker 1878-1887.
BEDFORD, F.; 7 Jeffreys Place, Camden Town Street, London. Advertised in 1900 as a reed organ maker.
BEDFORD, JOSEPH; 66 Weedington St., Kentish Town, London NW. Harmonium maker 1878-1892.
BEDWELL & SON; Cecilia House, Cambridge, England, later G.C. Bedwell Ltd. Pipe organ and harmonium maker.
BEER, JOH. GEORG; Erling bei Andechs, Germany. Listed as a harmonium maker in 1903, 1913, 1930.
BEESTON ORGAN WORKS; 141 Town St., Leeds, England; see *J.W. Sawyer*.
BEETHOVEN ORGAN CO.; Washington, NJ; successor to *Beatty Organ Co.*, incorporated 1885; later *Beethoven Piano Organ Co.*, owned by *Needham Organ Co.*, New York. Officers in 1897: John J. McDavitt, president; Charles M. Tuttle, sec.-treas. Purchased by John H. Seed about 1900. Sold direct to consumers. Closed about 1903.
BELL & CO.; Neumeyer Hall, Hart St., Bloomsbury, London. Manufacturer of American organs, 1883.
BELL, DANIEL, ORGAN CO.; Toronto, Ontario. Daniel Bell became manager of the *Canada Organ Co.* in 1875, and in 1877 was associated with the *Excelsior Organ Co.* He established the *Daniel Bell Organ Co.* in 1881 and operated it until 1886.
BELL, JOSEPH; (*York Harmonium Manufactory*.) Established 1847 in Petergate, York, England; in 1849 in 57 Gillygate, 24 Gillygate in 1861, 22 Feasegate in 1863, later at 28 Swinegate, then 14 Stonegate, all in York. An inventor and experimenter, he made harmoniums with reeds of wood, ivory and german silver. Succeeded by *Samuel Bell*, then by *Sarah Bell* at 14 Stonegate, York in 1894, still working in 1906.
BELL ORGAN & PIANO CO., LTD., see *W. Bell & Co.*
BELL, SAMUEL, see Joseph Bell.
BELL, SARAH, see Joseph Bell.
BELL, W., & CO.; Guelph, Ontario; started in 1864 by the Bell brothers, William and Robert, in the upper story of a building on Upper Wyndham St., producing one "Diploma" melodeon per week. Later they moved to

W. Bell & Co. two manual organ from the Fluke collection.

Carden St. In 1867 produced 80 instruments per year. William assumed management in 1865; the name *W. Bell & Co.* was used at least as early as 1871 when a new three story factory was opened on Market Square. In 1881 with 200 employees the capacity was 1,200, and in 1906 was 6,000 organs per year. An English syndicate bought the company in 1888 and changed the name to *Bell Organ & Piano Co.*, and in 1907 changed it again to *Bell Piano & Organ Co.* This group also owned *Neugebauer Nachf. C. Bell & Co.* of Germany. Made a variety of models including the "Bellolian", a player reed organ, and held the patent on the "Serophone", a device which gave the reeds a wood-pipe character. Organ production was discontinued in 1928 and the plant was sold to John S. Dowling of Brantford and resold in 1934 to the Lesage Piano Co.

Serial numbers:

1883—22539	1896—77107
1884—26000	1898—79932 (May)
1890—52239	80717 (July)
1892—60810 (Jan.)	82384 (Oct)
63416 (May)	1900—89615 (Jan.)
65557 (Nov.)	90602 (Mar.)
1893—61997	1902—96766
1894—64200	1904—109092
1895—75440	1907—122817

BELL & WOOD CO.; Guelph, Ontario.
BELL, see *Chicago Cottage Organ Co.*
BELLACK, JAS., & SONS; 1129 Chestnut St., Philadelphia, PA, 1860. Piano maker and dealer. Organs dated 1867 with this name have been seen.
BELMONT organ; Philadelphia, PA. Instrument seen in Cape May, NJ.
BENDER, C.C.; established 1850 by C.C. Bender, Sr., who died in 1878. He had four sons, one of whom emigrated to Buffalo, NY and is said to have established an organ factory. The other three continued the business located at Hoogewoerd 90, factory at Rijnstraat 4, Leiden, Netherlands. In 1894 a branch office was located at Damrak 74/76, Amsterdam. Proprietors in 1903: J.J. and J.C. Bender. Maker of American (suction) organs. The firm is still in existence.
BENDON, GEO.; St. Croix, Switzerland; music box with reeds.
BENDZKO, FRITZ; (also Bentzko). Hinter Rossgarten 14, Königsberg, Prussia, Germany. Harmonium maker, founded about 1923, operated at least through 1940.
BENGZON, see *Berggreb & Bengzon.*
BENHAM'S Cottage Organ.
BENNETTS & BENNETTS; 62 Norfolk Terrace, Westbourne Grove, W. London 1880-1883. Piano and harmonium maker.
BENSON, A.; Hessleholm, Sweden 1895. Harmonium maker 1890-1930.
BENT, GEO. P.; 81-83 Jackson in 1883; Washington Blvd. & Sangamon St., 281-289 Wabash Ave., 323-333 South Canal St., Chicago, IL; Crown organs; George Payne Bent started in 1870 as a sewing machine retailer, added organs and in 1880 began manufacturing organs and later pianos. In 1902 the factory had a capacity of 12,000 organs per year. He was active in trade associations and after retirement was the author of "Four

The "Bent Block," erected by the Geo. P. Bent Company in 1895.

Score and More," a book which he published containing reminiscences of old-timers in the music business. Fond of puns on his name, he gave out his personalized cigars saying, "Have a Bent cigar." Renamed *Geo. P. Bent Co.* in 1908; probably discontinued organ production in 1915. Later acquired by the *Adler Mfg. Co.* Serial number: 1901—8514, 1906—89519.

BENTLEY, H.D.; office and salesrooms at 1400 Old Colony Building, Chicago, IL, factory at Freeport. Office located at 195 Wabash Ave. in 1901. IL Parlor organ maker. O.D. Weaver, Jr., manager in 1894. Also listed as *H.D. Bentley Piano & Organ Stool Factory*. At least some Bentley organs were made by W.W. Kimball. Active at least from 1888 through 1901. See *O.D. Weaver.*

BENTLEY, J.; Small Heath, England.

BENTON, SAMUEL; Stanhope Square, Sheepscot, Leeds, England. Harmonium maker 1880-1892.

BENTZKO, see *Bendzko.*

BENVENUTI, CARLO; San Giovanni in Croce, Italy, 1903.

BERGGREB & BENGZON; Seffle, Sweden ca. 1909.

BERGMANN JUN., ANTON; Zakupy, (Reichstadt), Czechoslovakia, 1930; established 1850. Another Bergmann made Physharmonikas ca 1830, location unknown.

BERLINER HARMONIUMFABRIK GMBH, Alexandrinenstr. 22, Berlin; Eduard Scheidel, director; made the Skala harmonium; established in 1902. Succeeded in 1903 by *Skala Harmonium Gesellschaft*, Hamburg, Germany.

BERLIN PIANO & ORGAN CO.; Berlin, (later Kitchener), Ontario. Organized about 1890 by J.M. Staebler and F.G. Gardiner. The company erected a three story white brick factory building at 246 King St. West in 1891. In the early 1900s it was renamed William Snyder & Co., and in 1906 it was sold to the Foster-Armstrong Co. By 1906 fifty factory workers were employed, producing 25 instruments per week. The factory building was torn down in 1955. The city of Berlin, Ont. was renamed Kitchener in 1916. Serial numbers: 1891—592, 1898—802.
BERNARD; Rouen, France. Harmonium maker, 1896.
BERNTSEN, ANTON; Ørstedsgade 19, Vejle, Denmark; estab. 1901; in 1909 listed at 19 Jorstedsgatan, Vejle.
BERRUTI, LUIGO; 180 bis, Strada Casale, Turin, Italy, 1930.
BERRY BROTHERS. (No other information available.)
BERRY & THOMPSON; New York. Made the Choral Organ.
BERTEK, JOHANN; Gemer Sajavsky, Czechosovakia; est. 1903.
BERTHEAUX FRÈRES; Belleville, Paris.
BERTHION-HÉDOU; France. Reed maker, absorbed by Estève.
BERTRÁN, MIGUEL; 70 calle de Torrijos, Gracia-Barcelona, Spain, ca. 1930.
BETHLEHEM ORGAN CO.; Westminster, NJ
BETTEX, FRIEDRICH; Steinsfurt, Kr. Heidelberg, Germany; established 1913, still extant 1930.
BEVERSLUIS, P.; Dortrecht, Netherlands 1862; Tiel, Netherlands 1863. Showed "Semi-Melodeons" at the London Exhibition of 1862.
BEYER, LOUIS MORITZ; Wiehe, Thuringen, Germany in 1920, Bielefelder Str. 46, Brackwede, Germany in 1940, the firm is still in operation at Artur Ladebeck Str. 185. Established in 1920. Also *Otto & Moritz Beyer* shown at the same address. Made both pressure and suction instruments. Production ended in 1968.
BEYER, PAUL, see *Vitus Gévaert*.
BILDÉ, CH.; 3 ave. de Chambéry, Annecy, France in 1900; 129-bis rue de la Pompe, Paris; factory in Orly-Seine in 1903; 17 rue de Lancry, Paris in 1920. Established 1892. Gabriel Clément, proprietor.
BILHORN BROTHERS ORGAN CO.; founded 1885; 56 Fifth Ave.; 518-20 Fifth Ave.; 207 N. Wells St.; 1414 McLean Ave., 77 W. Lake St. in 1932, Chicago, IL; music publishers and makers of folding organs; also *Bilhorn Organ Co.*; Peter Philip Bilhorn, proprietor and George E. Bilhorn. Made organs for *Sears, Roebuck* in 1902. Bought reeds and reed boards from *Hinners Organ Co*. Active at least through 1941. Serial number: 1900—1094, 1900—1107, 1903—2858, 1933—322175.

The Bilhorn Telescope Organ

Style A—Single Reed 3¼ Octave   -   -   -   Listed $50.00
Style B—Double Reed 3¼ Octave   -   -   -   Listed $60.00
Style C—Double Reed 4 Octave   -   -   -   Listed $70.00

Description On Back Pages

Bilhorn Brothers, Manufacturers, Chicago, Ill., U. S. A.

BINA MUSICAL STORES; Nai Sarak, Delhi, India. Currently making table harmoniums.
BIRMINGHAM ORGAN CO.; Derby, CT, see *Sterling Organ Co.*
BISHOP, CHILD & CO.; Cleveland, OH 1853, also *Bishop & Co., Bishop & Child, Child & Co., Clark & Bishop*. Serial number: 1857—200.
BISHOP, E.M.; Painesville, OH. Melodeon maker, ca. 1860.
BISHOP & HEALEY; Goshen, NY, 1880.
BISWAS & SONS; 5 Lower Chitpore Road, Calcutta, India in 1930.
BLACK, A.D.; Chelsea, MA; organettes, 1883.
BLAKE, JOHN P., & CO. (No other information available.)
BLAKE, R.W., see *Loring & Blake, Sterling Organ Co.*
BLAKEMAN & GIBBS; corner Rose and Main Streets, Kalamazoo, MI, 1860. William P. Blakeman and Isaac Gibbs. "An extensive Factory for the manufacture of Melodeons, which, for tone, finish and price, cannot be excelled." See *Wm. P. Blakeman & Co.*
BLAKEMAN & PHILLIPS; 18 N. Rose, Kalamazoo, MI, 1869; Detroit, MI. William P. Blakeman and Delos Phillips. See *Wm. P. Blakeman, Delos Phillips.*
BLAKEMAN, WM. P., & CO.; Detroit, MI 1850-54, later *Simmons & Blakeman, A.A. Simmons & Co., Delos Phillips,* probably the same as *Detroit Melodeon Co.* (qv).
BLAKER, A.; 9 Whitfield Street, Tottenham Court Road, London, 1900; 20 Whitfield St. in 1914; 39 Store St., Tottenham Court Road in 1921. Made portable harmoniums.
BLANGENOIS; rue Frère-Orban 35, Brussels, Belgium. Piano and harmonium maker, 1914.
BLATCHFORD, G., ORGAN CO.; Galt, Ontario 1895, Elora, Ontario 1896. George Blatchford, proprietor. Made piano-cased organs. Awarded reed organ patents 1875, 1878.
BLESSING, reed organ made in China.
BLISS AMERICAN ORGAN CO.; 263 Oxford St., W. London in 1887; 151 Oxford St., London in 1889. Not working in 1891.
BLODGET & HORTON; Akron, OH, patented a reed organ in 1848 and 1849; see *Henry B. Horton.*
BLOE, C.; 11 Charles St., London in 1879, (this is the same address as *Charles Kelly & Co.*). In 1880 he was located at 16 Mortimer St., London. Not working in 1886.
BLONDEL, ALPHONSE; France. Maker of pianos and the Piano-Orgue, a piano plus a large harmonium.
BLOOMFIELD ORGAN CO.; 451-3 Bloomfield Ave., Bloomfield, NJ.
BLOUNT, H.A.; King St., Derby, England.

BOCA, G.; Via S. Chiara 43, Turin, Italy. Listed in 1903 and 1909.
BOCCESE, see *Schone & Bocchese*.
BOCK, A.; 41a Southampton Road, Gospel Oak, London, 1905.
BOCKMANN, see *Beckmann*.
BODAU; 225 chaussée d'Ixelles, Brussels, Belgium. Piano and harmonium manufacturer, 1914.
BODGE, HENRY; 97 E. 23rd St., New York, NY 1861. Melodeon maker.
BOECKX, THEOPHILE; Ruisbroek near Hal, Belgium; 427 chaussée de Wavre a Etterbeck, Belgium; 37 rue Witteberg a Saint-Gilles, Brussels, Belgium. Organ and harmonium maker. Worked with *Cloetens* in Brussels. In 1929 his son Jan was working with him.
BOGG, WM., & SONS; 31-33 John Dalton St., also 23 and 25 Corporation St., Manchester, England 1878-1896. Makers of Regent organ.
BÖHLITZ-EHRENBERG, see *Leipziger Pianofortefabriken Böhlitz-Ehrenberg*.
BOHM, FRANZ; Fabrikstr. 35, Volary (Wallern), Czechoslovakia, 1930; founded 1924.

BOHN, J. EDMUNDO; Rua Marques de Souza, Novo Hamburgo, Rio Grande do Sul, Brazil. Considered to be the best of the Brazilian harmonium makers. Made pipe organs and harmoniums from at least 1920 until 1984. Continues as an accordion and harmonica maker.
BOKUMS, BRÄLI; 24 Jürmalas ielā, Liepaja, Latvia ca. 1930.
BOLENDER, see *Heede & Bolender*.
BOLLERMANN, DOMINIC LEOPOLD; Badergasse 454, Schlossgasse 4 in 1847, Dresden, Germany. Pianoforte, harmonium, physharmonica and aeolodicon maker ca. 1838-44. Said to have gone to

America about 1848, although he continued to be listed in directories through 1852.
BOLLINGER, R.C.; Fort Smith, AR. Parlor organ maker.
BOMAN, see *Lawson & Bowman, Howland & Boman*.
BONATO, ANTONIO; Vicenza, Italy. Awarded a bronze medal at Arezzo, Italy in 1882.

Type O Harmonium, made by Harmoniumfabrik Bongardt & Herfurth, Wiehe/Unstruttal, Germany, 1972.

BONGARDT & HERFURTH HARMONIUMFABRIK; Rossleben 84, Wiehe, Germany. Established 1885, Max Herfurth, proprietor in 1930. Made a total of 7,500 harmoniums. Still in operation in 1994 as a piano string maker.
BONNEL, G.; 9 rue Saint-Ambroise, Paris. Made suction harmoniums 1919.
BONS, EGIDE; rue Goffart 52 a Ixelles, Brussels, Belgium. Harmonium maker 1899.

BOOSEY & CHING; 24 & 28 Holles St., Tottenham Ct. Rd., London; 1859, 1866, 1890. Founded in January of 1859. By October of that year the factory was moved to Wells Street; the showrooms and offices remaining in Holles St. Makers of Evan's English Harmoniums. See *Wardle Eastland Evans*. Awarded a medal at the London Exhibition of 1862 for "excellence of harmoniums on the Evans principle." A separate business, Boosey & Sons, was founded at the same address in 1859 to produce military band instruments. John Boosey published "The Musical World" from the same address.

BORGER, HERMAN; Vriezenveen, Netherlands, 1953, 1955. Made book-operated reed organs and a portable organ.

BORK, H.; 56a Crogsland Road, Chalk Farm Station, London. Made portable harmoniums in 1900, American organs in 1902.

BORGMAN, CHARLES H., see *Ling & Borgman*.

BOSANQUET, R.H.M.; invented an enharmonic harmonium with 53 equal intervals in 1872-3 which had 84 keys arranged as seven tiers of levers. Each tier communicates through a row of squares with a row of horizontal stickers. The organ, built by *T.A. Jennings* of London, is in the Science Museum, South Kensington, London.

BOSSI, VICENZO; Via S. Lazzaro, Triest, Austria-Hungary. Piano and harmonium maker, 1883.

BOSTON ORGAN CO.; 6 Avery St. Boston, MA in 1866, later *New England Organ Co.*

BOSTON PIANO & ORGAN CO.; Coshocton, OH. J.A. Compton, pres.; H.J. Barron, V.P.; A.E. Jones, secretary; F.R. Martin, treasurer, 1903.

BÖTTCHER; Stettin, Germany. Piano maker, made combination piano-harmoniums in 1864.

BOUCHIER; France; reed maker.

BOURGUIGNON-BOONANTS ET FILS; 59 rue du Moulin, Grammont, Belgium, 1930.

BOURLET; 106 rue d'Enfer, Paris. Successor to *Martin de Provins*. Exhibited in Paris in 1867, showing a harmonium with vertical action and a large case with a pipe top. Won a bronze medal at the Paris Exposition in 1878 for a transposing harmonium.

BOUS, JULES; rue Goffart a Ixelles, Brussels, Belgium, 1873-1880. Showed three harmoniums at the Brussels Exhibition of 1880. His brother E. Bous worked with him.

BOUTEVILIN, L., & CO.; 119 rue de Montreuil and 99 rue de Charonne, Paris 1863 until at least 1889, succeeded by *Cottino & Tailleur*. Won a bronze medal at the Paris Exposition in 1878 for a two-manual harmonium.

BOUTIN, LOUIS; Paris. Established 1863.

P. BRANTZEGS

Physharmonika (Harmonium).

3.

I Orretræes-Kasse, sort eller jakarandapoleret.

Størrelse: 1 Al. 17½″ bredt, 1 Al. 11″ høit og 20″ dybt.

5 Octavers Omfang fra C til e med 2 Stemmer 8 og 16 Fods Stemme med 8 Registre.

Pris 90 Spd.

Med 3 Stemmer, 4, 8 og 16 Fods Stemme med 10 Registre.
Pris 120 Spd.

I Jakarandatræes Kasse 10 Spd. Tillæg.

BOWITZ, C.A.; Breslau, Germany, 1825.
BOWLBY, CHARLES P.; Washington, N.J.; made organs under his own name at least from 1882-1889; see *Alleger, Bowlby & Co., Lawrence Organ Co., Bowlby's Sons Piano & Organ Co.*
BOWLBY'S SONS PIANO & ORGAN CO.; Easton, PA 1906; established about 1905 as successor to *Lawrence Organ Mfg. Co.* and *C.P. Bowlby Co.*
BOWMAN, see *Larson & Bowman, Howland & Boman.*.
BOWMANVILLE ORGANS; Bowmanville, Ontario, Canada. Active in 1875.
BOYD LTD.; also Boyd Organ Co., 407 Harrow Rd., London; 11 Powis St., Woolwich, London; 19 Holborn Bars, London; factory at Warwick Gardens, Harringay, North London. Made an exact replica of the *Mason & Hamlin* "Baby" organ, also player pianos. Discontinued organ production before 1921.
BOYER & MARTY; France. Won a bronze medal at the Paris Exposition of 1878 for a two-manual harmonium with one manual enharmonic.
BOYNTON, see *C.W. Eaton & Boynton*.
BRACHOT, JOSEPH; Namur, Belgium, 1885-1910. Harmonium maker, also worked at the *Balthasar-Florence* factory. Awarded a bronze medal at Anvers in 1885, a bronze medal at Liege in 1905 and a silver medal at Brussels in 1910.
BRADLEY, ISAAC; Haverhill, MA 1845; 41 Pleasant St, Newburyport, MA 1851-55; seraphine maker.
BRAENDLE, FRIEDRICH; 25 Poststrasse, Stuttgart-Untertürkheim, Germany. Established before 1914. Operating at least through 1930.
BRAINARD'S SONS CO., S.; 20 E. 17th St., New York and 298-300 Wabash Ave, Chicago. Music publisher. Organs with the Brainard name are probably made by others with the Brainard stencil.
BRANDRUP, CLAUS S.; Brooklyn, NY. Church and parlor organ maker 1899-1907.
BRANTZEG, PAUL CHRISTIAN; Christiania (now Oslo), Norway. Established 1850. Pipe organ, harmonium and piano builder until about 1900. Produced a total of 400 harmoniums.
BRANZ E CIA.; 21 via S. Martino, Trento, Italy in 1930.
BRASTEAD, H. & R., London, also Brasted. A piano maker, also made the *Cecelian* organ, (qv).
BRATTLEBORO MELODEON CO.; Brattleboro, VT; organized 1867 with Silas M. Waite, President; J.J. Estey, Treasurer; and A.A. Cheney on the executive committee. J.J. Estey, son of Jacob Estey, had also been appointed treasurer of *J. Estey & Co.* in 1866, and Waite had been a partner in that company up to that year. Waite, president of the First

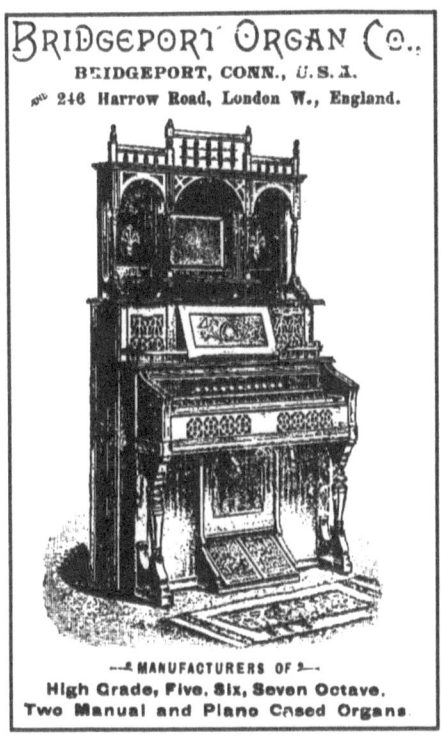

BRIDGEPORT ORGAN CO.
BRIDGEPORT, CONN., U.S.A.
246 Harrow Road, London W., England.

— MANUFACTURERS OF —
High Grade, Five, Six, Seven Octave,
Two Manual and Piano Cased Organs

National Bank of Brattleboro, was also a partner with Riley Burdett in *R. Burdett & Co.*, established in Chicago in 1866 as a result of the reorganization of *J. Estey & Co.*, and was later involved in a lengthy and bitter lawsuit against Estey. Waite's bank failed in 1880 and he hurriedly left town. The name later changed to *Brattleboro Organ Co.* and *Brattleboro Organ & Piano Co*, and was in business at least until 1901.
BRAUN, JACOB; Forststr. 53, Stuttgart, Germany; reed maker, 1883.
BRAUNER, W.E.; Bahnstr. 11, Mährisch-Neustadt, Austria-Hungary; Wilh. Brauner, proprietor in 1903; estab. 1881. In 1930 shown as *Wilhelm Brauner & Cie.* See *Swoboda & Brauner, Fr. Ketzer*.**BREDSHALL ORGAN CO.**; Chicago, IL, 1885, see *Hillstrom*.
BREEKOW, C.; Stargard, Germany. Physharmonium maker, 1840-45.
BREINBAUER, LEOPOLD, see *Willhelm Zika*.
BREMER ORGELBAUANSTALT GEHLHAR & CO.; Bremen, Germany; H.M. Hauschild.
BRÉMOND, B.J.; Geneva, Switzerland; music box with reeds.
BRESSANI, GIOVANNI; Bolzaneto, Italy, 1909.
BRIDGEPORT ORGAN CO.; Howard Ave. & Spruce St., Bridgeport, CT, established 1877, (1880 POPG). J.T. Patterson, proprietor in 1899;

factory capacity then 2,400 organs per year. Also sold organs as *James T. Patterson*, (qv). Had London showrooms at 18 Finsbury Pavement in 1921. Awarded a third prize at Sydney, Australia in 1878.
BRIDGEPORT ORGAN ENGINE CO.; corner Beaver and Middle Streets, Bridgeport, CT. Manufacturer of the Forrester hydraulic organ blowing engine, patented 1869.
BRIDGES, JOHN; 55 Collier St., King's Cross, London 1878, 1883; in 1884 at 249 Pentonville Road, London; at 240 Pentonville Road 1885-1900. Harmonium and American organ manufacturer.
BRIFFETT, GEORGE BENJAMIN; Brook Road, Ashley Road, Bristol, England. Organ and harmonium builder. Born Feb. 19, 1857, died Nov. 21, 1925. Made only a few instruments, including a portable and a larger American organ.
BRISTOL ORGAN CO., see *J.W. Punter*.
BRITISH AEOLUS, a two-manual and pedal organ made in 1886.
BRITISH REEDS LTD.; Perren Street, London. Reed maker, listed in 1947, 1950. G.H. Best, managing director, H.R. Dawson, director.
BROBERG & CO.; Amal, Sweden. Organs and harmoniums, 1909.
BROOKLYN ORGAN CO.; 1883, see *Green & Savage*.
BROOKS, C.; Albany, NY; seraphines & melodeons.
BROOKS & CO.; 31 Lyme St., Camden Town, London, 1910. Established 1810. Maker of piano actions, keys, stools, canterburies, reed organ cases and all music furniture.
BROOKS, F., & CO.; 194 Mare St., Hackney, London 1884-1886. Piano and harmonium manufacturer and dealer.
BROOKS, see *Herrburger Brooks*.
BROTHER MUSICAL INSTRUMENTS CO. LTD.; 9-35 Hotta-dori, Mizuho-ku, Nagoya, 467 Japan. Brother was established in 1908 as a sewing machine manufacturer, and is now one of the largest in Japan. It began manufacturing the Brother reed organ in 1969 through its subsidiary *Atlas Piano*. The Brother organ was designed for use in schools and by children. It had 2 ranks of reeds, 61 keys, C scale, with an electric blower. A total of 530,000 instruments were sold from 1969 through the end of production in 1980.
BROWN, A.; 20 rue des Fossés du Temple, Paris. Harmonium maker, made the Mélophone in 1850.
BROWN, ABNER; Montreal, Quebec 1848-74; melodeons.
BROWN BROS.; Union, ME.
BROWN, COLIN; Glasgow, Scotland; made an enharmonic reed organ called the Voice Harmonium based on *Henry Poole*'s design. Examples are located in the Science Museum, South Kensington, London, and in the Reed Organ Museum at Saltaire Village, Shipley, West Yorkshire, England. Another instrument is in a museum in Tacoma, WA.

BROWN & SIMPSON; Worcester, MA. See *Worcester Organ Co. (II)*.
BROWN & SONS; England. Honorable mention at the Paris Exhibition in 1878 for good value and sweet-sounding harmoniums.
BROZ, JOSEF; 29 Spalena ul, Prague, Czechoslovakia, 1930.
BRUCE-HASELTON; West Townsend, MA, melodeon maker ca. 1845. Also *Bruce & Haselton*. See *D.H. Haselton & Co.*
BRUCE, J.M., & G. CHARD; 515 Washington St., Boston, MA in 1869; Mozart Organs; closed 1878. See *Granville Chard*.
BRUCKMANN, H.; Stuttgart, Germany; reed maker, 1883.
BRUNER, FIDELIS; Warsaw, Poland. Made the Aeolmelodikon in 1818 for Prof. Hoffman.
BRUNI, FRANCESCO; 15 rue des Tournelles, Paris; orgue-expressif 1847; harmoniums, transposing keyboards.
BRÜNING & BONGARDT; 29 Gemarker Ufer, Barmen, Germany, 1920. Harmonium wholesaler and distributor. Reed organs, presumably made by *Hermann Hildebrand*t (qv), for resale with this stencil.
BRUNT, W., & SONS; 9 St. Augustine's Parade, Bristol, England, 1921. Sold organs made by *Smith-American* with the Brunt stencil.
BRUSH, ALEXANDER M.; Clayton, NY. Made melodeons about 1850-1871. His son Fred later joined the firm which was then called *A.M. Brush & Son*.
BUCHNER, O.; Bergen, Norway 1907-16, Oslo, Norway 1917-26. Mainly a piano maker, but also made harmoniums.
BUCK, HEINRICH; Bayreuth, Germany. Organ and harmonium maker, 1882.
BUFF-HEDINGER, ADOLPH, see *Neue Leipziger Musikwerke*.
BULL, HARRY M.; Main St., Preston, CT. Maker of parlor and vestry organs. Active 1877.
BUNGERT, E.; 3 rue de la Poste, Arlon, Belgium, 1869-1902. Succeeded by *J-P Bungert* from 1902 to 1921, located at 28 rue du Palais de Justice, Arlon until 1914, then 3 rue de la Poste and 28 rue du Gouvernement, Arlon. Maker and retailer of pianos and harmoniums. Succeeded by Bungert-Charlier from 1921 to 1953, a retailer only.
BURDETT ORGAN CO. LTD.; Sedgwick Street, Chicago, IL; Riley Burdett, formerly Burditt, had been the head of *J. Estey & Co.'s* Chicago branch, *Estey & Burdett*. In the 1866 reorganization of the Estey company, Burdett and Silas M. Waite left and formed the *Burdett Organ Co. Ltd.*, the first of the Chicago reed organ builders, building organs for *Lyon & Healy*, and in 1867 formed the *Brattleboro Melodeon Co.*, (qv). The Chicago factory burned in the Chicago fire of 1871, started again at 12th and Walnut Streets in Erie, PA in partnership with C.C. Converse 1872-1888; then moved to Freeport, IL in 1894. Built a three-story building on Manufacturers' Island which was occupied until 1898 when

the factory was moved to the Johnson Wheel Co. building in the Northwest part of Freeport, where it had a capacity of 400 organs per month. In 1901 the property and name were acquired by the *Hobart M. Cable Co.*, and the piano scales were acquired by the *Edna Organ Co.* In 1907 Cable sold the Burdett Organ Co. to *S.N. Swan & Sons,* (qv). Serial number: 1871—17331, 1898—58021.

BURDITT & CARPENTER; Brattleboro, VT 1850-1852, successors to *Jones & Burditt*; Riley Burditt and Edwin B. Carpenter, partners; succeeded by *I. Hines & Co.* See *Burdett.*
BURG, see *van den Burg*.

BURGER, HERMANN; Wilhelmstr. 781-783 in 1886, Wilhelmstr. 4-5 1890-1908, Bayreuth, Germany. Located at Kirchstr. 6 in Leipzig-Leutzsch in 1909-1912, Kurze Str. 6 in 1910, Kurze Str. 4 in 1912. Established in 1873. Awarded a gold medal for harmoniums at the 1895 Exhibition in Posen, Germany. Acquired by *M. Hörügel & Co.* and moved to Tanzplan 4, Leipzig by 1909, with Wilhelm O. Jurgens shown as proprietor. Still extant in 1930. See *Hörügel*.
BURLINGTON. (Name only, no additional data available.)
BUSCHMANN, GUSTAV ADOLPH; Barmbeck, Hamburgerstr. 173, Hamburg, Germany; Lindenstr. 20b, Hamburg. Also listed as *Buschmann's Instrumentenbau*. Piano, physharmonica and harmonium maker. Established in 1805 by J.D. Buschmann in Friedrichroda. Inventor of the Terpodion. Advertised a suction-operated physharmonica with expression. Invented a percussion action for suction reed organs in 1909. Displayed a harmonium at the Hamburg Exhibition in 1869, still extant in 1918.
BUSHNELL, O.P.; Worcester, MA.
BUSSELL, H.; 11 Westmoreland Street, Dublin, Ireland, 1865.
BUSSON, CONSTAND; 166 boulevard du Prince-Eugène, ci-devant 17 rue des Francs-Bourgeois (Marais), Paris in 1867; 166 boulevard Voltaire in 1883, 1892. Established 1835; made harmoniums, harmoniflûtes and finger barrel organs. Had 63 workers in 1863. Sales rooms at 24 passage Jouffroy, Paris. Awarded a bronze medal at the Paris Exposition of 1878.

Showed harmoniums and harmoniflûtes at the Paris Exposition of 1889. Extant until at least 1907.
BUTCHER, J.W.; 2-3 Ludgate Circus Buildings, London EC4. Two-manual reed organ.
BUTLER MUSIC CO.; Lafontaine, IN. See *Chute & Butler*.
BUTSCHER, AUGUST; Moltkestr. in Rudolstadt, Germany. Harmonium maker, 1913; founded in 1910.

C

CABINET ORGAN CO., see *Xavier Spang*.
CABINET PIPE ORGAN CO., THE; Onondaga and Gifford Streets, Syracuse, NY. 1872, 1874. Founded by *H.N. Goodman* (qv), who later sold out to James C. Mix and James Terwilliger. Made combination reed and pipe organs as well as conventional reed organs. *Xavier Spang*, (qv) was apparently also connected with this firm.
CABINETTO, a paper-roll operated street reed organ, made in England.
CABLE CO., THE; Chicago, IL; Fayette S. Cable, president in 1903, successor to *Chicago Cottage Organ Co.*, (qv); capacity 18,000 organs per year in 1903, 24,000 in 1906. Made the "Chicago Cottage" organ. Discontinued organ production about 1918.
CABLE, FAYETTE S., see *The Cable Co., Chicago Cottage Organ Co., Lakeside Organ Co.*
CABLE, HOBART M., CO.; H.M. Cable, president; successor to *Burdett Organ Co.* The organ factory, managed by S.N. Swan, was located in Freeport, IL, and had an annual capacity of 6,000 organs in 1903. The factory was sold to *S.N. Swan & Sons* (qv) in 1907. See *The Cable Co.*
CABLE PIANO CO., see *Collins & Armstrong*.
CADBY, CHARLES; 21 Alfred Street, Bedford Street, London in 1839; 33½ Liquorpond Street in 1848; Little Tothill Street, Little Gray's Inn Lane in 1867; Hammersmith Road in 1879. Piano and harmonium maker.
CADY & PHILLIPS; corner of Rose and Water Streets, Kalamazoo, MI, 1867. See *Delos Phillips, Star Organ Manufactory*.
CAECILIA organ, see *Emil Müller*.
CALAME, ROBERT V.; Salto Oriental, Uruguay, 1909. Piano and harmonium maker.

TO THE TRADE.

We beg to notify you that we have this day changed the name of the Chicago Cottage Organ Company to that of "THE CABLE COMPANY."

This has been done in order that we may transact our wholesale and retail business under one name. There will be no difference in the manner of transacting our business, and it will be under the same management as heretofore.

Thanking you for your liberal patronage in the past, and asking for a continuance of same under the NEW NAME, we are,

Yours very truly,

THE CABLE COMPANY.

Formerly CHICAGO COTTAGE ORGAN COMPANY.

March 12, 1900.

CAMP & CO.; Chicago, IL. Isaac Camp, music dealer. Organs with this name were probably made by others with the Camp stencil. Some Camp & Co. organs were made by *Columbian Organ Co.*, (qv). See *Story & Camp, Philpot-Camp.*

CAMP, GEO.; 106 Euston Road, London in 1865; 59 Gloucester Road, Regents Park, London NW. Harmonium manufacturer, 1865-1887.

CANADA ORGAN CO.; London, Ontario 1865. Reorganized as *Canada Organ and Piano Co. Ltd.* and moved to Toronto, Ontario in 1873 with R.S. Williams as president; directors: Daniel Bell of *Excelsior Organ*, Marshall Bancroft, William H. Williams, John Miller of *Miller and Karn*.

ČÁPEK, FRIEDRICH; Obere Vorstadt 165 in 1903, Untere Vorstadt 47 in 1930, Policka, Czechoslovakia. Formerly *B.F. Čápek*, established 1874. Succeeded by *Karl Čápek*, located at 47 Dolni Předměsti, Policka about 1930.

CAPITAL CITY ORGAN CO.; Opera House Block, Lansing, Michigan, 1885. W.S. Holmes, proprietor. Retail and wholesale dealer. Organs with this name were probably made by others with the Capital City stencil.

CAPPELEN, JERGEN WRIGHT; (1805-78). Started in 1829 as a book dealer located at Kirkeg. 15, Christiania (now Oslo), Norway. The business is still operating at that address as a book publisher and rare book dealer. Later started selling pianos and by 1840 opened a separate piano department. Also sold the Chicago Cottage, Mason & Hamlin, Carpenter, Gregorian, Putnam, Mannborg and other organs. Cappelens manufactured about 500 small upright pianos in the period 1953-59, and may also have made harmoniums.

CAPURON, see *Gentis & Capuron*.

CARHART, JEREMIAH; made his first accordion in 1836 and lap organ in 1839; granted patent No. 12,837 on the suction bellows on Dec. 28, 1846 while working for *Prince & Co.*, but it was later declared null and void. Co-founder with Elias P. Needham of *Carhart & Needham*.

CARHART & NEEDHAM; 172 Fulton St., 75-79 E. 13th St., New York, NY 1850-1855; *Carhart, Needham & Co.*, 97-101 E. 23rd St. 1861, 1865. See *Needham Piano & Organ Co.* Founded 1846 in Worcester, MA by Elias Parkman Needham and Jeremiah Carhart, moved to Stanton St., New York in 1848 and in 1850 moved to 13th St. between Third and Fourth Avenues, New York, occupying a part of John B. Dunham's piano factory. In 1855 Samuel C. Swartz was admitted as a partner and the company became *Carhart, Needham & Co.* In the same year the factory was moved to 143-147 E. 23rd St. Swartz died in 1865 and the name reverted to *Carhart & Needham* until 1868 when Carhart died. The company was then renamed *E.P. Needham & Son*. In 1880 Needham sold his patents and "practically" retired. Serial numbers:

1846—642	1853—2090	1860—4386
1847—820	1854—2520	1862—4970
1848—940	1856—3000	1863—5200
1850—1400	1858—3300	

CARLOSS, H., & CO.; in 1886 at 133 Dartmouth Park Hill, Highgate, London; in 1896 at 45 Holloway Rd. N, London. Harmonium and American organ manufacturer, still working in 1903.

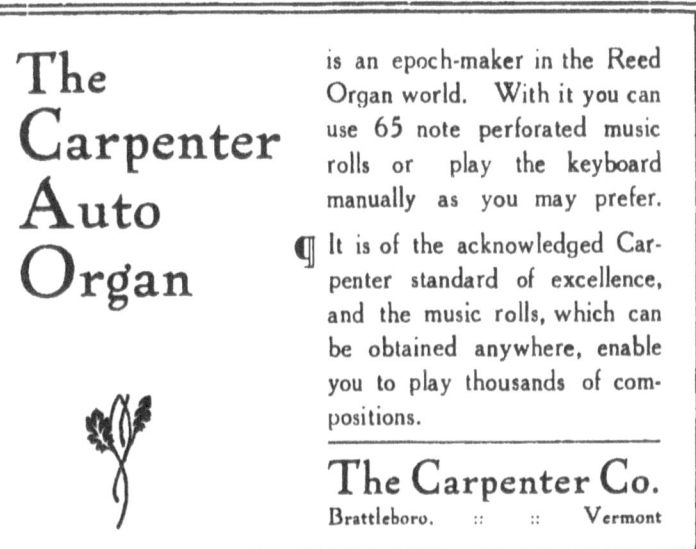

CARPENTER CO., THE; Brattleboro, VT.; see *E.P. Carpenter & Co.*
CARPENTER & COLEMAN; Syracuse, NY. See *U.S. Carpenter.*
CARPENTER, EDWIN B.; came to Brattleboro from Guilford, ME in 1850 and bought J.L. Jones' interest in *Jones & Burditt*; the firm name became *Burditt & Carpenter*. In 1852 Jacob Estey bought out Riley Burditt and the name changed to *E.B. Carpenter & Co.*, then Carpenter sold his interest to Isaac Hines. Later Carpenter associated with George Woods and Samuel Jones as *Carpenter, Jones & Woods*, still later sold out to Estey again and moved to Mendota, IL, where he went into partnership with G.W. Tewksbury in 1865 as *Tewksbury & Carpenter*, located at Washington and Main Streets. In 1866 they were located in the Dawson Building. In 1868 Eaken Smith and Abel Hoffman joined the company and it was renamed *Tewksbury, Carpenter & Co.*, now located at Sixth St. and Eleventh Ave. Tewksbury left in 1873 and the name changed to *Carpenter, Scott & Wise*, and in 1875 to *Western Cottage Organ Co.*, (qv). Carpenter sold out his interest and started manufacturing organs on his own as *E.B. Carpenter* from 1876 to 1882, when he renamed his company the *Carpenter Organ Co.* It was renamed *Mendota Northwestern Cottage Organ and Piano Co.* in 1887, closed out in 1889 and he returned to Vermont, where he died in 1891.

CARPENTER, E.P., & CO.; Worcester, MA 1850-66; founded by Edwin P. Carpenter, son of E.B. Carpenter. Bankrupt in 1866, indicted for concealment of assets in bankruptcy; doing business as *E.P. Carpenter* in Worcester in 1881, started again in Brattleboro, VT 1884, occupying the former *Brattleboro Melodeon Co.* factory on Flat St. Operated at least through 1917. W.E. Carpenter became general manager in 1894. Officers in 1899: George E. Crowell, president; C.H. Davenport, treasurer; Martin Austin Jr., secretary and general manager. Later became *The Carpenter Co.* George E. Crowell, president in 1911. E.P. Carpenter served as a judge of the musical exhibits at the World's Columbian Exposition in Chicago in 1895. Serial numbers: 1884—37478, 1900—98644, 1901—100715. Cumulative production figures:

1895—95000	1906—110000	1912—119000
1898—98000	1908—115000	1913—122000
1899—100000	1909—116000	1914—124000
1902—103000	1910—117000	1915—125000
1903—105000	1911—117000	1917—126000

CARPENTER ORGAN CO., Mendota, IL, see *E.B. Carpenter*.
CARPENTER, SCOTT & WISE; Mendota, IL 1873-1875, see *E.B. Carpenter*.
CARPENTER, U.S.; Syracuse, NY. See *Carpenter & Coleman*.
CARROLL, JAMES JOS.; 92 Bartholomew Rd., Kentish Town, and 91 Islip St., NW, London. American organ maker 1880-84.
CARTER, see *Van Dorn & Carter*.
CARY, ALPHONSE; Newbury, Berkshire, England; 1890.
CASA, ASET; 4 Mayor, Madrid, Spain, 1930.
CASE, WILLIAM, & CO.; made melodeons and flat top organs ca. 1878, probably in the United States.
CASILLAS, JOSE; Villanueva y Geltrú, Spain.
CASSINI, H.T.; 319 Goswell Road, London E and 1 Finsbury Road, Wood Green, N London. Piano and harmonium manufacturer 1864-84.
CATTERINI; Italy; maker of the Glicibarifon in 1837, a four-octave physharmonica.
CAUDERÈS, JEAN-JULES; Bordeaux, France. Awarded a bronze medal for a harmonium exhibited at the Bordeaux Exposition of 1882.
CAVAILLÉ-COLL, ARISTIDE O.; 13-15-21 avenue du Maine, Paris, Established 1830; later *Charles Mutin*. Perhaps best known as a great pipe organ builder, but also highly regarded as a maker of orgues-expressifs. Made the Poïkilorgue, an orgue-expressif, in 1834. Lefébure-Wély gave recitals on this organ. See *Cloetens*.

CECELIAN organ, made by H. & R. Brastead (or Brasted) of London, a piano maker. The Cecelian organ used steel reeds. The name was later taken over by Pigott's of Dublin, Ireland, who used it on reconditioned pianos and organs.
CECILIAN PLAYER, see *Farrand Organ Co.*
CEDERGREN, A.; Bjerges, Gotland, Sweden.
CELESTINA, a 20 note floor standing organette, roll operated.
CESARINI ET CIE.; rue de Richelieu, Paris. Harmonium maker, extant 1860 to at least 1884. The only genuine Cesarini instruments had "H.C.& E." around the margin of the nameplate.
CHABIN, M.; successor to *Couty & Liné*, Paris. Later shown as *H. Chabin Sr.*, boulevard Raspail 230, Paris.
CHALLENGER, G., & CO.; 57 Long Millgate, Manchester, England, and 136-138 Hampstead Rd., London, 1892 until at least 1900. Piano, harmonium and organ maker.
CHALLIOT, CHARLES; Paris. Reed maker, 1867.
CHAMEROY, EDMÉ-AUGUSTIN; France. Began manufacture of the orgue-expressif in 1829; in 1834 offered 3 to 6 octave models voiced as bassoon, oboe and flute; see *Fourneaux*.
CHAMPION PIANO & ORGAN CO.; Cincinnati, OH. Organized in 1878 with a capital of $12,000.
CHANCEL REED ORGAN AND PIPE ORGAN WORKS; Measham, Leics., England.
CHANDLER, G.S., & CO; over 7 Opera House Block, Detroit, MI in 1871; 5 Opera House Block in 1872. George S. and Edward S. Chandler, organ and melodeon manufacturers. George S. was shown as a melodeon tuner in 1862. Shown as *G.S. & E.S. Chandler*, musical merchandise at 45 Michigan Ave. in 1877. See *Ling & Chandler*.
CHANGUION, ALPHONSE; Paris 1846, originally from Lyon. Patented an orgue-expressif in 1846. Made a highly decorated model called "le Changuion" with carved figures, heads and inlays of brass, pewter and mother-of-pearl for Louis Philippe Albert d'Orléans, Comte de Paris, grandson of Louis Philippe I. This instrument was restored by *Alexandre* and is now in the Musée de la Musique of Paris.
CHAPERON, A.; 97 rue de Charonne, Paris, 1912, 1924; 31 bis, rue Victor-Masse, 1930. Successor to *H. Christophe & Etienne, Rodolphe Fils, & Debain* and *Cottino*, (qv).
CHAPERON, NOËL; Paris. Maker of orgues-expressifs 1840-50.
CHAPPELL & CO.; 50 New Bond Street, London; 14-15 Poultry, London in 1883. Piano and harmonium maker, exhibited a harmonium in 1862. Established in 1812.
CHARD, DAVID; 101 Border St., Boston, MA. Made the Mozart Cabinet organ.

CHARD, GRANVILLE; Boston, MA ca. 1874-5. See *Bruce & Chard*.
CHARLICK, R.; 4 Scholefield Bldgs., Scholefield Rd., Upper Holloway, London, 1897; 76 Duncombe Rd., Upper Holloway, London. Advertised as a reed organ maker in 1900, established 1892.
CHARTIER, C.; 12 Market Place, Oxford Market, London. Harmonium maker 1878-84.
CHASE, A.B.; 42-46 Newton St., Norwalk, OH; office and sales room at 16 West Main St. Founded by Capt. Alvin B. Chase in 1875. Chase died in 1876 and was succeeded by Calvin Whitney, an original stockholder, who was associated with the company until 1909. The original factory was located in the old Norwalk Barrel Co. building on Newton St. This building burned in 1880 and a new building was built on Newton St., which was later occupied by the Norwalk Furniture Co. Factory capacity in 1897: 3,000 organs per year. Chase made organs until about 1900, and continued making pianos. In 1922 it became a part of United Piano Co., which in turn became part of *Aeolian* in 1928. "Like a smile on the face is the charm of the Chase." Serial numbers: 1888—11325, 1895—32605.
CHASE, AUSTIN C.; 62 South Salina Street, Syracuse, NY. Began making melodeons under his own name after his partnership with Henry R. Phelps broke up in 1864. See *Phelps & Chase*.
CHASE & BABCOCK; Syracuse, NY. Melodeon maker.
CHAUFFER; Paris. Harmonium maker, including a small five-octave instrument without stops called the "Chaufferette."
CHAZELLE, P.; Avallon, France. Harmonium maker ca. 1896.
CHEIN & CO.; Burlington, NJ. Organette maker.
CHENEY, J.D.; 135½ Middle St., Portland, ME in 1861; Stevens Plains, ME in 1877. Made portable melodeons and cabinet organs. The reed organ business separated as *Small & Knight* before 1866 and J.D. Cheney continued on his own, later as a dealer at least through 1883.
CHIAPPA & FERSANI; 6 Little Bath St., Eyre-street Hill, Clerkenwell, London. The partnership was dissolved in 1880, succeeded by *Giuseppe Chiappa & Son*.
CHICAGO CABINET ORGAN CO.; Chicago, IL. (No other information available.)
CHICAGO COTTAGE ORGAN CO.; started in the fall of 1879 as the *Wolfinger Organ Co.* by F.R. Wolfinger, president, John A. Comstock, secretary, and Herman D. Cable, treasurer. Originally located in a two-story building at Randolph and Ann Streets, Chicago. About 1885 Comstock sold his interest to E.E. Wise and George W. Tewksbury, both formerly connected with the *Western Cottage Organ Co.*, and the name changed to *Chicago Cottage Organ Co.* W.N. Van Matre (qv) also came in as sales manager and a stockholder in 1885, remaining until 1895.

A few years later Wolfinger sold his interest to G.K. Barnes. A large building was acquired for the factory at 22nd and Paulina Streets. E.E. Wise sold his interest to Cable and Tewksbury, Cable becoming president. Barnes sold his interest in 1889, and Fayette S. and H.M. Cable came into the business, which after H.D. Cable's death in 1899 became *The Cable Co.* with F.S. Cable as president. A second factory was built in St. Charles, Ill. in 1899, and an office building at 215-221 Wabash Ave., bringing the capacity to 16,000 pianos and 18,000 organs per year. Chicago Cottage made stencil organs for many music dealers such as *Capital City Organ Co.*, Lansing, MI; *Bell,* Saginaw, MI; and *Grinnell Bros.*, Detroit, MI. F.S. Cable left the company about 1904 and bought the *Lakeside Organ Co.*, changing its name to the Fayette S. Cable Piano Co., which later became the Cable-Nelson Co. Hobart M. Cable left The Cable Co. and bought the *Burdett Organ Co.*, changing its name to *The Hobart M. Cable Co.* Serial numbers: 1892—43315, 1894—118189, 1907—250783.

The Chicago Cottage Organ Co. booth at the Columbian Exposition, Chicago, 1895.

CHICAGO MUSIC CO.; 150 Wabach Ave. in 1886; 195-7 Wabash Ave., Chicago, IL; maker of the Leslie Organ.
CHILD & CO.; Cleveland, OH 1859-1861. See *Bishop & Co., Bishop & Child.*
CHILVERS, W. & J.; Bedford Street, Norwich, Norfolk, England. Organ and harmonium maker 1878-82.
CHING, see *Boosey & Ching.*
CHISE, GIUSEPPE, E FIGLIO; Pratovecchio, Arezzo, Italy. Harmonium makers from 1837 until at least 1909. Also shown as *Chisci* and *Ghisci.*

CHORETTA; Germany. Portable "suitcase" organ with steel reeds, 1959.
CHRISTENSEN, N.C.; Thisted, Denmark, 1909. Organ and harmonium maker.
CHRISTOPHE, H., & ÉTIENNE; 11 rue de Charonne, 97 rue de Charonne in 1883, 1903 and 1912, Paris. Organ and harmonium makers, established in 1861, had 51 workers in 1872. Both principals had previously been foremen at *Alexandre's*. Succeeded by *A. Chaperon*. Awarded a gold medal at the Paris Exhibition of 1889.
CHURCH, JOHN; 66 West Fourth St. from 1859 to 1885, then 72-74 West Fourth St., Cincinnati, OH. Music dealer and publisher, also sold the John Church organ, presumably made by others with the Church stencil.
CHUTE & BUTLER; established in 1901 at La Fontaine, IN, removed to Peru, IN in 1906; also located in Marion, IN at one time. Hiram E. Chute, secretary, treasurer and general manager. Made the Piolian Organ. See *Chute, Hall & Co.* Serial numbers:

```
1900—1860    1905—1881    1910—1908
1903—1872    1909—1885
```

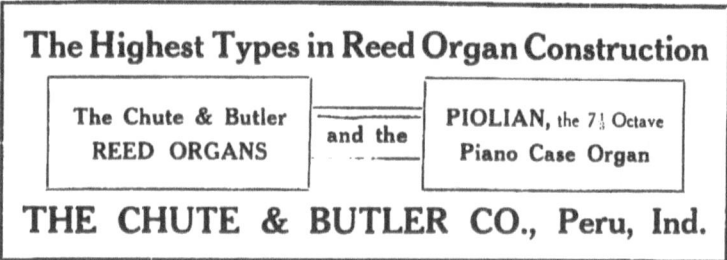

The Highest Types in Reed Organ Construction

The Chute & Butler REED ORGANS and the PIOLIAN, the 7¼ Octave Piano Case Organ

THE CHUTE & BUTLER CO., Peru, Ind.

CHUTE, HALL & CO.; 97 to 107 Water Street, Yarmouth, Nova Scotia 1883-94. Founded May 1, 1883 by Hiram E. Chute and Thomas Hall. W.F. Shaw was also active in the company. Manufacturers of reed organs, organ actions and piano stools, also dealers in pianos and music books. After a disastrous fire in 1892 in which the factory was destroyed, Hall and Shaw withdrew from the company, which continued under the name of *H.E. Chute & Co.*, with offices and showrooms in the Oddfellow's Building on the corner of John and Second Street. The business probably closed in 1894 since the Yarmouth Directory of 1895 shows no listing for *H.E. Chute & Co.*, and H.E. Chute is shown as an agent. In 1901 Chute appears as a principal in *Chute & Butler*, (qv).

CIOFFI, VINCENZO; via S. Sebastiano 18, Naples, Italy, 1903.
CITY HARMONIUM WORKS; Nr. Jaganmoham Palace, Mysore, India. C.S.N. Swamy & Son, proprietors, 1930.
CITY TRADING CO.; Saghir Chowk, Noshera Rd., Gujranwala, Pakistan. Currently manufacturing Indian table harmoniums.
CLARABELLA organ, see *C.E. Hale.*
CLARABELLA ORGAN CO.; Toronto, Ontario. Serial Numbers: 1898—9356, 1900—5188.
CLARABELLA ORGAN MANUFACTORY; Worcester, MA. Active at least from 1885 to 1900. In 1885 advertised four new models in the Trades Review (UK): Gothic, Aesthetis, New Empress and Grand Orchestral.
CLARK & BAUGHM; Quincy, IL. (Probably Melville Clark) Active about 1877-1880. Succeeded by *Clark & Rich.*
CLARK & BISHOP; Cleveland, OH, 1869. Melodeon maker.
CLARK, HUGH ARCHIBALD; Philadelphia, PA. Granted US Patent 105780 on a melodeon in 1870.
CLARK, LEWIS C., & CO.; Worcester, MA.
CLARK, MELVILLE; started an organ factory under the name of *Clark & Co.*, located at 10th and Franklin, Oakland, California in 1875, sold out in 1877 and went to Quincy, IL (see *Clark & Baughm*) and then to Chicago, where he formed another organ factory under the name of *Clark & Rich* in 1880. He was apparently associated in some way with *Story & Camp*, since his patented tilt-top case design is featured in their 1882 catalog. Clark & Rich was succeeded by Story & Camp in 1882. He then joined with Hampton L. Story to form *Story & Clark* (qv) in 1884. The Story & Clark catalog for 1885 credits Clark with building the first organ factory in Chicago. He left Story & Clark in 1900 to devote himself to the player piano business under the name of the *Melville Clark Co.*, located in De Kalb, IL, which sold the Apollo push-up player in 1901.
CLARK & RICH; 42 S. Canal and 22 S. Jefferson (1881), 687-695 S. Canal, corner of 16th St. (1882), Chicago, IL. Melville Clark and George W. Rich, partners. Founded in 1880, succeeded by *Story & Camp* in 1882.
CLARK, R.W.; 86A Leighton Rd., Kentish Town, London. Organ and piano key maker. Formerly *Sebright & Clark.*
CLARK, T.C., & CO.; 49 Causeway, Boston, MA, Melodeon maker, 1853.
CLARK, WILLIAM; Little Dockray, Penrith, Cumberland, England 1878-87. Harmonium maker.
CLARK, see *Nunn & Clark.*
CLARKE & SONS; Kirton Lindsay, Lincolnshire, England. Organ and harmonium builders, 1882-87.

CLARRY, W.W.; 23 Hertford Drive, Liscard, Cheshire, England. Pipe and reed organ maker, established 1875.

CLAUDE, CH., & SONS; 154 Ossulston St., Euston Rd., London; factory at 11 Parkers Place, Middlesex Street, Somers Town, London. Harmonium manufacturer 1853-1881.

CLAUS, F., FILS; 96 rue Ange-Blaize, Rennes, France, 1930.

CLAY CITY ORGAN CO.; Uxbridge, Ontario; located in Zanesville, OH in 1903, 1907.

CLEVELAND MELODEON CO.; Cleveland, OH. (Name only, no other data available.)

CLEVELAND ORGAN CO.; Cleveland, OH. (Name only, no other data available.)

CLINTON ORGAN CO., see *Oakes Organ Co.*

CLOETENS, GEORGES (1870-1949); 37 rue de Lausanne, Saint-Gilles-lez-Bruxelles, Belgium in 1901; 14 rue Belvedere, Brussels, 1903. Pipe organ builder, also made combination instruments such as l'Orpheal in 1925, a piano, organ and harmonium. In association with *Cavaillé-Coll* produced instruments labelled "Orpheal Cavaillé-Coll Paris." Cloetens filed for a patent on a harmonium with glass beating reeds.

CLOUGH & WARREN CO.; Detroit, MI 1850-1899; Adrian, MI 1899-1923. Started as *Wm. P. Blakeman* in 1850; then *Simmons & Blakeman*; became *A.A. Simmons & Co.* in 1854; then *Simmons & Whitney* in 1859; located at 168 Woodward Ave. in 1863; opened sales office at 104 Jefferson Ave. in 1865; *Whitney & Co.* in 1860 and 1866; then *Simmons, Clough & Co.* with James E. Clough in 1868, located at 15-19 Miami Ave.; *Simmons & Clough Organ Co.* at 6th & Congress Streets in 1873; *Clough & Warren Organ Co.* in 1874; and *Clough & Warren Co.* 1892-1923. George P. Warren became a partner in 1874, retired 1899, then his brother Joseph A. Warren became sole owner. The company went bankrupt in 1911, reorganized in 1913, discontinued organ production in 1916. The Warrens had previously worked for *Estey*. In 1879 Queen Victoria bought a Clough & Warren organ for the people of the Pitcairn Islands. The inscription said, "A present from the Queen to her loyal and loving Pitcairn Island subjects, in appreciation of their domestic virtues." It was sent on H.B.M.'s frigate Opal. In 1889 Clough & Warren received an order from Melbourne, Australia for eleven cartloads of their organs. See *Granville Wood*, also *Detroit Melodeon Co.*

Estimated total production:

1850-1865	100 organs per year	1,500
1866-1872	200 organs per year	1,400
1873-1883	5,000 organs per year	50,000
1884-1898	7,000 organs per year	98,000
1899		600
1900-1916	5,000 organs per year	80,000
1917-1923		700
	TOTAL	232,200

Serial numbers:

1876—25698	1890—90300	1905—119083
1879—28340	1891—93045	1907—114120
1881—38027	1892—95989	
1889—79342	1898—105146	

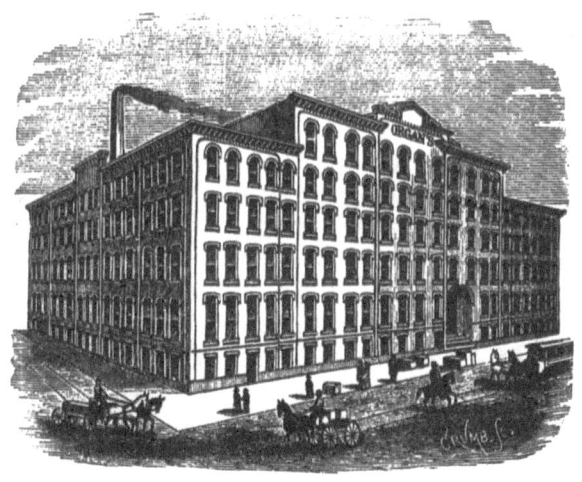

The Clough & Warren factory, Detroit, Michigan.

CLYDE MANUFACTURING CO.; Clyde, OH, 1885.
CNOBLOCH-BAR, G..; 4 rue de l'Empereur, Brussels, Belgium. Maker and repairer of pianos and harmoniums, late 1900s.
COBDEN PIANOFORTE CO.; 18 Eversholt St., Camden Town, London. Piano and harmonium maker, 1883.
COCKS, ROBERT, & CO.; 6 New Burlington St., London; 19 Park St., Camden Town, London. American organ manufacturer 1878-79, after that a dealer.

COD'HANT; awarded a bronze medal for an orgue-expressif at the Paris Exhibition of 1847.
COHNEN; 8 quai de la Batte, Liege, Belgium, 1875-1876. Maker or retailer of harmoniums and accordions.
COLBURN, see *Sommers & Colburn*.
COLCLOUGH & SCOTT; 138 Hampstead Road, NW London. American organ manufacturer 1887-1889.
COLEMAN, ABED; patented a combination piano and organ which was produced by *T. Gilbert* (qv). The Coleman reed attachment was also used on some pianos made by R. Nunns & Clark.
COLEMAN, CHARLES ALFRED; 25 New Road, Rothenhite, London. Piano and harmonium maker, 1883.
COLEMAN, J., & SONS; Toronto, Ontario, 1867-1890. Reed and pipe organ makers.
COLES, see *Prosper & Coles*.
COLLA, ERNESTO; Vicomoscano, Cremona, Italy. Harmonium and barrel organ maker. Exhibited at Arezzo, Italy in 1882.
COLLARD & MOUTRIE; 90 Southampton Rd., London, 1883; 50-52 Southampton St., London. See *Moutrie*.
COLLET, A.; 14 rue Jules-Dalou, Malakoff, France, 1930.
COLLINO, VITTORIA, E CIA.; 11 via S. Francis de Paolo, Turin, Italy, 1930.
COLLINS; Omaha, NE. (Name only, no other information available.)
COLLINS & ARMSTRONG; 302-304 Houston St., Ft. Worth, TX. Incorporated Dec. 1, 1890 with H.D. Cable, Chicago as vice-president. Sold organs made by *Chicago Cottage Organ Co.* with the Collins & Armstrong stencil 1890-92. After that sold Chicago Cottage Organs. In 1899 became *Cable Piano Co.* with Elmon Armstrong, manager.
COLLINS ORGAN & PIANO CO.; Ellingfort Rd., Mare St., Hackney, London. Established 1882 by C.H. Collins; advertised in 1900 as a piano and American organ maker. See *Imperial Organ & Piano Co.*
COLLINSON, WILLIAM; 1 Herbert Road, Chooter's Hill, Woolwich, London. Piano and harmonium maker, 1883.
COLSETH, PETER, & CO.; Moline, IL 1877-1881; see *Moline Cabinet Organ Co.*
COLUMBIA ORGAN CO.; New York. Serial No.: 1903—21891.
COLUMBIAN ORGAN CO.; Grand Crossing, IL; also *Columbian Organ & Piano Co.*, Wabash Avenue, Chicago, IL. Serial number: 1893—1479.
COMMAILLE, AUGUSTE; Bordeaux (Gironde), France. Harmonium maker ca. 1896.

> *ENTHUSIASTICALLY ENDORSED*
>
> ## Compensating Pipe Organs
> BY THE TRADE, THE PROFESSION AND THE PUBLIC. SOLD ONLY THROUGH THE TRADE. TERRITORY RAPIDLY TAKEN UP.
> WRITE FOR PARTICULARS
>
> ### Compensating Pipe Organ Co., Ltd.
> BATTLE CREEK, MICH., U. S. A.

COMPENSATING PIPE ORGAN CO.; Battle Creek, MI, Toronto, Ontario 1900-1910. Made a combination pipe and reed organ. Acquired by *Lyon & Healy*.
COMUS S.P.A.; viale Don Bosco 35, 62018 Potenza Picena (MC), Italy. Made the Bontempi organ, an electrically-blown reed organ, 1985.
CONFERBRE; Paris. Harmonium reed maker.
CONLEY CHURCH ORGAN CO.; Madoc, Ont. 1890. Sold organs made by *Berlin Organ Co.* with the Conley stencil. See *Cowley*.
CONN, C.G.; Elkhart, IN. Charles G. Conn, musical instrument manufacturer. Made the Wonder portable organ, patented 1901.
CONRAD, MARTIN & TÖRSTE; Aurelienstr. 56, Leipzig-Lindenau, Germany; also shown at Lützner Str. 33, Leipzig. Established in 1925. Richard Conrad, W. Martin and A. Törste, proprietors in 1930. Conrad had previously worked for *Popper & Co.*
CONSTRUCTION D'AUTOMATES ET D'INSTRUMENTS DE MUSIQUE MECANIQUES; rue des Danvions, 70000 Vesoul, France. J.F. Saire, owner. Maker of paper-roll operated organettes, 1988.
CONTI, ENRICO; Florence, Italy. Piano and harmonium maker, 1883.
CONTI, GIO., & FIGLIO; Milan, Italy, 1883. Harmonium and piano maker.
COOK, DAVID C.; David C. Cook Publishing Co., 36 Washington St., Chicago, IL, 1900. Organs with this name were made by others with the Cook stencil. At least some were made by the *Chicago Cottage Organ Co.*
COOK, GEO., & CO.; New Haven, CT. Lyre-legged melodeon, about 1855; also a flat-topped organ ca. 1870.
COOK & MARTIN; Rochester, NY. Organ made for them by *Taylor & Farley*.
COOK, RICHARD, & CO.; 133 Fenchurch St., London. Piano and harmonium maker, 1883.
COOL, ISAAC, & SONS; in 1882 at 46-47 Clarence Place, Newtown, Bristol, England. Organ and harmonium maker. Closed 1888.
CO-OPERATIVE ORGAN CO.; Mendota, IL, 1889.

COOPER, JAMES, & CO.; in 1879 at Greenman St., Essex Road, Islington, London; in 1883 at Peabody Yard, Essex Road, Islington; in 1886 at 70 Shepperton Road, Islington. Still working in 1906. Made the Chorister reed organ.

COPE, M.L.; Souderton, PA. Made the Excelsior parlor organ, 1910.

CORBEEL; France. Harmonium keyboard maker. Awarded a silver medal in 1878 at the Paris Exposition.

CORDLEY, J.; South Main St., Adrian, MI, 1870. Organ and melodeon manufacturer. See *Pruden & Cordley*.

CORNEGLIO, G.; Caselle Torinese, Italy, 1909.

CORNISH & CO.; factory on Hornbaker St., corner of Washington Ave., Washington, NJ 1879 to about 1921. Founded by Joseph B. Cornish, who sold organs in the 1870s. In 1879 he bought out *Dawes & Wyckoff*. He was later joined by his son Johnston Cornish. Sold direct to customers, said to be the only one of the Washington, NJ organ builders who made money. Factory capacity in 1900: 8,000 organs per year. Organ actions, keys, etc. were bought from others. Alvin F. Florey, general manager. Discontinued organ production about 1917. Serial numbers:

    1897—86492   1906—139279   1913—176886
    1899—104374   1906—146035   1914—177891
    1900—108241   1907—150718

CORNISH, WINTER & CO.; Washington, NJ; predecessor of *Cornish & Co.*

CORNWALL, G.W., & CO.; Huntingdon, Quebec; established before 1889. Acquired by the *Pratte Piano Co.* in 1895. Built reed organs at least through 1912.

CORWALL & PATTERSON ORGAN CO., see *Patterson*.

COTRINA; Vitoria, Spain. Name of maker uncertain. Harmonium with transposing keyboard, located in the Iglesia de Santiago, Calle Granada, Málaga, Spain.

COTSWOLD organette. Currently made by Peter K. Watts, 14 Rock Hill, Chipping Norton, Oxon. OX7 5BA, England.

COTTAGE GEM; organ in the Conklin Museum collection, serial number 33391. Possibly of British manufacture.

COTTAGE QUEEN organ, see *Wm. Stires & Son*.

COTTIAU, P.F.J.; Paris. Reed maker, 1862. Honorable mention at the London Exhibition of 1862 for good work on harmonium tongues.

COTTINO, JOSEPH; 47 Basset St., Kentish Town, London, 1883.

COTTINO & TAILLEUR; 119 rue de Montreuil, Paris; successors to *Boutevilin*. Also shown as *Cottino*. In 1921 advertised an instrument called "l'America, the perfect French system. Tone: soft and round and

harmonious," with a transposing keyboard and 2½ rows of reeds. Awarded medals at the Paris Expositions of 1878 and 1889. Established in 1863; in business at least until 1922. See *Chaperon*.
COURSER, see *Morrison & Courser*.
COURTIER; Paris. Made the Eoli-Courtier, a two-manual free reed organ in 1844.
COUSE, A.; Detroit, MI; melodeons, ca. 1845.
COUTY & LINÉ; 58 rue Bonaparte, Paris 1883. Established 1858, succeeded by *M. Chabin*. Awarded a silver medal at the Paris Exposition of 1878.
COUTY, MAISON, see *Gentis & Capuron*.

COUTY & RICHARD; 89 rue Nve. des Petits-Champs, Paris. René Couty and Jules Richard. Awarded medal of honor at Paris Exposition, 1867. René Couty first worked with *Alexandre*. Listed as a piano and harmonium manufacturer in 1868 at 82 Boulevard Sébastopol, Paris. Split up by 1878. See *Couty & Liné, J. Richard & Cie.*

COWLEY CHURCH ORGAN CO.; Madoc, Ont. 1890. Spelling uncertain, possibly *Conley*, (qv).

COX, ALFRED J., & SON; 17 Fortnam Rd., Upper Holloway, London. Builder, tuner, voicer and repairman 1881-1914. Continued working as repairman until 1941 when he retired at age 82.

COX & PIERCE; Pittsfield, MA. Melodeon makers. See *Wm. Pierce*.

CRABB, WM. R.; 147 Upper Kennington Lane, London. Harmonium maker 1878-1886.

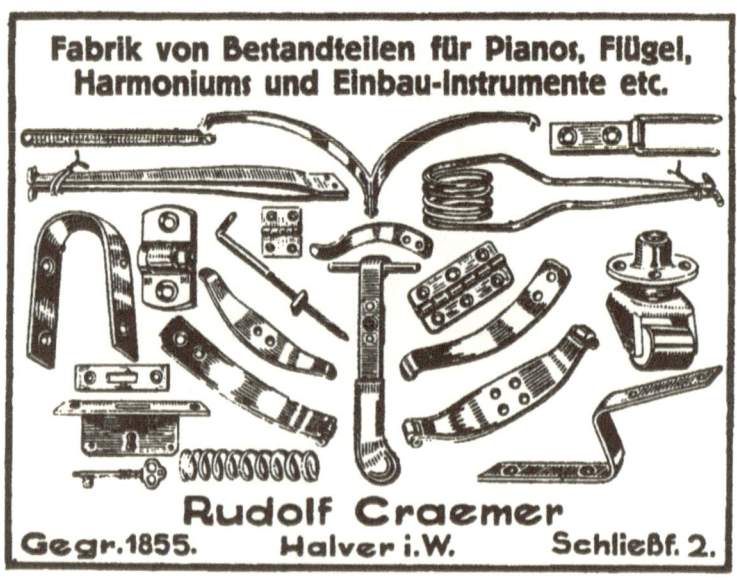

CRAEMER, RUDOLF; Berliner Str. 61, Halver, Germany; maker of springs and metal components for harmoniums. Established 1855, still working in 1930.

CRAMER, J.B., & CO. LTD.; 201-207-209 Regent Street, London W and 64 West Street, Brighton, England; factory in Lyme Street, Camden Town, London in 1871; in 1921 located at 139 New Bond St. Manufacturer and dealer in pianos, organs, harmoniums and American organs. Made harmoniums from one-stop four-octave to 24 stop 2mp models. Listed in directories 1868 through 1921. In 1889 the following notice was published: "Messrs Wood & Peach, trading as J B Cramer &

Co. of Regent Street & Notting Hill, dealers in musical instrs, dissolved partnership Jan 1st 1889. The debts will be collected and paid by Mr George Wood, who continues the business."
CRANE & SONS; Wexham, England. Discontinued organ production before 1921 when they were listed as dealers at 149 Oxford St., London.
CRAVEN & CO.; London. Harmonium manufacturer.
CRAWFORD, F.; Broadway, Eltham Park, London, 1900-1914; then at 14 Heavitree Road, Plumstead, London. In 1921 located at 37 Shooters Hill Gardens, Eltham Park, London. He was previously an employee of *J.W. Sawyer*.
CRESCENDO HARMONIUM, see *Osc. Ericson, Kbh.*
CRESCENT; Evansville, IN.
CRESWELL & BALL, (name only, no other information available.)
CRISTINI, GIUSEPPE; Acciano, Aquila, Italy.
CRODA ORGAN KABUSHIKI GAISHA; Okusawa, Setagaya-ku, Tokyo. Established in 1959 as *Tōyō Densi Gakki Kenkyujo* by Ichiro Kuroda. Made the Crodatone reed organs until 1965. These organs used small reeds similar to those in the harmonica, enclosed in dust-proof containers and electronically amplified in a manner similar to the Everett Orgatron. The current models of the Crodatone are fully electronic. Also presently building pipe organs. Croda produced the following quantities of reed organs: 1959—2, 1960—1, 1961—7, 1962—3, 1963—2, 1964—10, 1965—7.
CROGER, RICHARD; 184 White Chapel Road, London. Established about 1836. Still in business in 1909 as a music dealer, operated by Croger's son.
CROGER, THOMAS; 17 Devonshire St., London 1859; died in 1863 and his widow Emma took over. Manufactured instruments and sold parts.
CROKAERT, SEBASTIEN; 155 West St., Sheffield, England, also York. Made a combination piano and harmonium. Extant 1880-1896.
CROSBY MANUFACTURING CO.; Cambridgeport, MA; stop knobs. Active 1883.
CROWN ORGAN, see *Geo. P. Bent*; name also later used by *Sears, Roebuck*.
CULLUM, CHARLES FREDERICK, & CO.; in 1878 at 76 Euston Rd., NW London. In 1882 the extension of the Midland Railway required him to relocate to 98 Euston Road—called the Midland Showrooms. In 1886 located at 108 Euston Road. Harmonium maker 1859-1896.
CUONZO, VINCENZO; Bitonto, Italy, 1930.
CURRIER, see *Whitney & Currier*.
CURTIS, CHARLES; 28 & 29 Baker St., London. Piano and harmonium manufacturer 1880-1896.

CRAMER'S
AMERICAN ORGANS.

CRAMER & CO. are the only Manufacturers in England of the American Organs. The tone is most agreeable, and, although produced from the ordinary vibrator, is nearer to that of the metal pipe than has hitherto been obtained from the Harmonium.

The following are the varieties at present Manufactured by CRAMER & CO.:

Black Walnut or Oak,	Knee Swell,	5 octaves	...	£12 0 0
,, ,,	,, 2 stops, ,,		...	15 0 0
,, ,,	,, 4 ,, ,,		...	22 0 0
,, ,,	,, 6 ,, ,,		...	28 0 0
Rosewood or Walnut,	,, 8 ,, ,,		...	34 0 0

**HARMONIUM & AMERICAN ORGAN ROOMS,
201, REGENT STREET, LONDON, W.; and WEST STREET, BRIGHTON.**
CRAMER, WOOD & CO., Moorgate Street, London; & Dublin & Belfast.

CURTIS, GEORGE H., Concord, NH 1856; later *Ballou & Curtis*. In 1864 he was employed by *Dearborn, Severance & Co.*, and in 1867 by *Parker & Secomb*.
CZERNY, see *Hoffman & Czerny*.

D

DALE, DANIEL; 143 Albany Road, London in 1850; 3 Albany Road in 1855; 368 Albany Road in 1863; became *D. Dale & Son* in 1871. Harmonium maker, succeeded by *Samuel Dale* in 1872.
DALES & DALTON; Newmarket, Ontario 1870; melodeons. See *R.H. Dalton*.
D'ALMAINE, T., & CO.; a piano maker established in 1785; in 1853 located at 20 Soho Square, London, selling Alexandre harmoniums. In 1880 advertised as a piano manufacturer at 5 Finsbury Pavement, London. In 1889 advertised as a piano and American organ maker at 91 Finsbury Pavement. In 1913 moved to 244 Tottenham Court Road, and in 1921 shown at 135 Finsbury Pavement, London. T. d'Almaine died in 1877 and the business was continued by R.F. Robertson. Still in business as a reed organ maker in 1931.
DALTON, R.H.; Toronto, Ontario, from 1867 until 1890. Partner in *Dales & Dalton*.
DANIELL, WILLIAM; melodeons, 1865. (No further information.)
DANIELS, EDWARD; 65 Gooch Street, Birmingham, England. Harmonium maker 1879-1882.
DARD-JANIN; 3 rue de la République, St. Etienne, France. Piano and harmonium maker and dealer, 1883.
DARLEY & HOSKIN, see *Dominion Organ*.
DARLEY & ROBINSON, see *Dominion Organ*.
DARLING, JOSEPH L.; 331 Broadway, St. Louis, MO 1861. Melodeon manufacturer.
DATYNER & SZPECHT; Warsaw. Exhibited harmoniums at the Paris Exhibition of 1889.
D'AVENIA, LUIGI; via Tribunali 3, Naples, Italy, 1903.
DAVIE, JACKSON & CO.; Chicago, IL. Charles H. Davie and William Jackson patented and built a combination reed and pipe organ in 1870.
DAVIES, WM. H.; 55 Great Newton Street, Pembroke Place, Liverpool, England. Piano and harmonium maker 1878-1882.

DAVIS, A., & CO.; Worcester, MA. Reed maker, successor to *E. Harrington.*

DAVIS, J.D., & CO.; Chicago, IL; see *Treat & Linsley.*

DAWES, WILLIAM; 2 Kingston Grove, Leeds, England; also at 2 Ridge Terrace; factory located at Bagby Mills, Leeds. Maker of Melody attachment, first patented 1864, and used at least on the following harmoniums: *Alexandre, Archibald Ramsden, Schiedmayer* and *Mustel*. Patented a pedal bass attachment in 1868.

DAWES & WYCKOFF; Belvidere Ave., Washington, NJ. Succeeded by *Cornish* in 1879. John M. Wyckoff then became factory superintendent for *Daniel Beatty*. Factory located in the Van Doren warehouse along the canal on Belvidere Avenue.

DAWKINS & CO.; 205-207 City Road, London EC, 17 Charterhouse St., Holborn Circus, London in 1900. Reed organ maker and importer, established 1780.

DAY & MYERS; 37 Poultry, London; manufacturers of Aeolophon and Seraphine. Extant 1836.

DAYTON, ARVID; Wolcotville, CT. Born 1814, son of *Jonah Dayton* (qv), made both pipe and reed organs. Exhibited at the Wolcotville Fair in 1866. He was a key witness in the Burdett vs. Estey case, 1883. His brother Justus and son William H. worked for him.

DAYTON, JONAH; Wolcotville, CT. Made pipe and reed organs in the early 1840s, then reed organs with his son Arvid after 1846.

DEARBORN, ANDREW P.; Fayette St. in 1844, 45 Pleasant St. in 1850, Concord, NH.

DEARBORN & BARTLETT; 180 Main St., Concord, NH, 1844-47; David M. Dearborn and D.B. Bartlett.

DEARBORN, DAVID M.; Concord, NH 1847-1853; see *Austin & Dearborn, Liscom Dearborn & Co., Dearborn & Bartlett, Dearborn & Severance.*

DEARBORN, SEVERANCE & CO.; Concord, NH, 1860-64; David M. Dearborn & A.F. Severance.

DEBAIN, ALEXANDRE-FRANÇOIS; (1809-1877); in 1839 at boulv. St. Denis, Paris; in 1843 at 76-78 rue de Bondy, Paris; in 1845 at 53 & 15 rue Vivienne, Paris; in 1856 at 24-28 place de La Fayette; in 1865 and 1883 at 116-118 place de La Fayette; in 1888 listed as *Rodolphe Fils et Debain* at 15 rue Chaligny, Paris; factory at St. Ouen, France. Established 1834; had 105 workers in 1872, absorbed by *Rodolphe Fils* in 1896. Debain became superintendent of the Johann Pape piano factory in Paris in 1832 at age 22, and made many contributions to piano and reed organ design. He coined the name "Harmonium" for his reed organ patented in 1842. Debain's Harmonium differed from its predecessor the orgue-expressif in the arrangement of the casework, hinging of the various sub-assemblies, the resonating chambers, the stop arrangement, the designation of the stops by number, name and range on the stop face, and the division of the reeds into bass and treble parts. Other makers were quick to copy the instrument as well as to appropriate the name "harmonium" as a generic name. He also made a wide variety of reed organs, mainly pressure-operated, but including the "Organophone," a suction instrument, and the "Harmonicorde," a combination piano and organ. Serial numbers: 1867—17372, 1873—26207/19213.

DECKER JR., CHRISTIAN; 316 Sycamore, Evansville, IN. Piano maker, tuner and repairman at least as early as 1858. He began making melodeons about 1868, and is listed as a piano and organ maker through 1892.

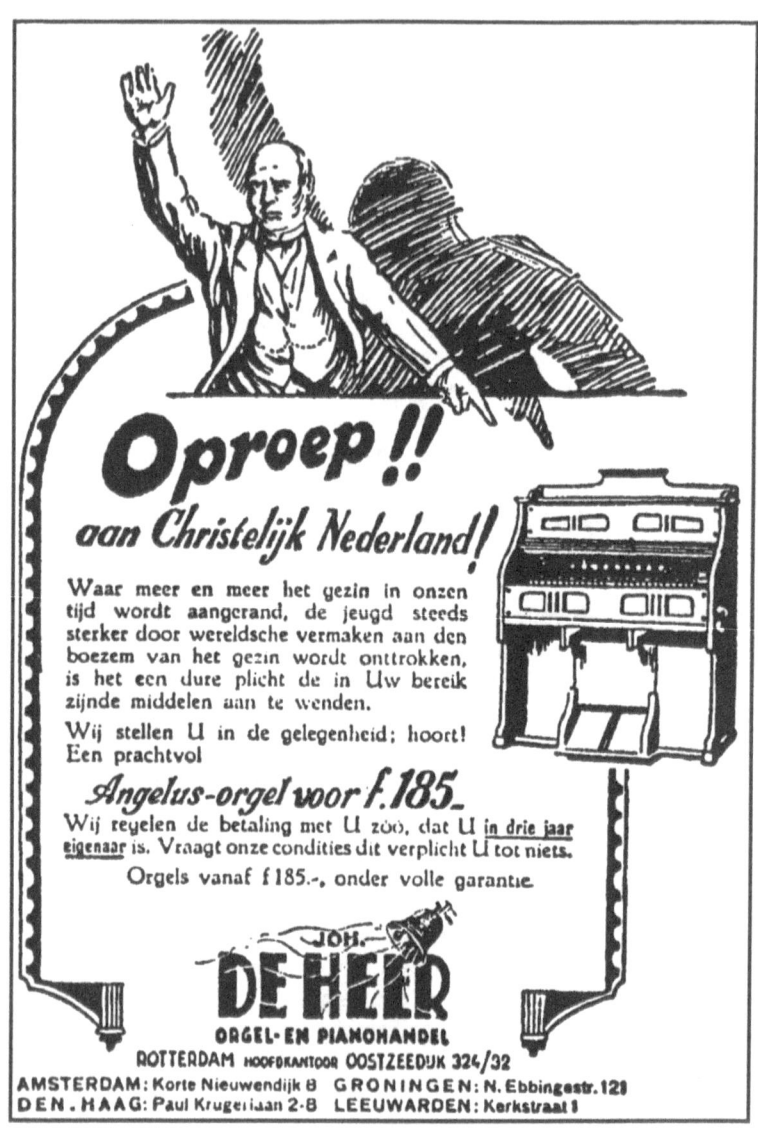

DE GROMARD, ARTHUR QUENTIN; France. Made the "Cecilium" in 1867, a free-reed instrument resembling the Mélophone of Pellerin. Awarded a bronze medal at the Paris Exposition of 1878.

DE HEER, JOHANNES; Ooszeedijk 324/32, Rotterdam, Netherlands, branches in the Hague, Amsterdam, Utrecht, Arnhem and Leeuwarden. Piano and organ dealer from 1898 until at least 1980. Manufactured the

Angelus Harp-organ in 1913 and a portable organ about 1938. DeHeer was noted for his appeals to Christian values in his advertising.
DEKKER, A.S.J.; Goes, Netherlands. Made the two-manual and pedal Sonora organ.
DELHAUTEUR, JOSEPH; 3 chemin de la Sarte, Huy, Belgium, 35 Grand-Place, Huy from 1910 to 1921. Established 1874. Maker and retailer of pianos and harmoniums.
DE LIL, ALBERT (b. 1896); 101 rue Theodore-Verhaegen, Brussels, Belgium. Organ and harmonium maker, established 1923. Succeeded by his son Paul (b. 1931). Their last harmonium was sold in 1968 to a mission in Burundi. The business is being continued as a retail store under Paul's son Jean (b. 1959).
DELMARCO, IGINIO, & CO.; via Suffragio 9 in 1935, via Roma 15, Trento, Italy. Made 18 different models of suction style reed organs. Established 1935.
DELMOTTE, THEOPHILE, & FILS; 26 chaussee de Lille, Tournai, Belgium. Harmonium maker, established in 1840. C. Delmotte is shown as an organ builder in Saint-Leger, Belgium in 1883.
DEMENY; instrument located in Bugyi, Hungary; origin unknown.
DENISON BROTHERS; Deep River, CT. Stop knob makers.
DERBAYNE & CO.; 41 Rathbone Pl., London. Piano and harmonium manufacturer, 1883.
DETHLOFF; Basel, Switzerland, 1883.
DETROIT MELODEON CO.; Monroe Ave., Campus Martius, Detroit, MI 1861. Manufacturers of melodeons with Carhart's patent. See *Blakeman & Co.*
DETROIT ORGAN CO., see *Farrand & Votey*.
DEUTSCH-AMERIKANISCHE ORGEL-HARMONIUM-FABRIK R. METZNER; Mühlenstrasse 40-42, Leipzig-Plagwitz, Germany 1903; Lauchstädter Strasse 38-42 in 1911; established in 1902, made the Aeolus harmonium, a suction-operated instrument. See *R. Metzner, Marie Dietz*.
DEUTSCHE HARMONIUM-ZUNGEN-FABRIK; Pegau, Germany; established 1911 by Theodor Mannborg, made "Jubilate" reeds, reed pans, mutes, couplers and other components for the reed organ trade. Some of the reed-making machinery was sold to *Gebruder Dix*, an accordion reed maker. This factory eventually was taken over by the German Democratic Republic and combined with the other reed makers into *Deutsches Tonzungenwerk* (qv). The reed-making machinery was acquired by *Lindholm* in 1961 and later broken up for scrap when Lindholm itself was taken over by the state.
DEUTSCHE PIANO-UNION BÖHLITZ-EHRENBERG, VEB, see *Leipziger Pianofortefabriken Böhlitz-Ehrenberg.*

DEUTSCHES TONZUNGENWERK; Gera, Germany; reed maker, 1961. Made the "Jubilate" and "Harmola" reeds. See *Deutsche Harmonium-Zungen-Fabrik, Gebruder Dix, Klingenthaler Harmonika Werke.*

DEUTSCHMANN, JAKOB; Laimgrube 32 in 1825, Lumpertgasse 821 in 1840, Wienstr. 39 in 1883, all in Vienna, Austria. Maker of seraphines and harmoniums. See *Peter Titz.*

DE VILLEROI, M.; showed the "Harmonine," a three-octave instrument at the London Exhibition of 1851.

DE VOLDER FRERES, CHARLES ET LEON; Terarckenstraat 9, Brussels, Belgium in 1883; 23 avenue de Watermael, Boitsfort, Belgium 1903. The family firm was established in 1790, and the brothers Charles and Leon began making harmoniums in the latter half of the 19th century.

DE VOS, JOSEPH; 14 rue Haberman, Brussels, Belgium in 1868, 9 place Robyt in 1873, 9 place du Concordat in 1880, rue d'Odon 6 in 1895, steam factory at boulevard de l'Abbatoir 30, Brussels.

DEWINGLE; 70 rue Amelot, Paris. Piano and harmonium maker, 1883.

DE WIT, see *Wit, de.*

DEXTER, F.N.; West Winfield, NY, 1880. Instruments with this name were possibly made by others with the Dexter stencil. Freeman D. Dexter was granted US Patent No. 588713 on a reed organ in 1897. See *New American Organ.*

DIBBLE, GEORGE H.; Granby, CT 1861. Melodeon manufacturer.

DICKENSON-GOULD ORGAN CO.; Lexington, MI. Operated in the period 1882-1886 by Joseph H. Dickenson and his father-in-law Hezekiah Gould. A large Dickenson-Gould chapel organ was displayed at the Cotton Centennial in New Orleans in 1884 as an example of the progress of blacks in manufacturing. Dickenson had previously worked for *Clough & Warren* and returned to that company in 1886. He later went to Aeolian in Garwood, NJ. See *Gould & Sons.*

DICKS & CO.; 70 Mortimer St., Cavendish Sq., London. Piano and harmonium manufacturer 1878-1880.

DIETZ, CHRISTIAN; made an improved version of *Haeckl*'s Physharmonica in 1828.

DIETZ, MARIE; Wolffstrasse 27, Leipzig, Germany. Made the "Aeolus" harmonium. See *Deutsch-Amerikanische Orgel-Harmonium-Fabrik R. Metzner.*

DINGER, GUSTAVE, & SÖHNE; Zeitz, Germany; keyboard maker, 1930.

DIPLOMA organ, see *W. Bell & Co.*

DITSON, OLIVER, & CO.; 277 Washington St., Boston, MA, music publisher and investor in *Mason & Hamlin, Lyon & Healy* and probably in the *Mechanical Orguinette Co.*, later *The Aeolian Co.* The Oliver

> **Gustav Dinger & Söhne, Zeitz**
> **Klaviaturenfabrik**
> Fernsprecher: 370
>
> liefern
> Klaviaturen für Flügel – Pianos und Harmoniums
> ◀ jeder Art in erstklassiger Beschaffenheit. ▶

Ditson Co. folding organs were undoubtedly made by others with the Ditson stencil.

DIX, GEBRÜDER; Gera, Germany. Maker of Harmola brand reeds and components for harmoniums, 1930. Established 1866, still operating in 1947. See *Deutsches Tonzungenwerke* and *Klingenthaler Harmonikawerke*.

DOBUNKAN; Kanda, Tokyo. A bookseller and publisher; Kikuro Shirai was an adviser in this enterprise. Started selling *Ikeuchi* school organs under the Dobunkan name in 1896, although probably had their own factory in Tokyo at one time. Stopped selling organs after the 1923 earthquake.

DODGE & LORD; Attica, NY. Melodeon makers.

DODSON, WM.; 85 Liverpool Road, Islington, London. Piano and harmonium manufacturer 1878-1880. Works located at 22 Bryan Street, Caledonian Road, London.

DOERR, ALFONS; Karlstr. 7, Salgau, Germany in 1930. Formerly *Carl Doerr*, established 1876. Maker of harmonium cases.

DOHERTY, W., & CO.; Clinton, Ontario. Started as Doherty & Menzies in 1868, a furniture and music retailer. Made a few organs in 1875 and the next year built a small shop employing eight men. In 1879 a second building was constructed alongside the other and production reached 100 organs per month. This original factory complex was located in the block bounded by Princess, Raglan and Rattenbury Streets. In 1898 the entire plant burned, but within three months a new factory consisting of two buildings at the corner of East and Irwin Streets was built with a capacity of four hundred organs per month. The buildings are still in existence. Piano production began about 1905 and the firm was renamed *Doherty Piano & Organ Co.* in 1908, *Doherty Piano Co.* in 1913 and *Doherty Pianos Ltd.* in 1917. Fires in 1901 and 1905 also caused serious set-backs. Acquired by *Sherlock-Manning Organ Co.* (qv) in 1920 when William Doherty retired, but continued to operate under the Doherty name. Made folding organs used by missionaries and also by the military

in World War II and the Korean War. Capacity in 1906: 6,000 organs per year. Organ production declined after about 1910 and came to an end during World War II. Serial numbers: 1887—5678, 1889—11429, 1901—36239, 1902—39023.

DOLGE, ALFRED; Dolgeville, NY, also *Dolge & Son* in 1895; felts and organ materials 1880; author of "Pianos and Their Makers" in 1911 and 1913, (two volumes).

Dobunkan School Organ, 1897.

DOMINGOLLE; awarded a bronze medal for an orgue-expressif at the Paris Exposition of 1847.

DOMINION ORGAN CO.; established in 1872 by A.M. Darley and Wm. Robinson in Oshawa, Ontario as *Darley & Robinson*, later *Darley & Hoskin*, then *Oshawa Organ & Melodeon Mfg. Co.* Jesse H. Farwell of Detroit is shown as president and principal owner in 1872; he was also a partner in *Simmons & Clough*. The factory moved to Bowmanville, Ontario in 1873 under the management of Darley and O'Hara. Renamed the *Dominion Organ Co.* in 1875 with Messrs. Piggot, Russell and Wesley as management. Awarded a bronze medal in Paris in 1878. Capacity in 1880: 100 to 125 organs per month. In 1879 the town council of Bowmanville granted the company a bonus of $5,000 to erect a piano factory, and in 1880 the name was changed to *Dominion Organ & Piano Co.*, then *Dominion Organ & Piano Co. Ltd.* in 1886. On the death of Mr. Piggott in 1890, Mr. Farwell again resumed control until 1895 when the company was purchased by Messrs. Alexander, Kydd and McConnel. Alexander became sole proprietor in 1901. Officers in 1906: J.W.

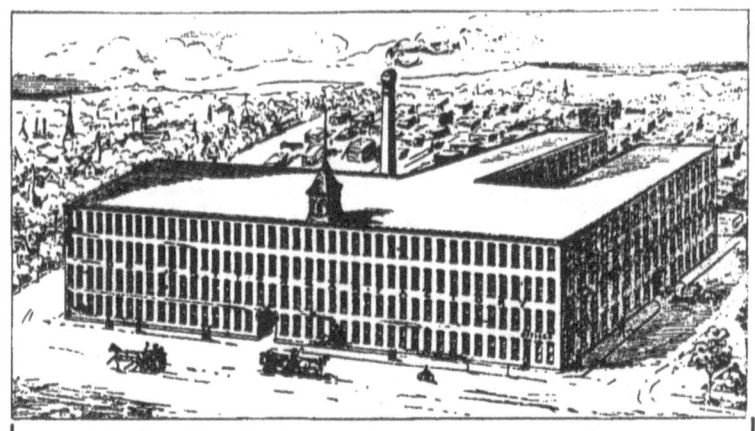

Alexander, president and general manager; C.J. Rowe, secretary-treasurer; J.B. Mitchell, vice-president and superintendent. Dominion manufactured organs with the Scribner Patent Qualifying Tubes under an agreement, presumably due to Jesse Farwell, with *Clough & Warren*, owners of the patent. Production ceased about 1930, the firm was declared bankrupt in 1936 and closed in 1937.

DONZELLI, RAFFAELE; Campli, Italy, 1903.

DORF, OLE; 426 Second Ave., New York, NY 1861. Melodeon maker.

DORNHEIM, F.W., & SOHN; Eichfeld b. Rudolstadt; Schwarzbergerstr. 14, Rudolstadt, Germany. Organ, harmonium and keyboard maker. Established 1842.

DOUGHTON & SAYRE; Camden, NJ, 1880. Doughton was a lumber merchant and the proprietor of a blind and sash factory, which was turned into an organ factory capable of producing 300 organs per week.

DOUILLET, A.; 59 rue de l'Ourcq, Paris in 1921. Manufacturer of actions and keys for pianos and harmoniums.

DOURTE, JUAN; Bilbao-Begona, Spain, 1930.

DOWNS, A.R., & CO.; East Dereham, Norfolk, England. By 1906 called *Euterpe Works*, located at High Street, East Dereham. American organ manufacturer 1889-1906.

DRAPER, JOSEPH MARK; in 1906 at Higher Audley Street, Blackburn, Lancs., England. Organette maker, established 1878.

DREAPER, see *Rushworth & Dreaper*.

DREHER, A.; Cleveland, OH. Granted US Patent 137350 for a reed organ in 1873.

DREHER, B.; 25 Prospect, Cleveland, OH 1870-1872; see *Kinnard, Dreher & Co.*

DREXLER, C.; reed organ with serial number 13083. (No further information).

DUBUS, FR.; France. Made an orgue-expressif in 1841, exhibited at the Paris Expositions of 1844, 1847, 1849 and 1855. He was awarded a Bronze Medal in 1847.

DUCASSE ET OLIVEAU; Paris.

DUCKER, M.; 618 Broadway, New York, NY, 1861. Manufacturer of Melodeon Triolodeons. These organs used steel reeds and had a triple touch arrangement in which the volume of sound could be controlled in three distinct gradations by means of increased or decreased pressure on each key. Thus a melody might be accompanied by a chord and the melody made to be heard more distinctly by using increased pressure on the melody keys and less on the chord. Shown at the Great Exhibition of 1862 in London.

DU COMMUN-GIROD, F.W.; 15 quai des Etuves, Geneva, Switzerland. Frederick William Du Commun married Jeanne-Catherine Girod and used both names for his music box firm, which made some music boxes with reeds. Established 1828, dissolved 1868.

DUCROQUET, PIERRE ALEX.; France, pipe organ builder, successor to *Girard et Cie.*, in turn succeeded by *Jos. Merklin & Schutze*, a pipe organ and harmonium maker in 1855.

DUFFIELD, WM. H.; Gloucester House, 108 Leighton Rd., N.W., London in 1897 and 1903. Established 1881, still working in 1909. Maker of harmoniums and American reed organs and a supplier of leather, felt, reeds and fittings.

DUFFILL, CHARLES; harmonium maker in York, England. Active in the 1880s.

DUFF & TATE; 2620 Shields Ave., Chicago, IL 1899, 1901.

DUMONT, L., ET FILS; France. Established 1857. Possibly a precursor to Dumont & Lelièvre.

DUMONT & LELIÈVRE; Les Andelys, France. Manufactured the Orgue Médiophone, which had large qualifying tubes. Some had a transposing keyboard. Also made harmoniums and other instruments. Awarded a gold medal at the Paris Exposition in 1878 for the Orgue Médiophone. Established 1857, still working in 1913 as *Dumont & Cie.*

DUNN & NICHOLLS; 482 Hackney Road, E. London. Piano and harmonium maker, 1878. By 1879 the firm was taken over by *Edward Nicholls* and moved to 118 Mile End Road, E. London. See *Nicholls*.

DURAND & CIE.; 177 route d'Espagne, Bordeaux, France, 1909.

DURAY, H.; 70 rue de Stassart, 18 rue de la Paix, Brussels, Belgium 1878-1880. Maker and retailer of pianos and harmoniums.

DURNER, CHARLES; Quakertown, PA; pipe organ builder, also built a few reed organs. Founded by Charles Frederick Durner (1838-1914) and continued by his son Charles E. (1863-1932).

DURRAND; Portland, OR. (No further information available.)

DUTTON & PLUMB; West Halifax, VT. Seraphine and melodeon makers in 1849.

DYER & HUGHES; Mechanic St., Foxcroft, ME; Boston, MA; 1866-1894; Thomas Franklin Dyer and his nephew John F. Hughes operated a grocery and hardware business. Dyer had an interest in music and was the founder and leader of Dyer's Band. He began building and selling reed organs and later pianos with such success that in 1885 they dropped the original business to concentrate on reed organs and pianos. The original factory was built on Mechanic St. in 1869. Dyer retired in 1894, Hughes bought him out and the firm name became *Hughes & Son*. Serial number: 1888—34855.

E

EARHUFF, JOHN G.; factory at 197-199 Wells St. in 1883, 51-55 Pearson St. in 1886, office and warerooms at 161 Superior St. in 1883, Chicago, IL. Established in Chicago in 1876. In 1886 J.S. Foley came into the company and the name changed to *J.G. Earhuff & Co*. In 1888 the factory was moved to North St. Paul, MN, taking over the plant of the Beach Wagon Co. At this time the company was renamed *J.G. Earhuff Organ & Piano Co.*, with J.G. Earhuff as president and F.H. Engstrous, secretary. Officers in 1897: John G. Earhuff, president; G.A. Earhuff, secretary. Factory capacity in 1897: 3,600 organs per year; made organs for *Kimball* 1876-80; made the Peerless Organ. Last listed in 1906. Serial Numbers: 1898—32852, 1902—9748.

EASON, ALEXANDER; 217-219 Kentish Town Road, London. Harmonium maker, 1871.

EASTERN HARMONIUM FACTORY; 11 Colootola Street, Calcutta, India. Harmonium maker, 1930.

EATON, C.W., & BOYNTON; Bristol, NH. Seraphine and melodeon makers. ca. 1920.

EBBLEWHITE, JOHN HENRY; 4-5 Ald Gate, High St., London.
Piano and harmonium manufacturer, 1883.

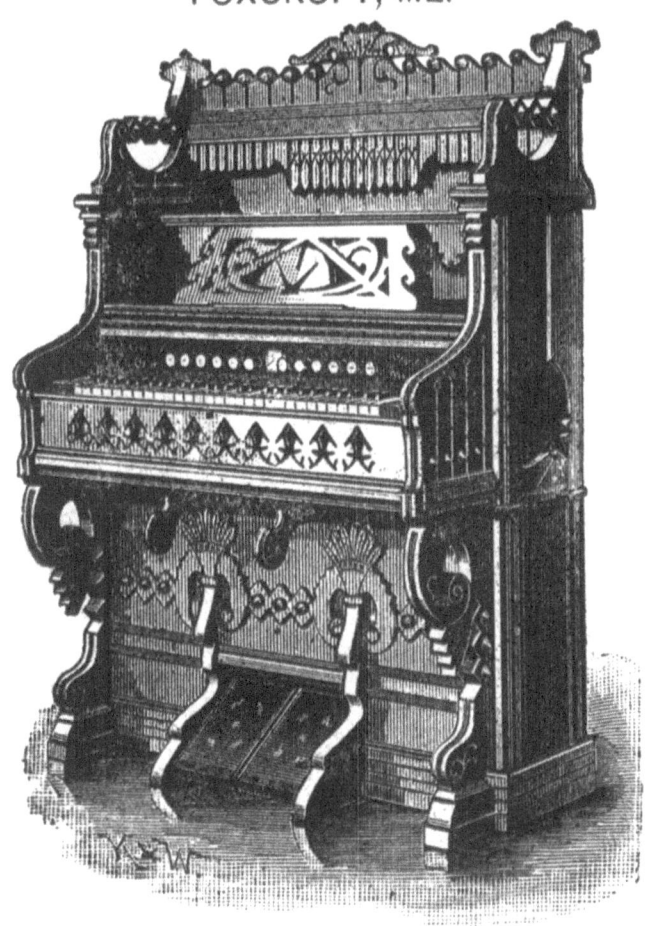

Mr. & Mrs. R.A. Acheson and daughter in their home near Watertown, Nebraska, 1903.

EBEN-EZER ORGAN CO.; Clifford, Ontario 1935.
ECKERT, CHARLES, & CO.; between Beecker & Amity Streets, New York, NY, 1861. Manufacturer of keys for piano, organ and melodeon.
EDER, ANTON JULIUS; Franzlskanerplatz 4, Budapest, Austria-Hungary. Piano and harmonium maker, 1883.
EDNA ORGAN CO.; established 1886 in Massillon, OH, incorporated there 1889, in 1890 moved to Monroeville, OH. Changed name to *Edna Piano & Organ Co.* Officers in 1897: John A. Baldwin, president; John Hosford, vice-president; H.E. Koontz, secretary; M.C. Price, general manager. Factory capacity in 1900: 1,200 organs per year. Purchased the *Burdett Piano Co.* in 1897. Renamed *Burdett Piano Co.* in 1906.
EESTI KLAVEIRIVABRIK A/S 'ASTRON'; 16 Kalda t., Tartu, Estonia 1930.
EHRHARDT, C., & CO.; 38 & 39 Brooke St., Holborn, London; American organ actions, keys, sounding boards, 1896.
EHRLER, ALFRED; Steinpleis, Germany, 1930; established 1923.
EHRLICH, PAUL; Mockernsche Str. 30B-30D, Leipzig, Germany. Later known as *Leipziger Musikwerke*, then *Neue Leipziger-Musikwerke A. Buff-Hedinger* in 1904. Made the Ariston organette with reeds starting in 1876. Founded by Frederick Ernst Paul Ehrlich.
EICHLER, MAX; Löbauerstr. 36, Görlitz, Germany; established in 1861, still in business in 1912.

EISENWERKE L. MEYER JUN. & CO.; Harzgerode, Germany; B. Rosenthal and F. Huth, proprietors, established 1871; harmonium components, 1930.
ELCKÉ, F., & CIE.; 47 rue de Babylone, Paris 1889; established 1846 by Frederick Elcké, later made harmoniums.
ELDER, WILLIAM; 97 E. 23rd St., New York, NY. Melodeon action maker, 1861.
ELDREDGE, O.H., & CO.; Cherry Valley, NY; established about 1851, later sold to *Alex Fea & Sons*, who operated it until 1874.
ELFSTROM, C.; Ljungby, Sweden, 1909.
ELLIS, A., invented the Harmonical, an enharmonic organ built by *Moore & Moore*. See Enharmonic organ.
ELM, PAUL; Werdauer Str. 17, Gera-Zwotzen, Germany; harmonium cases.
EMENEE INDUSTRIES, INC.; New York. (No further information.)
EMMER, WILHELM; 23-25 Berliner Str., Madgeburg, Germany in 1886; 19 Seydelstr. 20, Berlin, Germany. Established in 1870 as a reed organ maker, still in business as a retailer in 1930.
EMPIRE ORGAN CO.; Brattleboro, VT; Canton, OH. This is probably a separate company from the following listing.
EMPIRE ORGAN CO.; 87 Main St., Kalamazoo, MI 1867-70; 65 Monroe St., Grand Rapids, MI 1870-1878. George Piggott and Asa Filer Burch, owners. Used the Scribner qualifying tubes. See *Piggott, Burch & Allen*. Piggott was also interested in the *Dominion Organ Co.*
ENDERBY, EDW.; 11 Church St., Boston, England. Established in 1867; by 1909 appears as *Enderby & Son*.
ENDSLEIGH ORGANS, see *J. Humphreys & Sons*.
ENGLAND ORGAN & PIANO CO.; Houston, TX. James R. England, proprietor. Active 1907.
ENGLE, LEONHARDT; Bahnhofstr. 125, Oettingen, Germany, 1903. Reed maker, established 1877.
ENGLISH SERAPHONE CO.; made a roll-playing organette.
ENHARMONIC organ, see *Joseph Alley, R.H.M. Bosanquet, Boyer & Marty, Colin Brown, A. Ellis, T.A. Jennings, Johannes Kewitsch, Moore & Moore, Arthur von Oettingen, Henry Ward Poole, J. & P. Schiedmayer, Robert Snell, Franz Steirer, J. Straube, Dr. Shohei Tanaka, James Paul White*.
EPWORTH ORGAN, see *Williams Organ Co.*
ERBE, JACOB WILHELM; Altstadtstr. 9, Alexanderstr. 50, in 1903, Georg-Euckenstr. 28, Eisenach, Germany. Piano maker, established 1881. Made and patented a combination piano-harmonium, 1888.
ERICHSEN, P.; Ringebu, Norway. Harmonium maker from the 1860s to 1876. Produced 61 instruments.

ERICSON, FRANS OSCAR; Copenhagen. Working 1939-43.
ERICSON, OSC., KBH.; Denmark. Made the Crescendo harmonium.
ERIKSEN, AMUND; Norway. Pipe organ builder, also made a few harmoniums.
ERIKSEN, L.; 2 Bragernaes Torv., Drammen, Norway. Established in Drammen in 1913. The firm is said to have been founded previously in Sweden by A.N. Östlind and his brother-in-law, Mr. Nelson, who had previously had a leading position in the *Packard Organ Co.* of Fort Wayne, IN. Eriksen bought the factory and moved it with machines and employees to Drammen, where Nelson became the factory superintendent. By 1914 they were producing 300 instruments per year, and by 1925 had produced a total of 1,500 harmoniums. At that time the factory was enlarged and new machinery installed. Still in business in 1930.
ERIKSSON, A.; Kage, Sweden, 1909.
ERIKSSON, E.; Gefle, Sweden, 1909.
ERIKSSONS, J.; Kyrkogatan 7, Ostersund, Sweden, 1903.
ERSTE PRODUKTIV-GENOSSENSCHAFT DER HARMONIUM-MACHER WIENS; Hartmanngasse 10, Vienna, Austria; established in 1884 by Josef Strizik at Hartmanngasse 15; J. Witeck, director in 1903.
ERSTE VOGTLÄNDISCHE HARMONIUMFABRIK, see *Tröger, Max Hugo.*
ERSTE WURTTEMBERGISCHE REPARATURANSTALT, HARMONIUM- & PIANO-FABRIK J.G. GSCHWIND; Gutenbergstr. 95, Stuttgart, Germany; Lucie Gschwind, prop. in 1903. Still active in 1913. Established in 1858 as *Pross, Gschwind & Co.*
ESCHENBACH, BERNARD; Königshofen, Germany. Made the Organo-violine in 1814, one of the first free-reed instruments.
ESSIG, RUDOLF, & CO.; Stuttgart, Germany. Leipzig-Gohlis, Mittlere Georgstr. 4, Leipzig, Germany; Rudolf Essig & Richard Müller, proprietors, 1902. Made both pressure and suction instruments. Patent for harmonium, 1890.
ESTADELLA, CAYETANO; 58 calle de Martinez de la Rose, Barcelona, Spain, 1930.
ESTEE, a name reported by J. Estey & Co. in its 1880 catalog as having been used by "an irresponsible party in the West... on a lot of cheap instruments with the intent of deluding buyers into the belief that they are genuine Estey Organs."
ESTÈVE; Paris; reed maker, established 1840. Amalgamated with *Berthion-Hédou*, later succeeded by *Léon Pinet,* (qv). Introduced a new alloy for reed-making in 1852. Had 44 workers in 1872. Awarded a bronze medal at the 1878 Paris Exposition for excellent precision work. Awarded a first prize at Sydney, Australia in 1880.

ESTEY & GREEN; Brattleboro, VT 1855-1863; successor to *I. Hines & Co.*, Jacob Estey and Hatsell P. Green, partners; the Main St. factory burned in 1857, a new factory was built 1858 on the site later occupied by the Brattleboro House; succeeded by *J. Estey & Co.*

ESTEY, J., & CO.; Brattleboro, VT 1863-1872; successors to *Estey & Green*, the original partners were Jacob Estey, Riley Burditt, Silas Waite and Joel Bullard. A new factory was built in 1866 on Flat St. and the business reorganized with Jacob Estey, his son Julius J. and son-in-law Levi Fuller as partners. As part of the reorganization Riley Burditt and Silas Waite organized the *Burdett Organ Co. Ltd.* in Chicago. A new factory was started in 1869 on Birge Street at the Dickenson Farm, later called Esteyville; reorganized as *Estey Organ Co.* in 1872 and as the *Estey Corporation* in the early 1930s, closed in 1959. Estey made a folding suitcase-type organ for *Lyon & Healy*, (qv). Estey made most of the chaplain's organs used during World War II as well as the model M-1945 introduced at the end of the war or shortly thereafter. The Estey name survives (1994) on electronic organs sold by Fletcher Music Centers, Clearwater, FL. Serial numbers:

1850—400	1882—127000	1905—350789
1855—2400	1883—135997	1906—355000
1860—5600	1884—146000	1908—365000
1864—8700	1885—157498	1910—375000
1865—9500	1885—161917	1911—377721
1867—12545	1885—164196	1911—383488
1867—14000	1886—170695	1912—385000
1869—17025	1887—178997	1915—400000
1869—23006	1888—196879	1916—401174
1871—23368	1889—215352	1918—408000
1871—26941	1890—221000	1920—441884
1872—36200	1891—234319	1923—437391
1873—36955	1891—235429	1925—430201
1873—38222	1892—243981	1926—433000
1874—46538	1893—257335	1934—443820
1875—52199	1894—270908	1935—427303
1876—62000	1895—280144	1935—444603
1877—71498	1897—291978	1936—446349
1878—79000	1898—296115	1937—449217
1879—90180	1900—322000	1941—457999
1880—100000	1901—326050	1950—493343
1881—106640	1902—334000	1953—501290
1881—114498	1903—340000	1955—506000
1882—122000	1904—345597	

Estey Chaplains' Organ M-1945, designed at the end of World War II. Charles Robison collection.

ETIENNE, see *Christophe & Etienne*.
EUPHONIKA MUSIKWERKE; Leipzig, Germany.
EUTERPE WORKS, see *A.R. Downs & Co.*
EVANS, WARDLE EASTLAND; Cheltenham, England in 1839, relocated to 28 Market Place, Great Portland St., London by 1865; built a reed organ with steel reeds called the Organo-Harmonica. in 1839, (some sources say 1844), but was unable to manufacture it. It was later made and sold by *Boosey & Sons* as Evan's English Harmonium. He held many patents including the "Genouilliere," a knee-lever to control a pedal bass (held jointly with R. Smythe), and an 1881 patent on an expression stop for suction instruments.
EVANS, WM., & CO.; Lockport, IL. Made melodeons and pipe organs 1855-1860.

EVERETT PIANO CO.; South Haven, MI; established 1934, manufactured and sold the Orgatron (qv), a hybrid reed and electronic organ. It was surpassed in sales by the popular Hammond organ, and Everett sold the rights to *Wurlitzer* in 1945.
EVERHART ORGAN & PIANO CO.; York, PA. Active 1909.
EXCELSIOR ORGAN CO.; Washington, NJ. Made the Gem organ for *Sears, Roebuck & Co.* See *Daniel Bell Organ Co.*
EXCELSIOR organ, see *F.S. Fieman; E.C. Leidy; M.L. Cope; Jefts, Greble & Co.*

A Farrand organ in the parlor of a home in Scranton, Iowa, May 1940.

F

FABBRICA ITALIANA PIANOFORTI; 55 via Moretta, Turin, Italy, 1930. Piano and harmonium maker.
FABER, HOMO; factory 325 So. Robey St., office 2066 Flourney St., Chicago, IL; folding and portable organs. Established about 1905, operated until at least 1930. Associated with *Marshall Brothers*.
FABIANEK, FRANZ; Rájec (Raitz), Czechoslovakia, 1930. Also shown as *František Fabránek*.
FÁBREGA, ALFREDO; Albox, Almería, Spain, 1903.
FABRIK LEIPZIGER MUSIKWERKE; Möckernsche Str. 30b-d in 1900-03, Möckernsche Str. 29-33 in 1904, Leipzig-Gohlis, Germany. Formerly *Paul Ehrlich & Co.*; Paul Ehrlich, proprietor. Established 1877. Made the "Daimonion," a combination piano-harmonium, in 1894. Made an automatic harmonium with organ action by *Mannborg* in 1910.
FARFISA; Castelfidardo, Ancona, Italy. Two accordion makers, Soprani and Scandalli, combined to form Farfisa, primarily an accordion manufacturer but also a maker of small harmoniums. Made the Harmo-Transposer, an electrically-blown portable harmonium with a four octave transposing keyboard and a single set of reeds; the Pianorgan with a three-octave keyboard and bass chord buttons; and the "Golden Voice Regale" as recently as 1965.
FARLEY & HOLMES. (No additional information available.)
FARLEY, PEARSON & CO.; Old Burnside Bldg., Main St., Worcester, MA 1847-1852. John A. Farley, John G. Pearson and Milton M. Morse were partners. Morse had previously worked for *Prescott* and Farley came from Concord, NH. See *Pearson & Loring*, also *Taylor & Farley*.
FARRAND ORGAN CO.; Detroit, MI; 1897 until at least 1908; see *Farrand & Votey*.
FARRAND & VOTEY; 12th St. & Grand Trunk Railway, Detroit, MI; started as the *Detroit Organ Co.* in 1881, a worker-owned enterprise which proved unsuccessful and was bought out by Detroit music dealer C.J. Whitney and organ builder Edwin S. Votey, a former *Estey* employee, in 1883 and incorporated as the *Whitney Organ Co.* W.R. Farrand joined the same year as financial manager. Whitney retired in 1887 and the name changed to *Farrand & Votey*. Started building pipe organs in 1888 and in 1889 acquired the patents of Frank Roosevelt, successor to Hilborne Roosevelt. Acquired the Granville Wood Pipe Organ Co. in 1890. Votey did pioneering work on piano players, developing the famous Pianola. In 1897 the company split up, Farrand remaining with the reed organs as the *Farrand Organ Co.*, and Votey

taking the pipe organ and player piano business into the *Aeolian Company* where he became a vice-president. The *Farrand Organ Co.* later brought out its own piano player, the Cecilian, and went bankrupt in 1915. Serial numbers:

1888—15471	1892—29300	1902—79646
1888—20000	1893—33000	1906—106001
1889—21000	1894—35200	1908—122812
1890—23000	1895—38000	
1891—26000	1896—41000	

..THE..
Farrand Organs
ARE THE BEST

BECAUSE—they have the clearest and the sweetest tone—they pump the easiest—they are built with the famous

"SEPARABLE FEATURES"
(found in no other make)

they are built in an honest, careful manner—built to last and give satisfaction for a life-time.

FARRAND ORGANS FOR SALE BY

A. V. SCHLUEMBACH,   Martinsburg, Pa.

FARRANT, HENRY; 22 Gardner Street, Brighton, England; also 195 Western Road, Brighton, Sussex. Pipe organ and piano maker 1878-96, also made harmoniums.

FARRIS, JOHN; Hartford, CT. Active about 1880. (See *John Harris*.)

FAVRE, J.; Lyon, France. Showed "Harmonichords" at the London Exhibition of 1862.

FAZERIN, see *Musikki Fazerin Pianotehdas*.

FEA, ALEX, & SONS; Cherry Valley, NY; successor to *O.H. Eldredge*; business closed in 1874.

FELDNER, C., & CO. Gutwoehne bei Oels, Germany, 1885.

FELT, CHARLES F., see *Joseph Foster*.

FENTON, CHAS. E.; 20 Culmore Road, Asylum road, Peckham, SE London. Piano and harmonium manufacturer 1878-1883.

FERAT ET GAME; France, 1875. Won a bronze medal at the Paris Exposition of 1878 for a two-manual eleven-stop harmonium in a 13th century style case intended for a church in La Palisse.

FERNANDEZ, P.J.; Kalbadevird, Bombay, India. Harmonium maker.

FERRIS & RAND; Geneva, Ohio. A reed organ using the "Clarabella" reed was invented by Charles Newell Rand. Ferris, a cousin of Rand's and maker of the Ferris wheel, provided the financial backing.

FERSANI, see *Chiappa & Fersani*.

FEUCHT, see *Trefz & Feucht*.

FEUHR & STEMMER; two-manual and pedal reed organ, probably made in the U.S. (No other information available.)

FIDLER, J.; 56 Burton Street, London. Harmonium maker 1864.

FIEDLER, CARL E.; also *Harmonyphon-Musikwerke*, Graslitzerstr. 21B, Klingenthal, Germany, 1903. Carl Emil Fiedler, Proprietor. Established 1901; made music box actions with reeds.

FIEDLER, GUSTAV; Poniatowskystr. 4 in 1900, Sedanstr. 17 and Fregestr. 5-7 in 1906, Leipzig, Germany; Karl-Heine-Str. 82, Leipzig-Lindenau in 1905. Paul Kretzschmer, proprietor in 1905. Eugen Zimmermann and Theodor Ansinn, proprietors in 1930, established 1871 as a piano maker. Harmonium maker beginning in 1903. Closed in 1935.

FIEMAN, F.S.; Mount Etna, PA in 1903; in 1913 located in Myerstown, PA; established in 1876. Probably closed in 1914. Maker of the hand-made "Excelsior" organ. See *M.L. Cope, E.C. Leidy*.

FINDLAY, ALEXANDER; 110 West Nile Street, Glasgow, Scotland. Harmonium maker, established 1878, still working in 1906. Made the "Seraphium." After Alexander's death manufacturing was discontinued, but his sons Alex and Robert carried on with sales of pianos and reed organs.

FINK, J.J., see *Hinners & Albertsen*.

FISCHER, KARL J.; Werderstr. 15 in 1937, Palmstr. 21, Schorndorf, Germany, 1940. Established about 1914. Made suction harmoniums.
FISHER, A.; 260 Goswell Road, London. Harmonium fittings dealer, 1900.
FISHER, H.M.; Reading, PA 1899, Allentown, PA through 1908. Made both reed and pipe organs.
FISK, C.W., & CO.; Ansonia, CT, melodeon, 1850-1868.
FISK & RANDALL; Woodbridge, CT.
FITTLER, SANDOR; 20 Hatar ut., Budapest-Pesterzsebet, Hungary, 1930.
FITZ; harmoniums. (No other information available.)
FLETCHER & CO.; 177 and 161 City Road, London EC in 1900; advertised as *H.J. Fletcher & Co. Ltd.* at the Bridge Works, New North Road, London NI in 1931. Supplier of reed organ parts, established 1879.
FLOREY BROS.; Washington, NJ. Made small grand pianos for *Cornish* and others as well as a few reed organs. Alvin F. Florey was also general manager of *Cornish.*
FOERSTER, CARL; 1801 Lloyd St., Milwaukee, WI; made reed and pipe roller organs, 1889-1910.
FOLEY & WILLIAMS ORGAN CO.; 121-123 W. 5th St., Cincinnati, OH; made the Peerless organ. Also controlled the *Moore Organ Co.* The factory was moved to Kankakee, IL in 1902. In business at least through 1919.
FOLSOM, SIMEON; Limerick, ME; seraphine ca. 1850.
FONROBERT, GEBRUDER; Potsdamer Str. 26, Berlin, Germany; Gillaume Fonrobert, proprietor, maker of rubberized cloth for harmoniums, 1930. Established 1885.
FORBES, E.E.; A music dealer who sold organs made by others with the Forbes stencil. Bought out the *Jesse French* music stores. Serial number: 1904—67468.
FOREST GATE ORGAN WORKS, see *Robert Slater & Son.*
FÖRSTER, AUGUST; Georgswald, Czechoslovakia 1903, 1930; proprietors: Frau Margarete Förster, Gerhard & Manfred Förster; also at Albertstr. 14, Lobau, Germany 1903, Casar Förster, prop. in 1903; established 1859. Made the "Viertelton," an enharmonic harmonium.
FÖRSTER, HEINRICH EMIL; Rittergasse 43, Jüdengasse 150 in 1831, Neumarkt in 1832, Zeitz, Germany. Jüdengasse in Zeitz-Wasservorstadt, 1837. Piano maker, also made physharmonicas.
FÖRSTER & NICOLAUS; Butzbacher Str. 5 (now Kolnhäuser Str.), Lich, Germany. Founded 1842 by J. G. Förster. Made both pressure and suction harmoniums. Merged with *Nikolaus & Pappe* in 1927. Also see *Straube & Co.*

FORT WAYNE ORGAN CO.; Fairfield Ave. & Organ Ave., Fort Wayne, IN 1871-1899. Made the Packard organ; changed the company name to *Packard Organ Co.* in 1899 and later to the *Packard Piano Co.* Went out of business in 1930. The former factory site is now Packard Park. Isaac T. Packard, founder, S.B. Bond, a banker, president, and his son Albert S. Bond, general manager from 1886. Factory capacity 5,000 organs per year in 1897. See *Packard Bros.* Serial numbers:

1876—12000	1886—20001	1893—35200
1878—14600	1888—24100	1902—57639
1882—16400	1890—28000	1910—73187
1884—17900	1892—31392	

FORWARD. (No other information available.)

FOSS, CALVIN, see *Packard Bros.*

FOSTER, JOSEPH; a pipe organ maker in Winchester, NH, he built his first reed organ in 1831. In 1842 he took Albert Thayer into partnership and the firm name became *Foster & Thayer*, making lap organs. The firm was dissolved in 1845, and Foster moved to Keene, NH where he continued to build reed organs in partnership with Charles F. Felt under the name *Foster & Felt* until Felt's death in 1857. In 1866 Joseph Foster's brother Ephraim joined the firm which then became *J. & E. Foster* until Joseph's death in 1875. Ephraim continued in business until he died in 1889.

FOSTER & THAYER, see *Joseph Foster, Samuel H. Jones.*

FOUCHER, G.; 29 Picadilly, London, 1881. Made mechanical harmoniums and organettes.

FOURNEAUX, J.-B. NAPOLÉON; Paris. Maker of free-reed instruments, established 1835. Had a patent for a two-manual orgue expressif with reeds in a vertical position in 1840, made the "Orchestrion" in 1844—an orgue-expressif with a cylinder and keyboard. Successor to Chameroy, 1838; succeeded by his son *J.-L. Napoléon Fourneaux* in 1846; author of "Petit Traité de l'Orgue-Expressif," a book on the orgue-expressif and on tuning. Had 46 workers in 1860. Listed as *Jean-Nestor Fourneaux* in 1866. Located at 64 & 70 Galerie Vivienne, Paris in 1844; at 33 avenue de Saint-Cloud, Paris in 1851 and at 89 boulev. St.-Michel in 1883.

FOWLER; Chicago, IL. (No additional information available.)

FRANKLIN, see *James & Franklin.*

FRANSSEN, GEBR.; Christoffelstr. 10, Roermond, Netherlands; Anton Franssen, proprietor, 1903. Maker of church organs and American (suction) organs.

FRATTI & CO.; Buchholzerstr. 1, Berlin. Band organ, street piano and harmonium manufacturer, 1883.

Jesse French

FRENCH, JESSE, PIANO & ORGAN CO.; 240-242 North Summer St., Nashville, TN; started 1872 as a piano and organ retailer, later manufactured organs. At least some of the Jesse French organs were made by the *Chicago Cottage Organ Co.* with the French stencil, others were probably made by *Kimball.* Incorporated 1887, Jesse French, president; John Lumsden, St. Louis, MO, vice-president; O.A. Field, St. Louis, MO, secretary-treasurer.

FRENCH, see *Wagoner & French.*

FRENZEL, FRITZ; Südstrasse 61, Leipzig, Germany in 1921. Also shown at Scharnhorststr. 59 in 1925.

FRIEBORGH; portable harmonium made ca. 1953 by *Hermann Burger.*

FRIEDRICH & SCHULZE, HARMONIUM-FABRIK; Lützener Str. 8 in 1906, Lützener Str. 24 in 1907, Leipzig-Lindenau, Germany. Factory located in Leipzig-Lindenau at Siemeringstrasse 30 from 1912 to 1926, Aurelienstr. 4 in 1926. Established in 1902.

FRIEMEL, JOH.; Vienna, Austria, barrel-operated melodeons.

FRISBIE & TREAT, see *Whitaker & Frisbie.*

FRISBIE & WHITAKER; New Haven, CT 1847, see *Whitaker & Frisbie.*

FRÖHLICH, ERNST; Dragsdorf-Zeitz, Germany. Harmonium manufacturer, founded 1923. Working at least through 1940.

FROMENTIN; Paris. Reed maker, 1867.

FULDAER ORGEL-, HARMONIUM-, UND PIANOFORTEFABRIK MAIER & CO.; Friedrichstr. 16, Fulda, Germany; Ernst & Rich. Maier, directors, 1930.

FULLER, LEVI KNIGHT; started a sewing machine factory in Brattleboro, VT in 1863, but the shop burned at the time of the Estey fire in 1864. He started again but sold it when he entered the Estey firm. Eventually became vice-president and partner in *J. Estey & Co.* and son-in-law of Jacob Estey. Still later became a state senator, lieutenant governor and governor of Vermont and was instrumental in establishing the standard musical pitch of A=435 Hz. in the United States.

FUMMO, A.; Naples, Italy, 1862. Piano-melodium and vertical melodium.

G

GABORIAUD, see *Richard et Cie.*

GAERTTNER, G.F., & CO.; Ann Arbor, MI. (Also Gartner, Garttner.) Gottlieb Friedrich Gaerttner (1822-1878) learned pipe organ and harmonium building at *E.F. Walcker & Co.* in Ludwigsburg, Germany; emigrated to Ann Arbor in 1867 and began making reed organs at his home on West Seventh Street. In 1869 he moved his shop to Liberty Street between Main and Ashley Streets and began making pipe organs

Levi K. Fuller, about 1859.

in addition to reed organs. In 1871 he sold out to his son-in-law, *David Allmendinger*, (qv), worked for Albert Charles Gemunder in Columbus, OH, as an organ builder and about 1872 joined the Derrick & Felgemaker Co., organ builders, in Erie, PA as superintendent and head tuner.

GALANTE VASSEUR & CIE.; 40 rue de Paradis Poissonnière, Paris. Harmonium manufacturer, advertised from 1878-83.

GALLMANN, G.; Sechaus 1, Holligen siehe Bern, Switzerland, 1903. Established 1866.

GALLY, MERRITT; 9 Spruce St. in 1879; 25 E. 14th St. in 1883, 95 Nassau St., all in New York. Inventor of the Universal printing press and also of the Orchestrone, a roll-playing organ or organette. Both types had pneumatic valves which operated the pallet valves, permitting the use of very compact rolls in contrast to most other organettes which used the paper-as-a-valve system, requiring rather large rolls. Gally himself manufactured some organs and organettes and others were licensed to the *Munroe Organ Reed Co.*
GALVAN, EGIDIO; 100C Vittorio Emanuaele III, Borgo de Valsugana, Italy. Listed in directories for 1903, 1930.
GAMÉ, see *Ferat et Gamé.*
GANZEVOORT; Zwolle, Netherlands, 1954.
GARDNER, C.A.; Grand Rapids, MI.
GARDNER, WILLIAM P.; Peckhammer Building, George St., New Haven, CT in 1840, later moved to Bridgeport, CT for one year then returned to 216 Wooster St., New Haven. Located at 29 Cherry St., New Haven in 1861. Melodeon and pipe organ maker.
GARNIER, MARCEL; 16 rue Ernest-Cresson, Paris, 1930.
GARVIE & WOOD; 12 Union Square, New York, NY; sold the musical sewing machine cover or Dulciphone, a small roll-playing organette which was attached to a sewing machine cover and operated by the treadle. The Dulciphone was made by the *Munroe Organ Reed Co.* about 1885.
GASPARINI, ALEXANDRE; 17-19 rue de la Véga, Paris. Fairground organ maker, listed as a harmonium maker in 1903.
GATELY MANUFACTURING CO.; 72 Pearl St., Boston, MA. M.R. Gately, proprietor. Organette maker in the 1890s.
GATES ORGAN & PIANO CO.; also *Gates Brothers.* Three brothers, Winslow J., Austin L. and Charles E. Gates, began building pianos and organs in Melvern Square, Annapolis County, Nova Scotia about 1872. In 1882 they moved to Truro, NS to what is now the Moffatt Bros. Ltd. building on Court Street, and continued until at least 1897.
GATEWOOD ORGAN CO.; High Point, NC. A name used by *Shipman Organ Co.*
GAVIOLI, C., FILS; 15 rue des Charbonniers, St.-Antoine, Paris. Harmonium and harmoniflûte manufacturer, 1883.
GAVIOLI & CIE.; 2 avenue Taillebourg, place du Trône, Paris, 1883; 175 bis rue de Bercy and 11 quai de la Râpée in 1903; founded by Ludovic Gavioli. A. Gavioli and P. Yver, proprietors in 1903. Known mainly for its fairground organs, Gavioli also made harmoniums and street organs with free reeds. Awarded a bronze medal at the Paris Exposition of 1878.

GEAKE, HENRY & RICHARD; St. Thomas, Launceston, Cornwall, England. Also shown at Westgate St. in 1883. Organ and harmonium makers, 1878-1885.

GEBHARDT, J.; 1 rue Madame, Paris in 1920, later at 239 rue de Paris, Clamart, France. Aeoliphone portable harmoniums.

GEFLE ORGEL- & PIANO FABRIK; N. Kungsgatan 25, Gefle, Sweden; L.E. Barlein and P. Östlund, proprietors, 1903.

GEHLHAR & CO., see *Bremer Orgelbauanstalt Gehlhar & Co.*

GEISSLER, BRUNO; Elisenstrasse 42, Leipzig, Germany. Organettes.

GEM ORGAN CO.; also *Gem Piano and Organ Co.* in 1886, Washington, NJ; established 1859.

GEM ROLLER ORGAN CO.; organettes, Ithaca, NY; see *Autophone*.

GENTIS & CAPURON; (*Maison Couty*), quai la Rouselle, Saintes, France, 1903. Later listed as *Maison Couty, Liné & Klein, H. Chabin Sr.*, boulevard Raspail 230, Paris.

GENUNG, SETH J.; Waterloo, NY 1857; melodeons, see *Stilwell & Genung*.

GERAER KLAVIATUREN, VEB; Gera, Germany. Manufacturer of keyboards and components for harmoniums, 1961.

GERL, DR. F.M.; Hindelang, Germany; maker of Dr. Gerl's Hand-Harmonium, 1903, 1913; established 1892.

GERMANIA-INDUSTRIE GMBH; Berlin, 1921.

GEROME, L.; 105 rue Feronstree, Liege, Belgium in 1910; in 1925 located at 18 rue de la Province, Liege. Retailer and maker of pianos and harmoniums. In 1880 Gerome was manager of the *Balthasar-Florence* establishment at 97 rue Feronstree.

GERRISH, WM. H.; 1790 Washington St., Boston, MA in 1870; at 2130 Washington St., 2nd Floor, in 1880; 147 Tremont in 1883; established in 1868, in business at least until 1888.

GÉVAERT, VITUS; 36 rue Digue de Brabant, Ghent, Belgium. Inventor of the Harmonista (patented 1872), established 1846, in business at least through 1890. His brother *Charles Louis Gévaert* also manufactured pianos and harmoniums. Charles and his sons Paul and Fernand-Joseph opened showrooms at rue St. Paul 17 in Liege in 1870, and in 1879 opened another showroom at 20 rue des Dominicains in Liege. Showed a Harmonista at the Brussels Exhibition in 1880. Awarded a Diplome d'Honneur at the Anvers Exhibition of 1885 for a two-manual harmonium with Harmonista. Later operated by *Paul Beyer* at 63 Schoonzichtstrasse, Ghent, Belgium.

GEYZEN, ACHILLE; rue Dewez, Namur, Belgium. Successor to *Balthasar-Florence* as a manufacturer of pianos and harmoniums in 1920; closed in 1926.

The Gerrish Cabinet Organ, Style No. 4.

GHISCI, GIUSEPPE; Bratovecchio, Arezzo, Italy. Awarded a bronze medal for harmoniums at Arezzo, 1882. Also shown as *Chise*, (qv).

GIBBS, B.A.; 41A Southampton Rd., Malden Rd., London NW. Piano, organ and harmonium keymaker, 1921.

GILBERT; 115-113 rue de Vaugirard, Paris; established 1840; made "Melodian" organs. At least some of the Gilbert organs were made by *Hörügel*. Succesor to *Alexandre Rousseau*, (qv).

GILBERT, TIMOTHY, & CO.; 406 Washington St., Boston, MA 1847; made pianos with reed organ attachment patented by Abed Coleman. Serial number: 1851—4712.

GILDERSLEEVE, J., & CO.; 26 Angel Hill, Bury Saint Edmunds, Suffolk, England, 1892 & 1909, 20 Torbay St., Kentish Town, London 1891 & 1896; reed and pipe organ builder.

GILDERSLEEVE, R.; St. John's St., Bury Saint Edmunds, Suffolk, England. Pipe organ builder who made some reed organs. Advertised from 1890 to 1906.

GILMOUR, JAMES; Glasgow, Scotland. Granted patent for harmonium improvements, 1864. *James Gilmour & Son* showed two harmoniums at the Paris Exhibition of 1867.
GINOCCHIO, A., & BRO.; 41 Hester St., New York, NY, 1861. Manufacturer of cylinder organs and melodeons.
GIRARD & CIE., France, see *Ducroquet.*
GIULIANO, VITTORIO; Monteoliveto 61, Naples, Italy, 1883. Harmonium and organette maker. Awarded a First Order of Merit at Melbourne, Australia in 1880 for a harmonium.
GJELLESVIK, see *Kaland.*
GJERMSTAD; Ytterøya, Norway. Founded 1877 by Anton Gjermstad, who built pressure-type instruments until his death in 1892. His brother Sefanias then moved to Trondheim and opened an instrument repair shop.
GLASER, S.; Andreasgasse 9, Vienna, Austria, 1883.
GLASSL, EGYD; 13 Weingasse, Komotau, Czechoslovakia, 1930.
GLAVATCH, V.J.; St. Petersburg, Russia. Exhibited pianos and harmoniums at the Paris Exhibition of 1889.
GLOBE ORGAN CO.; New Bedford, MA. Incorporated 1884, with S.T. Viall as president.
GLORIA, a small harmonium with a two-octave keyboard and 14 bass chord buttons, made by *Wilhelm Spaethe*, (qv).
GLOTTON, G., see *Louis-François Debierre.*
GODAULT; awarded a bronze medal for good workmanship on an orgue-expressif shown at the Paris Exposition of 1847.
GODBY, WILLIAMS; 227 Haydens Rd., South Wimbleton, London, 1897; 19 Wynell Road, Forest Hill, S London, 1909.
GODEFROID-VOSSAERT, B.; 23 rue d'Eyne, Audenarde, Belgium, 1930
GODERICH ORGAN CO.; Goderich, Ontario 1890 through at least 1924. Serial number: 1924—15911.
GOGGIN, THOMAS, BROTHERS; Galveston, TX. Established 1866. Organ made by *Kimball* with the Goggin stencil.
GOLD MEDAL ORGAN, see *Alleger, Bowlby & Plotts.*
GOLDSCHMEDING; Warmoesstraat 141, Keizersgracht 305, Amsterdam, Netherlands. In business at least from 1898 through 1940. Retailer of reed organs from all over the world, some with the Goldschmeding stencil. Also a publisher of reed organ music.
GOLL, HERMANN, see *Süddeutsche Harmoniumfabrik Voigt & Goll.*
GOODMAN & BALDWIN; Rear No. 53 Chapel St., New Haven, CT, 1856. Melodeon maker. See *Whitaker and Frisbie.*
GOODMAN & FRISBIE, see *Whitaker and Frisbie.*

GOODMAN, HORATIO N.; New Haven, CT 1853, Syracuse, NY 1870; made the Pan Harmonicon, a combination pipe & reed organ. Patented a two-manual melodeon in 1853. See *Cabinet Pipe Organ Co., Phelps & Goodman.*

GOODRICH, EBENEZER; (1782-1841). Cambridge St., Boston, MA; pipe organ and piano maker; brother of William Goodrich who was also an organ builder. Ebenezer built a few reed organs, including one said to have been made in 1809 for the painter Gilbert Stuart, as well as pipe organs with free-reed ranks, one of which, made in 1829, is still extant. He is also credited with inventing a type of reed used in reed organs.

GOODWIN, T., see *Manchester Piano & Organ Works*.

GOUDGE, see *Jarret*.

GOULD & SONS ORGAN FACTORY; Lexington, MI. Founded by Hezekiah Gould about 1860. Hezekiah Gould also had a foundry and made stationary engines and farming utensils. In 1882 he took his son-in-law into partnership, renaming the firm *Dickenson-Gould Organ Co.* Dickenson, who had previously worked for *Clough & Warren*, returned to that company in 1886. Gould & Son continued in business with Hezekiah and his son John L. Gould until the factory was destroyed by fire in 1894. A firm named Cooley & Gould is listed in Port Huron, MI in 1893, but it is unclear whether this is the same Gould. See *Dickenson-Gould*.

GOULDEN, H.J.; High Street, Canterbury, Kent, England. Piano and harmonium maker 1884-88. In 1889 the firm became *Goulden and Wind*, which apparently only continued for one year.

GOUVERNEUR; Paris. Reed maker, 1867.

GRÄBNER, W.; Breite Str. 7, Dresden, Germany. Music dealership founded in 1823. Harmonium maker 1913-19. Proprietor in 1930: F. Gräbner.

GRAF, HERMANN; Reichenhainer Str. 11, Chemnitz, Germany in 1912; Nordstr. 2, Augustusburg, Germany 1925-35; established 1908. Piano and harmonium maker.

GRAHAM ORGAN CO.; Glasgow, Scotland.

GRAHAM, WALTER; 24A Risinghill Street, Pentonville, London until 1896, then at Moon St. off Theberton Street, Islington, London at least through 1906. Harmonium and American organ maker. Established in 1882, listed in 1900 as "late *Graham Brothers*." Also shown as *Walter Graham & Sons*.

GRAHAM, WM.; 4 Malboro' Works, Malboro' Rd., Upper Holloway, London. Reed organ maker, 1900.

GRANDJON, J.; 105 boulev. de Sébastopol and 74 rue Réaumur, Paris, 1883. Made pipe organs, harmoniums and barrel organs.

GRANITE STATE MANUFACTORY; Fisherville, NH, (now Penacook). Jacob B. Rand, principal, ca. 1860.

GRATIAN, H.; 1 Ferndale Rd., Upton Park, London E. Established 1870, advertised as a reed organ maker and piano dealer in 1900.

GRAVES, HENRY; 79 Harford St., Mile End Road, London. Piano and harmonium manufacturer, 1883.

GREAT WESTERN ORGAN CO.; organs made by *W.W. Kimball Co.*, Chicago, 1912.

Great Western Organ, Style 30. Made by W.W. Kimball Co., Chicago, Illinois, 1912.

GREEN, D.C.; 81 Haggerston Rd., London 1900, 1903. Portable harmonium maker.
GREEN, H.P., see *Estey & Green*.
GREEN, JOHN; 28 Norfolk Street, Strand, London; Soho Square, London in 1833; established 1830. Seraphine maker.
GREEN, OLIVER M.; Townsend, MA. Seraphine maker 1860. See *Smith & Green*.
GREEN, RUFUS H.; Poultney, VT; established 1835. Received US Patent No. 7113 on 19 Feb. 1850 for a seraphine.
GREEN & SAVAGE; Camden Rd., London. In 1878 moved the factory to North West Gate, Metropolitan Cattle Market; shown there in 1879,

1883, 1897, 1906. Manufactured the Brooklyn organ and a combination piano and organ. In 1921 shown as *Brooklyn Piano Co.*
GREENWOOD; Warrington, England. Maker of the Windsor organ.
GREEN, see *Smith & Green.*
GREGORIAN organ, the name used in Europe for the instrument sold in the United States as the Vocalion. See *The Orchestrelle Co.*
GREGORY, JOHN; 27 Lister Gate, Nottingham, England. Harmonium and accordion maker 1878-1889.
GRENIÉ, GABRIEL-JOSEPH; France. Demonstrated an orgue-expressif with free reeds in 1810. This instrument is generally considered to be the first free-reed organ.
GREULING, GEBR., & HINKEL; Hedelfingen, Germany, 1925.
GRIFFIN, E.C.; 171 Great College Street, London NW. Harmonium maker 1885-1892. Awarded a prize medal in the International Inventions Exhibition of 1885.
GRIMES, ARTHUR; 17 London Street, Derby, England. Piano and Anglo-American organ builder 1878-1880.
GRIMES, T., & CO.; Cheap Street, Sherborne, Dorset, England. Piano and harmonium maker 1878-1883. Succeeded by Mrs. Grimes, who operated the business until 1885.
GRINNEL BROTHERS; 1515 Woodward Ave., Detroit, MI. Piano maker. Organs with this name were probably made by others with the Grinnel stencil. See *Chicago Cottage Organ Co.*
GRINSTEAD, W.F.; Kilkenny, Ireland. Pipe organ maker, also made folding reed organs.
GROSSMAN; Kiev, Russia. Organ and harmonium maker, 1883.
GROSSMANN, F.; Hamburg, Germany. Made a combination piano-harmonium in 1886.
GROSSMANN & LEIDECK; Hallesche Strasse 118 in 1902, Sophienstrasse 22 in 1903, Leipzig-Gohlis, Germany. Listed as *Heinrich Grossmann Harmiumfabrik* 1903-05.
GROTEAU; New York. (No additional information available.)
GROVER & GROVER; 157-159 Kingsland Road, London. Piano and harmonium makers from 1878 to 1880, when Avill and Smart took over and apparently only produced pianos. In 1887 W. & F. Grover advertised as piano and harmonium makers at 150 The Grove, Stratford, E. London.
GROVER & WOOD; 62 Glengall Rd., London, 1887-1895.
GROVESTEEN & TRUSLOW; New York, NY. Piano maker, 1856; also probably made melodeons.
GRUCKER & SCHOTT; Strasbourg, France. Physharmonica makers, 1830.

The Gulbransen Magnatone electric reed organ, about 1940.

GRUNOW, AD.; Frankfurter Str. 52 in 1890, Frankfurter Allee 150 in 1912, Berlin. Harmonium maker, established 1879. Margarethe Grunow, director in 1912. Made a miniature harmonium and an accord-harmonium.
GRUNZWEIG & SCHLESINGER; Cöpenicker Str. 80-82, Berlin, Germany; Georg Wolff and H. Levi, proprietors; makers of rubberized cloth for harmoniums.
GRUS, ALPHONSE, see *Vygen Jeune*.
GSCHWIND, J.G., HARMONIUM & PIANOFORTEFABRIK; Lindenspürstrasse 45, Stuttgart, Germany; successor to *Pross, Gschwind & Co.* before 1883. Johann Georg Gschwind, proprietor. Established in 1851; Lucie Gschwind, director in 1912; Adolph Gschwind Erben, director in 1926; closed in 1928. See *Erste Wurtt. Reparaturanstalt, Harmonium- & Piano-Fabrik J.G. Gschwind*.
GUELPH MELODEON AND ORGAN CO.; Guelph, Ontario, ca. 1872. Associated with *Bell Organ Co.*
GUÉROULT; France. Awarded bronze medal at the Paris Exposition of 1878.

GUESNÉ, J.; 40 Faubourg du Temple, Paris. Made the Piano-Euphonium, a combined piano and harmonium, patented in 1867.

GUICHENÉ, L'ABBÉ FRANÇOIS; St.-Médard Les Landes, France. Invented a mechanism for playing full chords on the harmonium as accompaniment for melody, patented 1856. Used on the *Alexandre* harmoniums.

GULBRANSEN CO.; 3232 W. Chicago Ave., Chicago, IL; established 1906; officers: A.G. Gulbransen, president; C. Gulbransen, vice-president; Edward B. Healy, secretary. Made a modernized melodeon ca. 1930. About 1940 made the Magnatone, originally a suction instrument, later changed to pressure for quicker response. Used *Estey* reeds with electric valve action developed by *S.K. Ketterman* (qv), then chief engineer and assistant to the president.

GUNA, JULIUS; Veterna ulice 16, Prešov, Czechoslovakia.

GUNN, JAMES A.; Kelseyville, CA. Born in London, 1841; came to Lake County, CA in 1880. He established a planing mill and later the first organ and furniture factory in Lake County.

GUNTHER & HORWOOD; Camden Town, London ca. 1825. Seraphine maker.

GYS, PIERRE; Molenbeck-Saint-Jean, Belgium. Showed a harmonium at the Brussels Exhibition of 1847.

Organist at the Latter Day Saints Church, Mendon, Utah, 1940.

Brødrene Hals two-manual and pedal reed organ.

H

HAASE, RUDOLF; Lyczakowerstr. 48, Lemberg, Austria-Hungary, 1903. Established 1894.
HACK KLEINHARMONIUM; Göttingen, Germany, 1949. Dealer, sold instruments with this stencil made by others.
HAECKL, ANTON (also *Hackel*); Ungargasse 330, Vienna, Austria; piano maker. In 1818 made the four-octave Physharmonika, one of the earliest reed organs. This instrument was intended to be placed beneath the right side of a piano keyboard and played with the right hand while the left hand played accompaniment on the piano.
HAIG, WILLIAM; 13 Sixth Ave. in 1827, 48 Hammond St. in 1832, New York, NY; reed maker.
HALE, C.E.; West Didsbury, Manchester, England, 1903.
HALE, see *Hughes & Hale.*
HALIFAX PIANO & ORGAN CO.; Halifax, N.S., Canada. At least parts of these organs were made by *W. Doherty & Co.*
HALL, see *Chute, Hall & Co.*
HALLMAN, JACOB C.; 80 Alpine, Kitchener, Ontario. Made electronic reed organs 1950-69. Previously located at Waterloo, Ontario.
HALONEN JA KUMPP; Jyväskylässaa, Finland.
HALS, BREMER OLSEN; Norway. Built a "melodika" in 1819, thought to be an early reed organ.
HALS, BRØDRENE; showrooms at Storthingsgaden 24-26, factory at Klingenborggd. 1b og 3, Christiania (now Oslo), Norway. Karl Hals trained in piano manufacture in Copenhagen, Hamburg and Paris 1842-46 and returned to Norway to work in J.W. Cappelen's piano store as a tuner and repairman. He established Norway's first and largest piano factory in 1847 and the next year his brother Petter joined the business which was then named *Brødrene Hals* (Hals Brothers). Petter died in 1871 after which Karl continued the business with the help of his sons Olav and Thor. In 1880 the firm opened a concert hall and concert bureau, expanding into the music publishing business in 1885. A third son, Sigurd, joined the firm in 1883 upon the untimely death of Olav. Thor and Sigurd became partners in 1888; Karl died ten years later. The firm was incorporated in 1900. In 1908 the publishing department expanded further, acquiring the name Norsk Musikforlag in 1909. The concert hall closed in 1919. By the time piano production was discontinued in 1925 Brødrene Hals had produced about 27,000 pianos. A total of 1,337 harmoniums were made over the period 1886-1918. Norsk Musikforlag today is Norway's foremost music publisher and dealer in printed music.

HAMAMATSU MUSICAL INSTRUMENT MFG. CO. LTD.; Hamamatsu, Japan. Made the Westminster organ.

HAMILTON ORGAN CO.; 85-89 West 14th Place, Chicago, IL in 1899; sold in 1889 to *D.H. Baldwin & Co.* Made the "Monarch" organ. Discontinued organ production probably in 1913. Serial numbers:

1889—1000	1898—23000	1906—50382
1890—2090	1907—57149	1908—62748
1891—4010	1899—26000	1909—65574
1892—6300	1900—31000	1910—67181
1893—8000	1901—34000	1911—68773
1894—11000	1902—37000	1912—70388
1895—14000	1903—40000	1913—71722
1896—17000	1904—40001	
1897—20000	1905—45931	

HAMILTON VOCALION ORGAN CO.; Worcester, MA 1886-1889, see *James Baillie-Hamilton* and *Vocalion*.

HAMLIN, EMMONS; foreman at *Prince*'s, co-founder of *Mason & Hamlin*. Said to be the originator of reed voicing, but did not patent it. See *Alfred Little*.

HAMLIN, see *Smith & Hamlin*.

Hammond Reed Co., Manufacturers of Organ Reeds, Reed Boards and other Organ Supplies. Worcester, Mass., U.S.A.

HAMMOND, A.H., & CO.; May St., Worcester, MA. Andrew H. Hammond, successor to *Redding & Harrington*; reed maker 1885, 1889. Also made the "Louis" fan tremolo, patented 1856, 1862, 1867, 1868, 1870 and 1871. Made reeds and parts for *Sears, Roebuck & Co.* as well as complete instruments. Shown as Hammond Reed Co. in 1909. Hammond sold out to *Hinners Organ Co.*

HANCOCK, WM., & SONS; Wiveliscombe, England. Organ serial number 98733 in the Heiss collection.
HANDMANN, G.E., NACHF. HUGO HOPP; Munzstr. 2, Berlin, Germany; harmonium components, 1930; established 1837.
HANDS, C.W., & CO.; Harpur St., Bedford, England; also Midland Road, Bedford, 1903. Established 1866. Manufactured both suction and pressure-operated instruments.
HANDWERCK, ADOLF; Mittlegasse 13, Vienna, Austria 1919 until at least 1930.
HANEL; Zwickau, Germany.
HANSEN, F., & SON; Raadhusstraeds 8, Nykøbing, Denmark, 1909.
HANTZSCH, GEORG; Schlolfegergasse 33, Nurnberg, Germany; reed maker, 1883.
HARBACK ORGANINA CO.; 809 Filbert St., Philadelphia, PA. Made the Harmonette, a hand-cranked organette.
HARDIN ORGANS & MELODEONS; (spelling uncertain, possibly Harder, no other information available.)
HARDTE, WALTHER FERDINAND; Thomasiusstr. 17, Leipzig, Germany. Established 1891. Harmonium maker, listed in 1913 as a pianoforte maker.
HARDY, A.S., & CO.; Guelph, Ontario, 1874.
HARDY, CHAS.; Lancashire Hill, Stockport, Cheshire, England. Organ builder and harmonium maker 1879-1896. Had works in Penny Lane, Stockport.
HARGRAVE, J.W.; 20 Hornsey St., Holloway Rd., London N. American organ and harmonium maker, 1921.
HARGREAVES, WM.; in 1879 at 61 Dale Street, Manchester, England also 11 Booth Street, Picadilly, Manchester in 1897; in 1887 *Hargreaves & Co.* at 19 Vernon Street, Broughton, Manchester. Working until 1893.
HARLAND, ALFRED JOSEPH; 76 East Road, City Road, London; in 1921 shown at 106 Wenlock Street, New North Road, Hoxton, London. Established 1879, piano and portable harmonium maker.
HARMONIUMBAU ALBRECHT, GMBH; Heutingsheim, Germany. Established in 1919. Office at Blumenstr. 22, Ludwigsburg from 1925. Moved the factory to Mathildenstr. 21, Ludwigsburg in 1928. Doing business as *Harmoniumbau GmbH*, (qv).
HARMONIUM-BAUANSTALT RATZKE, see *Ratzke*.
HARMONIUMBAU GMBH; Mathildenstr. 21, Ludwigsburg i. Württbg., Germany; E.H. Wever, manager.
HARMONIUMBAU LUDWIGSBURG, see *Walcker-Mayer, Werner*.
HARMONIUMBAU PETER; Metzgerstr. 3, Reutlinger, Germany. Pipe organ, piano and harmonium maker, tuner and repairman, established 1877, Xaver Peter proprietor. Located in Eger/Böhmen in 1945.

Established 1919, production discontinued in 1965, closed 1975. See *Walcker-Mayer*, also see *Teck-Harmoniumfabrik*.
HARMONIUMFABRIK ZU NEISSE; Neisse, Germany; 90 Viehweg 90, Mühle, Germany in 1886. Made the Caecilian harmoniums.
HARMONYPHON-MUSIKWERKE, see *Carl E. Fiedler*.
HARRINGTON, E., & CO.; Worcester, MA, 1858; later *A. Davis & Co.*, reed maker.
HARRINGTON, see *Redding & Harrington*.
HARRIS, JOHN; Hartford, CT; made the "Parlor Grand" organ, ca. 1865.
HARRISON, THOMAS, & SON; 168 Drummond St., London, 1890, 1900; 17-18 Little Edward St., Albany St., London NW, 1921, 1931. Manufacturer of turnery and metal fittings for pipe organs and harmoniums; established 1830.
HARTMANN, OTTO; Werdau, Germany. Porcelain stop face maker, extant 1916-1929.
HARTUNG, ROBERT; Ludolf-Colditz Str. 10, Stötteritz, Germany in 1920; Hallische Strasse 155, Leipzig-Gohlis, Germany, 1929. Established 1905, closed 1928.
HARWOOD; Kansas City, MO. A Harwood chapel organ dated 1890 also carries the name J.W. Jenkins Sons Music Co. on the stop board.
HASELTON, D.H., & CO.; West Townsend, MA. Lyre-legged melodeon ca. 1860. Also shown as *Bruce-Haselton*.
HASLEVS HARMONIUMFABRIK; Jernbanegade 24, Haslev, Denmark; also *Mølgaard-Jensen*.
HASTINGS, WILLIAM P.; 144½ Exchange St., Portland, ME; established 1850 as *Hastings & Philbrook*. Located at 89 Federal St., in 1861. Made melodeons, seraphines, cabinet organs, chamber organs. Shown as a music dealer in 1883.
HATTERSLEY BROS.; Trenton, NJ, 1883.
HATTERSLEY, WM., & CO.; Regent Street, Westminster, London, established 1845. Shown at 22 Great Street as *Wm. Hattersley & Son* in 1850; at 5 New Bridge Street, Vauxhall as *Wm. Hattersley & Co.* in 1853; in 1854 at 3 Darlington Place; and in 1856 at Wilton Place, Pimlico. Piano and seraphine maker. His son, William P., was in business as *W. Hattersley & Co.* at 10-12-14 Bow St., Sheffield, England from 1868 until at least 1883, as a piano dealer and harmonium maker.
HAUGEN, BERNT M.; Volda, Norway. Harmonium maker, previously in partnership with Lars E. Ulvestad. See *Ulvestad & Haugen*.
HAUSCHILD, H.M., see *Bremer Orgelbauanstalt Gehlhar & Co.*
HAY, SAM.; 21 Bridge Street, Glasgow, Scotland. Piano, harmonium and organ manufacturer 1878-1884. After that moved to 91 Renfield Street and apparently discontinued making reed organs.

Farm girl playing the organ at home in McIntosh County, North Dakota, November, 1940.

HAYNES ORGAN, USA. No other information available.
HAYASHI, SAIHEI; Nihonbashi, Tokyo. Reed maker.
HAYDN organ, see *Beale & Co.*
HAZELTON, see *J. Reyner*.
HEALY, PATRICK J., see *Lyon & Healy*.
HEATH, R. & E.; 14 Crockherbtown, Cardiff, Glamorgan, Wales. Piano, organ and harmonium makers 1880-1889. After that moved to 51 Queen Street and apparently stopped making harmoniums.
HECHINGER; Munich, Germany, 1835. Harmonium maker.

HEDÉN, A.A.; Tampere, Finland. Learned organ making in Germany. Began making harmoniums in the 1860s, later joined by his brother J.E. Hedén. In 1928 the firm moved to Vihdin-Nummela and became *Hedén ja Kumpp* and later *Nummelan Harmoonitehdas*, finally going out of business in 1969.

HEEDE, CARL VOM, & BOLENDER; Priorei, Germany; metal components for harmoniums, 1930.

HEER, DE, see *DeHeer*.

HEES & CO. PIANO-EN HARMONIUMFABRIEK NV; Delft, Netherlands 1900. Made the Jubal organ.

HEINL, ANDR.; Klingenthaler Str. 738, Kraslice, (Graslitz), Austria; maker of "Accordionette" miniature harmoniums, 1930.

HEINRICHSDORFF, OTTO; Poggenpfuhl 76 in 1912, Neuer Weg 8 in 1925, Danzig, Germany. Piano and harmonium maker from 1832 until at least 1913.

HELBIG, JOHANN JACOB; Römhild, Germany, 1829. Äolodicon maker.

HELFERT, ANTON; Rahmgraben 139, Tachov, (Tachau), Czechoslovakia, 1930; established 1864.

HELLER, J.H.; Berne, Switzerland; music box with reeds.

HELMKAMP, ANTHONY G.; Chicago, IL. Piano and reed organ maker. Established 1847.

HEMLOCK, F.M.; Cincinatti, OH, 1875.

HEMPERLY, G.; Palmyra, NY. Active in 1900.

HEMSTEAD, H.N.; melodeons and harmoniums, 1865-1866.

HENDERSON ORGANS, connected with *Ann Arbor Organ Co.*, (qv).

HENRY & CIE.; Paris. Harmonium maker, 1895.

HENRY, JUSTIN; Kirchstr. 43, Urbeis (Orbev), Alsace, Germany and France, 1912, 1930. Cabinet maker and harmonium maker.

HEPBURN, JAMES; Pictou, N.S., Canada, 1854-60. Exhibited in the Nova Scotia Industrial Exhibition, Halifax, 1854.

HEPPERLE & RIETHEIMER, see *Teck-Harmoniumfabrik*.

HEPWORTH ORGAN CO.; 45 Hampstead Rd., London 1897; see *Jenkinson & Co.*

HERFURTH, see *Bongardt & Herfurth*.

HERMANN; London. Harmonium makers, 1876.

HERMANN, ALBIN; Mittelstr. 6, Werdau (Chemnitz), Germany. Established 1906, closed 1914. Made the Mozart harmonium, "Amerikanisches System."

HERMANN, HEINRICH; Bernau bei Berlin, Germany; miniature harmoniums, organettes, 1903.

HERNGREN, C.A.; Lindköping, Sweden, 1909.

HERRBURGER BROOKS; Meadow Land, Longeaton, Nottingham, England, 1896. Manufacturer of organ keys, still extant.
HESSE JR, CARL, & CO.; Raab, Austria-Hungary. Organ and harmonium maker, 1883.
HEUBESCH, WENZEL; Poricerstr., Prague, Czechoslovakia; mechanical musical instruments and harmoniums, 1883.
HEURE; France; reed maker.
HEYERICK, JOS.; 16 quai Porte aux Vaches, Ghent, Belgium; estab. 1885.
HEYL, G.; Brühl-Kirchgasse 156-58 in 1886, Brühl 27 and Kirchstr. 27 in 1912, Brühl 27 in 1925, Borna-Leipzig, Germany. Established in 1828, operated until at least 1930. Walther and Friedrich Heyl, proprietors in 1912. Made combination piano-harmoniums with organ actions by *Mannborg* and *Lindholm*.
HICKS, H.; Launceston, Cornwall, England. Reed organ maker 1912, 1913.
HIGEL, OTTO, CO. LTD.; corner of King & Bathurst Streets, Toronto. Made practically all keys, reeds and reedboards used by Canadian manufacturers. Officers in 1906: Otto Higel, president; Charles E. Clinken-Broomer, vice-president; Robert H. Easson, secretary.
HIGHAM, THOS.; 76 Bridge Street, Deansgate, Manchester, England. Harmonium maker 1878-1883.
HIGH POINT ORGAN CO.; High Point, NC. Predecessor of *Shipman Organ Co.*, (qv).
HILDEBRANDT, HERMANN; 82 Halle, Rossleben 15, and 206a Rosslebener Str., Wiehe, Germany. Established 1881 as a pipe organ builder, made harmoniums from 1899. *Brüning & Bongart* (qv) had a financial interest in 1925. Harmonium production was discontinued about 1949.
HILDRED BROS.; Boston, MA; makers or importers of harmoniums.
HILL, R.S., CO.; 4600 Louisville Ave., Highland Park Station, Louisville, KY; Richard Stott Hill, president, E.T. Schmitt, vice-president, Geo. W. Grant, secretary in 1914; factory at Mohawk St. and L&N Railroad. Hill was born in Huddersfield, Yorkshire, England in 1870, and as a child travelled on the concert circuit in the eastern United States as "Richard Hill, Boy Organist." He graduated from Purdue University with a degree in music and mathematics. In 1894 he was in Fort Wayne, IN, possibly with the *Fort Wayne Organ Co.* and later designed organs for *Beckwith* in Louisville, KY before establishing *R.S. Hill & Co.* Some organs are said to have been produced with the name *Beckwith & Hill.*
HILL, WILLIAM, & SON; London, made Vocalion organs under the *Baillie-Hamilton* patents.

```
┌─────────────────────────────────┐
│                                 │
│    R. S. Hill Company           │
│          INCORPORATED           │
│                                 │
│        MANUFACTURERS OF         │
│                                 │
│         REED ORGANS             │
│                                 │
│       HIGHLAND PARK STA.        │
│        LOUISVILLE, KY.          │
│                                 │
└─────────────────────────────────┘
```

HILLIER, JAMES & CO.; 12-15 Kings Rd, Camdentown, London in 1883 and 1889, 228 York Rd, N. London in 1897 & 1906; *Hillier Piano & Organ Co.* in 1903; established 1855, still extant 1909. E.S. Hillier, proprietor in 1903. Awarded a gold medal at the Antwerp Exhibition of 1894. At the Paris Exhibition of 1878 they showed the "Orchestrophone," a two-manual 25 stop instrument with one manual on pressure and one on suction, for which they were awarded an honorable mention. Hilliers were agents for Hammond reeds in 1888.

HILLSTROM & BREDSHALL; 64 North Carpenter St., 329 W. Ohio in 1880, Chicago, IL. Established in 1872 by Charles Oscar Hillstrom and his brother John August Hillstrom with a Mr. Bredshall. C.O. Hillstrom had learned organ building in his native Sweden. In 1880 moved to Chesterton, Indiana. See *C.O. Hillstrom & Co.*

HILLSTROM, C.O., & CO.; 2-28 Main St. (now Broadway), Chesterton, IN. Established in 1880 as the successor to *Hillstrom & Bredshall*. Founded by Charles Oscar Hillstrom and John A. Hillstrom, natives of Sweden, and H.H. Winger. The estimated total production was over 40,000 organs, and at its peak the company employed 125 people. Hillstrom also manufactured organ stools for sale with its own organs as well as for sale by *H.D. Bentley* of Freeport, Illinois, who contracted for 4,000 stools per month. Hillstrom presented an organ to King Oscar II of Sweden and it is said that King Edward VII of England owned a Hillstrom organ. After C.O. Hillstrom's death in 1896 the company declined and in 1898 came under the control of Leeds & Harper and later Mr. A.L. Harper. Part of the factory building was used by the Russell Lane Piano Co. of Chicago, and pianos were also built under the Hillstrom name.

Organ production was greatly reduced by 1908 and probably discontinued in 1913. The factory building was destroyed by fire in 1923.

HINES, ISAAC, & CO.; Brattleboro, VT 1853-1855; successor to *E.B. Carpenter & Co.* Partners: Jacob Estey, Isaac Hines, H.P. Green; succeeded by *Estey & Green* (qv).

HILL, WILLIAM, & SON; London, made Vocalion organs under the *Baillie-Hamilton* patents.

HINKEL, ERNST; office at Promenade 30, Ulm an der Donau, Germany; factory at Kämpffergasse 3-5; Dipl. Ing. Karl Rossler, manager in 1930. Established in 1880 by Ernst Peter Hinkel (1850-1924). In 1883 listed as *Hinkel & Silberhorn*. Production of suction reed organs begain in 1886, the same year that Peter's son Heinrich was admitted to the firm. Heinrich Hinkel took over management of the firm in 1922. Heinrich's son Heinz Hinkel entered the firm in 1930 after four years of training at Steinmeyer & Co. Hinkel produced 5,000 organs by 1892, 60,000 by 1924. In business at least as late as 1951.

HINNERS & ALBERTSEN; 341 Court St., 2nd floor, in 1879; Court & 5th Streets, 2nd floor, in 1883; 129-131 Court Street in 1885; all in Pekin, IL. Only the 341 Court Street building is still in existence. John L. Hinners, who had previously worked for *Mason & Hamlin,* started in 1879 making reed organs for *Fred Schaefer,* a music dealer. Schaefer retired in 1881, his business, presumably the music dealership portion only, continued as Koch Brothers. In the same year Hinners went into business for himself as *Hinners Reed Organ Co.* J.J. Fink became a

The First Hinners Organ Co. factory was on the second floor of this building at 341 Court Street in Pekin, Illinois in 1879, (1996 photo).

partner later in 1881 and the company was then known as *Hinners, Fink & Co.* Ubbo J. Albertsen joined in 1885, buying the interest of J.J. Fink and other partners. The company became *Hinners & Albertsen* in 1885. Sales were oriented toward the German-American community. Hinners acquired the capability to make its own reeds by buying out *A.H. Hammond & Co.* Albertsen retired in 1902 and the business was then incorporated as *Hinners Organ Co.* John L. Hinners died in 1906 and was succeeded by his son Arthur W. Hinners. Over 3,000 pipe organs, mostly trackers, were produced between 1890 and 1936. The reed organ business was continued under the name *Hinners Reed Organ Co.* by Louis C. Moschel until his death in 1940. The company was formally dissolved in 1942. A total of about 20,000 reed organs had been built.

HINTERMEISTER UNITED ORGAN CO.; 198-200 Terrace, Buffalo, NY 1887; Oil City, PA 1899. Established in 1884, succeeded by *Pittsburg Organ & Piano Co.* in 1901. M.J.H. Hintermeister, a native of Zurich, Switzerland, chairman; his son, F.A. Hintermeister was manager. Last listed in 1901. See *Ithaca Organ Co.*

HIRAMATSU GAKKI; shop at 5-3 Iidamachi, factory at 198 Sendagi, Hongo, both in Tokyo. Established 1898, operating at least through 1908.

HISSA, JAAKKO; Isokyla, Lapua, Finland. Established 1890, in business at least through 1903.

HOFBAUER, CARL HEINZ; (Orgelbaumeister Hofbauer), Rosdorfer Weg 14, D3400 Göttingen, Germany. Established 1923, currently making hand-cranked street organs operating from paper rolls, mostly with pipes but some reed instruments.

HOFBERG, MAGNUS; Turnerstrasse 49 in 1893, Lütznerstr. 24-26 in 1901, Lützenerstr. 22 1903-7, Leipzig-Lindenau, Germany. Then located at 20-22 Klingenstrasse in Leipzig-Plagwitz, Germany 1902-10. Established 1891. Maker of harmoniums and "Choral" organettes; Lars Magnus Hofberg, proprietor. Made both pressure and suction instruments. Lars Magnus Hofberg was born in Sweden in 1862 and came to Germany with Theodor Mannborg and Olof Lindholm. Hofberg worked for *Mannborg* until establishing his own factory in 1891. Hofberg died in 1919 and the business continued to be operated by his heirs until 1930 when it was sold to *Lindholm*. Serial numbers:

1895—3100	1920—22200	1950—29600
1910—14300	1930—28500	1955—30000

HOFFMANN, BENEDICT; Coselstr. 102, Oberglogau, Germany 1903; established 1843. In operation at least through 1909.

HOFFMANN, G.; Schönhauser Allee 178, Oranienburger Str. 83 in 1890, Berlin.

HOFMANN & CZERNY; Linzer Str. 174-180 in 1930, Vienna, Austria; piano and harmonium manufacturers, founded 1902. Claimed to be the largest harmonium factory in Austria-Hungary, with 500 workers. Serial numbers may include instruments other than reed organs:

1924—19000	1940—37500	1958—44000
1925—21000	1950—38200	1960—46000
1930—31600	1955—41200	
1935—35900	1956—42000	

HOGGSON & PETTIS MANUFACTURING CO.; 64-66 Court St., New Haven, CT; stop knobs.

HÖGNER, FREYER & BEER; Taubenpreskeln b. Gera, Germany, 1924-1931.

HOHNE, see *Willi Pucklitzsch*.

HOHNER, MATTH.; Trossingen, Germany, 1903. Manufacturer of accordions, harmonicas and several models of reed organs, including: the Hohner-Organa, a four-octave electrically blown portable organ; the Organetta, a 2⅓ octave table top organ, also electrically blown; and the Multimonica II, a combination reed and electronic organ in which the

lower manual had three rows of reeds, electrically blown, and the upper manual played electronic tones.
HOLDERNESS & HOLDERNESS; 105 New Oxford Street, London. Piano and harmonium manufacturers, 1883.
HOLLÄNDER, GEORG; Feuchtwangen, Germany, 1903, 1930. Established 1885.
HOLLERAN, see *Roth, Holleran & Miles.*

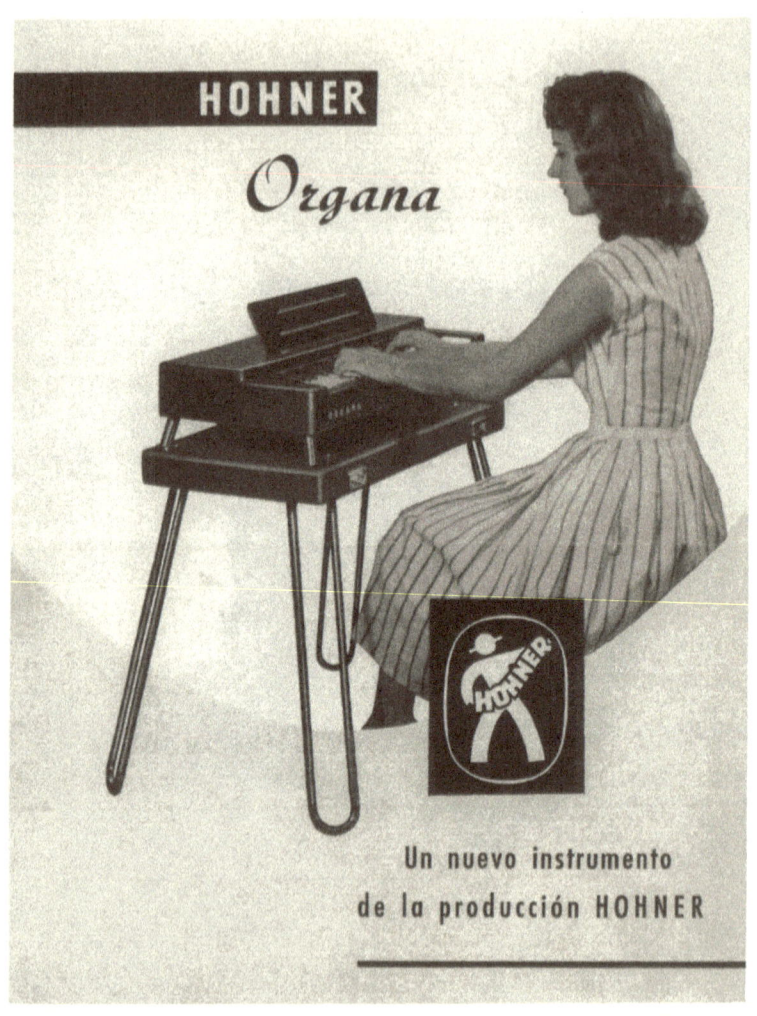

HÖLLING & SPANGENBERG; Am Rossmarkt, Zeitz, Germany, 1878. Established 1841. D.H. Friedrich Hölling and Friedrich Franz Spangenberg, proprietors. Patented a small portable reed organ. Made a combination piano-harmonium.
HOLMES, W.S., see *Capital City Organ Co.*
HOLMES, see *Whitney & Holmes, Farley & Holmes.*
HOLSTEBRO ORGEL-HARMONIUMSFABRIK K. KAMSTRUP; Holstebro, Denmark, 1930.
HOLT, JOHN; 62 Upper Gough St. in 1882; 81 Latimer St. in 1890; 176 Station St. in 1901; 12 Station St. 1907-1946, all in Birmingham, England; also at Clarence Road, Birmingham. Established in 1875 by

John Holt, who died in 1932; he was succeeded by his son John Wm. Holt, who died in 1946. John's daughter Doris M. Holt was also active in the firm. Built a variety of instruments from one to three manuals, and a four-manual instrument made only 32" deep to get through the doorway in the Islington Exhibition Hall in 1896. The factory was called the *Pioneer Organ Works*, and some of the organs were called "Pioneer." Built organs until at least 1938. Serial numbers:

1904—1287	1925—1477	1933—1534
1917—1416	1926—1479	1934—1540
1919—1430	1928—1504	1936—1548
1922—1454	1929—1509	1937—1552

JOHN HOLT,

Pioneer Organ and Piano Works,

CLARENCE ROAD,
AND
STATION ROAD, HARBORNE,
BIRMINGHAM.

JOHN HOLT also makes One Manual Reed Organs from 6 Guineas, and High-Class Pianos from 18 Guineas.

REPAIRS AND TUNINGS AT MOST MODERATE CHARGES.

Established 1875.

HOLZINDUSTRIE PAUL ZIMMERMANN, see *Zimmermann, Paul*.
HOMBERG, JULIUS; Zeitz, Germany; maker of organ benches 1872 until at least 1930. Established 1863.
HOPLEY, WM.; 58-60 Brunswick Road, Liverpool, England. Piano and harmonium manufacturer 1879, still in business in 1896 although apparently had already discontinued making reed organs.
HOPP, HUGO, see *G.E. Handmann*.
HORBIGER, ALOYSIUS; Atzgersdorf, Vienna, Austria, 1862.
HORN, MAX; Speigelstr. 23, Zwickau, Germany in 1925; Turnhallenstr. 1, Werdau 1927-29; Mühlenstr. 2 in Eisenberg, 1929-39; Berliner Str. 81a, Leipzig in 1941. Established 1909. Also listed as *Werdauer Harmoniumfabrik Max Horn*.

HORNBAKER, ROBERT; Hornbaker St., (now South Lincoln Ave.), Washington, NJ 1852.

HORTON, HENRY B.; Akron, OH 1852-55; built the Melo-pean, sold out and moved to Ithaca, NY where he became one of the founders of *Autophone*; see *Horton & Rose, Blodget & Horton, John M. Scott*.

HORTON & ROSE; Akron, OH; Henry B. Horton and Ira Rose.

HÖRÜGEL, M.; Am Tansplan 4 in 1893, Charlottestrasse 88 in 1901, Kirchstrasse 6 in 1903, Kurze Str. 4 in 1925, Leipzig-Leutsch, Germany; factory located in Ruckmarsdorf. Paul Hörügel, proprietor in 1895, joined by Wilhelm Oscar Jürgens in 1903. Jürgens was the remaining proprietor in 1930; founded 1872 or 1893 (sources vary). Acquired *Hermann Burger* in 1908. "Largest harmonium factory on the European continent" (1903). Annual production 2,000 instruments in 1904. Specialized in suction instruments, also made a three-manual and pedal harmonium. Went out of business in 1952. Serial numbers:

        1905—8634   1925—36792   1950—44680
        1910—18486   1928—40000   1951—44900
        1913—25000   1931—42830   1952—45100
        1915—28951   1935—43380
        1920—31948   1940—44000

Hörügel das Qualitäts-**harmonium**
Prämiiert mit nur goldenen Medaillen und ersten Preisen

HORWOOD, see *Gunther & Horwood*.

HOSKIN, see *Dominion Organ Co.*

HOTTA organ; sold by Otsuka Piano Shokai, 4-164 Motomachi, Naka-ku, Yokohama 231, Japan.

HOUCK; Nashville, TN. Stencil organ, possibly made by Cable.

HOUPAN, see *Tonzaa et Houpin*.

HOURK, O.K.; Memphis, TN, Little Rock, AR, 1907. See *Sterchi Bros.*

HOVEY & BACHELDER; Augusta, ME; maker of Nutting's Patent Aeolicon.

HOWARD, SAMUEL, & CO.; 577-579 Rochdale Road, also 1 New Cross, also 273 Broad Street, Pendleton, Manchester, England 1844-1899.

Made the Melody Organ which had a mechanical device for highlighting the melody over chords.

HOWE, HERMANN, & CO.; Gr. Frankfurter Str. 39 in 1903, Grosse Frankfurter Str. 44, Grosse Frankfurter Str. 50-51 in 1929, Berlin, Germany. Hermann Howe, proprietor 1903, 1909; established 1874. Church organ, street organ and harmonium maker.

HOWE, MAX; Blumenstr. 31, Berlin, 1912. Established 1870. Maker of church organs, street organs and harmoniums. Proprietor in 1912: Margarete Ascher.

HOWE, M.H.; Kleeburger Str. 16 in 1925, Kirchhofstr. 4 in 1929, Allenstein, East Prussia, Germany. Harmonium and street organ maker and dealer.

HOWECK; Odessa, Russia. Church organ and harmonium maker, 1883.

HOWLAND & BOMAN; 320 Clinton St., Chicago, IL. Established in 1875 as *Lawson & Bowman* (qv). Made the Garden City organ. In 1883 the business occupied a 30 by 100 foot three-story building and employed forty workers.

HOWLETT & SON; 10 Frith St., Soho, London. Established 1804, makers of name plates for harmoniums.

HOYLAND, JOHN; 23-25 Bow St., Sheffield, England. Harmonium manufacturer and piano dealer, 1879-1890. In 1889 began making concertinas. Also had premises at West Bank Lane, Sheffield and 21 Exchange Street, Sheffield.

HSINGHAI PIANO CO.; Beijing, China. Made organs until 1984.

HUG, GEBRÜDER; Switzerland, branches at Bruderstrasse in 1855, Königstrasse 16 in 1888, both in Leipzig, Germany. Became *Gebrüder Hug & Co.* in 1893, then *Hug & Co.* in 1917, located at Markgrafenstr. 10 and Schulstrasse 3, Leipzig. A retail dealer: organs with this name were made by others.

HUGHES, A.P.; Philadelphia, PA 1856. Flat top organ.

HUGHES & HALE; Philadelphia, PA. Melodeon maker.

HUGHES & SON; Foxcroft, ME, established 1894; successor to *Dyer & Hughes*. Also shown as Hughes & Son Piano Mfg. Co.

HUGHES; see *Vogel & Hughes, Dyer & Hughes*.

HÜLLER & CO.; Nürnberger Strasse 59, Leipzig, Germany; also listed as *Hüller & Stiegler*, Delitzscherstrasse 144, Leipzig, 1909. Made four-octave miniature harmoniums.

HULSHIZER, see *Shimer & Hulshizer*.

HUMMEL, FRANZ; Wenzelplatz, Prague, Czechoslovakia, 1883. Organ and harmonium maker, 1883.

HUMMER, H.A., & CO.; Frenchtown, NJ.

HUMPHREYS, A. & E.; Little Camden St., King St., Camden Town, London 1883 until at least 1931. Established 1883.

HUMPHREYS, C.; 15 Crawley Mews, Seymour St., London NW. Reed and pipe organ bellows maker in 1900, established 1866.

HUMPHREYS, JAMES; 198 Seymour St., Oakley Sq., London in 1883; shown as *J. Humphreys & Sons* at 35 Drummond St., Euston Sq. from 1896 until at least 1921. Located at 459-463 Caledonian Rd., London 1931-1935; made Endsleigh organs; established 1867. Built both suction and pressure instruments from portables to three-manual & pedal; also built a combination piano and organ with 58 stops and more than 1,000 reeds, with registers from 1 ft. to 32 ft.

HUNT, C.B., & CO.; 101 Bristol Street, Boston, MA 1870-1890; Bay State organs; started as *C.B. Hunt & P. Krause* in 1875 until some time before 1880; 39,000 organs sold by 1886. Serial number: 1888—39308.

HUNTING, W.S.; Boston, MA. Seraphine, 1840.

HUNTINGTON, W.D. (No other information available.)

HUPFELD, LUDWIG, A.G.; Hupfeldstr. in 1912, Böhlitz-Ehrenberg, Germany. Established 1882. Manufacturer of roll-operated pianos. Also made the "Clavimonium," a combination piano-harmonium in 1910 as well as player reed organs. The name was later changed to *VEB Deutsch Piano-Union*, Leipzig, Germany.

HUSSON-BUTHOD & THIBOUVILLE; 68-70 rue Réaumur, Paris. Manufacturer of organs, harmoniums and harmoniflûtes, 1883.

HÜTTNER, EDUARD; Stallbaumstr. 5 in 1902-05, Schachstr. 9 in 1906-08, Cöthener Str. 13 in 1912, Leipzig-Gohlis, Germany. Josephstr. 31, Leipzig-Lindenauer, Germany, 1909-11. Pipe organ maker from 1902, began making harmoniums in 1908. Karl Stock became the proprietor in 1911. See *Karl Stock*.

HYUNDAE MUSICAL INSTRUMENTS CO.; 853-13, Anyang-dong, Anyang City, Kyunggi-do, Korea in 1985.

I

IDEAL organ, see *J.W. Sawyer*.
IKEUCHI FUKIN; Osaka, Japan. Established about 1888 by Jinzaburo Ikeuchi. See *Tōyō Gakki Seizo Co. Ltd.*
ILJIN, N.J.; Jew Smoljenskoje, Schlusselburgsky 65, St. Petersburg, Russia, 1909.
IMPERIALE, portable organ with an art-deco style case; maker unknown.
IMPERIAL ORGAN CO. OF CANADA. (No other information available.)
IMPERIAL ORGAN & PIANO; 45-47 Ellingford Rd, Mare St., London 1903-1921; Established in 1902 as successor to *Collins Organ & Piano Co.*; still in operation in 1965. Made one- and two-manual and two-manual and pedal reed organs and the Pianorgan—a combined piano and reed organ produced about 1930.
INGALLS & CROCKET; 174 Main St., Concord, NH; Gustavus W. Ingalls and John K. Crockett.
INGALLS & EATON; Bristol, NH; established 1842 by G.W. Ingalls and Cyrus W. Eaton; made seraphines.
INGALLS, G.W., & CO.; 25 Hermon St., Worcester, MA 1866-1896, reed & component manufacturer; G.W. Ingalls worked for *Prescott*, later for *Charles Austin*, then associated with D.M. Dearborn as *Ingalls & Dearborn*; served in the Civil War; bankrupt 1896. His first name is shown originally as Gustavus and later as George.
INGLETON & CO., see *Wholesale Pianoforte & Organ Mfg. Co.*
IPPIG, A.; Theaterstr. 16 in 1903, Gartenstr. 29 in 1912, Insterburg, Germany.
ISAAC, F.W.; No. 17 Charlotte Street, Rathbone Place, London. Seraphine and organ maker, ca. 1845.
ISACHSEN & RENBJØR HARMONIUMFABRIKK; Levanger, Norway. Founded by Johann Cornelius Isachsen in 1852. The first organ was built in Isachsen's house in Eidesora, Skogn, Norway, and the firm later moved to Levanger about 1860. Petter K. Renbjør joined the firm about 1880 and later married one of Isachsen's daughters. After Petter died about 1935 his son Reidar took over. Reidar's son Leif succeeded him and shortly afterward in 1978 production ceased due to the unavailability of reeds. A total of about 5,000 harmoniums had been produced. Reidar died in 1981, and Leif Renbjør is still in business servicing pianos and harmoniums. The firm won a trophy cup in Levanger in 1866 and a gold medal there in 1936; it received the highest distinction at the Oslo exhibition of 1914, a gold medal at the Trondelag exhibition

Johann Cornelius Isachsen.

in 1930, a silver medal in Stockholm in 1897 and a bronze medal in Paris in 1900. Current address: Halsanv. 2A, 7600 Levanger, Norway. Serial numbers:

1867—50	1872—90	1877—126
1868—57	1873—95	1878—134
1869—75	1874—100	1879—142
1870—80	1875—112	1914—2470
1871—85	1876—119	

ISHII, HARUTARO; Awaza, Nishiku, Osaka, Japan. Exhibited at the 3rd Domestic Industrial Exhibition, Tokyo, 1890.

ISOARD; Paris. Free-reed instrument maker, established 1830.

ITHACA ORGAN CO.; Ithaca, NY, founded in 1877 by William L. Bostwick, president; H. Wegman, supt.; P. Frank Sisson, sec.-treas.; J.H. Hintermeister, gen'l agent, with the financing of Alonzo Cornell, son of Ezra Cornell, founder of Cornell University. Successor to the *Swiss Organ Co*. The company made conventional reed organs as well as the "Pipetta", a combination pipe and reed organette using the paper roll as the valve. Shown as *Ithaca Piano & Organ Co*. in 1881. The Ithaca Organ Co. went bankrupt in 1885, "wrecked by improvident liberality in selling its products without adequate security for payment." Serial numbers: 1878—574, 1879—1599, 1880—3387.

IVORY, HENRY A., & CO.; 23 Holborn Viaduct, London; steam factory at Wood Green, London. Made Robinson's patent harmonium attachment for pianos, for which they received a first award in the Sydney (Australia) Exhibition of 1879.

J

JACKSON, JOHN; Guelph, Ontario 1872-73, 1880.
JACKSON, see *Davie, Jackson & Co.*
JACOBS, J.A.; 15 Seymour St., Euston Square, London; reeds and fittings, 1896-1900. Established 1873.
JACOBSEN, J.; Hadersleben, Denmark. Showed the "Organ Aeolodican" at the London Exhibition of 1862.
JACOT, MICHEL; 2 Wood Lane, Birmingham, England, later 3 Cocks Lane, Offenham, Worcs. Harmonium maker, 1970-78.
JACQUES, R.; rue Aug-Blanqui, Choisy-le-Roi, France, 1930.
JAGLIOLI, MARCO; corso 4, Ancarano, Italy, 1903; established 1875.
JAHN & SOHN; Josephinenstr. 4 in 1871, Josephinenstr. 9 in 1880-90, Josephinenstr. 18 in 1895-1912, Dresden, Germany. Established as an organ builder in 1818. F. Jahn, proprietor in 1851, Julius Ferdinand Jahn in 1871, Johannes Jahn from 1912. Listed as organ and harmonium maker 1912-25, organ builder in 1930.
JÄHNERT, JULIUS; Holzhofgasse 4 in 1850, Katherinenstrasse 2, Dresden, Germany. Established 1845. About 1865 became *Julius Jähnert & Sohn*, succeeded by *E. Kannegiesser* in 1876.
JAKOBSEN, J. TH.; Lofoten, Norway. Harmonium maker, 1870s through the 1890s.
JAKOBSEN, REIDAR; Fredrikstad, Norway. Pipe organ and harmonium builder. Trained at Olsen & Jorgensen, a leading pipe organ maker in Christiania (now Oslo).
JAMARD; rue Quainaux 6, Brussels, Belgium. Maker and retailer of pianos and orgues-expressifs, 1914.
JAMES & FRANKLIN; Boston, MA. Made at least one miniature reed organ, ca. 1890.
JAMES, HENRY, & SON; in 1889 at 43 Balls Pond Road, Islington, London; 1890 at 150 Green Lanes, Stoke Newington, London, with factory at Kingsland Green, London. By 1896 located at 15 Warwick Court, High Holborn, London, with the factory at Wood Green, N London, but believed then producing only pianos. Established 1878; in business at least through 1909.
JAMES, T., & CO.; Guelph, Ontario, Canada. Made the Royal organ. Extant 1886.
JANKÓ, PAUL VON, a Hungarian by birth, he studied mathematics and music in Vienna, continuing under Prof. Helmolz at Berlin University. In 1882 he invented and patented a novel compact keyboard for a conventional single-manual organ or piano, consisting of six rows of rather short

A farm family gathers around the organ at Fort Kent, Aroostook Co., Maine, May, 1943.

keys. The linkage was so arranged that the hand could easily span two octaves. Jankó experimented with this keyboard on a standard parlor organ from 1882 to 1884 and in 1885 fitted it to a grand piano. Because of its compactness, a variation of the Jankó keyboard was used on some enharmonic organs, which require a large number of keys for each octave. See *Franz Steirer*.

JANSEN, TH. J.; Kerkstraat A. 118, 's-Hertogenbosch, Netherlands. Maker of decorative façades for harmoniums. Active 1878.

JANSSON, A.; 10 St. Nygt, Uddevalla, Sweden. Operating in 1930.

JARRET, RICHARD WILLIAM; 1 Eleanor Rd., London Fields, Hackney, London in 1883. Harmonium maker, previously worked with *Boosey*, later became *Jarret & Goudge*.

JAULIN, JULIEN; 11 rue d'Albouy, Faubourg St.-Martin, Paris in 1851; 59 rue du Fbg. St.-Martin, 27 rue du Château d'Eau in 1889. Made a portable harmonium and the Panorgue Piano, a very small harmonium intended to be placed under the keyboard of a piano thus making a combined piano and harmonium. At the Paris Exhibition of 1851 he was awarded a medal for the Panorgue and for improvements in free reeds. During the period 1844-1853 *Victor Mustel* worked with Jaulin, learning the manufacture of reeds. At the Paris Exhibition of 1889 he showed a "Harmoni-cor," adapted to the piano.

JAVELIER, LOUIS ANTOINE EUGENE; rue du Drapeau, Dijon, France, 1911. Piano and harmonium maker. Made pressure instruments including 2mp models.

JEFFREYS, GEORGE WILLIAMS; also *Jeffreys & Co.*; in 1878 at 38 Rosoman Street, N London; in 1883 at 32 Penton St., Pentonville, London until 1890.

JEFTS, GREBLE & CO.; Main St., Battle Creek, MI, 1870. Made the Excelsior organ. Instrument located at the Kimball House Museum, Battle Creek, MI.

JENKINSON & CO.; 45 Hampstead Rd., London in 1889 and 1896; Castle Rd., Kentish Town, London, 1903; see *Hepworth Organ Co.* In 1897 making the Hepworth Organ, and in 1898 the Super Octave Coupler. Not mentioned in 1906.

JENKINSON & JENKINSON; 5 Orchard Buildings, Haggenston Station, London, 1883.

JENKS, NELSON W.; one block east of Main St. on the railroad, Ovid, MI, 1885-7. Contractor, builder and organ manufacturer.

JENNINGS, T.A.; 127 Pentonville Rd., London; builder of enharmonic harmoniums, "harmoniums with one reed to each key, compass 4½ octaves," 24 to 84 keys per octave, 1876. See *R.H.M. Bosanquet*.

JENSEN, CLAUS; Norway. Pipe organ builder, also made a few harmoniums.

JENSEN, see *Haslev Orgelfabr.*

JEWETT & CO.; Leominster, MA; established in 1860 by Wade H. Jewett and George H. Allen as *Allen & Jewett; Jewett & Carpenter* in 1861. Later became *Jewett & Co., Jewett Piano Co.* Officers in 1897: W.P. Jewett, president; F.J. Woodbury, secretary-treasurer; W.G. Jewett, superintendent.

JEWETT & GOODMAN ORGAN CO.; listed as *Jewett, Goodman & Co.* at 195 Ontario St. in 1872, and as *Jewett & Goodman Organ Co.* at 66 Hayward in 1883, Cleveland, OH; in business at least through 1889; see *Peter Jewett.*
JEWETT, N.B., & CO.; Worcester, MA; established 1847 by Nathan B. Jewett.
JEWETT, PETER; Granby, CT 1830s-1847, also *Jewett & Hillyer*. Peter Jenner Jewett retired in 1847 and his two sons Stanley A. and Frederic Jewett and son-in-law Czar D. Goodman continued the business as *Jewett & Goodman* (qv), moving to Cleveland in 1866. S. A. Jewett was granted U.S. patent No. 18399 for a melodeon in 1857.
JOHANSSON, P.A., & SON; Sköfde, Sweden, 1909.
JOHNSON, WILLIAM ALLEN; Westfield, MA. Established 1844, became *Johnson & Son* in 1875 with William H. Johnson. Patented a combination reed and pipe organ in 1877.
JOHNSTON, D.S., & CO.; 56 West Fourth St., Cincinnati, OH. Music dealer. Probably sold organs made by others with the Johnston stencil.
JONES & BURDITT; see *Samuel H. Jones, Riley Burdett* (Burditt).
JONES, CARPENTER & WOODS, see *Samuel H. Jones, E.B. Carpenter, George C. Woods.*
JONES, F.; 145 York Road, Battersea, England. Advertised as a harmonium maker and instrument dealer in 1900. Established 1881.
JONES, GEORGE; 350 Commercial Rd., London; established 1850. Manufacturer of portable reed organs and concertinas. George Jones retired in 1899, and his sons Arthur George and Harry Sidney continued to operate the business as *George Jones & Sons*. The company failed in 1909.
JONES, JOHN, & CO.; 21-22 Bridge St., Bristol, England 1890, established 1864. Maker of the Choralion organ, available with one or two manuals or as a two-manual and pedal suction type American organ. In 1884 Jones patented a combined pressure and suction instrument, much like a large American organ in appearance. It had suction bellows at the top of the decorated case, and pressure bellows in the usual location for a harmonium. In 1885 a further patent reversed the arrangement with pressure bellows at the top. These instruments, called the Bristol organ, had separate sets of pedals for each bellows system and were available with one or two-manuals. Still in business in 1896.
JONES, JOSEPH L.; went to work for his brother *Samuel H. Jones* in Winchester, NH about 1844. When Samuel sold out in 1850, Joseph stayed with the firm, which eventually became *J. Estey & Co.*, until his death in 1901. During his service with Estey he made keys and keyboards, spent thirty-one years making bellows, and finally worked on pedals.

JONES, SAMUEL H.; went to work for *Foster & Thayer* in Winchester, NH in 1842 at age 20 making melodeons. When that firm dissolved in 1844, Jones made melodeons under his own name in Winchester until 1846 when he moved to Brattleboro, VT, locating in the Smith & Woodcock grist mill in Centerville. He took in John Woodbury and Riley Burditt as partners, calling the firm *S.H. Jones & Co.* Woodbury left in 1847 and the firm was renamed *Jones & Burditt*. In 1850 Jones sold his interest to E.B. Carpenter and left Brattleboro, (see *E.B. Carpenter*). Jones returned to Brattleboro in 1853 and organized a new firm called *Jones, Carpenter & Woods* with E.B. Carpenter and George Woods (the order of names depends on who is telling the story). In 1856 Jones and Woods sold out to *Estey & Green* and went to Boston.

JONES, WOODBURY, & BURDITT; Brattleboro, VT 1846-47; see *Samuel H. Jones*.

JORDAN'S Transposing Harmonium, see *J. Baynton & Co.*

JORDAN, W.C.; Hamilton, MO. (No other information available.)

JORIO, FRATELLI AMADEO E AUGUSTO; Giuliano di Roma, Italy. Listed in directories in 1903 and 1909.

JORIS, FRANÇOIS, & FILS; 179 rue de la Nouvelle Eglise, Renaix, Belgium 1927-1932; at 21 rue de l'Eglise in 1936. Manufacturer of pipe organs, pianos and harmoniums. François and his brother Joseph worked at *Anneessens* until they began their own business about 1900. *Joseph Joris* is listed separately at 31 Grande Place, Sichem, Belgium in 1903. Later François worked with his sons Edmond and Georges.

JORIS, LEO; Averbode, Belgium. Born 1906, a nephew of *François Joris*. Still active as a harmonium maker in 1955.

JOSEFSON, ADOLF; Gullspang, Sweden, 1903.

JUJIYA GAKKI-TEN; Ginza, Tokyo. Shigetaro Kurata exhibited an organette at the 3rd Domestic Industrial Exhibition, Tokyo, 1890.

JULIUS & MARCH; 22 S. George St., York, PA, 1884-99. John P. Julius was a music dealer, and Oliver L. March was a travel agent working for Julius. Organs with this name were undoubtedly made by others with the Julius & March stencil.

JUMANOW, E.A.; Permsche-Str., Perm, Russia, 1903; established 1886.

A D.W. Karn parlor organ.

K

KAHN, LEOPOLD, see *Stuttgart Harmonium Co.*
KAIHO, M.; Tokyo. Kaiho instruments were sold by Sanseido, Kanda, Tokyo. A 39 key baby organ is in the Meiji-mura Museum, Aichi prefecture.
KAILASH HARMONIUM WORKS; Egerton Road, Delhi, India, 1930.
KAIM & SOHN; Fabrikstr. 30, Wellingstr. 21, Alleenstr 3, Kirchheim u. Teck, Germany. Other firm names: *F. Kaim* (1819-1845); *Kaim & Günther* (1846-1883); *F. Kaim & Sohn* (1883-1922); *Kaim Pianoforte AG* (1922-1933); *Harmoniumbau Gebr. Kaim & Fritsche*; *Erste Deutsche Meister-Harmoniumfabrik*; *Ritz-Kaim*. Established in 1819 as a piano maker, began making harmoniums in 1900. Made pressure and suction instruments as well as mechanically played harmoniums.
KAKEGAWA KOGYO; near Hamamatsu, Japan. Reed manufacturer; machinery broken up in 1989.
KALAND, EINAR, ORGELHARMONIUMFABRIK; Olaf Kyrres Gade 16, Bergen, Norway in 1909; 31 Vaskerelvsgade, Bergen in 1930. Established in 1897 as a music dealer and publisher, started making harmoniums in 1900. From 1915 to about 1925 he produced a total of 1,500 instruments. Reorganized in 1974 as *Petterson & Gjellesvik*.
KALBE, J.F.; Gipstrasse 13, Berlin, Germany in 1890. Established in 1840, manufactured accordions, concertinas, mouth organs and harmoniums.
KÄLLMANN, A.; Lapua, Finland. Established 1897.
KALTSCHMIDT, FRIEDRICH WILHELM; Stettin, Germany. Established 1840; pipe organs, street organs and physharmonicas.
KAMPMANN, see *Kanpmann*.
KAMSTRUP, K., see *Holstebro Orgel-Harmoniums-fabrik K. Kamstrup*.
KANGASALAN URKUTEHDAS; Kangasala, Finland. Established in 1843 by A. Thulé who had come to Finland from Sweden. He was succeeded in the business by his son B.A. Thulé, his grandson M. Tulenheimo and his great-grandson P. Tulenheimo. The firm continued in business until 1984. Approximately 10,000 harmoniums were made by the firm.
KANNEGIESSER, E.; Grosse Plauensche Str. 18 in 1876, Hahnebergstr. 3 in 1877, Sternplatz 1 in 1881, Güterbahnhofstr. 5 in 1884, Steinplatz 1 in 1886, Johannisplatz 5f in 1888-90, Palaststr. 2 in 1891, Katechetenstr. 2 in 1892, also Katherinenstrasse 2, all in Dresden,

Germany. Founded by Eduard Gotthard Kannegiesser in 1830. Listed as *G. Kannegiessert* in Paris. Absorbed *J. Jahnert & Sohn* in 1876.

KANPMANN, A.W.; Neue Friedrichsstr. 34 in 1886 and 1890, Carnapstr. 50 in 1903, Carnapstr. 48a, Wuppertal-Elberfelde, Germany. Piano dealer, organ and harmonium maker. Established in 1850. By 1903 the firm name was *Heinrich Emil Kanpmann*. Also shown as *W. Kampmann.*

KÄNSÄLÄ, ALEKSI; (1868-1939), Finland.

KANSAS ORGAN CO.; Leavenworth, KS, 1885.

KANTNER, DR. FRANKLIN J.; Reading, PA; active 1882-1887. Son of *Joel Kantner*, who had made pipe and reed organs in the 1860s. See *Reading Organ Manufactory.*

KAPS, ERNST; Seminarstr. 20, Dresden, Germany. Established 1858. Piano, harmonium and American organ manufacturer, although the reed organs may have been made by others with the Kaps stencil. The following serial numbers may include both reed organs and pianos:

1868—500	1895—18000	1930—37500
1879—6000	1901—24000	
1889—14000	1908—30000	

KÄRCHER, KARL FRIEDRICH; Augustenstr. 9½, Stuttgart, Germany. Harmonium maker, established 1868. Associated with (Ludwig) *Emil Krauss* (qv) in 1871.

KARG-ELERT harmonium, named for Siegfried Karg-Elert, 1877-1933, composer who wrote extensively for the harmonium; see *Johannes Titz.*

KARLOFF, J.C.; 19 James St., Syracuse, NY 1861. Melodeon manufacturer.

KARLSAUNET, KRISTIAN; Å, Norway. Made six harmoniums from 1894 to 1915. May have produced a few later.

KARN, D.W., CO., LTD.; 532 Dundas St., Woodstock, Ontario. Established in 1867 when Dennis W. Karn joined John M. Miller, forming *Miller & Karn*, also known as the *Woodstock Organ Factory*. Karn bought out Miller in 1870 but retained the Miller & Karn name for several years before changing it to *D.W. Karn Co*. Exhibited in Barcelona, Spain in 1888. Acquired the *S.R. Warren & Son* organ factory of Toronto in 1896, and in 1909 became the *Karn Morris Piano & Organ Co*. In the early 1920s the company went through several changes of ownership ending in bankruptcy. The assets were acquired by *Sherlock-Manning* in 1924. Officers in 1906: D.W. Karn, president; T. Drew Smith, secretary-treasurer. Serial number: 1890—24098.

> # The D.W. Karn Co., Limited
> HEAD OFFICE AND FACTORIES:
> Woodstock, Ontario, Canada.

KÁŠ, ADALBERT; Neugasse 8, Brünn, Austria-Hungary, 1903; established in 1898. Later shown at Neugasse 25, Brünn, Hungary.

KASRIEL, MAURICE; established in 1839, 20 passage Vaucouleurs, Paris in 1883, 92 rue d'Angouleme in 1895, 9 passage de Ménilmontant in 1903. Succeeded by *Les Petits-fils de Mce. Kasriel*, 6 rue Tolain, Paris; still operating in 1951. Awarded a silver medal at Toulouse in 1863, a gold at the Paris Exhibition of 1878 for portable harmoniums and harmoniflûtes of good value and ingenious work, and a silver medal at Paris in 1900. In 1951 Kasriel was producing two- and three-octave guides-chants and harmoniums from a four-octave portable to a five-octave instrument with 4½ sets of reeds and a transposing keyboard.

> # LES PETITS-FILS DE M. KASRIEL
> 6, Rue Tolain — PARIS (20')
>
> Téléph. : DIDEROT 13-30   R. C. : Seine N° 161 528 bis
>
> Fondée en 1839, la Maison
> **"LES PETITS-FILS DE M. KASRIEL"**
> est une des plus importantes manufactures d'orgues et d'harmoniums du monde.

KATHOLNIG, HEINRICH; Sigmund-Haffner-Gasse 16, Salzburg, Austria, 1940.

KATZ, GEBRÜDER; Langestr. 143 in 1912-25, Langestr. 42 in 1930, Völksen, Germany. Established in 1905 by Heinrich and Conrad Katz. Church organs and harmoniums. Operating in 1930 as *Heinrich Katz*.

KATZER, FRANZ; Bahnhofstr. 11, Unicov, (Mährisch-Neustadt), Czechoslovakia in 1930; located at Olmützer Str. 57, Mährisch-Neustadt, Sudetenland, Germany in 1940. Formerly *W. Brauner & Co.*

KAUFFMANN, JOHANN MARCEL; Robert Hamerling-Gasse 30, Vienna, Austria in 1912; by 1930 shown as *Johann Josef Kauffmann*. Established 1877.
KAUFMAN, F., & SOHN; Ostra-Allee 19 in 1886-90, Dresden, Germany; mechanical and street pianos and harmoniums. Made physharmonicas in 1855.
KAWAI GAKKI SEISAKUSHO CO., LTD.; current address 200 Terashima-cho, Hamamatsu-shi, Shizuoka, Japan 430. *Kawai Gakki Kenkyusho* (Kawai Musical Instrument Laboratory) was founded in 1927 by Koichi Kawai, formerly chief engineer of *Yamaha*; renamed *Kawai Gakki Seisakusho* in 1929, then *Kawai Gakki Seisakusho Co. Ltd.* from 1951 to the present. At one time Kawai made its own reeds. Shigeru Kawai is now chairman and president. Until recently made seven electrically-blown and four foot-pumped reed organ models. The following serial numbers may include both pianos and organs:

1925—4200	1955—29590	1975—791000
1930—6000	1960—42776	1976—878000
1940—9600	1972—603325	1977—968000
1950—14200	1974—718000	

KELLER, HEINRICH; Staatestrasse, Oberhofen bei Thun, Switzerland. Acquired the reed organ business of *H. Otzinger* in 1925; in operation as a manufacturer through 1970; continued as a repair service through 1977. Founded by Heinrich Keller Senior (1880-1945), who was succeeded by his son Heinrich Junior (1912-1991) in 1945. "A reliable company for a good Swiss reed organ." Production quantities: 1925-1944—180, 1945-1970—720.
KELLMER, PETER; 1883, 1885, 1889; later *Kellmer Organ Co.* and *Kellmer Piano & Organ Works*, Hazleton, PA.
KELLY, CHARLES, & CO.; 10-11 Charles St., also 11 Cavendish St., Cavendish Square, and 14-16 Mortimer St., W. London in 1897. "Makers of harmoniums to H.M. the Imperial family of France." In business at least from ca. 1855 to 1906. Some Kelly harmoniums were made by *Constant Laurent*.
KELSON, P. ERN.; France. Harmonium maker 1845-1873. Exhibited a barrel-operated orgue-expressif in the Paris Exhibition of 1855.
KEMMLER, C., & CO.; 26 Wigmore St. & 23 Barrett St., London. C. Kemmler and E. Benard, proprietors in 1903; established 1884.
KEMP, ROBERT ALEXANDER; 50 New Bond Street, London. Patented a combination reed organ and piano in 1885. Author of "Tuning and Regulating the Alexandre Harmonium."

電動オルガン
KB-2A

標準価格　69,000円
(専用イス・カバー付)
61鍵／Cスケール／総2列笛／重音
最高音部＝ピッコロリード／
ソフトレバー
(風量風圧自動調整装置付)／
バスペダル／メロディペダル／
楽譜入れ／オートストップ
式スイッチ
高さ＝75.2cm
間口＝96.8cm
奥行＝42.7cm
重量＝35.5kg
定格電圧AC100V
定格周波数50/60Hz
定格消費電力35/45W

The Kawai model KB-2A organ.

KENNEDY BROTHERS; instrument restored by Pro Musica. Probably the same as *Kennedy & Morse* and *Vrom & Kennedy*.
KENNEDY & MORSE; Washington, NJ. Melodeon makers.
KENNEDY, see *Vrom & Kennedy*.
KENT ORGAN CO.; Buffalo, NY, 1885. William J. Kent probably worked for *Prince* prior to establishing his own business.
KENT, WILLIAM BARKER; Earl Soham, Wickham Market, England; harmonium with pipes, 1883.
KENWOOD; The Cash Buyers Union First National Cooperative Society, Chicago, IL, sold Kenwood organs through its mail order catalog of 1905/6. Some of these organs appear to have been made by the *Adler Organ Co.* and by *Lyon & Healy* with the Kenwood stencil.
KENYON, R.B.; West Killingly, CT. Melodeon maker, ca. 1860.
KEPSZELY, JOHANN; Neusohl, Austria-Hungary, 1903.
KERCHER, FRIEDRICH; Obere Jägerstr. 143 in 1869, Rosenbergstr. 35 in 1871, Stuttgart, Germany. Harmonium maker.

KERKHOFF, JEAN-EMILE (1859-1921); 7 rue de la Pepiniere, 155 avenue de la Reine, 11 place Masui, Brussels, Belgium. Shown at 17 place Masui 1930-1949. This location was later a private mansion and workshop and is now an annex of the Musée Instrumentale in Brussels. Manufacturer of pipe organs and harmoniums with 15 to 20 workers in the factory, established 1905. Kerkoff had many inventions for harmoniums. *Van den Kerkhoven* is shown as a harmonium maker at rue de la Pepiniere in 1883.
KEROPHON; Germany. Roll-playing reed organ.
KESNER & TURNER; 172 Seymour Street, Euston Road, London NW, 1906.

Vous avez besoin d'Instruments de Musique?
Instruments à vent en cuivre, et en bois, Instruments à cordes,
Pianos, Harmoniums, Orgues etc. etc.
 Adressez vous alors
à la Manufacture Royale
M. J. H. KESSELS, Tilbourg, (Hollande)

KESSELS, M.J.H., (*Koninkluke Nederlandsche Fabriek Van Muziekinstrumenten*); factory located at Tilbourg, Netherlands from 1898. Manufacturer of pianos, player-pianos, harmoniums and organs from 1886 until about 1940. Founded by Mathijs J.H. Kessels.
KESTEREN, see *van Kesteren*.
KETTERMAN ORGAN CO., INC.; 214 North Walnut St., Muncie, IN 1945-50; until recently: *Sylvan Ketterman's Enterprises*, 322 N. Mulberry St., Muncie, IN 47305; Sylvan K. Ketterman, proprietor. Formerly with *Gulbransen*, (qv). Manufactured a single-manual reed organ with electrically operated stops, a new valve action and an electric suction unit. Also manufacturer of the Orgavac, an electric suction unit for reed organs.
KEWITSCH, JOHANNES; Wilhelmstrasse 2 in 1883-86, Potsdammer Str. 27b in 1901-03 and 1930, Berlin. Established 1836. Piano and harmonium maker, also made an enharmonic organ.
KEYSTONE ORGAN CO.; probably made in Pennsylvania. Instrument seen with "*Mellor, Koene & Kenricks*" on the stop board.
KHIMJI, MISTRI MEGHJI, & CO.; Para Station Road, Rājkot, India. Harmonium makers and repairers.

Sylvan K. Ketterman at age 19 with the first Ketterman organ, the "Black Beauty."

Johannes Kewitsch
Flügel-, Pianino-
und
Harmonium-Fabrikant,
Berlin SW.
Wilhelmstrasse 2.

KIESSLING, NICHOLAS, & SON, (William J.); 416 Western Ave., Blue Island, IL 1909, 1913; school and folding organs.

KILGOUR, J. & R.; Hamilton, Ontario. Began as a dealer in 1872, then manufactured pianos and reed organs 1888-1899. Also *Kilgour Piano & Organ Co.*

KILNER, FRANK, & SONS; Camberwell, Melbourne, Australia. Made the Austral Electronic Organ, a reed organ with electronic amplification.

KIMBALL, W.W., CO.; S.W. corner of Wabash Ave. and Jackson Blvd., Chicago, IL; factory at Rockwell and 26th Streets. Founded by William Wallace Kimball. Started in 1857 as an organ and piano retailer in Chicago, built up an immense business as a jobber under the leadership of Edwin Stapleton Conway. Began manufacturing organs in 1881 and later pianos. Discontinued reed organ production in 1922. Also made organs for others such as *Bentley, Goggin, Thiery, J.V. Watson, Pacific Queen* and *Great Western*. Still survives as Kimball International, located in Jasper, Indiana See the next page for serial numbers.

Kimball serial numbers:

1881—26472	1895—167405	1908—318285
1882—31804	1896—178347	1909—328547
1883—43212	1896—184571	1910—339343
1884—57540	1897—189465	1911—350269
1885—67872	1898—200971	1912—359765
1886—77960	1899—211932	1913—369971
1887—88028	1900—222575	1914—376775
1888—97252	1901—237358	1915—380870
1889—107765	1902—248105	1916—385979
1890—118463	1903—258899	1917—391656
1891—130001	1904—268599	1918—396270
1892—142237	1905—279119	1919—401448
1893—149130	1906—291979	1922—403690
1894—157473	1907—304615	

KIMMERLING; Geneva, Switzerland; maker of music boxes with free reeds ca. 1860-70.

KINDŌ TODA, see *Toda, Kindō*.

KINNARD, DREHER & CO.; Cleveland, OH; started in 1857 as *Kinnard Melodeons* by William J. Kinnard; he also used the name *W.J. Kinnard*. He associated with B. Dreher and formed Kinnard & Dreher, which operated from 1859 to 1869. See *Dreher*. Serial numbers:

1858—1500	1862—3060	1867—4240
1859—1807	1863—3280	1869—5010
1860—2500	1865—4100	

KIRKMAN & WHITE; 67 Frith Street, Soho, London in 1822; 3 Soho Sq. in 1831; 9 Dean St. in 1846. Made a seraphine in 1836. Joseph Kirkman and Thomas White, principals. Kirkman died 18 October 1877, aged 87 years.

KIRKWOOD WAGON CO., THE; Elmira, NY; piano and organ wagon manufacturer.

KIRSCHEISEN, E. BRUNO; Fürstenplatz 1 in 1890, Zöllnerstr. 10 in 1930, Dresden, Germany. Established 1880. Organ and harmonium maker.

KIRSCHNIK; a Danish organ builder who used free reeds in pipe organs in the late eighteenth century.

KITLY & CO.; 14-16 Mortimer St., London, 1883.

KLAIS, JOHANNES; Kölnstr. 148, Bonn, Germany. Established 1882. Harmoniums with this name may have been made by *Mannborg, Lindholm* and *Teck-Harmoniumfabrik*.
KLASSMEYER, FRIEDRICH; Pappenstr. 22, Lemgo, Germany. Factory located at Kirchstr. 38, Kircheide b. Lemgo. Established in 1872, in operation at least through 1930.
KLEIN, ALPHONSE, & CIE.; Rouen, France. Made harmoniums with transposing keyboards as well as a combined piano and harmonium. Succeeded by Elilien Ledru, a music dealer located at 20 rue Jeanne d'Arc, Rouen by 1909.
KLEIN, GEORG; Sennefelderstr. 36, Stuttgart, Germany. Established in 1867, operated at least through 1883.
KLEIN, JOH.; Mariahilferstr. 86, Vienna, Austria, 1883. Awarded a medal at Vienna in 1873.
KLEIN, see *Weygandt & Klein*, also see *Chabin*.
KLEINERT, ROBERT; Quakenbrück, Germany. Made a combination piano and harmonium now in the Leipzig Museum.
KLEINJASPER, CHARLES; 23 rue Caumartin, Paris, 1883. Later located at 47 rue Notre-Dame de Lorette, Paris 9e.
KLINE, T.S.; Jackson, MI 1889.

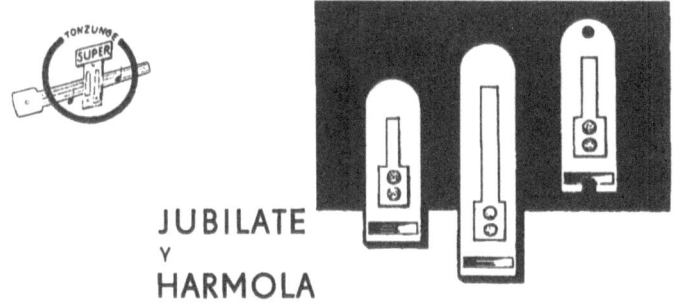

JUBILATE
y
HARMOLA

Dos marcas acreditadas, dos exponentes de calidad.
La nueva tecnología y los mejoras introducidas en la producción son los dos factores que determinan la calidad de nuestras

Lengüetas de latón para armonios.

VEB KLINGENTHALER HARMONIKAWERKE
Zweigwerk DEUTSCHES TONZUNGENWERK GERA

KLINGENTHALER HARMONIKAWERKE,; Klingenthal, Saxony, Germany. Also doing business as *Deutches Tonzungenwerke*, Gera, Germany. Manufacturing the "Jubilate" and "Harmola" reeds in 1961.

KLOCK, see *Stevens & Klock.*
KLOTZSCH, WILHELM; Jessnitz, Germany; harmonium with pipes. Shown as a dealer in 1890.
KNAUER, CHRISTOPHER; 618 Broadway, New York, NY 1861. Triolodeon maker for *M. Ducker.* Also shown in Philadelphia, PA.
KNIGHT, C.S.; Monroe, MI. Pipe and reed organ rebuilders.
KNIGHT, JOHN; 36-37 Dean Street, Birmingham, England. Piano, harmonium and American organ maker. Working until 1878.
KNIGHT, W.H.; Bishops Hall, Taunton, Somerset, England; also *W.H. Knight & Son.* In business at least from 1892 through 1908.
KNIGHT, see *Small & Knight, Levi K. Fuller.*
KNOTT, H., & SON; 111 Pentonville Road, London. Piano and harmonium manufacturer, 1883.
KNOTT, J.C.; Witton Street, Northwich, Cheshire, England. Piano and harmonium manufacturer 1879-82. In 1883 moved to 20 Castle Street, Northwich, Cheshire. Stopped making harmoniums in 1887.
KNUDSEN, JACOB; Bergen, Norway. With a background in furniture building, Knudsen learned piano and organ making in Germany and returned to Norway to start his own business in 1896. He built his factory in Bergen in 1917, expanded it in 1928, had a maximum of 60 employees. Made reed organs from 1919 until the 1950s, eventually producing a total of 4,000 organs, 9,500 upright pianos and a significant number of grand pianos. The firm also maintained sales stores in Oslo and Stavanger. Stopped production of pianos in 1975 and has since been dedicated to service and repair. Jacob Knudsen died in 1928 and the business was continued by his brother Wilhelm Knudsen until 1946 when his son-in-law Christen Faye took over. In 1977 Faye's son Fredrik succeeded him. Serial number: 1925—3200.
KOEFOEDS, H.P., EFTF.; Torvegade 10, Randers, Denmark; established 1876. By 1909 shown as *J.P. Koefoed.*
KOELLER-VANDENAKKER, ERNEST; 24 rue Vieille-Halle-aux-Bles, Brussels, Belgium in 1880; 105 rue du Midi in 1895; showroom and workshop at 9 rue du Midi in 1905, then at 9 rue des Moineaux. Harmonium and piano maker. Exhibited at the Brussels Exhibition of 1880.
KOHLER & CHASE; San Francisco. Possibly a stencil organ made by others.
KÖHLER, HARMONIUMFABRIK; Eisenbahnstr. 98 in 1920-24, Leipzig-Volkmarsdorf, Germany. Schloss Pretzsch in 1926, Bahnhofstr. 29a in 1951, Pretzsch, Germany. Edward Fritz Köhler, proprietor. Established 1921. Made both pressure and suction instruments. Still in business in 1990 as VEB Holzverarbeitung Pretzsch, a furniture maker.

The Köhler Model 34 harmonium.

KOLAŘ, BOHUMIL; Stiftgasse 12, Brünn, Mähren, Hungary, 1909.
KOLB, FRANZ, SÖHNE; Puste Zibridovice, (Wustseibersdorf), Czechoslovakia 1930.
KOLB, HEINRICH, see *Woerner & Kolb*.
KOLLER, LUKAS; Nasterzeile 53, Gmund, Austria-Hungary, 1903; established 1880.
KONIECZNY, ALOJZY; Wegierska 32, Přzemysl, Austria-Hungary, 1909. Established 1888.
KONINKLIJKE NEDERLANDSCHE FABRIEK VAN MUZIEKINSTRUMENTEN, see *M.J.H. Kessels*.
KORNER, see *Meinhardt & Korner*.
KORTENBACK. (No additional information available.)
KÖSSLING, JOHANN GOTTLOB; Grimmaesche Str. 5, Leipzig, Germany. Piano and physharmonica maker, 1834.
KOST, see *Paul & Kost*.
KOTYKIEWICZ, TEOFIL; Margarethenstrasse 61 in 1883; Straussengasse 18 in 1892, 1922 and 1930, Vienna, Austria. Originally founded in 1852 by *Peter Titz* (1823-1873), renamed and continued by his

son-in-law Teofil Kotykiewicz (1849-1920), who was in turn succeeded by his son Teofil Kotykiewicz (1880-1971).

> **K. u. k. Hof-Harmonium-Fabrik von Teofil Kotykiewicz**
> Wien V, Straussengasse 18.
> Lager von Harmoniums in allen Grössen.
> Specialität: **Grosse Salonwerke** in verschiedenen Dispositionen und in vollendet künstlerischer Ausführung stets vorräthig.
> 5 Jahre Garantie. — Illustrirtes Preisbuch gratis.

KRANZER, JOHANN; Ober Donaulange 41, Linz, Austria, 1940.

KRATOCHWIL, OTTO; Baumschulenallee 2a, Bonn, Germany, 1925-1930. Organ and harmonium maker.

KRAUS, see *C.B. Hunt & Co.*

KRAUSE, H.; Karlstr. 17, Berlin; Wilmersdorfer Str. 22 in 1912, Berlin-Charlottenburg. Harmonium maker and repairman, at least from 1903 to 1909.

KRAUSE, THEODORE; Handelstr. 19, Berlin, Germany. Designer of reed organs, ca. 1903.

KRAUSS, EMIL; Marienstr. in 1870, Augustenstr. 9½ in 1886-90, Stuttgart, Germany. Established 1870 as a piano maker. Began making harmoniums in 1871. Exhibited at the Vienna Fair in 1873. In business as late as 1929.

KREUTZBACH, JULIUS URBAN; Thomasiusstr. 22 in 1912, Leipzig, Germany. Piano maker, also made combination piano-harmoniums.

KRISTINEHAMS ORGELFABRIK; Kristinehamn, Sweden. Made the Alptona organ.

KROLL; Paris. Reed maker, 1867.

KROM, ANDR. L.; Utrecht, Netherlands. Made pedal actions for reed organs.

KRONIG, FRANZ, & CO.; Leipzig, Germany. 1922-3.

KRUMBHOLZ, PAUL; Lasurstr. 6 in 1938-40, Lange Str. 39 in 1963, Gera-Zwötzen, Germany. Established in 1928, closed 1974.

KRUSE, L. ED.; Steindamm 35 in 1886, Lüneburger Str. 3, Hamburg, Germany. Established in 1871. Piano, organ and harmonium maker.

KRZEMIŃSKI, JOSEF; ul. Dabrowska, Bendzin, Russia, 1909.

KUHN, THEODOR; Männedorf, Switzerland. Pipe organ maker, also sold harmoniums made by others with the Kuhn stencil. In operation at least from 1910 through 1925.

KUNKEL, WILHELM; Markplatz A21, Oettingen, Germany. Listed as a dealer in 1923, harmonium maker in 1940.

KUNZ, FRZ.; Trautenau, Austria-Hungary, 1883.

KUPER, ADOLF; Schkeuditzer Str. 16 in 1921, Breitenfelder Str. 91-95 in 1924-30, Leipziger Str. 91-95 in 1927, Leipzig-Gohlis, Germany. Established in 1918, made both pressure and suction instruments. Closed 1954.

KURZ, KARL FRIEDRICH; Wilchingen, Switzerland. Cabinet maker, also made reed organs beginning in 1915.

KUSTER, LOUIS; Paris. Harmonium reed maker, 1921.

KVARME, NIELS PEDERSEN; Voss, Norway. Pipe organ and harmonium maker, started building harmoniums in the 1860s.

A harmonium made by Paul Krumbholz, Gera, Germany, 1961.

L

LABROUSSE, J.; 41 Rue du Temple and 16 rue de Rivoli, Paris in 1903. By 1930 shown as G. Labrousse, 51 rue de Rivoli, Paris.

LACAPE, J.; 29 boulev. St.-Martin, Paris. Piano and harmonium maker 1883.

LADD, SENECA AUGUSTUS; Meredith, NH. Born 29 April 1819 in Louden, NH. He left school at age 13 and went with his older brother, Albert Warren Ladd, to learn the carriage, sleigh and painting business with a relative in Raymond, NH. In 1838 the Ladd brothers went to Boston where they worked in the piano factory of Timothy Gilbert. In 1839 Seneca went to Meredith to establish a carriage factory, which he operated until it was destroyed by fire in 1850. He then leased the building of a former cotton mill in Meredith and established a piano and melodeon factory, operating it until 1868. At that time he and others founded the Meredith Village Savings Bank, of which he became the first treasurer and secretary. A.W. Ladd remained with Timothy Gilbert until 1848, when he established his own piano factory.

LAGERQUIST & CO.; Norrgatan 22, Örebo, Sweden in 1903; Gustav Lagerquist, proprietor; established 1901.

LAHORE MUSIC HOUSE; Delhi, India.

A table harmonium made by the Lahore Music House, Delhi, India.

LAKESIDE ORGAN CO.; 246-256 West Lake St., Chicago IL; successors to *Tryber & Sweetland* about 1899; W.F. Tryber, president in 1903. Sold to F.S. Cable about 1904 and renamed the *Fayette S. Cable Piano Co.*; later renamed the *Cable-Nelson Co.*
LAMARTINE & CIE.; rue Lafitte, Paris. Organ and harmonium maker, active about 1880.
LAMBERF, VVE.; 79 rue de Bagnolet, Paris, 1930.
LAMMBRECHT, WILHELM; Berlin. Harmonica maker. Patented a table harmonium in 1842.
LÄMMLE, ALBRECHT; Stuttgart, Germany; made suction instruments ca. 1928.
LAMOUCHE, AUGUSTE-JOSEPH; reed maker, rue du Petit Musc, Paris. Established 1862. Lamouche originally worked for *Bruni*. In 1867 he and six other specialists formed "l'Association des Ouvriers Facteurs d'Anches Libres pour Orgues." The business was named *Société Lamouche et Cie.* and located at 45 rue Basfroid, Paris. Lamouche was the manager.
LANCASTER ORGAN MANUFACTORY, see *McKillips*.
LANDI, DESIDERIO; Corso Magenta, Brescia, Italy, 1903.
LANDFEAR, MERVIN T., (also Landfeur); Manchester, CT 1861. Melodeon manufacturer. On May 2, 1854 he received U.S. Patent No. 10848 for a "reed box."
LANDRIEN, ALPHONSE J.; workshop at 156 rue de Cologne, Brussels, Belgium; showroom at 39 rue du Cirque in 1870; showroom at 3 place de l'Universite in 1873. Piano and harmonium maker 1868-1875.
LANGDORF ET FILS; Geneva, Switzerland; music boxes with reeds.
LANGHAMMER, M.; Leipzig, Germany; maker of harmonium actions, 1930.
LANG & ROBINSON; Meredith, NH; melodeon cases 1861.
LAPUAN HARMONITEHDAS; Hirvensalmi, Finland.
LARCHE, E.; place Saint-Sauveur, Dinan, France in 1920; 27 rue Carnot, Dinan in 1930.
LARSON & BOWMAN; Chicago IL. Established in 1875 and still doing business under this name in 1880. By 1883 the name had changed to *Howland & Boman*, (qv). At that time the factory was located at 320 Clinton St., Chicago. Made the Garden City organ.
LARSSEN, OLE; Ofoten, Norway. Built a few pipe organs and harmoniums.
LATHAM, P.; 48a Stoke Road, Stoke on Trent, Staffs., England. Piano, pipe and reed organ builder, 1912-13.
LAUKHUFF, AUGUSTUS; Weikersheim, Germany in 1930; reed maker, established 1823. Still manufacturing organ parts and many parts for harmoniums including stop faces to specification.

LAURENT, CONSTANT; showrooms at 85 High St., Marylebone; factory at 7 Paradise Place, London. Established 1859, in business until 1887 when it was taken over by *F. Mesnage*, who advertised as the successor to Laurent until 1891.

LAVAUD, VVE. P.D.; 5 rue Lecourbe, Paris. Piano and harmonium maker 1883.

LAWRENCE, F., & CO.; 20 St. James Street, Islington, London. American organ maker 1892-1894.

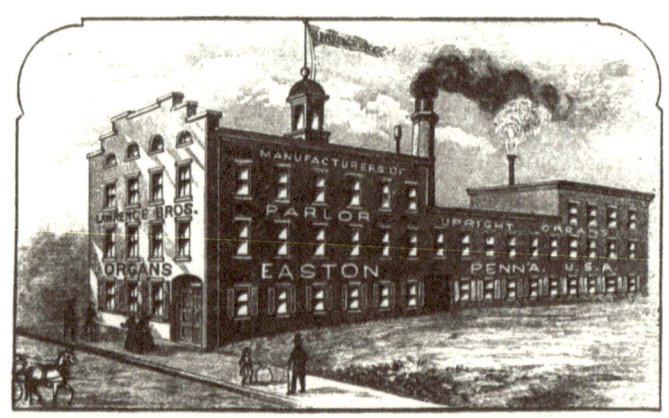

SIX AND SEVEN OCTAVE ORGANS
IN PARLOR UPRIGHT PIANO CASES.

Lawrence Brothers factory, Easton, Pennsylvania.

LAWRENCE ORGAN MFG. CO.; 320-322 S. 10th St. near Washington, Easton, PA; established 1888 as *Phillip J. Lawrence*. Also called *Lawrence Bros.* in association with F.W. Lawrence. In 1899 made the Beatty, Bowlby and Lawrence organs. Succeeded by *Bowlby's Sons Piano & Organ Co.*, Easton, PA in 1905.

LAWSON & CO.; 31 Fowler St., South Shields, Durham, England. Established before 1880, in business at least through 1909.

LAYLAND, C., & CO.; 268 Oxford St., London in 1868. In 1878 at 48 Alexander Road, Kilburn, NW London until 1879.

LAYTON, EDWARD; 12 Upper Street, Islington, London. Harmonium maker.

LEA & SON, 20 Newbold Rd., Chesterfield, England, 1883. Possibly the same as *Wm. Lea*, Liverpool, England, a reed organ dealer who sold organs made by others with the Lea stencil.
LEBANON ORGAN CO., see *Geo. S. Shepard*.
LECOMTE, A., & CIE.; 12 rue St.-Gilles, Paris. Manufacturer of salon organs and harmoniums, 1883.
LEDERER, GEORG; Oettingen, Germany. Reed maker, 1883.
LEE MUSIC MFG. CO.; Culver, OR; manufacturer of electric suction units for reed organs.
LE FAUCHEUR & CIE.; Ivry, France. Reed maker.
LEFERME, LOUIS-CAMILLE; Paris 1847. Made the Mélosymphonium.
LEGRIS, ALEXANDRE; Paris. Made an organino, a small orgue-expressif, in 1840.
LEHR, H., & CO.; 13th & Butler Streets, Easton, PA. Established in 1890 by Horace Lehr, his son Horace A. Lehr later joined the company. Partners in 1897: Horace Lehr, Jacob Diehl (factory superintendent) and Walter Lehr. Claimed to be the first company to make a piano-cased reed organ. Factory capacity in 1899: 1,200 organs per year. The factory burned in 1906, but production continued. Made both pianos and organs until 1942. By 1944 the company had converted to furniture making.
LEIDERITZ; Leipzig, Germany. Maker of orgues-expressifs about 1851.

Compliments of E. C. LEIDY,
Manufacturer Of
THE EXCELSIOR ORGAN,
Telford, Penn'a.

LEIDY, E.C.; Telford, PA. Manufacturer of the Excelsior parlor organ. See *M.L. Cope, F.S. Fieman*.
LEIPZIGER MUSIKWERKE; Leipzig, Germany, successor to *Paul Ehrlich* (qv). See *Fabrik Leipziger Musikwerke*.
LEIPZIGER PIANOFORTEFABRIK A.G.; Leipzig-Mölkau, Germany. Piano maker. Also made a combination piano-harmonium with organ action by *Lindholm*.

LEIPZIGER PIANOFORTEFABRIK BÖHLITZ-EHRENBERG, VEB; Leipzig, Germany, established in 1948 by the German Democratic Republic as the state-owned musical instrument making consortium. In 1968 it became *VEB Deutsche Piano-Union Böhlitz-Ehrenberg*, Julius Bluthner-Haessler, director. Successor to *Mannborg, Lindholm*, and many other musical instrument and component manufacturers.

LEISTNER, see *Sachsische Draht- und Metallwaren-Fabrik Leistner & Co.*
LELAND, S.R., & CO.; Worcester, MA, 1868, 1875.
LELIÈVRE, see *Dumont & Lelièvre.*
LEMAIRE; Paris. Reed maker. Reeds seen on an organ made by *Bertheaux Frères.*
LEMERCINIER, LOUIS; chausee de Liege 9, Jambes, near Namur, Belgium in 1940. Maker of pipe organs, harmoniums and pianos from about 1916 to about 1965.
LEMPEREUR; France. Harmonium maker. Advertised as sold by Thomas Dawkins, London between 1883 and 1889.
LENARCIC, JOS., & CO.; Oberlaibach, Austria-Hungary, 1903.
LENK, E.; Berlin. Harmonium maker, established in 1874. Operated as a street organ maker in 1893 by his widow.
LEONHARDT, MAX, & CO.; Kuhturmstr. 8 in 1921, Sebastian-Bach Str. 28 in 1922-30, Leipzig-Lindenau, Germany; Paul Haase, Max Leonhardt and Rudolf Oppitz, proprietors in 1930. Harmonium maker, established in 1920, in business at least through 1940. Also made instruments stencilled for the music dealer *Max Bannicke.*
LEROUX, ALEX., FILS; 2 galerie Véro-Dodat, Paris, 1883. Manufacturer of harmoniflûtes and accordions.
LESIEUR, AUG.; 56 rue Basse-du-Rempart, Paris. Piano and harmonium maker 1883.
LESLIE organ, see *Chicago Music Co.*

LETERME, C.; 192 rue du Temple, Paris in 1850. In 1883 listed as *C. Leterme Fils*, 25-27 rue de la Folie-Méricourt, Paris. Organ and harmonium maker, made the Mélophonorgue with two ranks of reeds in 1837, also made a foot-pumped harmoniflûte called the Organoflûte, as well as a number of unusual reed instruments such as the Accordéon-Guitare and a harmonium du violiniste called the Harpe-Éolienne.
LETTON, RAPHAEL E.; Quincy, IL. Active 1873-1883. Had numerous patents for reed organ improvements.
LEUTKE, HERBERT; Waldstr. 84 in 1921, Wilhelmstrasse 8-18 in 1922-25, Leipzig, Germany. Piano and harmonium manufacturer. Closed 1930.
LEWY, see *Friedrich Wimmer*.
LHOTA, AL. HUGO; Pragerthorstr. 231, Königgratz, Czechoslovakia; Karl Pich and Marie Julio, proprietors, 1903; established 1875.
LIBERTY organ, see *A.L. White Mfg. Co.*
LIDDIATT, THOMAS; Stanley Marsh, Gloucester, England. In 1879 shown as a carpenter located in Leonard Stanley; in 1885 listed as *Liddiatt & Son*, located in Kings Stanley. Maker of the Gothic and Stanley harmoniums. Extant at least through 1889.
LIDÉN & OLSSON; Vara, Sweden.
LÍDL & VELÍK; Vilova ctvrt 38, Moravský-Krumlov, Czechoslovakia; established 1921 by Jos. Velík, still in business in 1930.
LIEBIG, GUSTAV; Schiessgrabenstr. 2-4, Bismarckstr 159b, Schützenplatz 17-19 in 1920, Zeitz, Germany. Established 1882. Piano rebuilder and later piano manufacturer. Began making harmoniums in 1912. Fritz Gustav & Karl Liebig, proprietors in 1930. Still in business in 1958.
LIEBMANN, ARMIN; Neuestr. 14, Gera, Germany; Armin Liebmann and Richard Pfotenbauer, proprietors, 1903; organettes.
LIEBMANN, ERNST ERICH; Nestmannstr. 5 in 1903; Hainstr. 10 in 1912-30, Gera, Germany; established 1871. Manufacturer and dealer in harmoniums, melodeons, melotons, street organs and organettes. Made the "Liebmanista" harmonium player and the Kalliston organette from 1912. Emil Beyer and Richard Richter, proprietors 1905-1930. Closed 1947.
LILJERG, G.M.; O. Wittusgatan 14, Karlskrona, Sweden, 1903.
LIMONAIRE FRÈRES; 166 Ave. Daumesnil, Paris, 1903; manufacturer of fair organs (band organs), some of which used reeds rather than pipes, as well as harmoniums and harmoniflûtes. Established 1840.
LINARD, DR.; Vienna, Austria. Made a combination piano and reed organ called the Linardian, 1890-94.

LINDERMAN organs, sold by Northwestern Music House, Minneapolis, MN about 1905.

Lindholm

GEGRÜNDET 1894
FOUNDED 1894
CASA FUNDADA EN 1894

O. LINDHOLM · HARMONIUM-FABRIK · BORNA BEZIRK LEIPZIG

EXPORT NACH ALLEN WELTTEILEN
EXPORT TO ALL PARTS OF THE WORLD
SE EXPORTAN A TODOS LOS CONTINENTES

LINDHOLM, OLOF, HARMONIUMFABRIK; Breite Str. 5-11, Borna, Germany. Founded in 1894 by Olof Lindholm, a Swede who had come to Germany with Theodor Mannborg and Lars Magnus Hofberg. Lindholm worked for *Mannborg* until establishing his own factory. He retired in 1911 and sold the factory to Gustav Weischet, who operated a successful reed organ retail business in Wuppertal-Elberfeld. Gustav Weischet was succeeded by his son Hermann, who in turn was succeeded by his son Joachim Weischet in 1952. Lindholm made ammunition boxes during World War II and manufactured furniture for a few years after the war. By the late 1940s the reed organ business revived. Lindholm acquired *Hofberg* in 1930, *Mannborg* in 1961, and the reed-making machinery of *Deutsch Harmonium-Zungen-Fabrik* in 1969. Lindholm managed to operate as a privately owned business until 1972 when it was taken over by the German Democratic Republic and became a part of the state musical instrument making consortium *VEB Leipziger Pianofortefabrik Böhlitz-Ehrenberg*, (qv). The factory was restored to private ownership in 1993, and is now manufacturing historical keyboard instruments. The factory building also contains a harmonium museum. Gustav Weischet, proprietor. Serial numbers:

1905—4000	1952—23150	1963—56830
1910—7200	1954—23800	1964—57090
1920—12900	1955—53650	1965—57450
1925—16300	1957—54550	1966—57730
1930—20500	1959—55400	1972—59400
1940—22150	1961—56250	1974—60100
1950—22700	1962—56460	1976—60870

Modell 74

5 Oktaven F – F · Eiche - oak - chêne - roble - quercia - ek

LINDMARK & JONSSON; Mellerud, Sweden, 1909. In 1930 Shown as *Lindmark & Johnson*, Dals Rostock, Sweden.

LINDSAY, ADAM; 100 Renfrew Street, Glasgow, Scotland. Harmonium maker 1879-81.

LINSLEY, see *Treat & Linsley*.

LINÉ, see *Couty & Liné*.

LING & BORGMAN; 67 Monroe Ave., Detroit, MI 1870-72. Conrad Ling and Charles H. Borgman. Borgman apparently left the firm in 1872 when he became city clerk. See *Conrad Ling, Ling & Chandler*.

LING & CHANDLER; 17 Campus Martius, Detroit, MI, 1865-69, 67 Monroe Ave. in 1872. Conrad Ling and George S. Chandler, melodeon makers. See *Conrad Ling, G.S. Chandler*. Granted US Patent 71314 in 1867.
LING, CONRAD; 67 Monroe Ave., Detroit, MI, 1875-81. Music dealer and melodeon maker.
LINSTEAD, G.; 297 Upper Street, Islington, London N. Piano, American organ and harmonium maker 1891-95.
LISCOM, DEARBORN & CO.; Concord, NH, Levi Liscom and David M. Dearborn, melodeon makers, 1856-59.
LISCOM, LEVI; Concord, NH. Melodeon maker.
LISTER, see *West London Piano & Organ Co.*
LITTLE, ALFRED; worked for Charles Austin as a reed tuner and voicer about 1845-50. May have been the originator of reed voicing.
LITTLE, FREELAND; Adeline, IL. Granted US Patent 369725 in 1887 for a reed organ.
LITTLE SONIC Lightweight Table Organ, 3½ octaves, 1957. Used Swedish steel reeds.
LIUKKONEN, EINO; Hirvensalmi, Finland.
LIVINGSTON; York, PA. Serial No.: 1898—12839.
LIVINGSTONE, J.A.; Toronto, Ontario, 1877.
LJUNGQUIST, S.; Landvetter, Sweden, 1930.
LOCKE & SON; Mendelssohn House, 34-36 Great Ducie St., Manchester, England, 1883. Established 1842. Piano, harmonium and American organ maker and dealer.
LODUCA BROTHERS; Milwaukee, WI; portable organs.
LÖFFLER & CO.; Breitestr. 431b in 1903, Breitestr. 9 in 1929, Rittersgrün i. Erzgebirge, Germany. Established in 1919, closed 1945. Max & Fritz Löffler, proprietors 1930. Also known as *Sächsische Harmonium-Werkstäten, Löffler & Co.* Made the "Tannhäuser" harmoniums. Max Löffler had previously worked for *Hofberg* and *Hörügel*.
LONDON PIANOFORTE COMPANY LIMITED; Castle Road, Kentish Town, London, 1883.
LONDON & PROVINCIAL PIANO & AMERICAN ORGAN CO.; 55 Cleethorpe Road, New Clee, Grimsby, Lincolnshire, England 1885-1888.
LONG, JOHN H.; Lebanon, PA 1899, 1913.
LOOS, JOSEF; Seestadtl, Czechoslovakia, 1930.
LOPEZ, EUSEBIO; 2 calle Hurtado, Jaen, Spain, 1930.
LORD, see *Dodge & Lord*.

LORENZ SUPPLY CO.; Dayton, OH. Sold the "Regal Parlor and Chapel organs," almost certainly made by others with the Regal stencil, 1899.

LORET, JOSEPH LAEKEN; Brussels, Belgium. Showed two harmoniums at the Brussels Exhibition of 1847. Also shown in St. Nicolas, Belgium in 1835.

LORETO organ, see *Adler*.

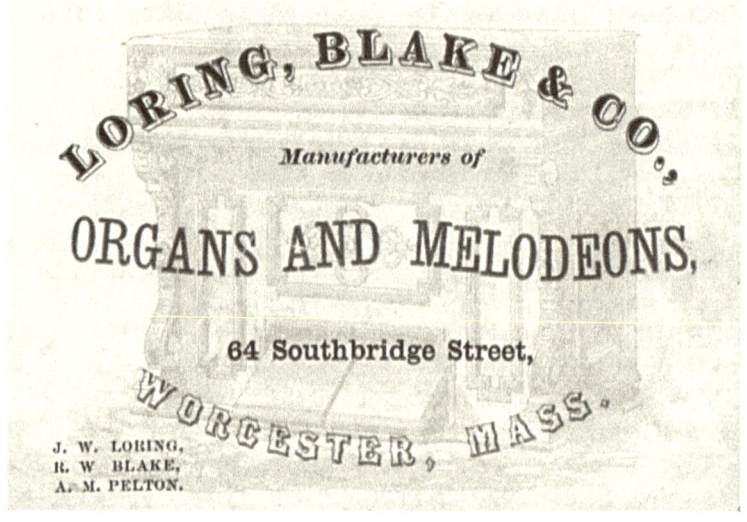

LORING, BLAKE & CO.; Worcester, MA, located at 64 Southbridge St. in 1868, then Hammond St., then to the Adams Block between Main and Southbridge St., in 1889 located at 19 Union St.; later moved to Toledo, OH. The name changed to *Loring & Blake Organ Co.* before 1881; made the Palace Organs. Partners: J.W. Loring and Rufus W. Blake, proprietors, formerly with *Taylor & Farley*, and *A.M. Pelton*. Blake left the company in 1873 to become secretary and general manager of the *Sterling Organ Co.* In 1881 the president was W.W. Whitney, the music publisher, the vice-president was W.H. Currier, and J.B. Woodford was secretary-treasurer and general manager. In 1899, Loring & Blake organs were being made in the *Taber Organ Co.* factory. Serial number: 1886—42379.

LOTUS organ, instrument of recent manufacture owned by Cal Rosenberg.

LOUISVILLE organ, probably of Louisville, Kentucky.

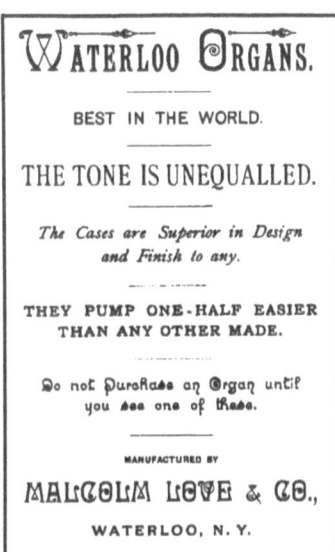 

LOVE, MALCOLM, & CO.; Waterloo, NY 1885 and 1889; see *Waterloo Organ Co.*
LOW, JOHN, & CO.; Aylmer, Ontario. Made the Elgin organ. Serial number: 1891—1366.
LOYELUXT ARMONIUMS; Azpeitia (Guipúzcoa), Spain.
LUCAS, M., & CO.; 90 Tremont St., Boston, MA. Church and parlor organ maker.
LUCHART. (Name only, no other information available.)
LUCILLA & CIA.; via Condotti 22, Rome, Italy. Piano and harmonium maker, 1883.
LUCK, WALTER VILLIERS, & CO.; Apollo House, Broadway, Stratford, England and 2 Stratford Grove, London, 1883. Piano, harmonium and American organ manufacturer.
LUDDEN & BATES; 140 Bull St., Savannah, GA. Ludden & Bates Southern Music House, a music dealership, was established in 1869 by William Ludden and Julius A. Bates. Publishers of the Southern Musical Journal, 1871-82. Both Ludden and Bates left the company in 1901, but it continued under different ownership for many years. Organs with this name were undoubtedly made by others with the Ludden & Bates stencil.
LUFF, GEORGE, & SON; 103 Great Russell St., Bloomsbury, London 1851, then 7 Caroline Mews, Bedford Sq., London 1861. Exhibited a harmonium and the Albert Cottage piano-harmonium at the London Exhibition in 1851. Also agents for *Debain*.

A George Luff & Son "Albert Cottage Pianoforte Harmonium."

LUMLEY, W.H.; in 1892 at Cleveland Road, Northampton, England; in 1895 at 32 Kettering Road, Northampton; in 1896 at 27 Abingdon Square, Northampton. Piano and American organ maker.
LUND, see *Akermans & Lunds Orgelfabrik Aktiebolaget.*
LUNDHOLM, C.A.V.; Hamnagatan 28 in 1897, Jacobsbergsgatan 39 in 1903, Stockholm, Sweden; established in 1870 by Carl Adam Victor Lundholm (1846-1935) initially as a piano store, later manufactured harmoniums.
LUTZ, J.A.; Churchville, Augusta County, VA.
LYON & HEALY; 156-164 State St., factory at Randolph St. & Union Park, Chicago, IL in 1864. Patrick J. Healy and George W. Lyon, former employees of *Oliver Ditson* in Boston, started a retail music business in Chicago in 1864 with the backing of Ditson, and in 1887 began manufacturing reed organs. Sold 217,249 reed organs in 1880. Patrick J. Healy died in 1905, aged 65. Discontinued organ production in 1907. In 1919 Lyon & Healy was the distributor for Estey in the Chicago area.

Sold a suitcase-style portable organ with the Lyon & Healy stencil manufactured by *Estey*. See *Kenwood*.
LYON, L.G.; England. Harmonium maker, still working in 1906. Probably the same as Louis George Lyon, 122 Camberwell Rd., London.

Mackie & Co.
82 STATE ST.,
Rochester, N. Y., U. S. A.

M

MACCHITELLA, TERIGI; 2 via Pergola, Brindisi, Italy, 1930.
MACILIUS, ANT.; 42 Vytauto g-ve, Marijampol, Latvia, 1930.
MACKIE & CO.; 82 State St., Rochester, NY; the "City Music Store" (retail) founded 1840. W.S. Mackie became sole proprietor in 1858 and in 1864 he took his son, H.S. Mackie, into partnership. W.S. died in 1865 and H.S. ran the business as a sole proprietorship until 1872 when *H.S. Mackie & Co.* was formed. Their building at 82 State Street was erected in 1884. Sold organs ca. 1878-80 with the name "Bell Treble," probably built by others with Mackie's stencil.
MACNUTT, A.; 115 N. Sixth St., Philadelphia, PA 1861, 1863. Melodeon manufacturer. In 1869 shown as *MacNutt Organ Co.*, maker of a desk organ. Also *MacNutt & Prior*.
MADER, F.; 84 boulevard de la Madeleine, Marseille, France, 1883. Piano and harmonium maker.
MADER, JOSEF, & SÖHNE; Petrovice (Petersdorf), Czechoslovakia; Josef Mader, proprietor in 1930; established 1880.
MAEKAWA; 19 Minami Kyuhoji machi Higashiku, Osaka, Japan, 1902 and 1909. Also shown as *Mayekawa*. Maekawa is a publisher and formerly a music dealer representing *Tōyō Gakki Seizo*, which made organs under the names *Ikeuchi Fukin*, *Tōyō Gakki Seizo* and Maekawa.

MAELZEL, JOHANN NEPOMUK, (also Mälzel); German musician and inventor. He exhibited his *Panharmonicon*, which used free-reed pipes, in Paris in 1807. A Panharmonicon was brought to the United States in 1811 and exhibited in New York and other cities under the supervision of Boston organ builder William Goodrich.
MAESTRO CO.; Eldridge, NY; self-playing attachment for organs, invented by Louis B. Doman ca. 1899.
MAFFEI, CARLO; via Cappellari 3, Milan, Italy.
MAGEN; 3 rue des Augustins, Agen, France, 1920.
MAGER, SIEGFRIED, & CO.; 9 Hacklandweg 9, Wuppertal-Elberfeld, Germany. Made the Mager-Straube Kleinorgel, a combination reed and electronic organ, ca. 1960. Closed 1975.
MAGNUS HARMONICA CORP.; also *International Plastic Harmonica Corp.*, 439 Frelinghuysen Ave., Newark, NJ. Founded by Finn Haakon Magnus during World War II to make harmonicas with plastic reeds, brass reeds then being unavailable. Later produced small electrically blown reed chord organs, a roll-operated organette, and numerous toy instruments, all with plastic reeds.
MAGNUSSON, OLOF; Quincy, IL. 1883.
MAIER, ALOYS; Friedrichstr. 26 in 1890, Friedrichstr. 16 and Rittergasse 4 in 1930, Fulda, Germany. Established 1846, in business in 1930 as *Fuldaer Orgel-, Harmonium-, und Pianofortefabrik Maier & Co.*, (qv).
MAILLARD & CIE.; 275 rue de Paris, Belleville, Paris; factory at 5 rue de Parc, Belleville, Paris, showrooms at 14 rue de la Douane. Jean-Baptiste Maillard, proprietor. Established in 1852. In 1854 made "l'Orgue-Piano." Manufacturer of Orgue-Melodiums and pianos, inventor of the Orgue Compositeur. Honorable mention at the Paris Exposition of 1855.
MAINGUET; Paris. Reed maker, found on Rodolphe harmoniums.
MAIOLO, GIOVANNI; Borgosesia, Italy, 1930.
MAISON COUTY, see *Couty*.
MAISON DU PARFAIT CLAVIER; 30 rue du Faubourg-Poissonnière, Paris; M. Arencibia, director; made piano-harmoniums, 1903.
MÄKINEN-TEHDASLIIKE; Sortavala, Finland (now in Russian territory); formerly *Eero Mäkinen*, Lauri Mäkinen proprietor in 1903; established in 1881 by Eero Mäkinen, who was also dean of the seminary.
MALCOLM, JOHN, & CO.; Regents Park Road; Erskine Rd. 1897 and 1903, London. Established 1891; made American organs (suction) and the Phoneon player organ. Merged with *Alfred Maxfield* in 1918, doing business as late as 1921.
MALCOLM, see *Malcolm Love & Co.* and *Waterloo Organ Co.*
MALHOIT & CO.; Simcoe, Ontario 1875.

MALKIN, E.; 34 Spencer Hill, Wimbledon, London; later at 6 Malcolm Road, Wimbledon. Manufactured harmoniums and a patent pedal attachment for pianos.
MALLEVILLE; 142 avenue de Versailles, Paris, 1930.
MALVESTIO, DOMENICO, E FIGLIO; 4 via Dietro Duomo, Padova, Italy, 1930.
MAMONTOW, A.P.; Wologda, Russia 1903, 1909.
MANCHESTER PIANO & ORGAN WORKS; (T. Goodwin), Brookside, Longsight, Manchester, England 1903.
MANGER, see *Mojon, Manger & Co.*
MANN, F.; New Briggate, Leeds, Yorkshire, England. Harmonium maker from 1878 (or before) until 1880.

Th. Mannborg, Leipzig.

Erste und älteste **Fabrik** für **Harmoniums** nach Saugwind-System in Deutschl.
13 patentierte und gesetzlich geschützte Konstruktionen.
Harmoniums in höchster Vollendung, von den kleinsten bis zu den allergrössten.
Grosser Prachtkatalog mit ca. 90 Modellen.

MANNBORG, THEODOR; Grimmaische Strasse 410, Borna, Germany in 1889; Kornerplatz 3 & 4 in 1903, Angerstrasse 38 in 1904, 1930, both in Leipzig-Lindenau, Germany. Mannborg was born in Karlstad, Sweden in 1861. He was apprenticed to *J.P. Nyström* in Sweden, emigrated to Germany in 1886 where he took additional training with the pipe-organ builder Urban Kreutzbach in Borna. He established his factory in 1889 in Borna, building the first suction organs produced in Germany. In 1894 he moved the factory to Leipzig and in 1904 opened a new factory at Angerstrasse 38 in the Lindenau district of Leipzig. Mannborg was instrumental in founding the Association of German Harmonium Manufacturers (Verein Deutscher Harmonium Fabrikanten). When Theodor Mannborg died in 1930 the business was operated by his son Karl until his death in 1941. The firm was taken over by the state-owned piano manufacturer Rönisch & Hupfeld in 1948, operating as a part of *VEB Leipziger Pianofortefabrik Böhlitz-Ehrenberg*. Acquired by *Lindholm* in 1961. See *Deutsch Harmonium-Zungen-Fabrik, Lindholm, Hofberg.*

Mannborg's Rococo Harmonium, Style 66.

Serial numbers:

1890—50	1930—49451	1958—65000
1900—5600	1935—52262	1961—66340
1905—11500	1940—58013	1962—66510
1910—20893	1945—59333	1963—66750
1920—34704	1950—60140	1964—67000
1925—41721	1952—61000	1965—67250
1928—45286	1955—63300	1966—67400

MANNING & NICHOLS; Salem, MA 1861. Melodeon manufacturers.
MANNING ORGAN CO.; Rockport, MA; Henry Dennis Jr., president; Joseph Manning, treasurer; William H. Manning, superintendent; William

A. Dennis, secretary. W.H. Manning obtained a patent in 1872 on a method for building parlor organs so that they could be taken apart in less than a minute without unscrewing a single screw, the price to be half the usual amount. He began manufacturing in 1873 in the rented upper stories of the Hide Seat Co. building. The business failed in 1875 and in 1876 the remaining stock was auctioned off and the patents sold to Rust & Marshall of Bristol, CT.
MANNING, see *Sherlock-Manning Organ Co.*
MANSONS, G.S.; melodeon Model 2500, May 19, 1857.
MARCH, see *Julius & March.*
MARCHAL & SMITH; 8 W. 11th St., 225 E. 21st St., 235 E. 21st St., 453 W. 36th St., New York, NY 1880 until after 1887; sold the University Organ. Established in 1859 as a piano manufacturer. Did not make reed organs, but represented a reed organ manufacturer and sold organs with the Marchal & Smith name directly to the public. Serial number: 1892—13912.
MARETKA, FRANZ; Elisabethstr. 35 in 1903, Vodni ul. 20 in 1930, Olomouc (Olmütz), Czechoslovakia.
MARIANI, ANTONIO; Corso Garibaldi 77, Milan, Italy, 1909.
MARION. Parlor organ. (No further information available.)
MARISTANY, RÓMULO; 12-14 Fontanella, Barcelona, Spain in 1883. Later shown as Hijos de Rómulo Maristany at 18 Plaza Cataluña, Barcelona. Established in 1870.
MARIX, LÉON; Grande Galerie at Passage des Panoramas, atelier at 131 rue Montmartre, Paris in 1842. Made harmoniums with up to 22 stops. By 1857 shown as *L. Mayer-Marix* at the same address, (qv).
MARKLOVE, see *Alvinza Andrews.*
MARKS; made a portable harmonium called the Marks-Celestine, 1870.
MARSH, C.H.; Temple St., Bristol, England; harmonium maker. Working in 1890.
MARSHALL BROS. LTD.; 24-25 Paternoster Row, Keswick House, London EC. Makers of Keswick Portable Organ and Universal Folding Organ.
MARSHALL, J.; 89 Great College Street, London. Maker and decorator of false front pipes for American organs, 1900.
MARSHALL, J.H.; Regent House, Regent Street, London. American organ manufacturer 1906.
MARSHALL, see *Manning Organ Co.*
MARSTON, A.B.; Campello, MA; bought out *Caleb H. Packard* in 1855, made reed organs in the same location until the building burned in 1859; built a new building on Depot St. in 1859. Shown in N. Bridgewater, MA in 1861.

MARTELLA, FLORENTIN; 1 rue Delpozzo, Nice, France 1903.
MARTIN, ALBERT; 38 rue des Ecluses-St.-Martin, Paris 1878, 1883. Awarded a bronze medal at the Paris Exhibition of 1878 for well-made harmoniums. Also awarded a third prize at Sydney, Australia in 1878.
MARTIN, CH.; Paris. Harmonium maker, 1913.
MARTIN, F., & CIE.; Magny-Cours, France, 1883.
MARTIN, LOUIS-PIERRE ALEXANDRE; of Sourdun, Provins, France. In 1851 located at 13 rue la Fontaine au Roi, Paris. Known as *Martin de Provins* or *Martin de Sourdun*, he was the inventor of the percussion device for harmoniums ca.1841; awarded a bronze medal at the Paris Exhibition of 1844. *Alexandre* bought the rights. Martin exhibited a percussion reed harmonium with expression at the Paris Exhibition of 1851. Succeeded by *Bourlet*.
MARTIN, W., see *Conrad, Martin & Torste, Cook & Martin*.
MARTINELLI. (No additional information available.)
MARTY, see *Boyer & Marty*.

A Mason & Hamlin Style K organ, 1910.

MASON & HAMLIN; Cambridge St., then 277 Washington St., then 134 Tremont St., Boston, MA 1854-1888. Renamed *Mason & Hamlin Organ & Piano Co.* in 1888. Founded by Henry Mason and Emmons Hamlin with funds provided by *Oliver Ditson* and Henry's father, Dr. Lowell Mason. Built about 450 organs per year from 1855-1861. Factory capacity 10,000 organs per year in 1902. In 1905 Mason & Hamlin made a contract with *Alphonse Mustel* in which he would make his home in Boston and supervise the manufacture of Mustel Harmoniums by Mason & Hamlin. While it is uncertain that Mustel ever went to Boston, twenty-five years earlier Mason & Hamlin had produced their "Orchestral" organ which had pressure bellows, expression, percussion action and the same specifications as a Mustel harmonium. Reed organ production ended in 1927. Catalogs and other sources give the following cumulative production quantities:

1873—100,000	1878—100,000	1884—150,000
1875—80,000	1880—102,817	1889—175,000

Serial numbers (not reliable):

1856—596	1874—24001	1892—112000
1859—1946	1876—34435	1894—117000
1861—2600	1880—45927	1899—212377
1863—3503	1881—50000	1900—214191
1865—5050	1883—58900	1903—223506
1867—8541	1885—73000	1906—229269
1870—10000	1887—81000	1916—239552
1872—12219	1888—86000	1899—212377
1873—17000	1890—103200	1904—225174

MASON & RISCH LTD.; 32 King St., Toronto, Ontario; established 1871. Acquired the manufacturing rights to the Vocalion in 1890 from the *New York Church Organ Co.*, and manufactured them at 5-11 Summer St., Worcester, MA. Sold the Vocalion rights to *Aeolian* in 1903. See *The Vocalion Organ Co.* for serial numbers.
MASONS, F.S.; melodeon maker. (No other information available.)
MASSABO; Paris. Reed maker, 1867.
MASSACHUSETTS ORGAN CO.; 43 Wash. St., 57 Wash. St., Boston, MA; factory in Chelsea, MA 1879-1885. Makers of the Mignonnette, Chesterfield organettes, the Imperial Cabinet Organ and the Gem and Phonographic Pianos. Affiliated with the *American Automatic Organ Co.*, (qv).

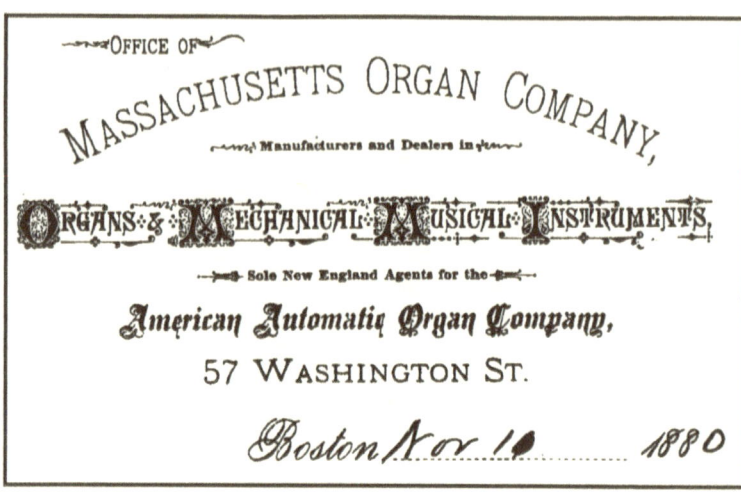

MATCHLESS ORGAN CO. (No other information available.)
MATHEWS, MASON J., an English mechanic who wrote extensively about reed organs in amateur scientific journals. After moving to the US in 1870 he patented mechanical devices which he then sold to *Mason & Hamlin, George Woods, Mechanical Orguinette Co.* and others. See *Mechanical Orguinette Co.*
MATHIAS ORGAN CO, see *Mathias W. Schulz.*
MATSCHKE, TRAUGOTT; Münchhausen bei Sonnewalde, Germany. Harmonium maker, 1913.
MATSUMOTO GAKKI GOSHI KAISHA; 5 Tsukishama, Nishinaka-dori 9-chome, Kyobashi-ku, Tokyo in 1902 and 1930. Also shown at 4 Chome, Bingo-Machi, Osaka, Japan in 1896, and at Hirano-cho-kado, Shinsaibashi-douri, Osaka in 1911, both probably show rooms. Shinkichi Matsumoto (1865-1941) started his career as a carpenter, then in 1887 was apprenticed to the reed organ builder *Nishikawa*. In 1893 he started making reed organs under his own name at Tsukiji, Tokyo. Made organettes (shikō-kin in Japanese) and American organs. In 1900 he studied piano making at the Bradbury Piano Co. in New York and in 1907 formed *Matsumoto & Co. Ltd*. In 1923 it became *Matsumoto Piano Co. Ltd.*, then *H. Matsumoto* until 1945, and is still in business making pianos as *S. Matsumoto* (Matsumoto & Sons), Chiba Prefecture, Japan. Also made reed organs with the Yamano stencil for *Yamano Music* (qv).
MATTIKA, E.H.; St. Dunstan's Buildings, St. Dunstan's Hill, EC London. Organette manufacturer 1887-1896.
MATTO, M.; Petersburger Str. 117, Dorpat (Jurjew), Finland. Established in 1891.

MAUGÉ; rue des Maraichers, Paris. Harmonium and reed maker, 1867.

MAVER, ROB.; 11 Renfield Street, Glasgow, Scotland. Harmonium maker 1879-1889. Also located at 27 rue de L'Empereur, Brussels, Belgium. Maker and retailer of pianos and harmoniums, 1905.

MAXFIELD, ALFRED; 326 Liverpool Rd., London; player reed organ 1898. Merged with *John Malcolm & Co.* in 1918.

MAYER-MARIX, L.; 48 passage des Panoramas, Paris in 1867. Established 1834. Made a portable harmonium in 1856, also made harmoniums, harmoniflûtes and barrel harmoniums. Succeeded by *A. Morhange* before 1883. See *Léon Marix*.

MAYER & TRUCHSESS; Jesingerstr. 22, Kircheim u. Teck, Germany. Established in 1920 by Rudolf Mayer and Th. Truchsess. Bought out by *Teck Harmoniumfabrik* (qv) in 1938.

MAZET, VICTOR, & CIE.; rue du Gentilhomme 25 in 1893; 19 rue du Gentilhomme, 1899-1903; rue Royale 170 in 1910, Brussels, Belgium. Invented an organ-harmonium with prepared combination registers.

MCCLURE, DR. A.R. A physician in Edinburgh, Scotland who became interested in a madrigal singing group. He found the equal-tempered scale unsuitable and tuned a piano to a 19 note per octave scale, then built a prototype reed organ and finally a pipe organ with the 19 note scale. This organ is now located at Edinburgh University, Scotland. His prototype was a single manual *Carpenter* organ now in the Victorian Reed Organ and Harmonium Museum, Saltaire Village, Shipley, W. Yorks., England. The notes per octave are: C, C♯, D♭, D, D♯, E♭, E, E♯, F, F♯, G♭, G, G♯, A♭, A, A♯, B♭, B, C♭.

MCKILLIPS, ALEX; 130 N. Arch St. in 1877, 320 N. Queen St. Lancaster, PA in 1879-82; later in Harrisburg, PA. Active 1877-1902. Also listed as *Lancaster Organ Manufactory*.

MCLEOD, WOOD & CO.; Guelph, Ontario 1869-72; later *R. McLeod & Co.*, London, Ontario, 1874-5.

MCNUTT, see *MacNutt*.

MCTAMMANY JR., JOHN; 511 Main St., Cambridgeport, MA 1886; also *McTammany Organette Co.*, Worcester, MA; self-proclaimed "greatest musical inventor of any age," and "the original inventor of the player piano," held numerous patents on mechanical musical devices, designed and sold organettes. The musical instrument industry was less impressed with his qualifications and never gave him the acclaim he sought.

MEAD, A.C., LTD.; 15 Foregate Street, Worcester, England, 1930.

MEANDLER, see *Schram & Meandler*.

MEANER. (No other information available.)

A fourteen-note organette made by the Mechanical Orguinette Co.

MECHANICAL ORGUINETTE CO., THE; 11 E. 14th St.; moved in 1880 to 1831 Broadway, New York and to Greenpoint, Long Island, NY in 1883; founded by William Barnes Tremaine in 1878. The organette was invented in 1878 by Mason J. Mathews, an Englishman who came to the U.S. in 1870, (qv). It was made by the *Munroe Organ Reed Co.* C.H. Ditson, son of Oliver Ditson, became treasurer in 1881. Tremaine later formed *The Æolian Co.* and acquired the *Munroe Organ Reed Co.*, setting the stage for the massive expansion carried out by his son H.B. Tremaine. The mechanically operated reed organ reached its highest development with the Æolian Orchestrelle, and it was Æolian which made the name Pianola a household word. The original Pianola was a push-up piano player. For an extensive history see the Encyclopedia of Automatic Musical Instruments by Q. David Bowers. Serial numbers of the Æolian Orchestrelle:

1898—1788	1903—8121	1911—8899
1898—1801	1904—7718	1912—5952
1901—2644	1905—8776	1912—8952
1902—2910	1906—7445	1914—8892
1903—4217	1907—7902	1914—8988
1903—7445	1909—8243	

MECHANICAL SYSTEMS, INC.; Lubbock, TX ; manufacturer of Equa-Vac electric suction unit for reed organs, 1985; Noble Stidham, proprietor.

MEE, CHARLES; Kingston, Ontario 1870; melodeons.
MEIDINGER, G., & CIE.; Mariengasse 12-20, Basel, Switzerland. Made reed organ blowers. Extant 1932.
MEIG; Madrid, Spain. Reed organ maker, 1825.
MEINL, ERNST; 124 Richard Wagnerstr., Graslitz, Czechoslovakia, 1930.
MEINVERE, VVE.; 10 rue de la Tour, Vanves (Seine), France in 1883; in 1909 shown at 10 rue de la Tour, Malakoff. Organ and harmonium manufacturer, 1883.
MEISSNER, BENJAMIN F., inventor of the Orgatron, (qv).
MEISSNER CO., THE; 110-120 Reed St., Milwaukee, WI. In the 1930s Meissner made a combination piano and reed organ with a built-in AM radio and record player
MELLOR, KOENE & KENRICKS, see *Keystone Organ Co.*
MELODY ORGAN CO., LTD., THE; 78 King St., Manchester, England; Samuel Howard, manager in 1903; made the "Melody Solo" American organ.
MELO-PEAN CO.; Akron, OH, see *Horton, Blodget, Scott.*
MELZER, JOSEF; Rudni ul, Kutná Hora, Czechoslovakia, 1930.
MENARD FILS; Flers, France, 1883. Piano and harmonium maker.
MENDOTA COTTAGE ORGAN & PIANO CO., see *Western Cottage Organ Co.*
MENDOTA NORTHWESTERN COTTAGE ORGAN CO., see *E.B. Carpenter.*
MENEELY & CO.; West Troy, NY. Operated a church bell foundry and also sold church, chapel and school organs made for them by others.
MENTASTI, PAOLO, & FIGLIO; via Torino, Casale Monferrato, Italy. In business at least from 1900 through 1909.
MENZENHAUER & SCHMIDT; Rungestrasse 17 in 1908, Rungestr. 18 in 1912, Berlin; Sedanstr. 47-48 in Berlin-Weissensee, 1925-30. Maker of the "Accordharmonium," with a two-octave manual and chord buttons for bass.
MERCIK, E.L.; 41 Great Pulteney Street, Golden Square, W London. Piano and harmonium manufacturer 1879-1882.
MERHAUT, ALFRED; Rosstr. 6 in 1890, Peterssteinweg 18 in 1900-13, Leipzig, Germany. Made the Sonorium harmonium. Working 1895-1910.
MERITAN & CIE., see *Léon Abeille.*
MERKLIN, JOS., & SCHUTZE; rue du Duc de Brabant 196, Ixelles, Brussels, Belgium. Established in Brussels as a pipe organ maker in 1843 by Joseph Merklin (1819-1905), also made harmoniums, mélodiums, orchestrions and pianos, probably only in Belgium. In 1847 his brother-in-law François Schutze joined him. At that time there were 20 to

25 workers in the factory. Renamed *Merklin-Schutze et Cie.* in 1853 when they had 200 workers in their factory, then located in Namur. Awarded a first class medal at the Paris Exposition of 1855. In the same year they bought out *Ducroquet*, a pipe organ builder in Paris, and moved that factory to boulevard Montparnasse, Paris. In 1858 styled "*Société Anonyme pour la Fabrication des Orgues - Etablissement Merklin-Schutze.*" Awarded a gold medal at the Paris Exhibition of 1867 and in the same year Schutze was awarded the Légion d'Honneur. Awarded another gold medal in Paris in 1878. Succeeded by *Pierre Schyven & Co.* (qv) in 1875, but both names were retained in use. Pierre Schyven previously had been a foreman with the company. Joseph Merklin retired in 1889 and in 1894 the Société was dissolved. Merklin's son-in-law Charles Michel took over the business at Lyon, which was then called *Charles Michel-Merklin.* The firm was still operating as *Michel-Merklin et Kuhn* at 11 rue Vendôme, Lyon as late as 1939.

MERLO, SIMONE; Corso Palestro, Vercelli, Italy, 1903.

MERRIAM, E.N., & CO.; East Poultney, VT. Established 1865 by two former employees of *Ross & Moore*: E.N. Merriam (1830-1908) and A.D. Ripley (1832-1900). Built the Union organ until about 1869.

MERRILL PIANO MFG. CO.; Boston MA; successor to *Smith-American Organ Co.*

MERTEL, HANS; 59 Neuhauserstr., Salzburg, Austria, 1930.

MESNAGE, F.; 85 High Street, Marylebone, London. Harmonium and American organ manufacturer. Successor to *Constant Laurent* in 1887. Working until 1891.

METIUS, K.; Leipzig, Germany; maker of rubberized cloth for harmoniums, 1930.

METZLER, GEORGE; 105 Wardour St., Soho, London in 1830; 37 Great Marlborough Street, Soho in 1842; 35 Great Marlborough St. in 1857; 38 Great Marlborough Street in 1858; also at 16 Great Marlborough Street in 1863; 36 Great Marlborough Street in 1864; 26-29 Great Marlborough Street in 1869. Established in 1781 as a piano maker, later made seraphines and finally operated only as a dealer. Metzler was the main dealer in the UK for *Alexandre* and *Mason & Hamlin*.

METZNER, RICHARD, ORGEL-HARMONIUM-FABRIK; Mühlenstrasse 38-42 in 1903-10, and Lauchstädter Strasse 38-42 in 1911-19, Leipzig-Plagwitz, Germany. Also listed as *Deutsch-Amerikanische Orgel-Harmonium-Fabrik R. Metzner*; Frohberg, Germany, 1930. Established 1902. Maker of suction harmoniums.

MEYER, see *Eisenwerke L. Meyer jun. & Co.*

MICADO CO., organ imported by *Joseph Riley & Sons*, (qv).

MIDMER, REUBEN; Brooklyn, NY, 1860-1895. Pipe organ builder, also made reed organs.

MIGLIA, GIUSEPPE; Caselle Torinse, Italy, 1930.
MIHARA, CHIKASUKE; Hongo, Tokyo, Japan. Honorable mention at 3rd Domestic Industrial Exhibition in Tokyo, 1890.
MIKI, S., & CO.; Kita-Kyuhoji-Machi, Shinsaibashi, Osaka, Japan in 1905. Sasuke Miki, proprietor. Dealer for *Yamaha* organs in western Japan. A reed organ with the Miki stencil was made by Yamaha.
MILES, L.; Syracuse, NY; see *Roth, Holleran & Miles*.
MILHAM, JOSEPH; 35 Landsdowne Place, Lewes, Sussex, England. Harmonium builder 1870-1890, made a combined reed and pipe organ.

MILLER AND SON; 208-210 Main St., Danville, IL. John M. Miller and his son Frield are listed in the Danville directories for 1876 and 1883 as proprietors of the Beethoven Organ Factory. By 1889 Frield Miller is listed alone as a piano tuner. The factory building is no longer in existence.

MILLER, JOHN M.; Dundas St., Woodstock, Ontario. Made about one organ per week until 1867 when he was joined by D.W. Karn, forming *Miller & Karn*.

MILLER & KARN; Dundas St., Woodstock, Ontario; established 1867; see *John M. Miller, D.W. Karn*.

MILLER ORGAN CO.; retail store at 738 Cumberland St., Lebanon, PA; established ca. 1873 by Adam ca. B. Miller; twostory factory built 1874, increased to four stories in 1883, son Abraham H. Miller joined ca. 1887. Factory capacity 1,800 organs per year in 1899. Also built pipe organs beginning in 1886. Renamed *Miller Organ & Piano Co.* in 1904, then located at Eighth and Maple Streets. Made organs at least through 1922. Serial Numbers: 1892—13561, 1895—16868, 1899—22184, 1903—27908.

MILLET ORGAN; four octave organ without stops.

MILSOM & SON; Bath, England.

MILWAUKEE, see *Thiery Milwaukee Reed Organ Co.*

A Minami organ, made by Tōyō Gakki Seizo Co. Ltd., Tatsuno, Japan.

MINAMI; Japan. The Minami organ was named for Yoshie Minami, an engineer for *Tōyō Gakki Seizo Co.* (qv), also a song writer and former professor at Tokyo School of Music. The organs were built by *Ikeuchi* and by *Tōyō Gakki Seizo Co.*
MINASI, C.; 3 St. James Terrace, Kentish Town Road, London, 1862.
MINNS, J.E.; 32 North Street, Taunton, Devon, England. Factory at Bishops Hull. Pipe organs and pedal reed organs 1886. No mention of reed organs in 1889 listing.

Brattleboro • Vermont

MINSHALL ORGAN INC.; Brattleboro, VT. Made a reed organ with electronic amplification. Later worked with the *Estey Organ Co.* as *Minshall-Estey Inc.* Minshall-Estey was sold to *Baldwin* in the late 1950s.
MITCHELL, C.C.; Concord, NH; melodeons.
MITROPOLSKY, D.A.; Novgorod, Russia, 1903.
MIWA ORGAN MANUFACTURING COMPANY; Nagoya, Japan, 1902 and 1909. (Miwa Gakkiten). Hakuya Miwa, proprietor. Exhibitor at 3rd Domestic Industrial Exhibition, Tokyo, 1890.
MIZUMA, TOYOSHINE; Shiogama, Miyagi, Japan. Exhibitor at the 3rd Domestic Industrial Exhibition, Tokyo, 1890.
MOELLER, FRIEDR.; Sondershausen, Germany, 1883. Established in 1857. Listed as *Frz. Moeller* or Möller at Friedrichstr. 1 in 1890 and at Fridrichstr. 18 in 1903 and 1912. Piano and harmonium maker.
MOGYOROSSY GUALA Royal Hungarian Registered Instrument Factory; Rakosczistreet 71, Budapest VIII, Hungary. Instrument located in Nagygoros, Hungary.
MOHN BROS.; 3 Lower Citpore Road, Calcutta, India, 1930.
MOJON, MANGER & CO.; Bartletts Buildings, London; manufacturer of music boxes and mechanical harmoniums.
MOLA, CAV. GIUSEPPE; via Nizza 82, Turin, Italy; established 1862. Awarded a Medal of Merit at the Vienna Fair of 1873, a bronze medal at the Paris Exhibition of 1878 and a third order of merit at the 1881 Exhibition in Melbourne.
MØLGAARD-JENSEN, N.P.; Jernbanegade 24, Haslev, Denmark; see *Haslev Orgelfabr.*
MOLINARI, G., & SON; wareroom at 153 Elizabeth St., New York, 1901. Made hand-cranked street organs with pinned cylinders, mostly with pipes but some models had reeds.
MOLINE CABINET ORGAN CO.; started as *Peter Colseth & Co.* in Moline, IL. From 1877-81 located at 630 Railroad Ave.; then *Moline Cabinet Organ Co.* 1881-88; corner of Illinois & Division 1882-85; then 4th Ave. & 7th St. in 1885; the name changed to *Moline Organ Co.*, also known as *Peterson, Thulin & Co.* 1888-94; then *Moline Organ & Piano Co.* 1894-99; then *J. Peterson & Co.* 1899 until at least 1920; often

referred to as the *Swedish Organ Co.* because of its orientation toward the Swedish-American market.
MÖLLER, FRANZ, see Friedr. Moeller.

M. P. MÖLLER, INC.
403 North Prospect Street ■ Hagerstown, Maryland 21740 ■ Phone 301-733-9000

MÖLLER, M.P.; Greencastle, PA, 1875-1880; 37 South Potomac St., Hagerstown, MD, 1880 to 1992. Founded by Mathias Peter Möller, made reed organs from 1875 until about 1909, although known principally as a pipe organ builder. Serial number: 1909—408.
MÖLLINGER, CHRISTIAN; Berlin. Made a free-reed keyboard instrument in 1814.
MONARCH ORGAN, see *D.H. Baldwin, Hamilton Organ Co.*
MONKHOUSE, S.I.; Camden, NJ 1861. Melodeon manufacturer.
MONTGOMERY WARD & CO.; Chicago, IL; Windsor organs, 1873. Serial number 1905—29571.
MONTI, CH.; Champigny-sur-Marne, France. In 1872 listed as Monti & Fils, 127 rue Oberkampf, Paris. Keyboards for harmoniums: 15 francs for a small harmonium keyboard in 1878. In 1905 listed as *Ferdinand Monti*.
MONTREE, J. & R.; Pentonville Road, King's Cross, London, 1900.
MOONEN, L.; Paris. Awarded first prize for a harmonium at Sydney, Australia, 1880.
MOORE & MOORE & CO.; 104-105 Bishopsgate, London, 1880, 1911. Factory at 28 Scrutton Street, London. Operated by J.H. and H.K. Moore. Built and sold the Harmonical, an enharmonic organ invented by A. Ellis. Exhibited at the 1885 Inventors' Exhibition in London. In 1911 Henry Keatley Moore invented an Indian scale harmonium with 23 tones per octave.
MOORE ORGAN CO., THE; 45-47 Jackson St., Chicago, IL 1892-93; 46 Jackson Place in 1899. Made the "Moore" and "Peerless" organs. Controlled by *Foley & Williams Mfg. Co.* in 1899. Last listed in 1920.

The Windsor Parlor Organ, Style L 105, sold by Montgomery Ward.

A Mott combination piano and organ from the Olthof collection.

MOORE, W.H.; King Street, Wellington, Shropshire, England. Harmonium maker in 1878.
MORANDI, JOS.; 6 Kingsland Road, E London. Harmonium maker 1879-1883.
MOREL, E.; 51 rue Franklin, Lyon, France, 1930.
MORGAN, WILLIAM; Great Barrington, MA 1861. Melodeon manufacturer.
MORHANGE, A.; 38 rue Vivienne, Paris, 1920. Also shown as *L. Morhange*. See *Mayer-Marix*.
MORRIS, H. & M.; Philadelphia, PA 1861. Melodeon manufacturer.
MORRISON & COURSER; Concord, NH.
MORSE BROTHERS; Union, ME. Shown as dealers in 1861 at Union and Rockland, ME.
MORSE, MILTON M.; Concord, NH, Worcester, MA 1847; later *Farley & Pearson*.
MORSE, see *Ross, West & Morse; Kennedy & Morse*.

MORTON, A., & CO.; 357 Coldharbour Lane, Brixton, London SW in 1896.
MOSCHEL, LOUIS C., see *Hinners & Albertsen*.
MOSSOUX, AD.; 32 rue du Pont, Andenna, Belgium, 1903.
MOTT, ISAAC HENRY ROBERT; 76 Strand, London. Made a combination harmonium and piano. Patented a seraphine 1845-46. Exhibited a piano-harmonium at the Paris Exhibition of 1851. Died 1868.
MOUCHE & CIE.; France; reed maker.
MOUTRIE, G.; 22 Werrington Street, Oakley Square, London. Harmonium maker, 1866. Joined with Collard to form *Collard & Moutrie*, (qv).
MOUTRIE, J.; 16 Henry Street, Pentonville, London. Harmonium manufacturer 1878-84. Advertised as *J. & R. Moutrie*, American organ manufacturers at 13 Garnault Mews, Clerkenwell, London 1890-1894.
MOZART organs, see *Bruce & Chard*.
MUDGE & YARWOOD MANUFACTURING CO.; Whitby, Ontario; established 1873. Alexander F. Yarwood was granted a reed organ patent in 1874.
MUDROCH, JAN.; Tisnov (Tischnowitz), Czechoslovakia, 1930. Established 1909.
MUELLER, see *Schmuller & Mueller*.
MUES, F.A.; Lenne, Germany. Organ and harmonium maker. Established in 1910, active at least through 1929.
MÜLLER; Feigengasse 8 in 1864, Palmstr. 32 in 1865, Dresden, Germany. Harmonium maker.

EMIL MÜLLER, WERDAU, Sachsen
Europas grösste Harmoniumfabrik nach amerik. System
Gegründet 1887 — Hervorgegangen aus der 1846 gegr. Bärmig'schen Orgelbauanstalt
Prämiiert auf vielen Ausstellungen

MÜLLER, EMIL; Friedhofstr. 40 in 1903; Pestalozzistr. 40-50 in 1930; Pestalozzistr. 42-46 in 1951; Industrieverwaltung 36 in 1947, all in Werdau, Germany. Kurt Müller & Arwed Brandner, proprietors 1930; made the "Cæcilia" harmonium and the "Transponier-Harmonista" harmonium player; established in 1846. In 1951 shown as *Werdauer Möbel und Harmoniumfabrik*. Discontinued reed organ production in 1952 and sold all remaining stock and materials to *Lindholm*.
MÜLLER, J.T.; Bärensteiner Str. 5, Dresden-Leuben, Germany in 1909-16; Fabrikstr. 115 in 1921-27; Werkstr. 59 in 1929. Established 1891. Made both pressure and suction harmoniums.

MÜLLER, SEBASTIAN; Augsburg, Germany. Made the Äoline.
MÜLLER, THÉODORE-ACHILLE; 42 rue de la Ville l'Evêque, Paris. A student of *Grenié*, he made harmoniums and a combination orgue-expressif and piano in 1834. Received medals at the Paris Exposition of 1834 and at the Valencia Exposition of 1835. In 1834 he made and patented a portable orgue-expressif, now in the Musée de la Vie Romantique, Paris. Awarded an honorable mention for two portable melodions at the London Exhibition of 1851. In 1892 patented the "Harmoniton" with Kebelac.
MUNCH; London. Made the Aeolophone in 1830, a six octave physharmonica.
MUNDUL & CO.; 3 Bow Road Bazar Street, Calcutta, India, 1930.
MUNROE ORGAN-REED COMPANY; Worcester, MA; established in 1860, incorporated Jan. 1, 1869 by William Munroe. Located at Hermon St. in 1869, 25 Union St. from 1879 to at least 1889. Reed and component manufacturer, made organettes for *Mechanical Orguinette, McTammany, Gally* and others; annual production reached 4,000,000 reeds in 1881, equivalent to 32,000 organs or about one-third of the total production in the U.S. Purchased by *Æolian* in 1892, but continued to operate under the *Munroe* name at least through 1900.
MURAKAMI, YASABURO; Matsuzaka, Mie, Japan. Exhibitor at the 3rd Domestic Industrial Exhibition, Tokyo, 1890.
MURCH & WHITE; Cincinnati, OH. Melodeon makers, ca. 1855.
MUSICAL PRODUCTS CORP.; St. Louis 8, MO. Made the Harmochord, an electrically-blown chord organ with steel reeds, forty chord buttons, 34 keys.
MUSIIKKI FAZERIN PIANOTEHDAS; Helsinki, Finland.
MUSILLON, E.; 61 rue Hermite, Nancy, France, 1920.
MUSTEL, VICTOR; also *Mustel et Cie.*, 80 rue de Bondy in 1853, at 42 rue de Malte in 1855, still at that location as *Mustel & Fils* in 1883, at 34 and 42 rue de Malte in 1889, at 46 rue de Douai, Paris from 1897 to 1914; *Mustel Père et Fils*, 4 rue Huntziger, Clichy, France in 1903; at 16 ave. de Wagram, Paris after 1914. He also had a factory at 14 rue Marie Anne Columbier, Bagnolet, (Seine). The Mustel company is still in operation (1996) as a musical instrument dealer. Victor Mustel (1815-1890) made his first harmonium in 1840, worked for a few years as a reed maker for *Jaulin* of Paris, then founded his harmonium factory in 1853. First exhibited at the Paris Exposition of 1855, where he won a silver medal. He became known for art harmoniums of the highest quality, and is credited with many inventions of improvements to the harmonium. In 1889 won the grand prize at the Paris Exhibition and in the same year was created a Chevalier of the Légion d'Honneur. His sons Charles (1840-93) and Auguste and grandson Alphonse also worked in the firm.

Alphonse was the author of "L'Orgue-Expressif ou Harmonium". See *Mason & Hamlin*. Serial numbers:

1867—104	1885—416	1904—1266/962
1875—223	1888—470	1908—1924/1057
1876—255	1894—806/607	1912—1924/1052
1880—311	1895—826/627	1913—2370/1233
1881—345	1897—851/650	1922—2748/1337
1882—349	1897—883/679	1925—3195/1455
1882—359	1898—887/682	1926—3206/1461
1883—384	1901—1100/832	1927—3244/1492
1884—395	1902—1179/892	1928—3417/1602

MUTIN, see *Cavaillé-Coll*.
MYERS & STORER; London; established 1837 by John Myers and Joseph Storer.
MYERS, see *Day & Myers*.

N

NAGAO, YOSHIZO; Matsuzaka, Mie, Japan. Exhibitor at the 3rd Domestic Industrial Exhibition in Tokyo, 1890.
NAGY, JOSEF; Strada Sfintilor 42, Bucharest, Rumania. Established 1867. Piano and harmonium maker.
NAISH, E.V.; Wilton, England. Supplier of piano and organ felts to the trade.
NAKAJIMA, YUKINOSUKE; Asakusa, Tokyo. Exhibitor at the 3rd Domestic Industrial Exhibition in Tokyo, 1890.
NAUTA, DIRK; Groningen, Netherlands. Patented a combination pipe organ and suction reed organ in 1934.
NEAL & PRATT; 71 E. Genesee St., Syracuse, NY 1861. Melodeon manufacturers.
NEDERLANDSCHE ORGELFABRIEK WORCESTER, NV; 185 Arnhemsche Weg, Amersfoort, Netherlands, 1890 at least through 1930. Also known as *Worcester Reed Organ Company*. Won a gold medal at the Rotterdam Exposition in 1907.
NEEDHAM, ELIAS PARKMAN, see *Carhart & Needham*.
NEEDHAM PIANO & ORGAN CO.; offices at 292 Broadway, New York, NY; factory in Washington, NJ 1891; made the Beethoven Organ; successor to *E.P. Needham & Son*. Officers in 1897: Charles H. Parsons, president; E.A. Cole, secretary. Factory capacity 17,000 organs per year in 1897. Also operated as *Beethoven Organ Co*. and *Beethoven Piano-Organ Co*. See *Carhart & Needham*. Serial number: 1877—21904.
NEEF, G.; Feuerthalen, Schaffhausen, Switzerland, 1862. Awarded an honorable mention for a church harmonium at the London Exhibition of 1862. Also shown as Gebrüder Neef.
NEEREMOLA Organ; table harmonium made in India.
NEIS; Viehweg Mühle 90, Schlesien, Germany, 1886.
NELSON, JOSEPH; 52 Cumberland Market, Regent's Park, London NW in 1883; 113 Cowley Rd., Oxford, England in 1903. Harmonium manufacturer, established 1866.
NELSON MANUFACTURING CO.; Mercer, PA.
NEPAL MUSICAL INSTRUMENT INDUSTRIES, (PVT) LTD.; 21-1-359 Khichapokhari, Kathmandu, Nepal. Prameswar Rajtandukar, proprietor. Currently a manufacturer of musical instruments including several models of Indian table harmoniums with two or three sets of reeds.

NESCHUTA, JOSEF; Burggasse 86, Vienna, Austria, 1883, 1903. Maker of orchestrions, physharmoniums and melodions (mouth organs). Shown as a pipe organ maker in 1903.

NESS, JOHANNES L.; Kvinnherad, Norway. Built a few pipe organs and harmoniums after 1895.

The Netzow Style 30 organ.

NETZOW, CHARLES F., MANUFACTURING CO.; Milwaukee, WI. Made the Bristol organ. Charles F. Netzow came to Milwaukee from Germany in 1883 as a gardener. He began selling organs, sewing machines and wagons in 1885 and later began manufacturing organs in a factory building on Second Street. This building burned about 1914 and he built a new three-story building on Palmer Street; discontinued organ production about this time. The business still exists (1994) as Netzow Pianos & Organs, a retail dealer, at 8837 W. North Ave., Milwaukee, WI 53226, although the company is no longer owned by the Netzow family.

NEUE LEIPZIGER MUSIKWERKE A. BUFF-HEDINGER; Leipzig, Germany. Successor to *Leipziger Musikwerke* and *Paul Ehrlich*..
NEUFEIND, R.; Friedrichstr. 215, Berlin, 1925-30. Established in 1888.
NEUFELD, DR. VERNON; Fresno, CA. Made 11 replicas of the *Mason & Hamlin* Style 110 organ ca. 1983.
NEUGEBAUER NACHF. C. BELL & CO.; 27 Andreasstr. 32, Aufg 3, Berlin. Established 1878. German branch of the *Bell Organ & Piano Co.* of Canada, which had been bought by a British group. See *W. Bell & Co.*
NEUMANN, E.; Berlin. Physharmonica maker, active from 1843 to about 1878.
NEUMANN, see *Weiser & Neumann.*
NEUSSER, JOHANN; 60 Mühlgasse, Neutitschein, Czechoslovakia. Active in 1930; probably the successor to *Karl Neusser.*
NEUSSER, KARL; Oberthorstr. 62, Neutitschein, Austria-Hungary. Established in 1827 and active at least through 1909.
NEW AMERICAN ORGAN; unusual instrument bearing the name of *F.N. Dexter*, West Winfield, NY, although probably not made by him. This organ has 17 sets of reeds on a single manual and three sets for the pedal. See *F.N. Dexter.*
NEW DOMINION ORGAN CO.; Saint John, New Brunswick 1875.
NEWELL, AUGUSTUS, & CO.; 42 Mich. Ave. in 1880, 93-113 Racine Ave. in 1885, Chicago, IL. Reed maker. Learned melodeon making in his native New Hampshire, then moved to Toronto, Canada about 1864 where he made reeds and reedboards. He moved his business to Chicago about 1870 and was caught in the great fire of 1871. He reestablished his Chicago business in 1874. The Racine Avenue factory, on the corner of Garfield Avenue, was built in 1882-83, after which he added the manufacture of celluloid piano and organ keys.
NEW ENGLAND ORGAN CO.; Marble Building, 1297-99 Washington St., Boston, MA 1871-80; 632 Harrison St. in 1881; 57 Washington St. in 1883; 32 George St., Roxbury until 1904; formerly *Boston Organ Co.*, later *New England Piano Co.*; acquired *Smith-American Organ Co.* after 1900 and was succeeded by *Merrill Piano Mfg. Co.* George B. Loring, pres., Daniel Needham, sec'y in 1880; George F. McLaughlin and Thomas F. Scanlon were proprietors in 1881 when the business was reorganized. McLaughlin continued the business and Scanlon left to go into piano manufacturing. Awarded a second prize at Sydney, Australia in 1878. Serial numbers: 1870—16143, 1881—57579, 1882—62360, 1887—98537.

 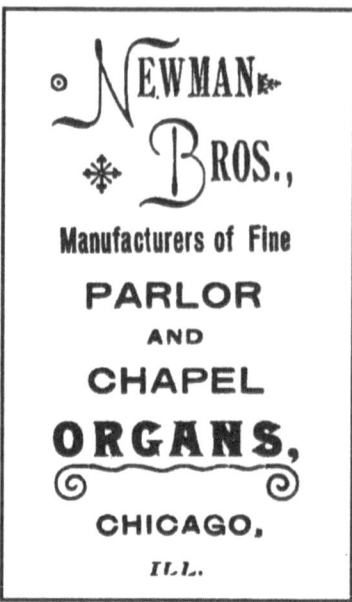

NEW ERA ORGAN CO.; North East, PA. Founded in the spring of 1873 by John A. Smith, who was superintendent and director, A.W. Blaine, president and director, and others. Organ Street in North East was named for the New Era Organ Co. Joseph H. Reed later joined the company, and the name was changed to *J.H. Reed* in 1880. It was seized by the sheriff in 1889. See *John A. Smith*.

NEW HAVEN MELODEON CO.; New Haven, CT. Established before 1860. Later renamed *New Haven Organ Co.* and active under this name 1881, 1883.

NEWMAN BROTHERS ORGAN CO.; 63-65 West Washington St. in 1883, 38-40 South Canal St. in 1889, West Chicago Ave. & Dix St. in 1899, Chicago, IL. Established in 1881 by John, Gustav R. and Charles W. Newman, incorporated 1892. Capacity in 1902: 4,000 organs per year. In business at least through 1920. Serial numbers: 1887—58955, 1920—76165/36345.

NEW WESTERN, organ auctioned in Concordia, KS in 1992.

NEW YORK CHURCH ORGAN CO.; Worcester, MA. Bought out *Hamilton-Vocalion Co.*, operated it for a few years and sold it to *Mason & Risch* in 1890; see *James Baillie-Hamilton*.

NICHOLLS, EDWARD, & CO.; 118 Mile End Rd., E London. Successor to *Dunn & Nicholls*. Harmonium manufacturer 1879-82. In 1883 became *Nicholls and Nicholls*, working at least until 1896.

A Newman Bros. parlor organ from the Gary Stevenson collection.

NICHOLS, ALGERON P.; Haverhill, MA. Reed and pipe organ maker, active in 1861.

NICHOLS, G.H.; VT. Melodeon maker ca. 1845-55, possibly as *Nichols Williams Co.*, (qv). George H. Nichols later moved to Wisconsin where he taught piano. In 1881 he is listed at 420 Nicollet Ave., Minneapolis, MN as a cabinet organ maker, with the factory at 110-112 Hennipin Avenue.

NICHOLS, M.O.; Clyde, Scotland, maker of the Dynamicon, 1881.

NICHOLS, M.O.; Syracuse, NY, established ca. 1850. Located at 293 Washington St., Boston, MA in 1850 and at 166 Washington St. in 1853. Claimed to be the "Original Inventor and Maker of the REED ORGAN." Became *Nichols & Woods* in 1852, later *Phelps & Chase*. Moses O. Nichols was granted US Patent 144409 on an organ reed in 1873.

NICHOLS WILLIAMS CO.; Barre, VT. Lap organ maker, 1845.

NICHOLS, see *Manning & Nichols*.

NICOLAUS & PAPPE, see *Förster & Nicolaus*, also *Straube & Co.*

NICOLAUS, RUDOLF; Grossfahner; Germany; established 1840; reed organ components.

NICOLE FRÈRES; rue Kleberg 17, Geneva, Switzerland; François and Raymond Nicole, proprietors, made music boxes with reeds; established 1839. Also made harmoniums at rue Vivienne, Paris.

NICOLE, GEO. H.; Prescott, WI.

NIEDERMAYER; Germany 1876.

NIHON FUKINSHA; 3-1 Nishikicho, Kanda, Tokyo. A mail order organ business, advertising in 1890.

NILSEN, AUGUST; Norway. Pipe organ builder, also made a few harmoniums.

NIPPON GAKKI CO., LTD.; P.O. Box 1, Hamamatsu, Japan. Successor to *Yamaha Gakki Seizo-sho*, 1897-1987; now called *Yamaha Corp.* (qv).

NISARD, TH.; Paris. Made a harmonium called the Clavier Grégorien, also made instruments with transposing keyboards. Exhibited at the Paris Exposition of 1855.

NISHIKAWA & SON; 30-Banchi, 2-Chome, Hinode-cho, Yokohama, Japan. Established 1885 by Torakichi Nishikawa (1846-1920). Awarded a third prize at the 3rd Domestic Industrial Exhibit in Tokyo, 1890. Nishikawa organs were among the highest quality made in Japan. Used Harmola reeds from Germany and Soprani reeds from the US. The instruments were sold by Hakubun-sha, Ginza, Tokyo and by Jujiya. Absorbed by *Yamaha* in 1921, becoming Yamaha's Yokohama factory. The Nishikawa name continued to be used at least as late as 1928. Serial numbers: 1895—1835, 1919—21216.

NOBLE, DON, & CO.; 316 S. Wabash Ave., Chicago, IL. Made a foot-pumped four octave C-scale folding organ, model 348, as well as electrically-blown models.

NORD, see *Wikstrom ach Nord*.

NORDDEUTSCHES METALLWERK WILLY SCHUMANN; Parkstr. 1, Finsterwalde, Germany; harmonium components; est. 1896.

NORDHEIMER ORGAN CO.; Toronto, Ontario.

NORLING, AUG.; Tradgardsgatan 15, Råå, Sweden. Established 1898. In 1930 shown at 15 Tradgaardsgatan, Sala, Sweden.

NORMANN, RUDOLPH; Neugasse, Reval, (now Tallinn), Estonia, 1903. Established 1845.

NORSK ORGEL-HARMONIUMFABRIKK; Snertingdal, Norway. Founded in 1870 or 1873 by Bernt Myrengen. He began building pipe organs on his farm in Vardal, eventually producing 63 instruments there. His son, Petter Berntzen, eventually took over the firm. Petter's son Bernhard continued the business, opening a piano store in nearby Gjøvik in 1916, and began making harmoniums in 1919. In 1928 Bernhard inherited a farm in Snertingdal from his mother's brother and moved the workshops there. Pipe organ production was resumed in 1937, by which time Bernhard's son Klaus had joined the firm. After World War II a new factory was built which continues in operation today, run by Klaus' son Hans and daughter Lilian Berntzen. Harmonium production was discontinued in 1976. Currently Norway's largest pipe organ manufacturer, located at 2826 Snertingdal, Norway. Serial numbers: 1951—3000, 1976—5456.

NOTHIG; invented the Harmonophone in 1895.

NUMMELAN HARMOONITEHDAS, see *Hedén*.

NUNNS, R., & CLARK; New York, NY. Maker of orgue-expressif, 1851. Also made a combination piano and reed organ using the *Coleman* attachment.

Mahogny — Bjerk — Alm — Eik,
Høyde 108 cm — Bredde 107 cm — Dybde 54 cm

Modell A.

Med denne modell har vi forsøkt å få fram et stilfullt møbel for hjemmet, samtidig som det vil være en pryd for enhver skole eller forsamlingslokale.

De lune og harmoniske linjer gjør at denne modell virker meget tiltalende, ved siden av at selve konstruksjonen gir inntrykk av solid, gjennomført håndverksmessig arbeide.

Denne modell leveres i tre forskjellige disposisjoner som omstående side viser.

𝔑𝔬𝔯𝔰𝔨 𝔒𝔯𝔤𝔢𝔩=𝔥𝔞𝔯𝔪𝔬𝔫𝔦𝔲𝔪𝔣𝔞𝔟𝔯𝔦𝔨𝔨 𝔄.𝔰
Snertingdal-Gjøvik

NUTTING, RUFUS; Hudson, OH, Romeo, MI; made the Aeolodeon, a combination piano and reed organ, patented in 1848; also inventor of the Aeolicon, made by *Hovey & Bachelder*. Rufus Nutting was originally from Randolph, VT, and was a brother of William Nutting, Jr. (1815-69), a pipe organ builder.

NYE, E.D. & G.G.; North Montpelier, VT. Makers of "seraphines, piano and cylinder key melodeons."

NYSTRÖM, C.G.; Spelmannsgatan 17, Kristinehamn, Sweden, 1903. Established 1875.

NYSTRÖM, J.P.; Karlstad, Sweden 1865 to at least 1903. Also known as *J.P. Nyström's Orgel & Pianofabrik*. In 1891 made and patented his Reform-Organ, a self-playing instrument with suction bellows, which used a cardboard disk.

Interior of a small church near Cedar Grove, North Carolina, May, 1940.

O

OAKES ORGAN CO.; Clinton, Ontario, Canada. Established in 1889. In 1890 the name was changed to *Clinton Organ Co.*
OAKES, see *Stimson, Oakes & Co.*
ODENBRETT, ABLER & CO.; Milwaukee, WI 1871-1888. Philip Odenbrett and Franz (Frank) Abler, pipe and reed organ makers.
OECKELEN, see *Van Oeckelen.*
OETTINGEN, ARTHUR VON; Leipzig, Germany. Designed and patented the Orthotonophonium in 1914, an enharmonic organ in which each octave contained 53 notes. The instrument was manufactured by *Schiedmayer.*
OKADA, YONEZO; Nishiku, Osaka, Japan. Exhibited at the 3rd Domestic Industrial Exhibition, Tokyo, 1890.
OKENFUSS, ANTON; Triester Str. 47, Vienna, Austria, 1909. Made hand-cranked street barrel organs with reeds.
OLBREI, J.; Jurjewstr. 461, Reval, Estonia in 1903; 6 Suur Tariu M, Tallin, Estonia in 1930. Established 1890.
OLIVER organ, sold by Northwestern Music House, Minneapolis, MN about 1905.

Playing an old organ for period dances at Turnbridge, Vermont, September, 1941.

ONO GAKKI-TEN; 3 Kita-Jinbo-cho, Kanda, Tokyo in 1929; 1 Tokiwa-cho, Kyobashi-ku, Tokyo in 1930. Harp maker. Made reed organs until the beginning of World War II.
ONTARIO ORGAN CO.; Toronto, Ontario 1884.
OOR, J.; 30 rue d'Arenberg, Brussels, Belgium. Established 1850. In 1930 doing business as *George Oor*.
ORCHESTRA SPOL SRO; 26 Jungmannova tr., Prague, Czechoslovakia 1930.
ORCHESTRELLE CO. LTD., THE; headquarters and sales rooms at Æolian Hall, 135-6-7 New Bond St., London; factory at Hayes, Middlesex, England 1911; subsidiary of *The Æolian Co.*, made the Orchestrelle and Gregorian Organs. See *The Mechanical Orguinette Co.*
OREAN Y CÍA.; 40 Ponzano, Madrid, Spain, 1930.
ORGANETTE, also orguinette, a small hand-cranked mechanical music box using reeds and a recording medium such as perforated paper rolls. In the earliest models, the perforations in the paper roll operated as valves, allowing air to flow directly to the reeds. Later models used pneumatic valves, permitting smaller perforations and consequently narrower rolls.

ORGATRON, an early electronic organ. Frederick Albert Hoschke worked on early versions, eventually patented by Benjamin F. Meissner and manufactured by *The Everett Piano Co.* It used conventional pallet valves to control air-blown vibrating reeds which acted as variable capacitors. The voltage across this capacitance was amplified and fed to a loudspeaker. *Wurlitzer* later bought the rights and produced a redesigned model in which the reeds vibrated continuously.
ORGAVAC, see *Ketterman.*
ORGELBAUANSTALT E.F. WALCKER & CO., see *Walcker, E.F., & Co.*
ORGEL-HARMONIUM-FABRIK RICHARD METZNER, see *Metzner, Richard.*
ORGEL- UND HARMONIUMBAUANSTALT MAX STIEHLER, see *Stiehler, Max.*
ORGUINETTE, see organette.
ORIENT ORGAN, brand name of *Ikeuchi Fukin* (qv) after 1906.
ORNTLICH, HANS; Postr. 8-9, Reval, Estonia. Piano and harmonium maker, 1896.
ORSZÁGH, SANDOR, & SÖHNE; Rákospalota Pazmany-Str. 33, Budapest, Hungary. Established 1861. Also shown as *Alexander Országh & Sohn*. Emerich and Ladislaus Országh, managers in 1909.
OSCHATZ, PAUL; Körnerstr. 49, Leipzig, Germany; Parkplatz 3, Zwickau, Germany in 1925. Harmonium maker.
OSHAWA ORGAN AND MELODEON MANUFACTURING CO.; Canada 1871-3; later *Dominion Organ & Piano Co.* See *Dominion Organ Co.*
ÖSTLIND & ALMQUIST; Esplanadgatan 125-6, Arvika, Sweden, established 1888 as a piano and harmonium manufacturer. Located at Vestra Hamngatan 18, Gothenburg, Sweden in 1903; A.N. Östlind and Anton Almquist, proprietors in 1903. See *L. Eriksen.*
OSTROROG, COMTE DE; 108 rue de Rivoli, Paris in 1860. Made a folding instrument for salon or portable use called the Mélodina, for which he was awarded a gold medal.
OTTO, F.G., & SONS; Jersey City, NJ. Made the Olympia organs.
OTZINGER, H.; Oberhofen bei Thun, Switzerland. Succeeded by *Heinrich Keller* in 1925.
OXFORD MANUFACTURING CO., INC.; 505 State St., Chicago, IL. Made the Oxford sewing machines, pianos and organs.

GENERAL SUGGESTIONS TO PERSONS PURCHASING

ORGUINETTES.

When one enters an Orguinette store, he is very likely to have the following questions on his mind. We will attempt to answer them in advance.

Question.—**Is the O. a musical toy or a real instrument?**

Answer.—The Boston firm who have turned their attention to selling it are not toy merchants. While the smaller instruments are capital playthings, they at the same time make good music; and the large Cabinet Instruments have all the capacity of a Reed Organ.

Question.—**Which style had I better buy?**

Answer.—The smallest instruments have quite enough reeds for the melody of popular airs. If you want a little expression, buy one a little more expensive; and if you wish a compact form in which to keep the slips containing the music, buy an instrument with rollers.

The "Cabinetto" has 25 reeds or two octaves. Of course that is an advantage for a parlor instrument, and the Cabinet Instruments, as they advance in price, give more and more variety.

Question.—**You say these are very durable. Does that mean that they cannot get out of order?**

Answer.—They are very simply, strongly, and durably made, and need but ordinary care. Of course, falling into the water or fire will be an injury, and being knocked about a nursery by young children is too much for the constitution of any machine. A very common trouble with reed instruments is caused by small substances, grains of sawdust, or of food, or pins, or bits of paper, falling into the reed box and stopping the vibration of the reeds. Such things are, very readily removed by a wire or needle. It is a good plan to place the smaller instruments, when not in use, in a secure box or drawer.

Question.—**For what can I use the Instrument?**

Answer.— First. "For fun!" The smaller ones, properly used, pay for themselves very quickly in the amusement they provide for a household. Also when brought forward in a company, they do their part very creditably in an evening's entertainment. As the smaller ones, which weigh but from 6 to 10 pounds, can be readily carried under the arm, they are just the things to have at a picnic, where they can serve as "band," can lead the "hymn singing," can provide good "boat music," and will do for "fiddler" at a dance.

Second.—As they have absolute pitch, they do very well to revive your memory as to any tune you have forgotten, and to keep you in tune. Also they will accompany informal "sings" well enough.

Third.—The largest instruments, skillfully managed, are quite competent to give fine and enjoyable music, and are well worth possessing by persons of fine musical taste, who cannot spend time to learn to play.

Fourth.—The Orguinette will answer an excellent purpose in a common school, for teaching new songs, etc.

REMEMBER THE NUMBER,

578 WASHINGTON STREET,

BOSTON.

Ditson, Haynes & Co.

Packard Organ Co. Style 371.

P

PACIFIC QUEEN organ; San Francisco, CA. Probably made by *Kimball* for a San Francisco dealer, *Philip Werlein*, 1212 Market St. (qv). Used "PipeTone Action." Serial number: 1902—256700.
PACKARD BROS.; Bridgewater, MA. Isaac T. and Edmund Packard. Melodeons were made under the Packard Bros. name as well as under each brother's name. For a time Isaac was in business as *Packard & Foss* and as *Packard, Foss & Co.* in North Bridgewater in 1850. In 1852 Isaac is shown at Campello, MA. In 1862 Edmund Packard sold his business to *Philip Reynolds*. Isaac moved to Chicago and formed *Packard, Keith & Talbot*, but the business failed at the time of the Chicago fire in 1871. Isaac then moved to Fort Wayne, IN where he formed the *Fort Wayne Organ Co.* (qv) with the backing of S.B. Bond, a banker. In 1900 the name was changed to *The Packard Organ Co*. At that time the factory had a capacity of 4,000 organs per year. The site of the former Packard factory in Fort Wayne is now Packard Park.
PACKARD, CALEB H.; Bridgewater, MA 1839 to about 1855. A melodeon maker, he was a cousin of Isaac and Edmund Packard. Sold out to *A.B. Marston* in 1855.
PAGE, POTTER & CO.; Ansonia, CT. Melodeon maker.
PAIN, ROBERT W.; 368 Second Ave., New York, NY 1861. Melodeon maker. Later associated with *Aeolian Organ and Music Co.*
PAJKR, RUDOLF, & CO.; Neu-Königgratzer Str., Hradec Kralové (Königgratz), Czechoslovakia 1930; Franz & Rudolf Pajkr, props. in 1903; M. Pajkr, proprietor in 1930, established 1894.
PALACE ORGAN CO.; Palace organs, see *Loring & Blake Organ Co.*
PALMER; Toronto, Ontario.
PANDHARPURKAR BROS., A.M.; Dandia Bazaar, Baroda, India, 1930.
PANHUBER, JOSEF; Ledererstr. 58, Ottensheim bei Linz, Austria, 1930; established 1920.
PAPE, CHR.; 8 rue Denis Papin, Asnières (Seine), France, 1883.
PAQUOT, S.; 46 rue Pioul, Huy, Belgium. Maker of pianos and harmoniums, 1914.
PARIS; Dijon, France. Made the Harmoniphon in 1836.
PARKER & SECOMB; Concord, NH 1866, 1867; Caleb Parker and Daniel F. Secomb, melodeon makers.
PARKER & TRACY; Concord, NH 1850; Samuel F. Parker and Luther Tracy.
PARKS, JAMES S.; Boston, MA 1855; melodeons.

PARTRIDGE & TABER; Worcester, MA; made reed organ cases for *Farley & Pearson* in 1847, see *Taber Organ Co.*
PASDELOUP & VIET; 16 rue Dauphine, Paris, 1883. Also shown as *Pas de Loupe & Cie.* Harmonium maker.
PASQUALE & CO.; 5 Phoenix Pl., Mount Pleasant, London, 1903, 1921. Piano and reed organ maker.
PATHÉ; chord organ with Italian steel reeds.
PATRIOT EXCELSIOR PIANO, ORGAN & HARMONIUM CO.; High Street, Chesham, Bucks., England, 1880-1885. Manager: Thomas Leadbetter.
PATSCHKE, J.W.; Hannover, Germany. Piano and harmonium maker, 1879.
PATTERSON, JAMES T.; Bridgeport, CT. Sold organs directly to the public and through clergymen, to whom he gave a 20% commission. Appears under this name in 1883 and 1889. Also shown as *Corwall & Patterson* in 1881 and as *Bridgeport Organ Co.* (qv) from 1877 at least through 1899.
PAUL & CO.; probably Germany. Maker of the Rigoletto harmonium and portable harmoniums, 1951.
PAUL & SONS; 2 Lower Chitpore Road, Calcutta, India, 1930.
PAULL & HAMILTON; 335-345 Church St., Lancaster, PA. Manufacturer of Lancaster organs. Listed in 1884 as church organ builders.
PAYNE, GEO., & CO.; Chicago IL.
PAYNE, W.T.; 208 Hoe St., Walthamston, London, 1906; 101 & 103 Approach Rd., London 1896. Harmonium and American organ manufacturers. By 1921 they were making pianos only.
PEACHEY, GEORGE; 72-73 Bishopsgate Street Within, E London, established 1828. Making and advertising seraphines in 1836. Piano and harmonium manufacturers to the Queen 1879-84.
PEAR, THOMAS; Carlton St., Cheltenham, England. Maker of a two-manual and pedal reed organ sold by Hickie & Hickie of Reading.
PEARL RIVER folding portable organs; China.
PEARPONT, E.A.; Derby (Ansonia), CT 1861. Manufacturer of melodeon keys, legs and cases.
PEARSON, JOHN G.; 203 Main St., Worcester, MA; established 1867; seraphines, melophines, Aeolians. Also *Farley & Pearson* (qv), and *Pearson & Loring*.
PEARSON & LORING CO.; Worcester, MA; successors to *Farley & Pearson*, 1852-67; Pearson sold out in 1867 and the firm became *Loring & Blake*.

PEASELEY, AARON MERRILL; Middle St., Boston, MA. Peaseley received a patent on Nov. 11, 1818 for a reed organ using either a suction or pressure bellows. This is the earliest reed organ patent in the United States and predates many of the early European developments. The patent document was destroyed in the Patent Office fire of 1836. It was not until 1884 that a copy appeared in the possession of the *Mason & Hamlin Company*, which sent it to Levi K. Fuller of the *Estey Organ Co*. Fuller in turn sent it on to the Patent Office, but it has since disappeared again.
PECCHIONI, REDENTO; Sissa, Italy, 1903, 1909.
PEDALION ORGAN WORKS; Amersfoort, Netherlands; see *van den Burg*.
PEERLESS organ, see *Foley & Williams*.
PELL, JOHN, & CO.; Globe Works, 194 Ashstead Row, Birmingham, England. Organ, piano and harmonium manufacturer, working until 1878.
PELOUBET, LOUIS MICHEL FRANÇOIS CHABRIER; maker of flutes, piccolos and clarinets, moved from New York to Bloomfield, NJ in 1836, located in Pierson's Mill at 3 Myrtle Court 1837-41, then at 86 Orange St. 1842-1869. Began making melodeons about 1842 and cabinet organs in 1849 when his son Jarvis joined him, the company then being known as *C. Peloubet & Son*. The factory burned 1869 and he erected two buildings across the street; formed the *Peloubet and Pelton Standard Organ Co.* in partnership with J.M. Pelton in 1873. The partnership broke up about 1882 and Peloubet continued operation as *Peloubet Standard Organ Co., Peloubet Columbian Organ Co.*, and as *Peloubet & Son*, with offices at 841 Broadway in New York. In 1888 began manufacturing the "Reed Pipe Top Organ." Chabrier died in 1885 and Jarvis continued operations as *The Peloubet Co.* until 1890 when he sold his business to *Lyon & Healy*, Chicago, and went to work for that company. Serial number: 1866—5307.
PELTON, JEREMIAH M.; 28 E. 14th St., New York, NY 1882; Excelsior organ; formerly a partner in *Peloubet, Pelton & Co.*
PENSO, VICTOR; 24-6 Duke Street, Brushfield Street, Bishopsgate, London. Piano and harmonium maker, advertised in 1898 and 1902.
PERÄLÄ, K.W.; Lapua, Finland. Also shown as *J.K. Perälä*. Established 1893.
PERCIVAL, J.; New York, NY. Also *J.P. Percival*, Auburn, NY. Seraphine maker.
PÉRICHON, ALEXANDRE; 10 rue de l'Odéon, Paris, 1883. Piano and organ maker. Honorable mention at the Nantes Exhibition in 1861.

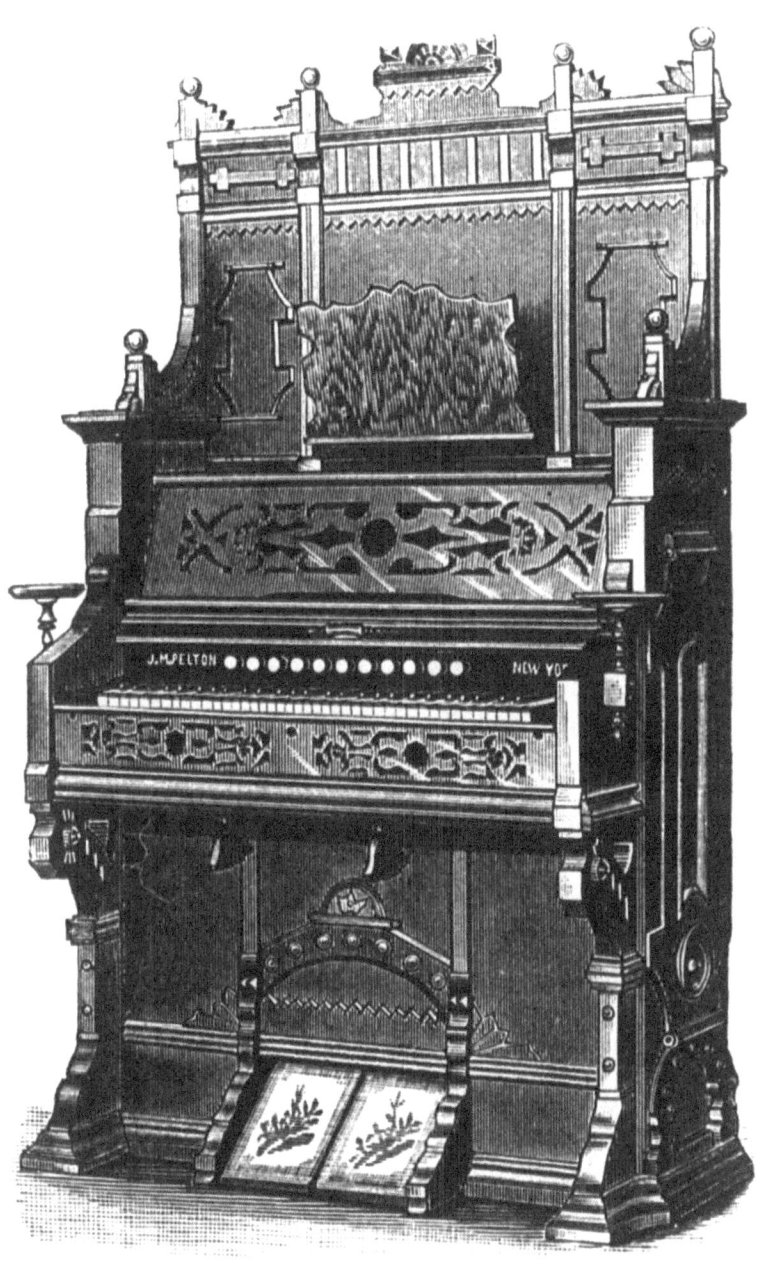

J.M. Pelton Excelsior Organ, Case No. 3, 1882.

PERL, BERNHARD; Dresdner Str. 107-109 in 1912, Dresdner Str. 117-121 in 1929, Waldheimer Str., Hartha i. Sachsen, Germany. Established 1882. Manufacturer of harmonium benches and harmonium players. Produced suction harmoniums from about 1909 to 1914.
PERMANAND; Nawad Shahad Sind, Pakistan. Made table harmoniums.
PERRY ORGAN CO.; Wilkes-Barre, PA., Scranton, PA. Listed in Wilkes-Barre directories from 1870 to 1888. In 1884, Joseph R., Tulbert H. and Lycus B. Perry, organmakers, are shown at 352 N. Main St., Wilkes-Barre. Moved to Scranton, where the factory building burned in 1889. Joseph R. Perry and his brother Samuel R. Perry were granted numerous reed organ patents during the period 1869-1878.
PETER, ANDREAS; Bahnhofstr., Hotel Neuberger, Eger, Czechoslovakia; established 1877. Still in business in 1957.
PETER, XAVER; see *Harmoniumbau Peter*.
PETERKIN, J.A.; 91 Union Street, Glasgow, Scotland. Harmonium maker 1879-80.
PETERS ORGAN CO.; St. Johns, Canada.
PETERSEN & STEENSTRUP; store at Kirkestrade 1, Copenhagen, Denmark, 1839-1920; 28 Bredgade, Copenhagen in 1930. Hans Axel Gilbert Steenstrup, proprietor, 1903. Harmonium manufacture began in 1884.
PETERSON, J., CO.; Moline, IL. Made the "Moline" organ. Active 1899-1920. See *Moline Cabinet Organ Co.*
PETERSON, THULIN & CO., see *Moline Cabinet Organ Co.*
PETITQUEUX-HILLARD; domaine de Biscaye, Lourdes, France, 1930.
PETRELLI, GIOVANNI; Talamona, Italy 1903, 1909, 1930.
PETROF, ANTON; Vorstadt Brünn, Königgrätz (Hradec Králové), Czechoslovakia. Harmonium and piano maker, established 1864. Awarded grand prizes at the international expositions in Ghent 1921, Barcelona 1929, Brussels 1935 and Paris 1937. Still in operation (1993) as a piano manufacturer. The following serial numbers may include both reed organs and pianos.

1900—13000	1960—87100	1967—124750
1920—33400	1961—89200	1968—134350
1930—46500	1962—92200	1969—145000
1940—58000	1963—95900	1970—156800
1950—67280	1964—102500	1971—169000
1955—75400	1965—108300	1972—182600
1957—80000	1966—116150	

*Seit Gründung 1864
über 55.000 Instrumente
erzeugt
Hervorragende
Erzeugnisse von Weltruf
Telegramme:
Petrof Königgrätz
Fernruf: Nr. 12
Postsparkassenkonto:
Prag Nr. 60.869
Fabriksfilialen:
Žilina, Masarykova 28
Fernruf Nr. 376
Pilsen, Wilsonstraße 14
Fernruf Nr. 1609*

ANT. PETROF

FLÜGEL- PIANINO-

HARMONIUM- UND ZUNGENORGELFABRIK

KÖNIGGRÄTZ, TSCHECHOSLOWAKEI

PETTERSON & GJELLESVIK, see *Kaland*.
PETTIS, see *Hoggson & Pettis*.
PEXTON, BARTHOLOMEW; York, England. Harmonium maker, active 1838-50.
PHELPS & CHASE; Washington Block, 65 South Salina Street, Syracuse, NY; successor to *M.O. Nichols* in 1852. Founded by *Austin C. Chase*, a piano dealer, and *Henry R. Phelps*. The partnership dissolved in 1864, and each one continued to manufacture organs under his own name. In 1866 Phelps went into partnership with H.N. Goodman.
PHELPS & GOODMAN; Syracuse, NY; melodeon makers 1866-69. Henry R. Phelps and H.N. Goodman. See *Phelps & Chase, H.N. Goodman*.
PHELPS, HENRY R.; 56 James Street, south side, between Pearl and Lock, Syracuse, NY; melodeon maker 1864-66. See *Phelps & Chase, Phelps & Goodman*.
PHILBROOK, see *Hastings & Philbrook*.
PHILIPP, GOTTLOB; Eulerstr. 533 in 1875, Cottbuser Str. 64 in 1899-1930, Forst i. Lausitz, Germany. Made pianos and a combination piano and harmonium. Operated until 1945.
PHILLIPS, DELOS; 18 N. Rose St., Kalamazoo, MI, 1867-81, 124 W. Main St., 1883-85. Music dealer, jeweler and organ manufacturer, established in 1854. Made the Star organ. Delos Phillips died about 1886 and was succeeded by George H. Phillips at the 124 W. Main St. address, probably retail only. See *Blakeman & Phillips, Cady & Phillips, Star Organ Manufactory*.

G. Philipp

in

Forst i/Lausitz,

Inhaber von Patenten und der gold. Medaille Frankfurt a/M. 1881.

Fabrik von **Pianinos** nach neuesten bewährten Erfindungen für alle Climaten, Discant mit Doppelscala. Mechanik schnell repetirend und sehr dauerhaft mit leichter Spielart. Auf Wunsch mit Prolongationspedal.

Specialität

die seit Jahren beliebt gewordene Combination:

Pianino mit Harmonium

PHILPOT-CAMP CO.; corner of Broadway and Ohio, Cleveland, OH 1872-78.

PHÖNIX MUSIKWERKE; Leipzig, Germany; organettes, see *Schmidt & Co.*

PIANOLA; originally a push-up piano player, invented in 1897 and patented in 1900 by Edwin S. Votey; see *Farrand & Votey* and the *Æolian Co.*

PIANO & ORGAN SUPPLY CO., THE; Corner Garfield and Racine Avenues, Chicago, IL 1912; reed and reed-board maker.

PIATRASRANTA, FIGLI; 4 via Sarzanese, Lucca, Italy, 1930.

PICARD; Paris. Maker of free-reed instruments, established 1830.

PICHLER, FRANCIS; 162 Great Portland Street, Oxford Street, London. Advertised 1851, 1862, 1863. Harmonium and pedal-harmonium manufacturer. Inventor and maker of the "Prize Medal Instrument" of 1851 and of the "Cottage Harmonium." Manufacturer to the late *W. Wheatstone*. Patented rounded black keys.

PICKENS, JAS., & CO.; 172 Hampton Street, Birmingham, England. Harmonium maker 1880-84.

PIEDMONT MFG. CO.; High Point, NC 1925; in business at least through 1930. Successor to *Shipman Organ Co.*, (qv)

PIERCE, LEVI M.; Chicopee, MA 1880; reed maker.

PIERCE, WILLIAM; 114 North St., Pittsfield, MA 1861, 1864. Established in 1846, possibly as *Cox & Pierce*. Later shown as *Wm. Pierce's Melodeon Factory*. Produced over 100 melodeons in 1859.

PIERCECCHI, VINCENZO; Campli, Italy, 1903.

PIGGOTT, BURCH & ALLEN; 85 Monroe Ave, Grand Rapids, MI, 1870. Listed as *George Piggott* in 1873, also shown as *Piggott & Burch* and as *Piggott, Sees & Johnson*. See *Empire Organ Co.*
PILCHER, W.; 19 Stockbridge Terrace, Pimlico, London.
PILVINEN, YRJÖ T.; (*Urkuharmooni- ja Pianotehdas Yrjö T. Pilvinen*), Tampere, Finland. Piano and harmonium manufacturer.
PINAULT; 21 rue d'Alsace, Angers, France.
PINET, LEON; 14 rue Morand, Paris about 1875; factory and warehouse at 64-68 cours de Vincennes 1913; showrooms at 52 rue de Bondy; had a branch in Belgium. Manufacturer of supplies for harmoniums and free reeds. Successor to *Estève* (qv), about 1875.
PIOLIAN ORGAN, see *Chute & Butler.*
PIONEER ORGAN CO.; High St., Crewe, England. Working until 1906.
PIRON; France. Made the Mélophilon in 1846, an orgue-expressif in the shape of a piano.
PITMAN, WILLIAM; instrument in the Lee Conklin Museum, Hanover, MI.
PITTALUGA E FIGLI; 17r via Gioffredo Mameli, Sampierdarena, Italy, 1930.

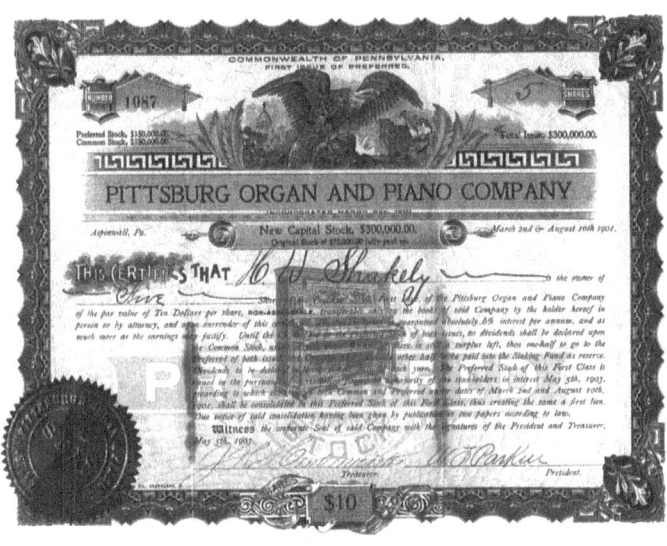

PITTSBURGH ORGAN & PIANO CO.; Aspinwall, PA in 1901; Shadyside Ave., Pittsburgh, PA in 1906. Incorporated March 2, 1901 as the successor to the *Hintermeister United Organ Co.*; W.F. Parker, president; J.H. Hintermeister, treasurer. Made the "Hintermeister" organ at least through 1912.

PITZSCHLER & CO.; Altenburg, Germany. Harmonium and harmonica retailer. Instruments with this name were made by others.
PIZENHOFFER, ALOIS; Deveeser, Austria-Hungary, 1909.
PLAG, LUDWIG; Schiessmauer-Weg 6, Knittlingen, Germany, reed maker, 1930; established 1881.
PLAYER PIANO CO.; current address 704 East Douglas, Wichita, KS 67202; Durrell Armstrong, proprietor; manufacturer of electric suction and pressure units and replacement parts for reed organs.
PLOTTS ORGANS; Washington, NJ, Ed Plotts, proprietor. See *Beatty & Plotts; Alleger, Bowlby & Plotts.*
PLYMOUTH MELODEON; organ with a rosewood case similar in shape to a square grand piano, with turned or octagonal legs. (No other information available.)
POHLMAN & SON; Princess Street and Hall Street, Halifax, Yorkshire, England. Piano and harmonium manufacturer 1878-80.
POINCTES; France. Made the Omni-harmoni-orgue in 1882. Alphonse Mustel said it had one name too many.
POIROT FRÈRES; Mirecourt, Vosges, France. Established ca. 1845. Maker of mechanical instruments including harmoniums.
POKORNY, JOSEF; Maria Theresia-Platz 3, Budapest, Hungary.
POLACEK, VACLAV; Rasinova tr., Rychnove nad Kneznou, (Reichenau a.d. Kněžna), Czechoslovakia. Active 1903-1905.
POLYPHON-MUSIKWERKE A.G.; Bahnhofstr. 61, Leipzig-Wahren, Germany. Established about 1890 by Gustav Brachhausen and Paul Riessner. Made the "Polyphon" disc music boxes. Also made a combination piano-harmonium, including an electrically operated model for movie theaters. In operation at least into the 1930s.
POOLE, HENRY WARD; Danvers, MA 1867-68; made a "Euharmonic Organ" with a special keyboard with 36 keys per octave, capable of playing 26 major and 13 minor scales. Poole received U.S. Patent No. 75753 on Jan. 28, 1868 for the keyboard. The organ itself was built by Joseph Alley of Newburyport, MA. See *Joseph Alley, Colin Brown, James Paul White, Enharmonic organ.*
POPPER, HUGO, & CO.; factory at Wittenberger Str. 8 in 1908-11, Bitterfelder Str. 14 in 1913, Leipzig-Eutritzsch, Germany; sales rooms at Reichstrasse 33-35 in 1900-11, Leipzig, German. Mechanical musical instruments including a player suction reed organ and the "Mystikon", a large player harmonium used in churches.
PORRO, DIEGO; Via S. Giuseppe, Brescia, Italy, 1903, 1930. Spelling uncertain, possibly Porre.
PORTER, GRAHAM, & CO.; 165 High Road, Lee, London, SE. American organ and harmonium manufacturer, 1896, 1900.
POSPISIL, JOS.; Pragergasse, Kolin, Hungary, 1903.

POTOCNIK, FELICE; via St. Antonio 13, Görz, Austria-Hungary, 1903.
POTTER, HERALD J.; (1798-1871), Bristol, CT. Originally a clockmaker, began making melodeons in 1849. Built a factory on Riverside Ave. Melodeon production ended in 1863 when the factory building was purchased by the Bristol Saw Co., later the Penfield Saw Works.
POTTER, see *Page, Potter & Co.*
POTVENIK, PIETRO; Görz, Austria-Hungary. Awarded a silver medal at Triest in 1882.
POUDRA. Reed maker, established 1840.
POWELL, FRANCIS; in 1880 at 47-48 George St., Euston Sq., NW London. After 1906 at 48 George St. American organ and harmonium manufacturer.
POWELL, H.; in 1878 at 46 Dollar St., Cirencester, Gloucester, England; in 1880 Powell & Sons; in 1882 at Dollar Street and Coxwell Street; in 1885 Powell W. Crown House, Stratton and Dollar Street; in 1887 at 120 Market Place, Cirencester; in 1894 until 1906 at 46 Dollar Street.
POWELL, see *Wood, Powell & Co.*
POWERS & STORY; Burlington, VT. Piano manufacturer, possibly also made organs. See *Story & Clark.*
PRANTE, JOSEPH; Chillicothe, OH. Active in 1889, last listed in 1903.
PRATT & COLBURN, see *Sommers & Colburn.*
PRATT, J.J.; Derby (Ansonia), CT 1861. Melodeon manufacturer.
PRATT, READ & CO.; Deep River, CT; manufacturer of organ keys and components. Predecessor company: George Read & Co.'s Ivory Comb Factory, established 1806, which became Ezra Williams & Co. in 1816, renamed George Read & Co. in 1829. In 1863 it combined with Pratt Brothers & Co. of Deep River and Julius Pratt & Co. of Meriden, CT to form Pratt, Read & Co. In 1938 it merged with Comstock, Cheney & Co., a piano action manufacturer of Ivoryton, CT and moved part of its operation to that town. George L. Cheney was president in 1925. It is still in existence as a major supplier of piano actions.
PRATT, see *Neal & Pratt.*
PRATTE PIANO CO.; 2461 St. Catherine in 1903, Montreal, Quebec 1889-1926. Founded by Louis-Etienne-Napoleon Pratte as a retail store in 1875. His younger brothers Antonio and Evariste were apprenticed to *Dominion Organ & Piano Co.* from 1882 to 1889 and also studied in New York. They began making pianos in 1889, and in 1895 formed the Pratte Piano Co. and acquired *G.W. Cornwall & Co.*, a reed organ manufacturer. In 1912 they introduced a harmonium with a transposing keyboard.

PREGNIARD, M.; Paris. Harmonium maker.

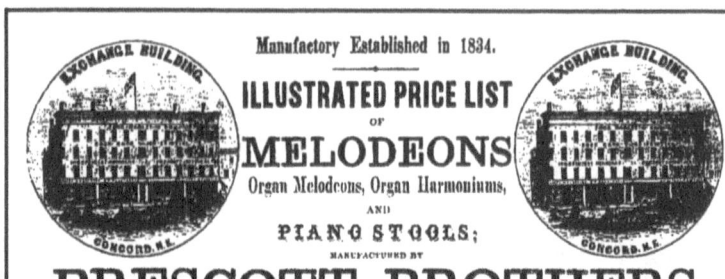

PRESCOTT, ABRAHAM; bass viol maker in Deerfield, NH from 1809 and Concord, NH from 1831; began making lap organs patterned after *Bazin*'s elbow melodeon in 1836, followed by melodeons; changed the firm name to *Abraham Prescott & Son* when his son Abraham J. came into the business in 1845. About 1849 the name *A. Prescott & Sons* was used. Abraham retired in 1850, and sons Josiah B. and Joseph W. joined the firm which was renamed *Prescott and Brothers*, and in 1853 *Prescott Brothers*, located at No. 3, Merchants' Exchange (upstairs) and later at the south end of Main St. near the railroad. *Joseph W. Prescott* withdrew from the company in 1853 and went into business for himself as a melodeon maker. Josiah died in 1857 and the youngest brother George D.B. Prescott joined in 1859. The name was changed to *Prescott Organ Co.* in 1871 and incorporated in 1881. They began manufacturing pianos in 1886 and in 1887 changed the name to *Prescott Piano & Organ Co.* When organ production ceased in 1891 the name was changed to *Prescott Piano Co.* In 1890 the office and factory were located at 71 South Main St. and the sales rooms were at 92 North Main St., Concord. The factory burned in 1896, and the company went out of business in 1912, ending the corporate life of one of the pioneers of the American reed organ industry. Serial numbers: 1845—515 & 541, 1848—1270.

PRESTO organ. Probably made by others with the Presto stencil.

PRESTON, BENJAMIN; York, England. Harmonium maker, active 1838-50.

PRESTON, J.; Chicago, IL 1880.

PREVOST; Paris. Reed maker, 1867.

PRICE, E., & SONS; 165 High Road, Lee, London SE, depots at Yeovil and Bournmouth. Harmonium dealer. An instrument with this name has been seen, indicating that Price was a harmonium maker or at least sold instruments made by others with its stencil.

PRICE, see *Totterdell & Price*.

PRIDHAM, W., & SON; Glaskins Mews, Clapton, London E. Harmonium and American organ manufacturer.

PRINCE & BACON; Buffalo, NY, established 1879; Samuel N. Prince, brother of George A. Prince, and *Charles E. Bacon* (qv), successors to *Prince & Co.*

PRINCE & CO.; 200 Main St. in 1846, Niagara and Maryland St. in 1851, later Pearl St., Buffalo, NY, also *Geo A. Prince & Co.*; closed about 1879. Founded in 1846. In 1849 Prince had 150 workmen and produced 75 to 80 instruments per week according to contemporary reports. Allowance must be made for nineteenth century puffery, as this volume does not correspond to actual production as revealed by the serial numbers shown below. Advertisements show the following cumulative production quantities:

| 1866—40,000 | 1869—45,000 | 1875—55,000 |
| 1868—40,000 | 1874—53,000 | 1876—56,000 |

Serial numbers:

1846—3870	1852—11200	1864—25000
1847—4700	1854—15200	1866—26400
1848—5400	1856—18070	1868—28000
1849—6200	1857—19604	1869—29100
1850—8000	1858—22068	1870—31000
1852—8885	1862—23900	1871—32595

PRINCESS organs; see *Chas. P. Bowlby*.

PRINZ, E.; Hohenstaufenstrasse 49, Schöneberg, Berlin, Germany. Organs possibly made by others with the Prinz stencil.

PRIOR, see *Barnard & Prior, MacNutt & Prior*.

PRITCHARD; Made a combination piano and harmonium, 1885.

PROCTOR, WILLIAM CHARLES, & SON; Wilson Place, Town Street, Bramley, Leeds, England, 1930.

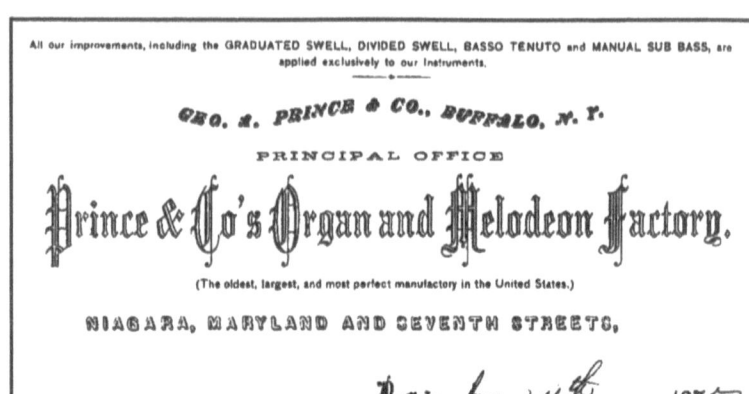

PROSPER & COLES; Paris. Harmonium with transposing keyboard.
PROSS, GSCHWIND & CO.; Stuttgart, Germany, established 1858 by C.H. Pross and Johann Georg Gschwind. Succeeded by *J.G. Gschwind Harmonium & Pianofortefabrik* before 1883.
PROSSER, HENRY J.; 20 Market Place, Frome, Somerset, England. Organ and harmonium manufacturer from at least 1883 to 1906.
PROUDMAN, J.D.; Measham, Derbyshire, England. Seraphine maker.

J.D. Proudman Seraphine.

W.W. Putnam & Co. parlor organ, case style 700.

PRUDEN & CORDLEY; northeast corner of Maiden St., Adrian, MI, 1859. Moses C. Pruden and Prof. J. Cordley, melodeon makers, also made organ actions for *J.R. Smith*, (qv). See *Prof. J. Cordley*.

PRZYIEMSKY; Bar-le-Duc, France. Piano and harmonium maker 1883.

PUCKLITZSCH, WILLI; August-Prebel-Str. 48, Zeitz, Germany 1930; formerly *G. Hohne*; harmonium case maker.

PUETZ, PETER J.; Milwaukee, WI 1860-69; melodeons.

PULKKILA, VELJEKSET; (Pulkkila Brothers), Kangasala, Finland.

PUNTER, JOHN WILLIAM, & CO.; showroom at 2 Old Market St., factory at High Street, Staple Hill, Bristol, England 1898, 1903, 1914. Also *Punter & Sons*. Made the Bristol organ.

PURNELLE, HONORE-JOSEPH (1872-1931); Noduwez, Belgium. Established in late 1900s, operated until 1931. Harmonium and piano maker. Awarded a silver medal at the Brussels Exhibition of 1910.

PUTNAM, W.W., & CO.; sales store at 103 West Main St., factory near C. & O. Railroad tracks in Staunton, VA; started in 1894 by William Wallace Putnam in a back room with two employees. Putnam, a native of Brattleboro, VT, had previously worked for *Estey*, then spent nine years with *Bell Organ & Piano Co.* in Guelph, Ontario. Later Herbert E. Fox, also of Brattleboro, became a partner. Fox had also worked for Estey and had been a partner in Bell Organ & Piano Co. By 1906 the company had 200 employees, 50,000 square feet of factory space and produced 6,000 organs per year. Made conventional parlor organs as well as the Little Giant folding organ. Later became *W. W. Putnam Co., Inc.*, and between 1920 and 1925 was absorbed by the Basic Furniture Co. of Waynesboro, VA.

Serial numbers:

| 1895—1117 | 1903—18956 | 1907—37923 |
| 1895—1320 | 1907—30876 | 1907—40065 |

Q

QUINCY ORGAN CO.; Quincy, IL.

R

RACELINA, J.; rue Gallieni, Tananarive, Madagascar. Harmonium maker, 1930.
RADAREED, an electromechanical reed organ demonstrated in Chicago in the late 1940s.
RADICE E FIGLI; 3 via Manzoni, Seveso S. Pietro, Italy, 1930.
RAFFIN, JOSEPH; (*Orgelbau Raffin*), Überlingen, Germany. Currently a builder of small hand-cranked street organs, mostly with pipes but some reed instruments. Reed instruments discontinued in 1996.
RAINER, see *Reyner.*
RAITH, GUSTAV; Gleditschstr. 1-1a in 1925, Charlottenburg 5, Fritschestr. 68 in 1940, Berlin, Germany. Piano and harmonium dealer in 1925, harmonium maker in 1940.
RÅLIN, A.G.; Birger Jarlsgatan 22, Stockholm; factory in Amal, Sweden, 1903, 1930.
RAMSDEN, ARCHIBALD; 12-13 Park Row, Leeds, England, also 103 New Bond St., London. A large musical instrument retailer, probably had organs made in Germany with the Ramsden stencil.
RAM SINGH, D.S., & BROS.; 344-48 Sardar Vallabhbhai Patel Rd., Bombay, India. currently manufacturing Indian table harmoniums.
RAMSPERGER, F.; An exhibitor of harmoniums at the Crystal Palace Exhibition of 1884 in London.

J. Ramsperger
Piano- und Harmonium-Fabrik
Stuttgart

empfiehlt seine anerkannt vorzüglichen Instrumente zu billigsten Preisen.
Specialität für Export. 5jährige Garantie.
Illustr. Preiscourante stehen zu Diensten.

RAMSPERGER, JOSEPH; Augustenstr. 9½ in 1875, Obere Heusteige 10 in 1879, Stuttgart, Germany. Piano and harmonium maker, 1883.
RAND, JACOB B.; Concord, NH 1856 through at least 1860. In 1857 employed 20 to 30 workers in his shop in Penacook, NH. Shown in Fisherville, NH in 1861. Manufacturer of the Granite State Piano Forte, melodeons, piano stools and pianoforte hardware.
RAND, JOHN, & CO.; 24a Cardington Street, Hampstead Road, London, 1848, 1855. Piano maker, also made the Aeolian Attachment, a reed organ device to be attached to a piano.
RANDALL, R.H.; Chicago, IL. A music publisher, also sold organs ca. 1893-94 with the Randall stencil, probably made by Kimball.

RANDALL, see *Fisk & Randall.*
RAPPE & CO.; Kingston, Ontario from about 1871 to about 1887.
RASKA, IGNATZ; Stramberggasse 595, Freiburg, Germany, 1940.
RATTI, EMILIO; Milan, Italy, 1883.
RATZKE, FERDINAND; Lissa, Germany. Organ and harmonium maker and piano dealer, 1883-90.
RATZKE, PAUL JR.; Lissa, Germany. Harmonium maker and piano dealer, 1883.
RATZMANN, FRIEDRICH HEINRICH; Ohrdruf, Germany. Äolodikon maker, active ca. 1829.
RAUTAVUORI JA SUOMEN URKUHUOLTO; Kangasala, Finland.
RAYGAERT FRÈRES; 27 rue Adam, Grammont, Belgium, 1930.

The United States Organ
THE FINEST IN THE LAND.
Manufactured by F. L. RAYMOND,
Cleveland, O.

RAYMOND, F.L.; 131 Windsor Ave., Cleveland, OH, 1889-1913; manufacturer of the United States Organ. In 1913 it was absorbed by the Janssen Piano Co., discontinued operation in Cleveland and apparently discontinued organ production. See *Whitney & Raymond.*
RAYNARD, S.A.; 35 calle Talleres, Barcelona, Spain, 1930.
RAYNER, see *Reyner, J.*
RCA VICTOR; reed organ made in the 1960s, probably in Japan; two ranks, electrically winded.
READING ORGAN MANUFACTORY.; Reading, PA, 1882-85. Factory located at the corner of Washington and Ash Streets, show room at 517 Penn St. (Ash Street has been renamed Madison St.) Dr. Franklin J. Kantner, proprietor. He was a son of Joel Kantner, a pipe organ builder.
RECHNAGEL, LEO; Fredensborg, Denmark, 1930.
REDDING & HARRINGTON; Worcester, MA; reed maker; *A.H. Hammond* bought a one-third interest and eventually bought control. The firm then became *A.H. Hammond & Co.*
REED, JOSEPH H., (1846-1923), North East, PA; see *New Era Organ Co.*

REED, J.W. & SONS; Handel Works, 32 Hanover St., Islington, London, established 1868. Later made pianos. Listed at 2a Elfort Street, Drayton Park, London in 1914.
REED & SON; 47 Dearborn St., Chicago, IL. Alanson Reed, Reed's Temple of Music, 1869.
REEVES & CO.; 131 New Cross Road, 15 Waterloo Bridge Road, London. Piano and harmonium manufacturer, 1883.
REGAL organ, see *Lorenz Supply Co.*
REGENT organ, see *William Bogg & Sons.*
REICH, Furth, Germany. Invented the Eolodicon, a six-octave type of physharmonica, about 1821.
REISER, J.H.; Cologne, Germany. Harmonium ca. 1860.
REISNER, PROFESSEUR A.; 5 passage Colbert, Paris. Established 1832. Orgue-expressif maker.
ŘEMEK, JOHANN; Poric 1039, Prague, Czechoslovakia, 1903. In 1930 shown as Jan Řemek at 13 Smečky, Prague.
REMLER, WILHELM, & SOHN; Friedrichstr. 235, Besselstr. 17 in 1886-90, Berlin. Äolodikon maker, about 1853. Pipe organ and harmonium maker, 1883.
RENBJØR, see *Isachsen & Renbjør.*
RENDALL, W.C.; Adelaide, Australia. Pipe Organ and reed organ maker, 1883. Awarded a first prize for a harmonium at the Adelaide Fair of 1881.
RENNER, JOSEPH; Regensburg, Germany. Organ dealer who sold organs made by others with his stencil, 1883, 1885. *Wilhelm Renner* was listed at Gartenstr. 22, Ludwigsburg in 1940, and *Louis Renner* is still in business at Fritz Reuter Strasse 18, Stuttgart D7000.
RENSON, A.J.; 16 rue des Guillemins, Liege, Belgium. Piano and harmonium maker, 1883.
RESTAGNO, VICENZO; 90c Vittorio Emanuele, Turin, Italy, 1930.
REVERCHON & MERLAVAUD; Saint-Etienne, France. Made the Odestrophedon in 1842.
REYNER, J.; (also Rainer, Raynor) Kingston, Ontario from about 1871 to about 1885; melodeons. Also shown as *Raynor, Sweatman & Hazelton* in 1875.
REYNER, JOSEPH; 21 Woodhouse Lane, Leeds, England. American organ maker 1879-81.
REYNOLD, J., & CO.; 11 Lindsay Street, Calcutta, India, 1930.
REYNOLDS ORGAN CO.; Chicago, IL.
REYNOLDS, PHILIP; probably Bridgewater, MA; successor to *Edmund Packard*, 1862.
REYNOLDS & THOMPSON. (No other information available.)

REYNS, S.G.; Slachthuiskade 2, Rotterdam, Netherlands. Founded by S.G. Reyns (1881-1977); produced organs until 1933.
RICH, see *Clark & Rich*.
RICHARD, J., & CIE.; 10 St.-Gilles, Paris; also *Couty & Richard*, 1867-78, then *J. Richard & Cie.* from 1878 until at least 1903, when the location is shown as Etrépagny, France. Jean Richard, proprietor. Awarded a bronze medal at the Paris Exposition of 1878. Succeeded by *R. Gaboriaud*.
RICHARDSON, GEO.; 44 Stonegate Street, York, England, 1858. Harmonium maker.
RICHARDSON, JOHN P., see *Treat & Richardson*.
RICHARTZ, HEINRICH; Hauptstr. 159 in 1912, Kölner Str. 159 in 1930, Kommern bei Euskirchen Germany. Established 1885. Organ and harmonium maker and dealer. Harmonium production ended in 1936.
RIESENBURGER, P.; 80 boulevard du Nord, Brussels, Belgium in 1889; 2-4 rue du Congres, 1897-1914. Harmonium and piano maker.
RIETHEIMER, C.; Heusteigstr. 19 in 1866, Heusteigstr. 21a in 1870, Stuttgart, Germany. Harmonium maker, 1883. Medallions: Amsterdam 1869, Graty 1870, Eger 1871, Linz 1871, Ulm 1871, Vienna 1873. Also see *Teck-Harmoniumfabrik*.
RIGOLETTO; a table harmonium with an electric blower, probably made in Germany.
RILEY, HENRY; instrument manufacturer, importer and dealer, 23-25 Constitution Hill, Birmingham, England in 1906. Listed as Henry Riley & Sons Ltd., piano and organ dealers, at the same address in 1921. See *Joseph Riley*.
RILEY, JOSEPH; 20B-C Constitution Hill, Birmingham, England in 1880, instrument maker; manufacturer and dealer at Constitution Hill & Hampton St. in 1884; at 25 Constitution Hill in 1890; manufacturer, importer and dealer at 23 and 25 Constitution Hill and 30 Corporation St. in 1896 and 1900. Established in 1851. See *Henry Riley, W. Joseph Riley*.
RILEY, W. JOSEPH; instrument manufacturer, importer and dealer, 56-58 Corporation St. and Martineau St., Birmingham, England in 1906.
RINKOWSKI, ALFRED; Weissenfelser Str. 18 in 1920, Weberstrasse 19 in 1930, Zeitz-Aue, Germany. Established in 1920, harmonium production ended in 1932. Harmoniums for church, school, concert and home in all sizes.
RISBERG, F.; Stockholm, 1883.
RISBERG, JOHANNES; Stampgatan 6, Gothenburg, Sweden 1903, 1909.
RISCH, see *Mason & Risch*.

RISSMANN, C.C.; Calenbergerstr. 39 in 1886, Stader Chaussee 32 in 1930, Hannover, Germany. Piano and harmonium maker. Established 1846.

RITZ, LOUIS, & CO.; Neuerwall 29 in 1886-90, Catherinenhof, Holzbrucke 7-11, Hamburg, Germany, 1930. Factory at Kircheim u. Teck. Established 1875.

RIVOREDA, G.; Via Ormea 34, Turin, Italy, 1903. By 1930 shown at 6 bis via Vittozzi, Turin.

ROBERTS, ALFRED G.; Laxon St., Long Lane, Bermondsey, London 1878, 1883. Made pedal harmoniums with 1, 2 or 3 manuals and portable harmoniums. Established 1848.

ROBERTSON & CO.; 69 Essex Road, London N. Advertised as an American organ maker in 1900.

ROBERTSON, R.F., see *T. d'Almaine.*

ROBERTSON, WILLIAM J.; 107 Tottenham Rd., London 1877. Established 1847. William Robertson died in 1883. No advertisements after 1885.

ROBINSON & SONS; Meredith, NH. Flat top and parlor organs, possibly made by *G.W. Ingalls. J.S. Robinson* active in Meredith 1899-1901. Serial Number: 1881—131.

ROBINSON, see *Darley & Robinson, Lang & Robinson,* and *H.A. Ivory & Co.*

RODEHEAVER CO., THE; 218 South Wabash Ave., Chicago, IL, 1930. Folding reed organs.

RODOLPHE, ALPHONSE, & FILS; 15 rue Chaligny, Faubourg St.-Antoine, Paris 1883; also at 64 rue Amelot, Paris; factory in Nogent-sur-Seine, France. Alphonse Rodolphe worked for *Fourneaux* before establishing his own business in 1848. Awarded a gold medal at the Paris Exposition of 1878. Advertised harmoniums in the "Franco-American Syste in 1889. Some harmoniums carry the name *Rodolphe Fils & Debain*. Became *Rodolphe Fils* in 1903, absorbed *Debain* before 1903, succeeded by *A. Chaperon* (qv).

RODRIGUEZ, RICARDO; 3 Ventura de la Vega, Madrid, Spain, 1903; established 1890.

ROETHINGER, E.A.; Schiltigheim, Alsace, 1913; 44 rue Jacques-Kable, Strasbourg, France, 1930. Established in 1893.

ROLFE, WILLIAM; 112 Cheapside, London. Seraphine maker, established 1797. In 1899 shown as *William Rolfe & Sons*.

ROSCHE, GEO. F., & CO.; Elmhurst, IL, a music publisher, active at least in the period 1915-28. Organs with this name were undoubtedly made by others with the Rosche stencil.

A William Rolfe seraphine from the collection of Leonard Mann, Chicago.

ROSE, IRA; Akron, OH 1855-59; successor to *H.B. Horton*.

ROSS & WEST; East Poultney, VT. Established in 1849 by Paul M. Ross (1800-1870) and Elijah West. Chester Brown joined in 1851 and the firm name became *Ross, West & Brown*. Brown left in 1852 and Joseph Morse (1792-1876) and his son Joseph Harris Morse (1819-1856) joined the firm, which became *Ross, West & Morse*, then *Ross, Morse & Co.*, and soon after *Ross & Morse*. The original factory building had formerly been a blacksmith shop, and is still in existence, occupied by the Poultney Historical Society. The factory also occupied a part of J.H. Morse's mill on the river. J.H. Morse was killed in an accident at the mill in 1856 and the company declined after that, eventually closing in 1864. L.F. Kellogg then joined Paul Ross to form *Ross & Kellogg*, which operated until 1875.

ROSSBERG, E.; Mathidlenstr. 35 in 1877, Munzgasse 11, Neugasse 11 in 1880, Neugasse 48 in 1888-1902, Ziegelstr. 2 in 1909, Neue Gasse 30 in 1930, Dresden, Germany. Instrument maker and tuner in 1877, listed as a harmonium and harmonium reed maker 1886-1912. Also listed as *Carl August Rossberg*.

ROTH, HOLLERAN & MILES; Waterloo, NY 1871; established in 1866 as successors to *Stilwell & Genung*. Also operated as *Waterloo Organ Co.*

ROTHE & SCHÖNBRODT; Wolfgang Str. 14, Eisenach i. Thur., Germany. American organs a specialty. Established in 1895 by Ernst Rothe and August-Franz Schönbrodt. Closed 1920.

ROUSSEAU, ALEXANDRE; 50 rue Notre-Dame des Champs in 1864; 19 rue Schomer in 1883; 113-115 rue de Vaugirard in 1919 and 1921, all in Paris. Won a gold medal at the 1900 Exhibition in Paris. Succeeded by *Gilbert* (qv).

ROUSSEAUX, W.C.; Jette, Brussels, Belgium. Piano and harmonium maker and retailer, 1914.

ROUSSELOT; France 1876.

ROWE, JOHN T.; Aylmer, Ontario. Active 1902-06.

RUCHE, J., & FILS: 19 rue Claudius-Pernet, Lyon-Montchat, France, 1930.

RUCK, JOSEPH; Boston, MA in the 1870s. Previously listed as an instrument maker in North Bridgeport, MA in 1861 and later as a music dealer in Roxbury, MA.

RUCK, Y.; melodeon maker.

RUCKH, BALTHASAR; Schuhhausgasse 5, Ulm a. Donau, Germany, 1930; established 1904. Listed as a harmonium reed maker in 1954 located at Hampfergasse 24. Harmoniums with this name were possibly made by others.

RUDD, A., & CO.; 74 Dean St., London W., established 1837. Piano and harmonium manufacturer 1878-96. An advertisement appeared in 1906 for *Rudd & Debain*.

RUDERT, G.; Gross-Zschocher, Schleussiger Weg, Leipzig, Germany; Gustav Rudert, proprietor, established 1898. also listed as *Rudert & Kunze*. Closed about 1914.

RUDOLPHE, H.; boulevard de Montparnasse, Paris.

RUDOLPHE, MAX, & SOHN; 15 Warwick Court, London, 1903, 1906.

RUSHWORTH & DREAPER; Great George St., 11-17 Islington (in 1938), Liverpool, England; manufactured the Apollo reed organ (qv) from about 1911 to 1940. Altogether they made about 336 reed instruments. Still in operation as Rushworth's Music House, Ltd., Whitechapel, Liverpoot 1, England. The pipe works is in St. Anne St., Liverpool 3.

Designed and BUILT by **Rushworth & Dreaper Ltd.** Church, Chamber and Concert ORGAN BUILDERS

Showrooms, 11-17 Islington, LIVERPOOL. Telegrams: 'APOLLO,' Liverpool.

LONDON:—The CHAPPELL PIANO CO. Ltd., 50 New Bond Street, W.1.

RUST, see *Manning Organ Co.*
RUTLEY, GEORGE; 15 Panton St., Haymarket, W. London 1878, printer of name tablets for harmoniums.

RUTT & COWING; London, ca. 1900. Founded by Robert Spurden Rutt and Bertram Cowing. Went out of business before 1909, when Rutt is listed as a pipe organ builder.
RYRFELDT, C.J.; Mellerud, Sweden, 1930.

S

SAARIMAA, JUHO; Lapua, Finland. Lapua was the largest harmonium making center in Finland in the late 1800s, with six factories. Juho Saarimaa and *Elias Sillanpää* (qv) made the first harmonium in Lapua.
SÄCHSISCHE DRAHT- UND METALLWAREN-FABRIK LEISTNER & CO.; Wurzer Str. 26-28, Leipzig, Germany; Alex. Claassen & Bruno Moding, proprietors, established 1890, in business at least through 1930; metal components for harmoniums.
SÄCHSISCHE HARMONIUM-WERKSTÄTTEN, see *Löffler & Co.*
ST. MARY'S ORGAN COMPANY; Cadogan Terr., London, 1883.

ST. PAUL ORGAN CO.; 280 Western Ave., St. Paul, MN. Joseph Lorenz, proprietor. Owned by Lugar Furniture Co. Last listed in 1901. This is the same organization as the St. Paul Pipe Organ Manufactory. Reed organs with this name are almost certainly stencil organs, possibly made by Kimball. Lorenz, a pipe organ maker, was previously active in Cincinnati.
SAITA, MITSUNORI; Japan. Made the first reed organ built in Japan from components of a *Mason & Hamlin* organ in 1881. This instrument is now in the museum of the Tokyo National University of Fine Arts and Music.
SAKAI GAKKI-TEN; 6 Monzen-cho, Nakaku, Nagoya, Japan, 1930.
SAKS, I.; 2 I. Toe tan, Parnu, Estonia, 1930.
SALAÜN, SCHWAAB ET CIE.; Paris. Awarded medal of honor at the Paris Exposition of 1867 for a 5½ rank harmonium.
SALEM BROS.; flat top organ. (No other information available.)
SAMES, JACOB; Birmingham, England, established 1855. Advertised as an accordion maker at 8 Suffolk St. in 1858; then as an accordion and harmonium maker at 6 Suffolk St. in 1861. In 1871 he is shown as a harmonium maker at 5 & 6 Suffolk St. and in 1878 as an American organ and piano maker at 5 & 6 Suffolk St. and at 6 Windmill St. By 1883 the firm name had changed to *J. Sames & Sons* and they were manufacturing American organs and harmoniums "by improved steam machinery" at 14 & 16 Holloway Head, Birmingham, and had a London showroom at 16 Long Lane, Aldergate St. In 1888 and '89 shown as *Wm. Sames* at 331 Euston Road, London, steam factories in Birmingham making 3,000 instruments per year. In 1890 the address is 14-16-18 Holloway Head; in 1900 it is *Wm. Sames Ltd.*, piano and organ manufacturer, 1 Holloway Head and 21 Ombersley Rd., Birmingham. In 1903 a sales room was established at 155-157 Corporation St., Birmingham, which remained in use through 1940. From 1910 through 1930 the Ombersley Rd. address was also shown for Wm. Sames Ltd., piano manufacturer.
SAMICK MUSICAL INSTRUMENTS MANUFACTURING CO., LTD.; 316-48 Hyosung-dong, Buk-ku, Inchon, Korea. Established 1958. Currently a maker of pianos, guitars, violins and reed organs. Hyo Ick Lee, president 1983.
SANCHEZ, ALFREDO; Albox, Almería, Spain, 1903.
SANDER, GUSTAV; Kreuzstr. 15a in 1884, Reichenstr. 22 in 1885-1908, Hildesheimer Str. 15b in 1909-16, Hildesheimer Str. 67 in 1917-39, Saarstr. 75 in 1940-62, Braunschweig, Germany; established in 1860. Later listed as *Gebruder Sander*, Hugo and Hans Sander, proprietors. Organ and harmonium makers.
SANSEIDO; 7,8 Jinbocho, Kanda, Tokyo. Factory at 22 Nishi-Edogawacho, Koishikawa, Tokyo; Mr. Kaiho, engineer. Received a gold

prize at the Japan and Great Britain Exhibition in Tokyo, 1910. Still in business as a book publisher.

SARDARFLUTE; Chaitsingh, Gurbaksing & Bros., 292 Sardar Vallabhbhai, Bombay, India. Table top organ.

SATO, T., & CO.; 360 Shimoyamate 7-chome, Kobe, Japan, 1930.

SAUNDERS; at E. Lachenal's Concertina Manufactory, 4 Little James St., Bedford Row, London WC. Harmonium maker ca. 1875.

SAUTTER, CHRISTIAN; Osterwiese 14 in 1910, Markgröninger Str. 11 in 1931 and 1951, Marbacher Str. 62 in 1949, Ludwigsburg-Eglosheim in Württemburg, Germany. Located in Spaichingen, Germany in 1883. Founded 1819. The following serial numbers may include both pianos and reed organs. Note the renumbering after World War I.

1825—401	1954—14800	1968—41450
1840—900	1958—19200	1969—43800
1870—2500	1960—23200	1970—46200
1880—3300	1961—23900	1971—48700
1900—5000	1962—26200	1972—51400
1910—6002	1963—28300	1973—54300
1914—6500	1964—32500	1974—57000
1919—100	1965—34800	1975—59600
1939—4500	1966—37000	1976—62300
1952—13200	1967—39200	1977—65000

SAWYER, J.W.; established 1885. Located at 141 Town St., Leeds 1900-1952; 21 Barton View, Beeston Hill, Leeds, England 1903; Ideal organ, see *Beeston Organ Works*. John William Sawyer died in 1907; his brother Percy Alfred Sawyer operated the company until his death in 1952. Built organs of all sizes up to a four-manual & pedal with 86 stops and 4,444 reeds and a three-manual and pedal with 92 stops and 5,000 reeds.

SAWYER, T. & E.; corner of Main and Water Streets, Nashua, NH., 1857-58. Edmund Sawyer was shown as a principal in *B.F. Tobin & Co.* (qv) in 1853 at the same address. Listed in Nashua directory 1857-58 as T. & E. Sawyer, Tristram Sawyer, Jr. and Edmund Sawyer, proprietors. Probably successors to B.F. Tobin. Employed ten hands, made about four melodeons per week. Later moved to Vermont.

SAX, ADOLPHE; Brussels, Belgium. In 1841 made a kind of reed organ driven by steam under five atmospheres of pressure.

SCHAEFER, AUGUST MAX; Creglingen, Germany. Organ and harmonium maker, 1909-29.

The... "IDEAL"
1, 2, 3, & 4, Manual and Pedal Organ

FOR THE

Organist's Home, Chapels, Mission Halls, Schools, Lodges, &c.

High-Class Instruments built to Customers' own specifications.

J. W. Sawyer,

Pipe & Reed Organ Builder,

Beeston Organ Works,

Leeds, . . .

Opposite Beeston Station, G.N.R.

(Established 1885.)

Specialities:

REAL ORGAN TONE, PROPER ORGAN POSITIONS.
ENLARGED SCALE REEDS ON THE MANUALS. . .
REVERSIBLE COMPOSITION PEDALS. . . . .
PISTONS & ALL PIPE ORGAN APPOINTMENTS.
EXTRA LARGE SCALE REEDS ON THE PEDALS.
SPECIALLY DESIGNED CASES WITH. . . . .
    ACOUSTICAL COMPARTMENTS AND . . .
    VIBRATING SOUND BOARDS ON . . . .
    AN ENTIRELY NEW PRINCIPLE. . . . .

SCHAEFER, FRED; Pekin, IL, 1880. "Manufacturer of Parlor and Chapel Organs and Dealer in Pianos, Organs, Musical Merchandise, Books, Stationery, Toys, Notions, Fancy Goods." Succeeded by *Koch Brothers, Inc.* in 1881.

SCHAEFFER, C.; 397 Kingsland Road, entrance on Derby Road, London NE, 1899. Advertised in 1900 as a reed organ maker.

SCHAFFNER, JACOB; 128 E. 27th St., New York, NY 1861. Melodeon maker.

SCHAKE, H.D.; Hannover, Germany. Harmonium maker, 1879.

SCHANTZ ORGAN CO.; Orville, OH; formerly *Tschantz Organ Co.*, well-known pipe organ builder, founded by Abraham J. Schantz in Kidron, OH. Made reed organs from 1873 to 1877.

SCHATZEL, JOSEPH; Vienna. Physharmonica maker.

SCHÄUFELE, FERDINAND; Martinstr., Webergasse 3 in 1892, Esslingen, Germany. Established 1879. Harmonium maker to 1930.

SCHEFFEL & STOLPE; Allentown, PA, 1869, 1875.

SCHEYTT, C.G.; Ensinger Str. 208, Illingen-Stuttgart, Germany; established 1878. Awarded an honorable mention at the Stuttgart Exposition in 1881. In business at least until 1930.

SCHIEDMAYER, J. & P.; Neckarstrasse 12, Ulrichstr. 1-5, Stuttgart, and Königgrazerstrasse 81, Berlin, Germany. Julius and Paul Schiedmayer were the younger sons of Johann Lorenz Schiedmayer, himself the son and successor of Balthasar Schiedmayer, the founder of the piano manufacturing firm *Schiedmayer & Söhne*. After studying harmonium making in London and then in Paris with Debain and Alexandre, they began building harmoniums in 1853 as J. & P. Schiedmayer. In 1903 listed as *Schiedmayer Pianofortefabrik*, Paul & Max Schiedmayer, proprietors. Max was Paul's son. Made harmoniums as late as 1950. Made both pressure and suction harmoniums as well as players. Also made the "Orthotonophonium", an enharmonic harmonium designed by Arthur von Oettingen. Associated with Schiedmayer & Söhne. The following serial numbers include both pianos and reed organs.

1853—1	1930—60200	1958—54132
1880—14300	1935—62100	1960—67000
1900—31000	1940—63400	1961—67200
1910—43000	1950—64200	1966—68900
1920—51800	1952—64800	1969—69618
1925—55600	1955—65550	

SCHIEDMAYER & SÖHNE; Necharstrasse 14-16 and Urbanstr. 27, Stuttgart, Germany; established 1809, operating in 1930. Associated with *J. & P. Schiedmayer*. The following serial numbers include both pianos and reed organs.

Älteste Klavierfabrik Süddeutschlands. Seit 7 Menschenaltern im Klavierbau tätig!
Balthasar Schiedmayer verfertigt 1735 sein erstes Instrument (ein Clavichord).
Älteste und Stamm-Firma

Schiedmayer & Soehne
Pianofortefabrik, gegründet 1809
Stuttgart, Neckarstrasse 16

Fabrikation von:
Flügeln, Pianinos, Kunstspiel-Pianos und Harmoniums
in vollendeter Ausführung
nach eigenen und nach Künstlerentwürfen

Export nach allen Erdteilen, besondere Bauart für Tropenklima

Filialen: Ulm a. D. und Saarbrücken

Adresse und Schutzmarke bitte genauest zu beachten!

1880—11068	1935—46017	1968—54797
1890—15157	1938—47200	1969—124593
1900—20011	1950—53100	1970—124866
1910—28611	1952—53180	1971—125163
1920—35321	1961—54132	1972—125457
1925—40130	1962—54293	1975—126131
1928—43372	1966—54600	1977—126375
1930—45037	1967—54700	

SCHIERKS, EGON; Nürnberg, Germany.
SCHINDLER, HARMONIUMBAU; Am Neuen Markt 26, Bremen, Germany, 1925-30. E. Schindler, prop. Organ and harmonium maker.
SCHIRLING, JOHANN A.; Kleinzschocher, Germany in 1921; Sophienstr. 7, Leipzig in 1924. Harmonium maker and dealer.
SCHLEICHER, J., & HOCHSTUHL; 55 Bristol St., Boston, MA; est. ca. 1881, maker of combination reed and pipe organs, Boston.
SCHLESINGER, see *Grunzweig & Schlesinger*.
SCHLIMBACH, BALTHASAR; Wurzburg, Germany. Built an Aeoline, 1854. Listed as Schlimbach & Sohn, organ builders in 1883.
SCHLIMBACH, JOHANN-CASPAR; Königshofen, Germany; also shown at Ohrdruff, Germany in 1816. Piano and organ builder, 1810-1840. Worked with *Bernard Eschenbach*, (qv). Made combination reed organ and giraffe pianos and the Aeoline.
SCHLIMBACH, MARTIN; Königshofen, Germany, ca. 1825-30. Son of Johann-Caspar Schlimbach.
SCHLOSSER, LUDWIG; Mittelgasse 2, Nieder-Ohmen, Germany, 1930; established 1926.
SCHLUNZIG, WILHELM, SEN. & JUN.; Untermhaus, Gera, Germany; reed maker, 1930.
SCHMID, G.; Germany. Äolodikon in the Deutsches Museum, Munich, Germany.
SCHMIDT & CO.; Leipzig, Germany; organette maker.
SCHMIDT, M.; 31 rue de Champ-de-Mars, 1858-1860; 9 rue de Champ-de-Mars, 1868; 188 rue de la Poste, 1895, Brussels, Belgium. *M. Schmidt Fils* listed as a maker of apparatus for photography and harmoniums. *M.A. Schmidt*, showrooms at 137 rue de la Poste and workrooms at 125 chausee de Haecht in 1899; 97 rue du Midi & rue de la Gouttiere in 1903; 16 rue de la Gouttiere in 1905; 84 rue d'Anderlecht in 1909, all in Brussels. Awarded a silver medal at the Brussels Exhibition of 1897.
SCHMIDT, W.; Wettinstr. 2, Borna, Germany, 1940.
SCHMIDT, see *Menzenhauer & Schmidt*.
SCHMOLLER & MUELLER; Omaha, NE. Identical instruments with the Kenwood and Lyon & Healy names have been reported.
SCHNEIDER & CO.; Magdeburg, Germany; later Zweigwerk Marterbüschel, Germany. Established 1834 by Traugott Schneider. Active through the 1890s.
SCHOFIELD, J.; 52 Bridges St., Ramsbottom, Lancs., England, 1903.
SCHÓIER, L.C.; Norregade 37, Odense, Denmark, 1904.
SCHOLEFIELD, J.F.; Park Works, Greenhead Road, Huddersfield, Yorkshire, England. Harmonium manufacturer 1886-88.
SCHONBRODT, see *Roth & Schonbrodt*.

SCHONE & BOCCHESE; 13 p. Aspromonte, Milan, Italy, 1930.

SCHÖNSTEIN, GUSTAV; Rathenaustr. 20, Villingen, Germany; reed maker, established 1896; Gustav Schönstein & Wilhelm Maiers Erben, proprietors, 1930.

SCHORTMANN; Buttstedt, Germany. Made an Aeoline.

SCHOTT, see *Grucker & Schott.*

SCHPIKIN, N.N.; Kirotschnaja 42, St. Petersburg, Russia, 1903.

SCHRAM & MEANDLER; melodeon and harpsichord makers.

SCHRAMM, M.J.; Rosenstr. 10 in 1886, Rosenstr. 5 in 1930, Munich, Germany. Pianoforte and harmonium maker, 1913. Made a combination harmonium and piano in 1871.

SCHREYER, MÜLLER & CO.; Unterwiesenthal, Germany. Makers of a suction harmonium now in the Heimatmuseum, Werdau, Germany.

SCHULZ, GUSTAV; Wiesenstr. 9b in 1912, later at Wiesenstr. 34, Frankfurt a. d. Oder, Germany. Established 1898, doing business at least through 1930.

SCHULZ, MATHIAS W.; 711 Milwaukee Ave., Chicago, IL 1876-99; factory at Morgan, Superior and Sangamon Streets. Started as a cabinet maker in 1869 with two partners, later made reed organs as the *Mathias Organ Co.*, bought out his partners in 1876; incorporated in 1889 as *M. Schulz & Co.* with his son Otto as vice-president. Capacity in 1898: 14,000 organs per year. Built a total of 120,000 organs. Made organs at least through 1914.

Established 1869. Incorporated 1891.
CAPITAL AND SURPLUS $500,000

OTTO SCHULZ, President
EMIL WOLFF, Vice-President
F. A. LUHNOW, Sec'y and Treas.

M. SCHULZ CO.

Manufacturers of High-Grade

Reed Organs

FACTORIES:
Erie, Curtis and Ohio Streets, Carpenter and Erie Streets

OFFICE AND WAREROOMS:
373 Milwaukee Avenue, CHICAGO, ILLINOIS

SCHULZE, see *Friedrich & Schulze.*
SCHUMANN & CO.; Karl-Heine-Str. 89-93, Leipzig, Germany; harmonium components, 1930.
SCHUMANN, see *Nord-deutsches Metallwerk Willy Schumann.*
SCHÜRER, ALBERT; Raunerstrasse 4, Kirchheim-Teck, Germany. Harmonium maker, established 1947. Succeeded by *Teck-Harmoniumfabrik* in 1967. Made a total of about 2,000 harmoniums.
SCHUSTER; Vienna, Austria. Made a free-reed instrument called the Adiaphon in 1819.
SCHUTTÉ, H.; 2 rue de la Plante, Namur, Belgium. Piano and harmonium maker, 1883.
SCHUTZ, M. (No other information available.)
SCHUTZE, see *Jos. Merklin & Schutze.*
SCHWAAB, see *Salaun, Schwaab & Co.*
SCHWARZBAUR, JULIUS; Bahnhofstr. 102-107, Mindelheim, Germany. Organ, piano and harmonium maker, Established in 1896, operated through 1925.
SCHWARZKOPF, CARL; Trossingen, Württemberg, Germany, 1909; Crailsheim, Germany in 1925; Friedrich-Hermann-Strasse 4, Ilshofen in 1930. Awarded a patent for a harmonium in 1909. Made suction and pressure harmoniums.
SCHWECHLEN, G.; Berlin. Harmonium and piano maker. Exhibited in Melbourne in 1880.
SCHYVEN, PIERRE, & CO.; 25 rue Francart a Ixelles, Brussels, Belgium. Pierre Schyven was apprenticed to *Merklin & Schutze* in 1843 and eight years later was the foreman. The firm of Pierre Schyven & Co. was registered in 1875 with Schyven and Armand Verreyt as administrators, both from Merklin & Schutze. This firm was the successor to *Jos. Merklin & Schutze*, but both firm names continued to be used.
SCOTCHER, C., & SON; 37 Bull St., Birmingham, England, 1883.
SCOTT, J.; 145 Church Road, Brighton, Sussex, England. Started making American organs in 1891, working until at least 1921 as a piano dealer. Also had premises at 10-11 George Street, Brighton.
SCOTT, JOHN M.; Cadiz, OH; see *Henry B. Horton.*
SCOTT, see *Carpenter, Scott & Wise.*
SCRIBNER, J.W.; inventor and maker of qualifying tubes used in *Bell, Dominion,* and *Clough & Warren* organs. U.S. Patent No. 104653, June 21, 1870.
SCRIBNER, see *Smith & Scribner.*
SEAGER, GEORGE; 66 Worship St., Finsbury, London, 1883.
SEALS; Birmingham, AL. Music dealer, sold organs with the Seals stencil, 1903.

SEARS, ROEBUCK & CO.; offices in Chicago. Sold the *Beckwith* organ, at first made by others with the Beckwith stencil; also sold the *Bilhorn* Telescope folding organ in 1902 and the Crown organ. Started

This Beckwith organ sold for $19.90 in Sears' 1905 catalog.

its own organ production by establishing the *Adler Organ Co.* in 1903 at the site of the former Bennett Furniture Works on Chestnut St. between 28th & 29th Streets, Louisville, KY. Sears also had a factory in St. Paul, MN, 1907. See *Adler Organ Co.*

SEBRIGHT, T.; 2 Harold Street, Malden Road, Kentish Town, London NW. Pianoforte, organ and harmonium key maker, doing business at least from 1878 through the end of the century. By 1887 the firm was known as *Sebright & Clark*. At that time they advertised special keys for India and the tropics, made of mahogany instead of lime, with the ivories riveted and using black screws. Succeeded by *R.W. Clark.*

SECOMB, DANIEL F.; Concord, NH; established 1849; see *Parker & Secomb.*

SEMPLE, J.W.; parlor organ manufacturer. (No other information available.)

SERGEANT, see *Stein & Sergeant.*

SEVERANCE, A.F., see *Dearborn & Severance.*

SEWELL & SEWELL; 8, 10, 16 Worship Street, Finsbury Square, London EC from 1896 to at least 1906.

SEYBOLD REED-PIPE ORGAN CO.; Peoria, IL; established by William Seybold in 1902, sold to *Strohber Piano Co.* in 1903 and moved to Elgin, IL. William Seybold died in 1904 and the company which bore his name was then operated by William Grote, president, and William F. Bieltmann, factory superintendent, who had learned organ building in Germany. Production began in Elgin with eleven employees; cases and some other parts were purchased from others. By 1905 Seybold, by then staffed with fifty employees, was producing ten instruments per day including cases. Renamed *Seybold Piano & Organ Co.* in 1908, capacity was ten organs and five pianos per day. In 1910 the work force was up to 80 and a total of 10,000 organs had been produced. In 1913 Seybold merged with *F. Engelhart & Sons Company*, owners of the Peerless Player Piano Company and the National Music Roll Company, to form the *Engelhart-Seybold Piano Co.*, with offices in Chicago, but the new enterprise went bankrupt 18 months later. The former Seybold plant was acquired by the E.P. Johnson Piano Co. in 1916 and used for piano production.

SEYDEL, FRANZ FRED; Spandauer Strasse, Berlin, Germany. Chord organ.

SEYDLER, RUDOLPH; Dresdner Str. 21 in 1925-30, Berlin. Established 1900, active at least through 1928. Piano and harmonium maker.

SEZERIE; Paris. Reed maker, 1867.

SHACKELL, see *Thompson & Shackell, Ltd.*

SHAEFER, C.; 27 Baxter Road, Essex Road, London, 1898. American and portable harmoniums.
SHANGHAI ORGAN & PIANO CO., Shanghai, China.
SHAW, M.L.; 5-1 Dharamtala Street, Calcutta, India, 1930.
SHEIB, W.B., & CO.; New York, NY.
SHENSTONE & CO.; Steamworks, Grange Road, Leyton, London. Key makers, 1896. Still working in 1921.
SHEPARD, GEORGE S.; Lebanon, PA; established 1863, maker of organs at least through 1912. Serial number: 1876—3200.
SHEPHARD, LUKE JAMES; Canton, MA. Seraphine, melodeon and (probably) piano manufacturer, active at least from 1856 through 1863.
SHERLOCK-MANNING ORGAN CO.; London, Ontario, Clinton, Ontario; started in 1902 by John Frank Sherlock and Wilbur N. Manning, former employees of *Wm. Doherty & Co.* Renamed *Sherlock-Manning Piano & Organ Co.* in 1910 and *Sherlock-Manning Pianos Ltd.* in 1930. They acquired the Doherty company's assets in 1920 and the assets of the former *D.W. Karn & Co.* in 1924 and continued making reed organs until about 1960. Capacity in 1906: 2,000 organs per year.

お子さまの夢を育てる

 島田楽器株式会社

静岡県島田市横井2丁目20番54号
電話〈05473〉7－4165(代表)

SHIMADA GAKKI CO., LTD.; current address 2-20-54 Yokoi Shimadashi, Shizuoka, Japan 427. Originally a furniture maker, began making reed organs after World War II and until recently made five electrically-blown and two foot-pumped reed organs. Shimada Gakki organs are sold by Zen-on in Tokyo. Shimada also made the Sister organ for the Yaesu Piano Co. (qv).
SHIMAZAKI, KUMAJIRO; 2 Shinminatomachi, Kyobashi, Tokyo. Exhibitor at the 3rd Domestic Industrial Exhibition, Tokyo, 1890.
SHIMER & HULSHIZER; Phillipsburg, NJ 1861. Melodeon and harmonium manufacturer.
SHINSEISHA; 1-14 Motomachi, Hongo, Tokyo. Advertised in 1888 as a maker of school organs. Dealer was Kinkodo, Nihonbashi, Tokyo.

SHIMADA ORGAN

SHIPMAN, E.; 30 Prince of Wales Road, London NW, factory located at Poynungs Road, Junction Road. Harmonium manufacturer 1877-96. In 1890 listed as *Shipman & Shipman*, harmonium and piano maker.

SHIPMAN ORGAN CO.; South Hamilton and East Green Streets, High Point, NC. William Gatewood Shipman and H.C. Barckhoff, owners. J.K. Link, Shipman's brother-in-law, was president from 1905 until his death in 1908. At that time E.A. Snow became president. Factory capacity 700 organs per month in 1915. Operated as the *High Point Piano & Organ*

Co. from 1905 until a fire in 1911 destroyed the factory. A new 50,000 square foot factory was built on the same site and the business continued as the Shipman Organ Company. Made organs under this name through 1924, when it was succeeded by the *Piedmont Mfg. Co.* The *Gatewood Organ Co.* was another name used by Shipman.

SHIRAI, KIKURO; a relative of Ren-Ichi Shirai and editor of the instruction book for the *Dobunkan* organ.

SHIRAI, REN-ICHI; a principal in the music dealership Kyoeki Shosha and a major stockholder in *Yamaha Hukin Seizo Sho*.

SHIRLEY, G.; 17 Ellesmere St., North St., Poplar, London, 1883.

SHIVCHARAN MUSIC HOUSE; 95 1st Floor, Mohan Singh Place, New Delhi 110001, India. Currently making Indian table harmoniums.

SHOEMAKER, W.H.; 11 S. Third St., Harrisburg, PA.

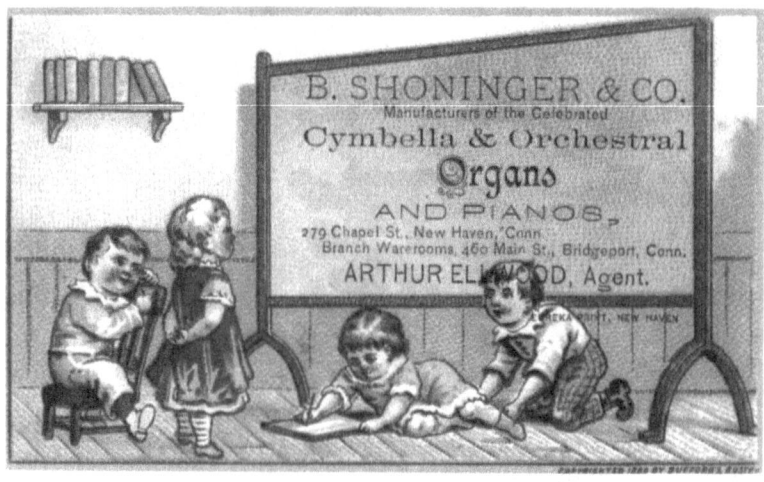

SHONINGER, B., & CO.; original factory at Woodbridge, CT 1850-65, burned in 1865 and Shoninger bought *Treat & Linsley*'s factory near the corner of Chapel and Chestnut Streets in New Haven, CT, later expanded to 97-123 Chestnut St.; sales rooms on Church St. in New Haven 1850-57, then 801 Chapel St. Bernard Shoninger was born in Bavaria and emigrated to the U.S. in 1847. In 1887 Bernard was still president and his son Simon B. was secretary; later renamed *B. Shoninger Organ & Piano Co.* Bernard Shoninger died in 1910. Serial numbers:

            1874—33954   1883—65000   1890—79413
            1876—46000   1884—76000
            1882—57000   1885—77000

SIEBER, J.P.; melodeons. (No other information available.)
SIEBER, PHIL.; Holzkirchen, Germany; J. & R. Sieber, proprietors, 1930. Organ and harmonium maker, established 1826, closed 1943.

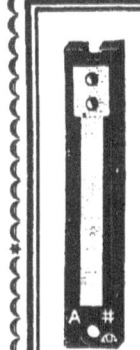

ERNST SILBERHORN
Gegründet 1877 Stuttgart 6 Gegründet 1877
Älteste Spezialfabrik für Orgel- und Harmoniumstimmen
GROSSES LAGER SÄMTLICHER
BESTANDTEILE FÜR DRUCK- U. SAUGWINDHARMONIUM
speziell gut gelagerte Stimmstöcke und Zungen, in den verschiedensten Dispositionen, Klaviaturen, Perkussionsmechaniken mit Hämmer, Gummituche, Filze, Leder, Federn aller Art usw.
● Fachmännische Reparaturen rasch und billig ●
Grösste u. einzige Spezialhandlung d. Harmoniumbranche Deutschlands
EXPORT NACH ALLEN LÄNDERN
Illustrierten Katalog auf Verlangen gratis!

SILBERHORN, ERNST; Böblinger Str. 195-197, Stuttgart 6, Germany. Specialized in reeds and components for harmoniums; Wilh. Silberhorn, proprietor. Established 1877, in business at least through 1930. In 1883 listed as *Hinkel & Silberhorn*.
SILLANPÄÄ, ELIAS; (1849-1909), harmonium maker in Lapua, Finland. Established 1875. Succeeded in 1894 by his son Vihtoripoika Sillanpää, (1871-1928). As a boy, Vihtoripoika began helping his father, and by age eleven built his own harmonium without help. He continued in business at least until 1916.
SIMMONS, A.A., see *Clough & Warren*.
SIMMONS & VAN DINTER; Kalamazoo, MI, 1875. The identity of Simmons is not certain. See *Van Dinter*.
SIMON; France; orgue-expressif 1846.
SIMON, A.; 8 avenue de Hannut in 1906; 59 rue Delimoy in 1913, Namur, Belgium. Maker, retailer, tuner and repairer of pianos and harmoniums. In business until 1940.
SIMPSON, JAS.; in 1879 at 141 Sauchiehall Street, Glasgow, Scotland; in 1882 at 559 Sauchiehall Street; in 1889 until 1890 at 284 Sauchiehall Street. Harmonium maker.
SIMPSON, see *Brown & Simpson*.

SIMS, H.C.; in 1882 at 23 Onslow Road, Southampton, England; in 1886 and 1903 organ works at Bellevue Terrace, Southampton; in 1906 *South of England Organ Works*, Bellevue Terrace. Organ builder, harmonium manufacturer and tuner.
SINDEL, HEINRICH; Crailsheim, Germany; established in 1873, in business at least through 1913. Harmonium maker and dealer.
SINGER ORGAN CO.; Chicago, IL, 1887. In 1894 became Singer Piano Co. at 235 Wabash Ave., Chicago.
SINGER, PETER; Salzburg, Austria. Made the Pansymphonicum, a combined piano and harmonium, and the Polyharmonium in 1839.
SINGH, ANAND; Delhi, India. Table organ maker.
SINGH, BABA KISHAN, & SONS; Bawian di Hatti, Clock Tower, Amritsar, India. "Makers of World Famous Harmoniums."
SISTER organ; made by *Shimada Gakki* (qv), sold by *Yaesu Piano Co.*
SITNIKOW, E.P.; Sarjadji, Hans Starkow, Moscow, 1903.
SKALA HARMONIUM-GESELLSCHAFT; Hamburg, Germany. Successor to *Berliner Harmonium-Fabrik* in 1903 (qv).
SKANDINAVISKA ORGELFABRIKEN; 41 Mastersamuelsg., Stockholm, Sweden. In 1930 shown as *Skandinaviska Orgel-och Pianofabriken*.
SKEWES, H.; Trelowren St., Camborne, Cornwall, England, 1903.
SKOGSAAS, JOH.; Vefsn, Norway, 1876. Harmonium maker.
SKOPEK, VINCENZ; Wilsonstr. 723, Tabor, Czechoslovakia, 1930.
SLACK, EDWARD; 12 Packers-row, Chesterfield, England. Piano and harmonium maker, 1883.
SLATER, ROBERT, & SON; Forest Gate Organ Works, Odessa Road, Forest Gate, London. Between 1920 and 1929 made 484 small portable harmoniums for Morgan & Scott, supply house for the Congregational Church. The son was Sidney Slater.
SLAYTON, see *Whitney & Raymond.*
SLESSKIN, J.W.; Pekrowka, Nishny-Novgorod, Russia, 1903.
SLIWINSKI, JOHANN; Kopernikusgasse 16, Lemberg, Austria-Hungary, 1903; established 1876.
SLOAN & CO.; melodeons, also shown as *A.L. Sloan*. (No other information available.)
SLOAN, J.E., & SON; Corunna, MI. Listed in 1875 and 1879. In 1883 shown as J.E. Sloan.
SLOOTMAECKERS FRÈRES; 155 rue Masui, Brussels, Belgium from 1905 to 1932; 218-219 avenue des Volontaires, Wolnwe-Saint-Lambert, Belgium until 1945. Served an apprenticeship with *Kerkhoff*, then established a workshop about 1900.
SLOWN, J.; Owen Sound, Ontario 1871-89.

SMALL, CHARLES W.; Worcester, MA. Granted reed organ patents 1870, 1871.
SMALL & KNIGHT; Stevens' Plains, Portland, ME. William Small and Franklin Knight, cabinet makers and organ repairmen from 1822, acquired the reed organ business of *J.D. Cheney* prior to 1866. Still in business in 1883 as dealers.
SMART, see *Avill & Smart*.
SMEETZ, J.; 129 quai de l'Industrie in 1878; 129 rue de l'Intendent in 1880; 10 Place de la Concordat from 1881 to 1900, Brussels, Belgium. Maker and retailer of organs, harmoniums and pianos. In 1895 listed as *Smeetz van Genechten* and in 1900 *P. Smeetz* is listed.
SMITH, A.; 56 Manchester Road, Burnley, Lancashire, England. Piano, harmonium and pipe organ manufacturer 1889-1890.
SMITH AMERICAN ORGAN CO., see *S.D. & H.W. Smith*.

SMITH & CO.; 107 Tottenham Road, Ball's Pond Road, London N. Established in 1850, advertised in 1900 as an American organ maker.
SMITH, DAVID W. AND CORNELIUS D., ORGAN CO.; Brome, Quebec established 1875.
SMITH & GREEN; Townsend, MA. Henry Smith and Oliver M. Green, 1850 to ca. 1856. Also possibly Alvin Green. See *Oliver M. Green*.
SMITH & HAMLIN reed organ. (No other information available.)
SMITH, HENRY; Townsend, MA. Maker of a melodeon located at Townsend Historical Society. See *Smith & Green*.
SMITH, HERBERT HARVEY; Church Street, Eckington, Worcestershire, England. Harmonium manufacturer and tuner, extant 1872.
SMITH, HERMANN; 29 Shaftesbury Road, Hammersmith, London; later 238 Oxford Street. Coinventor with Baillie Hamilton of the Vocalion. Built the Mechanics' harmonium and the Oberon. Published a

series of articles on how to build your own harmonium appearing in the English Mechanic (periodical) in 1867. Smith was quoted by Prof. Hermann Helmholtz in his classical study of acoustics, "Sensations of Tone as a Physiological Basis for the Theory of Music."

SMITH, H.H., & SONS; London. Portable harmonium makers.

SMITH, J.C., ORGAN CO.; 563 E. King St., York, PA, 1884-89.

SMITH, JOHN A.; Washington, NJ 1850; North East, PA 1873; Erie, PA 1881. Melodeon and reed organ maker. Had numerous reed organ patents. In 1899, Adam Fickes is listed as president, John A. Smith, treasurer and Frank Pl. Smith, secretary. See *New Era Organ Co.*

SMITH, JOHN R.; corner of State and Michigan Streets, Adrian, MI, 1859, 1867. Jonathan Rufus Smith, manufacturer of organs and melodeons.

SMITH, NATHAN D.; 75 Main St., New London, CT 1853, corner of Williams and Waxler Streets in 1857; also in 1857 shown as having a factory at North Main St. and a sales room at 23 Bank Street. Located at the corner of Williams and Cedar Streets in 1859. Melodeon maker. In 1882 he is shown in partnership with his son Frederick M. as *Nathan D. Smith & Son* at 21½ Bank St., probably as a music dealer only at this time.

SMITH & SCRIBNER; Chatham, Ontario 1864-65.

SMITH, S.D. & H.W.; Boston, MA. Started as *S.D. Smith* in 1852, then S.D. & H.W. Smith 1853-74 when Henry W. Smith joined the firm, then *Smith American Organ Co.* in 1883. Succeeded by *New England Organ Co.* and controlled by Merrill Piano Mfg. Co. of Boston in 1899. First located at 417 Washington Street, moved to 511 Washington St. in 1860. Built a new factory at 531 Tremont Street in 1868. In 1890 the address was 136 Boylston St., Boston. Also made organs with the *W. Brunt & Sons* (qv) stencil. Serial numbers:

1852—100	1863—4700	1882—57500
1853—400	1865—5200	1883—63000
1854—800	1866—5700	1884—68000
1856—1500	1867—6300	1885—73000
1858—2100	1868—7000	1886—77900
1859—2600	1869—7300	1887—88000
1860—3100	1870—7650	1888—97000
1861—3640	1872—8000	1890—118000
1862—4300	1881—53600	

SMITH & SMITH; 1 Chapel Mews, Chapel Street, Somers Town, London. Harmonium, American organ and bellows manufacturer, 1880.
SMITH, W.F., & CO.; 168 St. John St., Clerkenwell, London. American organ and harmonium manufacturer 1890-96.
SMITH & WHINCUP; 89 Cookridge Street, Leeds, West Yorkshire, England. Harmonium makers in 1882.
SMITH, WILLIAM; 22½ High Petergate, York, England. Harmonium maker, 1858.
SMITH, see *Marchal & Smith*.
SMYTH, JOHN M.; 150-166 West Madison St., Chicago, IL. A general merchandise mail order dealer, he sold reed organs made by *Lyon & Healy* and possibly others with the Smyth stencil.
SNELL, E. & W.; 402a Essex Road, Ball's Pond, North London in 1864; King St. North, Camden Town, London in 1883; 3 Colonnade Buildings, Holloway Road, London in 1884; Ledbury Road, Bayswater in 1887. Established in 1864, known as *Ed. Snell & Co.* at 54 Essex Road, Islington in 1898, and later that year as *Snell Bros.* at 383 Hornsey Road, London. Also shown at 305 Hornsey Rd., Seven Sisters Road in 1900; at Nightingale Works, Hornsey Road in 1902, at Seven Sisters Rd., London in 1903 and at 100 Blackstock Road, Finsbury Park in 1904. Made the Albany organ. Finally closed in 1907.
SNELL, HARRY; 97 Duncombe Road, Upper Holloway, London in 1895; Alberg Piano Works, 7a Andrews Road, Mare Street, Hackney, London in 1901. Piano and harmonium maker.
SNELL, ROBERT; Ball's Pond Road, London. Exhibited a bichromatic seraphine at the London Exhibition of 1851. This instrument had 24 notes

notes to the octave, producing perfect harmony in every key. It was controlled by an octave of pedals which, when depressed, would correct the scale for the key required. See enharmonic organ.

SOCIEDAD FRANCO-HISPANO-AMERICANA PARA LA CONSTRUCCIÓN DE PIANOS Y ARMONIUMS; 31 Canuda, Barcelona, Spain, 1930.

SOCIETÉ DES ORGUES D'ALEXANDRE PÈRE ET FILS, see *Alexandre Père et Fils.*

SOCIN, FIDEL; Bozen, Austria in 1883. Shown as *Egidio Socin*, located at Kaiserin Elisabethstr. 10, Bozen; Austria in 1903. In 1930 shown as *Fidel Socin* at 10 via Regina Elena, Bolzano Novarese, Italy. Established 1870, awarded a bronze medal at Triest in 1882.

SOLARI, JEAN; 43 rue des Visitandines, 1870; 11 rue Notre-Dame de Graces; 9 rue de Notre-Dame de Graces in 1875; 88 rue Blaes, Brussels, Belgium. Born in Boccolo, Italy in 1843, worked in the *Kanneguissert* factory in Paris, established his workshop in Brussels in 1870, continued in business as a maker and retailer of accordions and harmoniums until 1924. Awarded silver medals at the Anvers Exhibition of 1885 and the

Brussels Exhibition of 1897. Awarded Diplomes d'Honneur in 1905 and 1910 at Brussels.
SOMMER; Dresden, Germany. Harmonium maker.
SOMMER, W.; Kerksteeg 9-13, Gorinchem, Netherlands.
SOMMERS & COLBURN; Ansonia, CT ca. 1850-60; also *Pratt & Colburn*.
SONATA. A 49 note organ made about 1930. (No other information available.)
SONNTAG, HEINRICH; Hansweg 2, Altenburg, Germany; reed maker, 1903; established 1890.
SOPER, W.; 26 Conduit Rd., Plumstead, Kent, England, 1903.
SORA, DON CESARE; Quinzano d'Oglio, Italy. Organ and harmonium maker, 1909.
SORA, GIOVANNI, & FIGLIO; Mondolfo, Italy, 1903, 1909.
SOTYGA; 17 Gliwicka, Katowice, Poland. Harmonium and American organ maker, 1930.
SOUBEIRAN, J.; 5 rue Grignan, Marseille, France, 1920.
SOUTH OF ENGLAND ORGAN WORKS, see *H.C. Sims*.
SOUTHERN ORGAN CO.; Athens, TN; incorporated in 1883 as the Athens Furniture Works for the manufacture of furniture and as the Southern Organ Co. for the manufacture of organs and pianos; I.C. Mansfield, John A. McKeldin, Fred L. Mansfield, W.G. Wilson and W.T. Lane, owners.
SPAETHE, WILHELM; Bismarckstr. 1, Gera, Germany; Otto Spaethe & W.E. Spaethe, proprietors in 1903; established in 1859 or 1865 (sources vary); also *Thuringia Piano & Organ Comp. Wilhelm Spaethe*. Closed 1945.
SPAETHE, WILHELM ERNST; Gera, Germany. Established in 1927, closed 1956.
SPANG, XAVIER; 64 N. Salina St., Syracuse, New York; started making melodeons in 1860 at 64-66 N. Salina St. with son Rupert. Located at 2 & 4 Noxon St. in 1873. Firm named *Spang & Mertens* 1881-85. Shown as Xavier Spang again in 1886, still at the Noxon Street address; also named *Cabinet Organ Co*. Serial numbers:

1860—7000	1865—8600	1870—11000
1861—7500	1866—9007	1871—11690
1862—7764	1867—9503	1872—12100
1863—8100	1868—10500	1873—13100
1864—8450	1869—10789	1874—14000

SPANGENBERG, DANIEL; Washington, NJ.
SPANGENBERG, see *Holling & Spangenberg*.

SPENCE & CO.; 217, 219 Hyde Road, Manchester, England. Piano and American organ manufacturer 1896 through at least 1921, made the Cleveland reed organ and the Annexe, a combination piano and organ. The owner was E.J. Spencer, who shortened his trade name to Spence.
SPENCER, A., & HAILES; 104A Park St., Camden Town, London. Sound boards, 1896.

A·J·SPENCER LTD.
Established in 1855   96 UPPER BROOK STREET
MANCHESTER 13

SPENCER, ARTHUR JAMES; 96 Upper Brook St., Chorlton-on-Medlock, Manchester, England. Manufacturer of the University organ, Albaphon and 1, 2 and 3 manual and pedal harmoniums; established 1855, in business until at least 1963.
SPENCER BROS.; 81 Hyde Rd., Manchester, England. Pipe organ, piano and harmonium builder 1880-85.
SPOTLESS CO., THE; Richmond, VA. A mail order dealer, sold reed organs made by others with the Spotless stencil.
SPRAGUE, D.L.; West Townshend, VT. Derek L. Sprague began making melodeons and lap organs in 1844 in rented quarters. He began building a new shop by the brook in 1854 and moved into it in 1855. Moved to Chester, VT in 1857.
SPRAGUE, WILLIAM; 7 Finsbury Pavement, London in 1877; listed at 87 Finsbury Pavement in 1883. Also shown at 20 Little Moorfields, London. Established 1847 as a piano and seraphine maker. Closed in 1883.
SPRINGFIELD ORGAN CO., THE; Chicago, IL. In business at least from 1902 to 1913. Serial number: 1913—35873.
SPRöSSEL, W.; Leipzig. Germany. Harmonium maker ca. 1870.
STADLEZ, M.; St. Petersburg, Russia 1895. Made the Harmonicum, with 31 stops and four knee stops.
STAHL, see *Franz Steirer.*
STANLEY, EGERTON; Crystal Palace, Sydenham, London 1878-82.
STAR ORGAN MANUFACTORY; 18 N. Rose, Kalamazoo, MI, 1867. Founded by Delos Phillips in 1854; later *Blakeman & Phillips*, (qv). Also see *Phillips, Delos*.

STAR PARLOR ORGAN CO.; Railroad Avenue, Washington, NJ 1869-81, owned by H.W. Alleger. The factory burned along with *Daniel Beatty*'s factory in 1881; see *Alleger, Bowlby & Plotts*.

STATHER, ROBERT; 187 Seven Sisters Rd., London; also shown at 202 Liverpool Road, London in 1883. Established 1870, shown in 1914 as an organ repairman and piano maker, in 1921 as a reed organ maker and repairer at 181 Seven Sisters Road.

STECK, WILH.; Heslach, Germany, 1883. Reed maker.

STEENSTRUP, see *Petersen & Steenstrup*.

STEIGERMAN. Name used by *Yamaha* on some organs and pianos made for export.

STEIGLER, see *Huller & Co.*

STEIN, EMILE; Paris. Orgue-expressif maker ca. 1845.

STEIN, P., & P. SERGEANT; exhibited at the Paris Exposition 1849.

STEINART; (or Steinert), North Adams, MA.

STEINBRÜCK, FRIEDRICH; Langensalza, Germany. Aeolodikon maker, 1829.

STEININGER, GEBRÜDER; Obertrattnach, Austria. Established in 1886, in business at least through 1930.

STEINMANN, GUSTAV; Salzufelner Str. 160, Vlotho-Werendorf, Germany, 1927-35. Established 1909. Steinmann later joined Vierdag to form *Steinmann & Vierdag*. Organ and harmonium maker. See *Beyer*.

STEINMANN & VIERDAG; 79 Brinkstr., Enschede, Netherlands, 1921 through about 1930.

STEINMEYER, G.F., & CO.; Kellerstr. 134, Oettingen, Germany. Established in 1847 by Georg Friedrich Steinmeyer, organ maker. Began making (pressure) harmoniums about 1860, and in 1901 suction instruments. Awarded a gold medal at Nurenberg in 1882. When production ended in 1955, Steinmeyer had produced 6,000 harmoniums. Hans Ludwig, Gottlieb and Albert Steinmeyer, Wilhelm Strebel, and Fritz Steinmeyer, proprietors in 1930; also *Steinmeyer & Strebel*. Still doing business (1996) in repair and restoration of harmoniums.

STEIRER, FRANZ; Besigheim b. Stuttgart, Germany in 1925, Besigheim and Ludwigshafen in 1929, Walheim, Germany and 3 Ühlandstr., Beitigheim, Württemberg, Germany in 1930; still manufacturing in 1984 as *Steirer-Stahl*, H. Steirer, prop., located at Industriestrasse 11, 7120 Bietigheim-Bissingen, Germany. Pipe organ and harmonium builder, established 1920. Also made harmoniums with the Jankó enharmonic keyboards (qv).

STEMMER, see *Feuhr & Stemmer*.

STERCHI BROS.; Chattanooga, TN. Music dealer, sold organs with the Sterchi stencil probably made by *O.K. Hourk*.

STERCUS; England. Made a two-manual harmonium with an inclined swell keyboard and pedals.

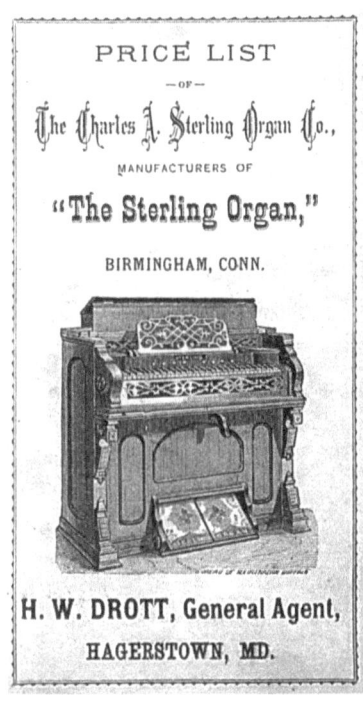

STERLING ORGAN CO.; established 1860, incorporated in 1866 by Charles A. Sterling as the *Birmingham Organ Co.*, located in Birmingham, CT; renamed *The Charles A. Sterling Organ Co.* in 1871. Moved to 218 Derby Ave., Derby, CT in 1873 and renamed *The Sterling Organ Co.*, later renamed *The Sterling Co.* Rufus W. Blake, formerly of *Loring & Blake* became secretary and general manager in 1873. Officers in 1897: R.W. Blake, president; J.R. Mason, secretary-treasurer. Factory capacity 7,000 organs per year in 1887; and by 1894 had produced 73,000 organs. Went out of business in 1902. Serial number: 1889—39205.

STEVENS, C.E.; 17 Cedar Street, New York, NY; manufacturer of a combination reed-pipe organ.

STEVENS, F.C.; 7 Green St., Cambridge Heath St., London, 1903.

STEVENS & KLOCK ORGAN CO.; Marietta, OH; factory located on Gilman Avenue, West Marietta. In business in 1885, became *Stevens Organ Co.* in 1897 when Orin C. Klock retired. Also shown as *Stevens Piano & Organ Co.* Collins R. Stevens had previously worked for Estey. Officers in 1899: D.B. Torpy, president; T.W. Moore, vice-president; B.F. Stricker, secretary; C.R. Stevens, treasurer and general manager. Capacity 600 organs per year in 1898 and 1,200 in 1902. Made reed-pipe organs in piano cases at least through 1919.

STEVENS, R.F., LTD.; 42b Hampstead Rd., London in 1897-1900; 82a Leighton Rd. Kentish Town in 1903. Other addresses: 170 Drummond St.; 343 Euston Sq.; Kelly Street, Kentish Town in 1931. Some references show it as established in 1853 although an advertisement in 1900 says it was established in 1869. Made both suction and pressure instruments and well as bellows and pans.   Production ended in 1966 and the company closed in 1980. Serial numbers: 1895—2573, 1928—25556, 1923—24130, 1945—29419.

R. F. Stevens, Ltd.

Factory: "Organ Works," Kelly Street,

ESTABLISHED 1853 Kentish Town, London, N.W.1

Telephone: GULLIVER 2745

Pedal Board R.C.O. Scale

STEVENS "STUDENTS" PEDAL ORGAN

STEVENS, W.W., MUSIC CO.; Lebanon, IN. Music dealer, sold organs made by *C.O. Hillstrom* with the Stevens stencil.
STEVENSON, FRANK; North York, Ontario 1867.

STEWART, C.A., & CO.; North Adams, MA. Melodeon maker.
STEWART, C.W.; Brattleboro, VT. (No other information available.)
STEWART, DR. A.; Roxbury, MA. Seraphine maker, 1838.
STIEHLER, MAX; Zollikoferstr. 10, Leipzig-Volkmarsdorf, Germany in 1921, Bismarckstr. 18, Leipzig-Borsdorf, Germany in 1925. Established 1919, closed 1932. Made both pressure and suction instruments.
STILWELL & GENUNG; Waterloo, NY, 1857; formerly *Seth J. Genung*. Succeeded in 1866 by *Roth, Holleran & Miles*.
STIMSON, OAKES & CO.; Westfield, MA 1861. Manufacturer of legs for pianos and melodeons.

STIRES, WM., & SON; Pittstown, NJ. Manufacturer of the Cottage Queen organ and a dealer in pianos and organs.
STOCK, KARL; (also Carl). Schachtstrasse 6-9, Leipzig-Gohlis, Germany in 1914-16; Herlossohnstr. 1-2, Leipzig in 1924-30. Formerly *Eduard Hüttner*; manufacturer of both pressure and suction harmoniums and harmonium cases. Established 1908. Also made stencilled instruments for harmonium dealer *Max Bannicke*. In business at least through 1943.
STOLPE, see *Scheffel & Stolpe*.
STOLTZ, EUGÈNE; 79 avenue de Breteuil, also 33 ave. de Saxe, St. Lazare, Paris. Established in 1846, in business at least through 1909.
STONE, P.; Churchville, NY.

STONEFIELD; London. Made a two-manual and pedal harmonium with Estève reeds, ca. 1900-20.

STORER, JOSEPH; 26 Picadilly, London. Inventor, patentee and manufacturer of seraphines and aeolophones. At the London Exhibition of 1851 he displayed a percussion aeolophon with two sets of reeds, 8' and 4'. Also displayed a portable aeolophon and the "Oeolomusicon" which had the tongue and plate of the reeds formed from a single piece of metal. See *Myers & Storer*.

STOREY, HENRY, & SONS; 22 Eversholt Street, Camden Town, London. Piano and harmonium manufacturers 1878-80. Still in business after that date but not making harmoniums.

STORY & CAMP; office and retail store at 188-190 State Street, Chicago, IL. Bought out the *Clark & Rich* factory at S. Canal & 16th Streets, Chicago, in 1882. Hampton L. Story and Isaac N. Camp, proprietors. Organs with this name are in the Conklin Museum. *Melville Clark* (qv) had some association with Story & Camp, probably as factory superintendant, as his patented tilt-top case design was shown in their 1882 catalog. Apparently Clark bought out Camp about 1883 when *Story & Clark* (qv) was formed.

STORY & CLARK ORGAN CO.; corner Canal & 16th St., Chicago, IL; after 1901 located in Grand Haven, MI; established in 1884 by Hampton L. Story and Melville Clark. Story was pre- viously a partner in Powers & Story, H.L. Story & Co. (1869) and in *Story & Camp* (qv), manufacturer, music dealer and agent for Estey. Story & Camp was dissolved in 1884 when H.L. Story retired to California. His retirement was short-lived, however, as he soon formed the Coronado Beach Company in association with Elisha Babcock, Jr. to develop the Coronado peninsula near San Diego. The showpiece of this development was the Hotel del Coronado, still in operation as a luxury resort hotel. At the time of his retirement in 1884 Story organized the Story & Clark Organ Co. with *Melville Clark* (qv), a reed organ builder,

Story & Clark Organ Co.
CHICAGO - LONDON

along with his son, Edward H. Story. The firm was incorporated in 1888 with E.H. Story as president and Melville Clark as vice-president. The Story & Clark catalog for 1885 credits Melville Clark with building the first organ factory in Chicago. Story & Clark organs are noted for their metal stop knobs, used from about 1885 until about 1890, and after 1890 for the beautiful pink porcelain stop knobs. In 1896 a new firm of Story & Clark and F. Kaim & Sohn Piano & Organ Co. Ltd. was formed in England, located at 62-65 Tabernacle Street, London. Organ production ceased about 1897-99. Clark left in 1900 to start the Melville Clark Co., and the business, trademarks and patents were sold to the *Ann Arbor Organ Co.* Serial numbers: (note that they do not follow a strict chronological sequence.)

1886—78496	1889—34004	1896—80250
1887—41579	1891—47712	1896—83009
1888—26716	1892—69854	1897—92076
1888—35151	1894—82412	1899—104755
1889—29722	1895—78875	1899—107332

STRAUB, ALOIS; Ithaca, NY, Akron, OH; made organs for *H.B. Horton* 1852-56, travelling salesman for *Horton and Rose* 1856-61, opened Akron's first music store 1861.

STRAUBE, J., & CO.; Wilhelmstr. 29, Berlin in 1883-90. Friedrichstr. 34 in 1912-18, Belle-Alliance-Str. 90 in 1929, all in Berlin. In 1903 listed as *Straube's Harmoniumbau-Anstalt* at Schönebergerstr. 27, Berlin; also at Friedrichstr. 34 in 1912-18 and at Bell-Alliance Str. 90, Berlin in 1929; and at Garbenteicherweg 15, Lich, Germany in 1930. Johannes & Karl Straube, proprietors, J. Straube, superintendent in 1903; Otto Pappe, proprietor in 1923, (see *Nicolaus & Pappe*); Reinhard Pappe, proprietor until 1972. Established 1869, closed 1972. In 1926 Straube built a Bichromatic Quartertone Harmonium for Mordecai Sandberg with white keys for the whole tones, black keys for the half tones and brown keys for the quarter tones. This instrument is now in the museum at York University, Toronto, Ontario, Canada. In 1929 he built another enharmonic harmonium called "Eine Quarte" with twelve and sixteen tones per octave with a transposing keyboard. This instrument was described by the Times of London as a "...fascinating but fearsome harmonium which has 192 keys to the interval of a perfect 4th." Made a complete line of harmoniums from a two octave portable to a two-manual and pedal with seven ranks of reeds. In the 1950s Straube, together with Siegfried Mager & Co. of Wuppertal made a combination electronic and mechanical harmonium called the Mager-Straube-Kleinorgel.

STRAUCH, CARL H.; Stallschreiberstr. 18, Berlin. Organ and harmonium maker, 1886.
STRAUCH, JOSEF; Vienna, Austria, 1930.
STREBEL, JOHANNES; Hinterer Bahnhof 7, Nürnberg, Germany. Church organ and harmonium maker. Established 1884. Wilhelm and Hermann Strebel, sons of Johannes, proprietors in 1908. Acquired by *G.F. Steinmeyer* (qv) in 1921.
STRIZIK, JOSEF; Vienna, Austria; succeeded in 1884 by the workmen of the firm under the name *Ersten Productiv-Genossenschaft der Harmonium-Macher Wiens*.
STRMISKO, MATTH.; Rybarnygasse, Uhirske Hradiste (Ungarisch-Hradisch), Czechoslovakia; established 1902, still in business in 1930.
STROBL, AUGUST; store at Proreznaja 8, factory at Jilanskaja 25, Kiev, Russia in 1903.
STROMENGER, J., & SONS; 169 and 206 Goswell Road, London EC. Piano and harmonium manufacturers 1878-95.
STURM, FRIEDRICH; Suhl, Germany. Made his first reed instrument in 1823, then the Aeolodicon in 1824. Became a full time instrument maker in 1827. In 1828 he moved to Berlin and in 1830 to Hamburg. Also shown in Schweinfurth in 1815 and later in Coburg.
STURMA, JOSEF; Palackeho ul. 295, Pardubice (Pardubitz), Czechoslovakia, 1930; established 1890.

**LEOPOLD KAHN.
STUTTGART HARMONIUM COMPANY.
GERMANY.**

STUTTGART HARMONIUM CO.; Reinsburstr. 21 in 1880, Schloss Str. 59b in 1883, Stuttgart, Germany. Founded by Leopold Kahn in 1875. Also listed as *Stuttgarter Pianoforte- Salon-Orgeln- & Harmonium-Fabrik Leopold Kahn*, 1879. Showed two harmoniums at the Paris Exhibition of 1878: one- and two-manual instruments with 26 stops, ten of which were combination stops. These instruments were made for Australia. Awarded a third prize at Sydney, Australia in 1878. Succeeded by *Trefz & Feucht* (qv) in 1875.
SUCTORIAN: an electric suction unit for reed organs invented by Harold T. Depue in 1923 and built by the Pipe Organ Service Company, Omaha, NE. The standard model of the Champion Electric Suctorian was 17½ inches square by 15½ deep, and was powered by a ¼ horsepower 1750 rpm motor, had an automatic control valve for regulating the amount of suction, and was intended for two-manual and pedal organs. The Junior

model was 17½ inches square by 13 inches deep, was powered by a 1/6 hp 1750 rpm motor and was intended for one- and two-manual organs with up to six sets of reeds.

SÜDDEUTSCHE HARMONIUMFABRIK VOIGT & GOLL; Frühere Kriegsspitalkaserne, Neu-Ulm, Germany in 1922; Lehenerstr. 346, Freiburg in 1924-32. Established in 1921 by Richard Voigt and Hermann Goll. Piano and harmonium makers.

SULZER, LEOPOLD; Heusteigstr. 43 in 1890, Guttenbergstr. 57 in 1903, Rotestr. 65 in 1909, Stuttgart, Germany. Harmonium and physharmonica maker. Closed by 1919.

SUNDAY SCHOOL UNION organs, see *Bailey.*

SUNDQVIST, LEON, & CO.; Jacobsgatan 21, Örebo, Sweden, 1905.

SURPETI; India. Floor model harmonium.

SVÆREN, JOHANNES P.; Hardanger, Norway. A teacher and organist, he built about 60 harmoniums.

SVENSSON, ALFRED, ORGELFABRIK; 12 Lästmakaregatan in 1898; Master Samuelsgatan 40, Stockholm, Sweden, 1903.

SWAMY, C.S.N., & SONS, see *City Harmonium Works.*

SWAN, AMOS L.; Cherry Valley, NY; established about 1849, discontinued at the time of the Civil War.

SWAN, S.N., & SONS; Freeport, IL. S.N. Swan, who had been manager of *H.M. Cable*'s reed organ business, purchased the former *Burdett* factory from the *Hobart M. Cable Co.* in 1907. Officers in 1910: S.N. Swan, president; G.E. Swan, vice-president; A.H. Anderson, secretary; C.J. Berg, superintendent. Officers in 1925: D.E. Swan, pres.; A.J. Swan, sec'y.; G.E. Swan, vice-president. Serial number: 1916—112872.

SWEATMAN, see *J. Reyner.*

SWEDISH ORGAN CO.; see *Moline Cabinet Organ Co.*

SWEET, A.S., & SON; Taunton, MA. Reed organ makers, established 1879.

SWEETLAND, E., CO., see *Tryber & Sweetland.*

SWENSSONS, A.; Eshof, Sweden, 1903.

SWISS ORGAN CO.; Ithaca, NY. Founded in 1876 by H. Wegman and J.H. Hintermeister. Reorganized the following year as the *Ithaca Organ Co.*, (qv).

SWOBODA & BRAUNER; Bahnstr. 11, Mahrisch-Neustadt, Austria-Hungary; Franz Josef Swoboda, proprietor; established 1881, in business at least through 1903. See *W.E. Brauner.*

SWOGER, T., & SON; Beaver Falls, PA. Sold direct to the public. Active 1888.

SYRENO, organette probably made by *Mechanical Orguinette Co.* and imported into England by Geo. White & Co., 143 Holborn Bars, London, 1889.

> Made by the Same Men for the Past Thirty Years
>
> # The SWAN Reed Organ
>
> Commands the attention and admiration of the buyer who wants a THOROUGHLY HIGH GRADE instrument, absolutely reliable and unqualifiedly guaranteed by the makers.
>
> S. N. SWAN CO. :: Freeport, Ill.

T

TABER ORGAN CO.; Herman St., Worcester, MA 1883; William B. Taber was a furniture maker in 1856, then a partner in *Partridge & Taber*, organ makers, later worked for *Loring & Blake*, eventually bought out the *Worcester Organ Co.* (I) and renamed it *Taber Organ Co.*; still operating in 1903.
TAGLIABUE, GIULIO; via Arena 29, Milan, Italy; organettes.
TAILLEUR, PIERRE; Paris. Harmonium maker, 1860.
TAILLEUR, see *Cottino & Tailleur*.
TAMPEREEN HARMOONITEHDAS SEKA HARMONITEHDAS A.J. TIAINEN; Uukuniemi, Finland.
TAMPLIN, AUGUSTUS LECHMERE; London, organist at St. James Marylebone. Inventor of double touch on harmoniums. Died in 1889.
TANAKA, DR. SHOHEI, (1862-1945); Tokyo. Eminent Japanese physicist and teacher. Studied at Tokyo University and in Germany, including work under Dr. Helmholtz in Berlin. Inventor in 1890 of a pure-temperament harmonium called the Enharmonium, built for him by *Philip J. Trayser & Co.* of Stuttgart. *Johannes Kewitsch* also made enharmonic organs for Tanaka. At the urging of Kaiser Wilhelm he designed an

TABER
ORGAN COMPANY,

WORCESTER, MASS., U. S. A.

☞ *Send for Catalogues.* ☜

W. H. PAIGE & CO.,
AGENTS,
607 Nain Street, . . . **TERRE HAUTE, Ind.**

enharmonic pipe organ, based on the same scale as the Enharmonium, which was built by *E.F. Walcker & Co.* of Ludwigsburg, Germany. After returning to Japan he had a number of Enharmoniums built at *Yamaha*'s Yokohama factory.

TANAKA FUKIN SEIZO-SHO; 4 Banchi, 3 Bancho, Kōjimachi, Tokyo. Kamekichi Tanaka, proprietor. Active 1890. Made seven styles of relatively inexpensive organs, from 39 to 61 keys.

TANNHÄUSER SÄCHSISCHE HARMONIUM- WERKE- STÄTTEN LÖFFLER & CO., see Löffler & Co.

TANSAIN HARMONIUM WORKS, THE; Gujranwala, Punjab, India, 1930.

TATE, JOHN; 5 Dickenson St., Kentish Town, London.

TATE, see *Duff & Tate.*

TAYLOR, A., & CO.; USA, 1890.

TAYLOR, ABRAHAM & GEORGE; USA. Melodeon and cabinet organ makers, 1829.

TAYLOR, C.R., & CO.; USA. (No other information available.)

TAYLOR, CHARLES; Milwaukee, WI, ca. 1877-78.

TAYLOR & FARLEY ORGAN CO.; 17 Hermon St., Worcester, MA, 1855-85. John A. Farley and Simeon Taylor, proprietors. Hermon St. factory built in 1865. Incorporated in 1870. Serial Numbers: 1866—2914, 1867—1624 & 4047, 1874—18150, 1884—34463.

TAYLOR, JAMES B.; USA. (No other information available.)

TAYLOR, P.H.; USA. (No other information available.)

TAYLOR, V.N. & J.E.; Chicopee Falls, MA 1861. Melodeon manufacturers.

TEALDO, ANTONIO; via Fontanelle, Vicenza, Italy in 1903; 20 Settembre 18, Vicenza in 1909. Harmonium maker and repairman.

TECK-HARMONIUMFABRIK; Oettlinger Str. 74, Kirchheim u. Teck, Germany in 1930; Kircheim, Teck in 1940, 1950 and 1964. Established 1925 as *Harmoniumfabrik GmbH* by Ernst Wissmann, Johannes Hepperle and Immanuel Reitheimer, proprietors. Made pressure and suction harmoniums. Harmonium production ended in 1975 and the firm was closed in 1990. Also listed as *Hepperle & Reitheimer. Reitheimer* also built organs under his own name (qv).

TEMLETT, W.; 95 Union Street, Borough, SE London. Harmonium manufacturer 1878-86. In 1887 expanded to 93-95 Union Street. In 1889 making banjos, no mention of harmoniums.

TEMPLE; New Haven, CT; St. Louis, MO.

TERINS; Ivry, Paris. Reed maker.

TESTÉ, J.A.; Nantes, France 1861. Organette maker.

TEUSCHER & WALTER; Schönauer Str. 16, Leipzig-Leutzsch, Germany. Harmonium maker, 1923-26.

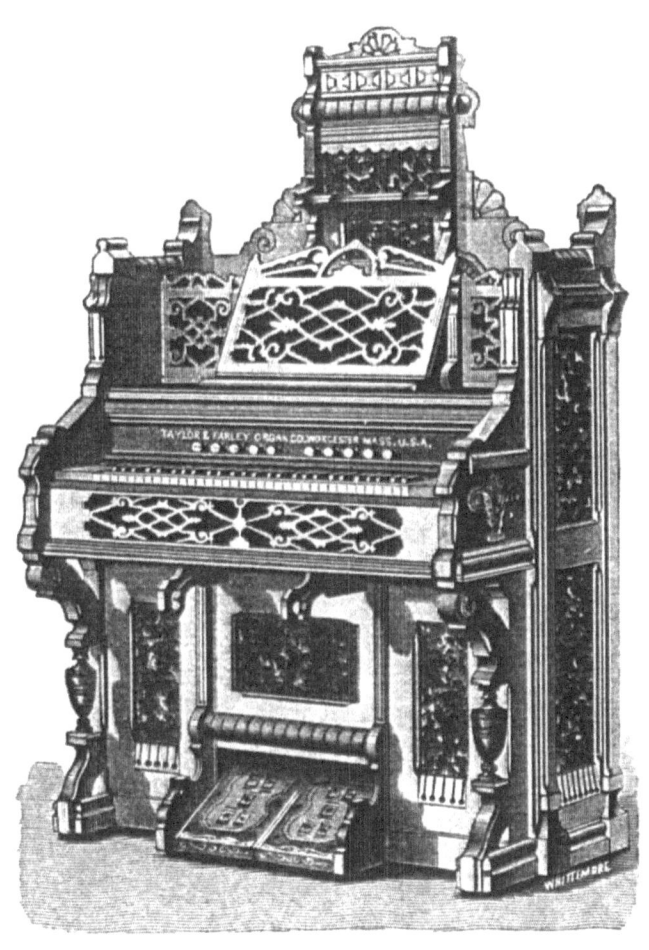

A Taylor & Farley parlor organ.

TEWKSBURY, GEORGE W.; Mendota, IL 1857-65. Made about a dozen melodeons 1857-65, then formed a partnership with *E.B. Carpenter* called *Tewksbury, Carpenter & Co.*, 1865-73. Tewksbury left in 1873 and the company became *Carpenter, Scott & Wise*, and in 1875 *Western Cottage Organ Co.*, (qv). In 1885 Tewksbury and E.E. Wise bought John A. Comstock's interest in the *Chicago Cottage Organ Co.* (qv).

THAYER, ALBERT; see *Foster & Thayer*.

THIBOUVILLE-LAMY, JÉRÔME, & CIE.; 140 rue St.-Charles, Grenelle, Paris; factory at 68-70 rue Réaumur, Paris, 1883, 1903; harmonium factory at 1 ave. Graillet, Mirecourt, Vosges, France. Made a wide variety of musical instruments including harmoniums and the Organina, a book-music organette; established 1790, still working in 1921.
THIBOUVILLE, see *Husson-Buthod & Thibouville.*
THIEL & TSCHIEDEL; Schmejkalplatz 2, Teplitz, Bohemia, Austria-Hungary. Established 1897. Listed as *Thiel & Sohn*, 14 Schulg, Teplitz, Czechoslovakia in 1930.
THIERY MILWAUKEE REED ORGAN CO.; Milwaukee, WI. J.B. Thiery, proprietor. Sold organs made by *Kimball* with the Thiery stencil. (See Kimball for serial numbers.) Active at least from 1907 through 1917. Serial number: 1917—385498.
THIES, WILLIAM, & SON; Huntingburg, IN. Made "Imperial" organs 1902.
THOMAS ORGAN CO.; Woodstock, Ontario. Founded in 1875 by Edward G. Thomas, a member of a large family of organ and piano builders. "Made by British labour in Britain's Premier Colony." James Dunlop became a partner in 1891 and owner in 1895 when the name changed to *Thomas Organ & Piano Co*. Capacity in 1900: 150 reed organs per month. In the 1920s made the Thomas Orchestral and Symphony reed organs and in the late 1920s produced a portable reed organ.
THOMPSON ORGAN CO.; Chicago, IL.
THOMPSON & SHACKELL, LTD.; Queen's Buildings Music Warehouse, Cardiff, Wales 1879-1906.
THOMPSON, see *Reynolds & Thompson, Berry & Thompson.*
THORKILDSEN, see *Torkildsen.*
THORNTON, JAMES, & CO.; Hamilton, Ontario 1871-89.
THULÉ, B.A., see *Kangasalan Urkutehdas.*
THULIN, see *Peterson, Thulin & Co.*
THURINGIA PIANO & ORGAN COMP.; Gera, Reuss, Germany; see *Wilhelm Spaethe.*
THÜRMER, FERDINAND; Meissen, Germany. Still operating at Friederikastr. 4, Bochum, Germany, Jan Thürmer, proprietor. Piano maker, established 1834. Made a combination piano and harmonium for which he was awarded a bronze medal at the Halle Exposition in 1880.
TIAINEN, A.J., see *Tampereen.*
TIDDER, W.H.; 228 Mile End Rd., London 1895, 1897, 1906; later *W.H. Tidder & Sons*. Seraphine, harmonium and concertina makers. In 1896 located at 144 Jamaica Street, London making steel reeds. In 1900 also shown at White Horse Court, White Horse Lane, E. London. In 1909

Style No. 11—Five-Octave Size

Thiery Milwaukee Reed Organ Co., Milwaukee, Wisconsin, 1907.

at 2a Whitehead Street, Cleveland Street, Mile End, London. In 1914 listed as an American organ and portable harmonium maker.

TIGER organ, see *Yamaha, Zen-on*.

TITZ, JOHANNES; Gerberstr. 126, Löwenberg, Germany. Established in 1880, closed about 1944. Frau verw. E. Titz, proprietor in 1930. Maker of the Karg-Elert harmonium.

TITZ, PETER; Vienna, Austria; served as an apprentice to *Jakob Deutschmann*, and in 1852 began making harmoniums under his own name. The factory was continued after his death in 1873 by and in the name of his son-in-law *Theophil Kotykiewicz* (qv).

B. F. TOBIN & CO.,
Manufacturers of
CARHART'S CELEBRATED PATENT IMPROVED
Melodeons, Seraphines, & Reed ORGANS,
Corner of Main and Water Sts., Nashua, N. H.

TOBIN, B.F., & CO.; 21 Factory St., then Corner of Main and Water Streets in 1853 Nashua, NH. B.F. Tobin and Edmund Sawyer listed as principals in 1853. In business at least as early as 1850. Made melodeons using the Carhart patent of 1846. Probably succeeded by *T. & E. Sawyer* (qv), who are listed at the same address in 1857-58.

TODA, KINDŌ; Japan. Made the Shikō-Kin from 1883 to 1910, a 14 note paper roll organette patterned after an instrument belonging to the Rev. Christopher Carrothers, a Christian missionary in Tokyo. Toda was also a partner in the music dealership Jujiya Gakki-Ten.

TODESCHINI; Bento Gonçalves, Santa Catarina, Brazil. Harmonium maker.

TOFANELLI, EMANUELE; via della Stella 67, Viareggio, Italy in 1903; at via Umberto I 83-85, Viareggio in 1909. Church organ and harmonium maker.

TOKYO FUKINSHA; 1-1 Nishikicho, Kanda, Tokyo. Advertised as an organ maker in 1889. The dealer was Shunseido, 1 Izumicho, Kanda, Tokyo.

TOLLIVER, O.; Pittsfield, MA. Melodeon maker.

TOMATI & CIA.; Corso Roma, Diano S. Pietro, Italy. Established in 1830. In 1909 the proprietor was Battista Tomati.

The Shikō-Kin, made by Kindō Toda, Japan.

TOMBO GAKKI SEISAKUSHO; 2-12-16 Shimo-Toda, Toda, Saitama, Japan; 8-853 Nippoli, Arakawa, Tokyo; presently located at 2-12-27 Toda, Toda City, Saitama, 335 Japan. Established in 1900 by Seijirō Mano (1872-1945) at Ueno, Tokyo. He designed many toy organs, and began making reed organs in 1937 which were sold through *Zen-on*. Although reed organ production has been discontinued, Tombo is presently one of the leading accordion and harmonica manufacturers in Japan.

TØMMERAAS, PEDER OLSEN; Harstad, Norway. Pipe organ and harmonium repairman. Built at least two harmoniums and received a silver medal at the exhibition in Harstad in 1895.

TONSYRENO organ, 46 note player organ probably made by *Mechanical Orguinette Co.* and imported into England by Geo. White & Co.

TØRKILDSEN, BRØDRENE (brothers); Åsen, Norway. Iver Torkildsen learned organ building from *J.C. Isachsen*, and began building harmoniums on his own in Åsen in 1879. In 1882 his brother Peder joined him and *Brødrene Tørkildsen* was formed. About 1920 Peder's sons Ivar and Karl took over the firm and about 1970 it passed to Ivar's sons Per Oyvind and Nils Harald. The firm built approximately 10,000 harmoniums, most of them in the period 1890-1910. Harmonium production stopped about 1952. The first instruments were of the pressure type, but in 1886 they switched over to the suction type after Peder had travelled to Chicago to study the "American system" with the Chicago Cottage Organ Co. Pipe organ production began in 1898, and the firm is now the second largest pipe organ builder in Norway. Current address: *Brødrene Tørkildsen A/S orgelbyggeri*, 7630 Åsen, Norway.

TORONTO MELODEON MANUFACTURING; Toronto, Ontario, 1862. See *R.S. Williams*.

TORONTO ORGAN CO.; Toronto, Ontario 1880.

TORONTO STANDARD ORGAN CO.; Toronto, Ontario, 1886. Operated by William H. Williams, brother of *R.S. Williams*.

TORSTE, see *Conrad, Martin & Torste*.

TOTTERDELL & PRICE; 2 Kingsland Green, London N. Manufacturer of harmoniums and American organs, June 1887.

TOURNAPHONE MUSIC CO.; 9 May Street, Worcester, MA 1885; organettes.

TOURNEUR, A.; 103 boulev. Ménilmontant, Paris. Harmoniflute maker 1883.

TOUZAA ET HOUPIN; 16 boulevard Saint-Germain, Paris, 1920.

TOWER, SYLVESTER; 139 Broadway, Cambridgeport, MA. Established 1853, in business until at least 1889; manufacturer of piano and organ keys.

TOWNSEND, WILLIAM; Hamilton and Toronto, Ontario; 1840-56.

TŌYŌ DENSI GAKKI KENKYUJO, see *Croda Organ Kabushiki Gaisha*.

TŌYŌ GAKKI SEIZO CO. LTD. (The Oriental Musical Instrument Mfg. Co. Ltd.); Tatsuno, Hyogo prefecture, Japan. Established Feb. 6, 1896. Jinzaburo Ikeuchi, chief engineer; Toyohiko Hori, a banker, was president. Made organs under the names *Ikeuchi Fukin, Maekawa, Minami, Tōyō Gakki Seizo* and *Orient*. Dealers were Yoshioka-Hōbun-Kan and Maekawa. Sold organs to the Tokyo School of Music and also exported. Made 1,500 instruments per year in 1915. Closed April 11, 1911.

TŌYŌ-SHA FUKIN; 3 Kamakura-cho, Kanda, Tokyo. Made reed organs from 39 to 61 keys, the latter with 15 stops. Active 1902.

TRACY, see *Parker & Tracy*.

TRANE & SONS; Wrexham, England.

TRAVIS, WM.; 109 Manchester Street, Oldham, Lancashire, England. Harmonium and piano maker 1879-85.

TRAYSER MELODEONS & ORGANS; Indianapolis, IN; established in 1849 by George W. Trayser, brother of *Philip J. Trayser* of Stuttgart, Germany. After serving an apprenticeship in the *Alexandre* factory in Paris, emigrated to the U.S.; moved to Ripley, OH in 1869 and then to Richmond, IN in 1872 when James S. and Benjamin Starr acquired an interest. Trayser retired in 1878 and Milo J. Chase entered the firm. Chase and Starr eventually separated, Chase forming the Chase Piano Co. and later the Chase Bros. Piano Co. The Trayser Piano Co. became a subsidiary of the Starr Piano Co.

PH. J. TRAYSER & CO.,
STUTTGART.

TRAYSER, PHILIPP J., & CO.; Neu Weinsteige in 1853, Gerberstr. 19 in 1854, Sennefelderstr. 6 in 1883, Rothebühlstrasse 100 in 1887-90; Reinsburgstr. 21 in 1903, all in Stuttgart, Germany. Established 1847 after Philipp J. Trayser had learned the harmonium business at the *Alexandre* factory in Paris. Julius Laemmert was the proprietor in 1903, by which time the company had produced 37,000 instruments. Built an enharmonic organ for *Shohei Tanaka*, (qv).

TREAT & LINSLEY; 21 Chestnut St., New Haven, CT 1856-65; John L. Treat and Nelson Linsley; factory on Franklin St. Linsley sold out to a Mr. Davis of Worcester, MA in 1864 and the firm became *Treat & Davis*. A few months later the factory burned, Linsley bought back his interest from Davis and moved the factory to Chapel and Chestnut Streets, and in 1865 sold out to *B. Shoninger & Co*. Serial number: 1861—10005.

TREAT & RICHARDSON; Boston, MA; James Elbert Treat and John P. Richardson, established 1875. Treat was primarily a pipe organ builder, but wanting to investigate the use of free reeds in the cabinet organ he went to work for *George Woods* 1871-74. In 1875 he formed a partnership with Richardson to build cabinet organs but sold out to Richardson in 1876 and accepted employment with pipe organ builders Hutchings & Plaisted.

TREE, CHAS. B.; 132 Petherton Road, Highbury, N London in 1879.

TREFZ & FEUCHT; Obere Heusteige 10, Stuttgart, Germany in 1873. Exhibitor at the Vienna Exposition of 1873. Established 1872 by Johannes Trefz and Johannes Feucht. Operated at least through 1883.

TREMAINE, HARRY B., president of the *Aeolian Co.*, son of William B. Tremaine.

TREMAINE, WILLIAM BARNES, founder of *The Mechanical Orguinette Co.* and the *Aeolian Co.*

TREMAUX, PIERRE; Charcey Nr. Bourgneuf, France. Exhibited a "Patent Improved Harmonium" at the London Exhibition of 1851. This instrument could "lessen at pleasure the sonorousness of low notes."

TRIUMPH DELUXE organ, made by others ca.1925 for Salvationist Publishing & Supplies Ltd., Judd Street, King's Cross, London W.C. 1, a part of the Salvation Army. Chapel, folding and suitcase models were available.

TRÖGER, MAX; Marknewkirchner Str. 18e in 1912, Zwota, Germany. Established in 1899, made harmoniums and table harmoniums through 1959. Also listed as *Erste Vogtländische Harmoniumfabrik*.

TROLL, SAMUEL; see *Geo. Baker & Co.*

TROST, E.; 263-4 Whitechapel Road, London. Harmonium and accordion maker, 1863.

TRUCHSESS, THEODOR; Stuttgart, Germany; patent for pressure harmonium in 1904; 22 Jesinger Str., Kircheim-Teck, Germany, 1930. Serial number: 1930—1284/8250. See *Mayer & Truchsess*.

TRUEMAN, PETER; England. Currently (1992) producing small handcranked street reed organs, both book and roll player models.

TRUSLOW, GROVESTEEN V.; New York, NY. Melodeon maker.

TRYBER & SWEETLAND; 246-250 West Lake St., Chicago, IL; made the Lakeside organ. Established 1882 by W.F. Tryber and F.R. Sweetland. Succeeded by *E. Sweetland Co.* and *Lakeside Organ Co.*, which was later absorbed by *Cable-Nelson*. Serial number: 1898—29718.

```
┌─────────────────────────────┐
│   Tryber & Sweetland,       │
│   246, 248 & 250 WEST LAKE ST.; │
│          CHICAGO.           │
└─────────────────────────────┘
```

TSCHANTZ, see *Schantz*.
TSCHANUN, B.; 7 chemin des Liles Servette, Geneva, Switzerland; established 1873.
TSCHANUN FRÈRES, G. & A.; 46 Grand Pré, Geneva, Switzerland, 1930.
TSCHIEDEL, see *Thiel & Tschiedel*.
TSUCHIYA, ICHITARO; Hamamatsu, Matsushiro, Shizuoka, Japan. Exhibitor at the 3rd Domestic Industrial Exhibition, Tokyo, 1890.
TSUJI PIANO & ORGAN FACTORY; Kishiwada, Osaka, Japan 1915.
TUBI, GRAZIANO; Castello, Lecco, Italy. Established 1860, in business until at least 1929; also *Fabbrica de Armoniums Dott. Graziano Tubi*. Exhibited a harmonium attachment for pianos at the World's Columbian Exposition in Chicago in 1895.
TUČEK, JOHANNES; Kuttenberg, Bohemia, Austria-Hungary, established 1869. Succeeded by *Jan Tuček*, located at St. Barbaragasse 47 in 1903; at Svatobarborská 210 in 1930, Kutná Hora (Kuttenberg), Czechoslovakia. Katharine & Zdenek Tuček, proprietors in 1930. By 1883 Tuček had produced over 5,000 harmoniums and 300 organs.
TUČEK, W.; Karolinenthal, Prague, Czechoslovakia, 1883; Jesuitengasse 25, Kuttenberg, Bohemia in 1885; Wassertorstr. 8, Glatz in 1912 (now Klodzko, Poland). Established 1860 in Prague. Organ and harmonium maker and piano dealer. Wwe. A. Tuček, proprietor in 1912.
TUCKER, W.B.; 95 King's Rd, Chelsea and 334 Euston Rd., London in 1903. Also shown at 329 Euston Road and at 95 King's Road, Chelsea, London. In business at least through 1914 as a portable harmonium and piano maker.
TULLER, A.; Melbourne, Australia. Awarded a Third Order of Merit at the Melbourne Exposition of 1880.
TURBAN & CIE.; France; reed maker. Awarded an honorable mention at the 1878 Paris Exposition.
TURNER, see *Kesner & Turner*.
TUSSELING, H.J.; Barneveld, Netherlands. Made the Barnova organ.

TYLER APPARATUS CO. LTD.; 15 Gerrard Street, London, 1915. Made the Tyler Orchestral Grand, a theater organ which included piano, reed organ, bells, zither and harp.

This Union organ was offered for $15.00 plus a list of 25 names in 1883.

U

UHLIG, CARL FRIEDRICH; Chemnitz, Germany. Learned accordion making with Cyrill Demian in Vienna. Physharmonica and accordion maker, established about 1830.

ULLMANN, CH. & J.; 11 rue du Faubourg Poissonnière, Paris. Established 1881 by Charles and Jules Ullmann.

ULLMANN, JOSEF; Lederergasse 23, Vienna, Austria; established 1839.

ULLRICH & PHILIPP; Nicolaistr. 2 in 1921, Dippoldiswalder Gasse 11 in 1929, Dresden, Germany. Established 1876, closed in 1931. Piano and harmonium maker.

ULVESTAD & HAUGEN; Volda, Norway. Established in the early 1900s by *Lars E. Ulvestad* and *Bernt M. Haugen*. They later split up and both produced harmoniums.

UMBREIT; 13 place de la Justice, Brussels, Belgium, 1913-20. Maker and retailer of pianos and harmoniums. In 1930 shown as a retailer only at 83 rue Hotel des Monnaies, Brussels.
UMLAUF, JOSEF; Rozasagasse 39, Budapest, Hungary, 1903.
UNION; located near Naka-Izumi, a station on the Tokaido railway line in Shizuoka prefecture, Japan. Active about 1946-65. The dealer for Union was Miyaji Shokai. A fire, which started in the glue process, burned the factory resulting in bankruptcy.
UNION ORGAN MANUFACTURING CO., THE; 90-94 South Water St., New Bedford, MA 1883, 1885; 8-10 Coffin St., office at 104 Union St.
UNITED STATES ORGAN, see *F.L. Raymond.*
UNIVERSAL folding organ, see *Marshall Brothers.*
UNIVERSITY ORGANS, see *Marchal & Smith, A.J. Spencer.*
UPTON & MILLER; Rochester, NY.
UXBRIDGE CABINET ORGAN CO.; Uxbridge, Ontario; established in 1872, later became the *Uxbridge Organ Co.* and in 1898 the *Uxbridge Piano & Organ Co.* Apparently went out of business about 1909. See *Clay City Organ Co.*

V

VALENTINE, LORENZO; Market Place and Scalford Road, Melton Mowbray, Leicestershire, England. Pipe organ, piano and harmonium maker 1882-90.
VALLA, ABBÉ; Charlieu, Loire, France. Made a transposing harmonium with suction bellows, 1850.
VALLÉ; rue du Vieux-Colombier, Paris. Made orgues-expressifs called Euphonicon and Euphonium, 1850.
VAN BEVER-LACKEN; Belgium. Exhibited in Antwerp, Belgium, 1885.
VANCOUVER ORGAN CO.; 3425 Pt. Grey Road, Vancouver, BC, Canada 1930.
VAN DEN BURG, R.; Arnhemsestraat 8, Amersfoort, Netherlands; makers of Pedalion and Clavion organs until 1968.
VAN DEN KIRKHOVEN, see *Kerkhoff.*
VANDERBURG; Vienna, Austria. Made the Oedelphone, probably a kind of Physharmonica, in 1818.

J. VAN DER TAK & Co.
Hooge Boezem.
FABRIKANTEN VAN
AMERIKAANSCHE ORGELS.

VAN DER TAK & CO.; Leuvenhaven in 1859, then Boerenvismarkt, Kipstraat, in 1880 located at Hoogeboezemkad 32, and in 1913 at Schoutenstraat 159, all in Rotterdam, Netherlands. J. van der Tak, proprietor. Annual production in 1900 was about 600 organs per year and total production is estimated to be in excess of 20,000 instruments by 1913. The factory burned in the 1920s and the firm went out of business. Most of the personnel then went to work for *S. G. Reyns*, (qv).

VAN DINTER, LOUIS, & CO.; (also van Deuter, van Duiter), Detroit, MI. Pipe and reed organ maker, 1883, 1929. See *Simmons & Van Dinter*.

VAN DOREN & CARTER: Washington, NJ. Flat top organ with painted panels of birds and flowers.

VAN DYKE, J.M.; 444 Broadway, New York, NY; New Yorker organ.

VAN GRUISEN, N.L.; rue St. Honoré, Paris and 17 Bold St., Liverpool, England 1855, 1867. The Liverpool address was probably a sales office.

VAN KESTEREN, J.; Gennep, Netherlands. Harmonium maker.

VAN MATRE, WILLARD NAREMORE; Beloit, WI. Music dealer 1877-85. Sold the Van Matre organ, made for him in Chicago. Became sales manager and a stockholder in the *Chicago Cottage Organ Co.* from 1885 to 1895. Later he was a principal in several piano companies.

VAN MINDEN, R.; New York, NY. (Also von Minden). Flat top organ.

VAN OECKELEN, CORNELIUS JACOBUS; Boston, MA. Born in Holland in 1798 to a family of organ builders and clock makers, he showed an early aptitude for mechanical innovation. At age 22 he won a bronze medal at the Ghent Industrial Fair for a mechanical piano. He emigrated to the Dutch East Indies in 1839 and in 1855 moved again to Boston. He made and patented several types of reed organs including the Melodium, a lap organ which won a silver medal at the Boston Exhibition. Some of his other inventions included a machine for packing chewing tobacco, a snow-sweeping machine, a life-saving apparatus for fire accidents and numerous musical instruments including the triolodeon, the improved banjo, the "night-melodeon" and the pedal violoncello. None of these inventions brought him financial success. He died in New York in 1865.

VAN RAAY, JOHANNES; (1775-1845). Amsterdam; Netherlands. A highly regarded piano maker, he also patented the Melodium in 1811 and the Aeolodicon in 1820. His sons Hein and Frans were also active in the firm.

VARETTO, PETER; Manchester, England. Reed barrel organ.

VAZ DE CARVALHO; Portugal. Showed a harmonium with a vertical reed pan at the Paris Exhibition of 1867.

VEB LEIPZIGER PIANOFORTEFABRIK BÖHLITZ-EHRENBERG, see *Leipziger Pianofortefabrik Böhlitz-Ehrenberg, VEB*.

VEGEZZI-BOSSI, CARLO; Corso S. Maurizio 79, Turin, Italy, 1903.

VÉGH, V. KÁROLY; 63 Rákóczy út, Budapest, Hungary, 1930.

VEIT, ANTONI; Dzika 47, Warsaw, Poland. Barrel organ and harmonium maker, 1903, 1909.

VELIK, see *Lidl & Velik*.

VENABLES & CO.; 187-189 Essex Road, London. Formerly in Lower Road, Islington, London. Harmonium maker 1869.

VENDITI, FRANCESCO; Cava de Tirreni, Italy, 1930.

VENERI, NESTORI; Sammarcello, Italy, 1903, 1909.

VENKAT & CO.; 130 Mint Street, Madras, India, 1930.

VERHAERT, A.; 100 Marche St. Jacques, Antwerp, Belgium; Wwe. A. Verhaert, proprietor, 1903.

VERHASSELT, FRANÇOIS (1813-1853); rue des Paroissiens from about 1838 to 1841; petite rue des Dominicains in 1841; vieille halle aux Bles 15 in 1843; vieille halle aux Bles 21 in 1848; rue Leopold 2 from 1853 to 1855, all in Brussels, Belgium. Maker of accordions, harmoniums, mechanical instruments and pianos. Awarded a bronze medal for an orgue-expressif at the Brussels Exhibition of 1841. In 1847 he showed three harmoniums at the Brussels Exhibition and was awarded a silver medal. In 1842 he married Marie-Anne-Elisabeth d'Outrelepont. After François' death in 1853 she continued the business until about 1855. Some of the instruments carry the label *Verhasselt d'Outrelepont*.

VERMEULEN, MART; Voostr. 27, Woerden, Netherlands, 1930. Made two-manual and pedal harmoniums.

VESTRE'S ORGELFABRIKK; Haramsøy, Norway; established in 1888 by Ludvig Vestre, who had previously built a few harmoniums beginning in 1885. He died about 1937 and his son Hans took over. Hans died in 1955 and was succeeded by his wife Jennie and their son Ludvig. Vestre's originally made only harmoniums but later expanded into pipe organs, and built a few pianos in the period 1947-54. Harmonium production was discontinued about 1970 after about 10,000 instruments had been built. The firm was incorporated in 1980 and went bankrupt in 1982.

VICTORIA ORCHESTRIONETTE, a hand-cranked music box with reeds, using perforated cardboard music books, made in Germany.

A Vocalion organ, about 1900.

VICTOR PIANO & ORGAN CO.; offices in the Bush Temple of Music, factory at 49th Ave. and West Lake St., Chicago, IL. Officers in 1903: Walter Lane, president; W.L. Bush, treasurer; B.F. Bush, secretary.
VIERDAG, see *Steinmann & Vierdag*.
VIRGIL folding organ, "new perfected clavier." Instrument sold at auction. (No other information available.)
VIROT, CHARLES; 67 Stanhope St., Euston Rd., London in 1878; in 1879 moved to 15 Seymour St., Euston Sq.; still there in 1883. Manufactured reeds and also harmoniums, including a two-manual with a retractable pedalboard.
VISHWAKARMA MUSIC CORP.; Railway Road, Phagwara, India. Table harmonium maker.
VITTINO, FRATELLI; Centallo, Italy 1883; Francesco Vittino in 1903 and 1909; established 1824.
VOCALION ORGAN CO., THE; Meriden, CT; 18 W. 23rd St., New York, NY 1900; see *Aeolian, James Baillie-Hamilton, New York Church Organ Mfg. Co., Mason & Risch, S.R. Warren*. The Vocalion organ was sold in Europe as the Gregorian organ.

Serial numbers:

1889—589	1893—1960/2030	1903—4258
1890—979	1895—2374/2476	1906—4801
1892—1001	1899—3245	
1892—1757	1900—3615	

VOGEL & HUGHES ORGAN CO.; Norwich, CT. C. William Vogel and George H. Hughes. *William Vogel* is listed alone as a musical instrument maker located at 103 Franklin St. in 1869, then Vogel & Hughes at White's Court in 1872 and in Thamesville 1873-75. After 1875 Hughes is listed separately as an organ tuner.

VOGEL, J.C., & SOHN.; Heinrichstr. 19, Ecke Schloss-Str., Plauen, Germany. Harmonium in the Weischet collection.

VOGLER, GEORGE JOSEPH, (the Abbé, 1749-1814); learned to make free reeds from Rachwitz, an assistant to the Danish organ builder Kirschnik. Vogler built a portable organ in 1784 which he called the orchestrion, using free reeds. He toured Europe with the organ, and built pipe organs with free-reed stops.

VOIGT; Schweinfurt, Germany. Maker of the Eolodicon in 1815, an early reed organ.

VOIGT, ARNO; Schlossäckerstr. 17 in 1930, currently at Schlossäckerstr. 34, Liebenwerda, Germany. Established 1905. Organ and harmonium maker.

VOIGT & GOLL, see *Süddeutsche Harmoniumfabrik Voigt & Goll.*

VON JANKÓ, see *Jankó, Paul von.*

VON OETTINGEN, see *Oettingen, Arthur von.*

VOTEY, see *Farrand & Votey.*

VOUGH PIANO CO.; Waterloo, NY; purchased the plant, property and business of the *Waterloo Organ Co.* in 1903.

VROM & KENNEDY; Washington, NJ 1861. Melodeon and Harmonium manufacturers. Also shown as *Vroom & Kennedy.*

VYGEN JEUNE; 12 rue d'Hauteville, Paris, 1883. Organ and harmonium maker, 1883, 1896. Alphonse Grus, successor.

W

WADDINGTON AND SONS; New Station Street, Leeds, England. Established in 1838. Making harmoniums at 9 Woodhouse Lane, Leeds in 1885 and 1897; also had premises at 44-66 Stonegate, York. Made a combined piano and harmonium in 1882. The sons succeeded to the business as *William Alfred and Walter Waddington*.
WAGE, L.; Hamburg, Germany.
WAGENHAUS, KARL; 279 Stretford Rd., Manchester, England, 1903.
WAGNER, P.J., & CO.; Neue Str. 24, Gera, Germany. Showed accordions and harmoniums at the London Exhibition of 1862.
WAGONER & FRENCH; Lead, SD; J.P. Wagoner and Brooks French, a former employee of *Ft. Wayne Organ Co.* French held U.S. Patent No. 254950 for a stop action.
WAITE, SILAS M., see *J. Estey & Co., Brattleboro Melodeon Co., Burdett Organ Co.*
WALCKER, E.F., & CO.; Cannstatt b. Stuttgart, Germany in 1780; Untere Kasernenstr. 14-22, Vordere Schlossstr. 41-43 and Postgasse 1-3 Ludwigsburg, Germany in 1903. Established in 1780 or 1820 (sources vary), still in operation as a pipe organ builder. Made harmoniums from 1838 to about 1914.
WALCKER-MAYER, WERNER; Ludwigsberg, Germany. Harmonium maker, 1954. Doing business as *Harmoniumbau Ludwigsberg*.
WALHORN, ANTON; Prinzipalmarkt 39 in 1890, Rothenburg 36 in 1903, Münster, Germany. Harmonium maker and piano dealer, established in 1871. Specialized in miniature harmoniums.
WALKER; Norwich, CT 1840; seraphines.
WALKER, SAMUEL; 92-100 Leeds Road, Bradford, England.
WALKER, T.W.; Oxford St., Ripley, Derbyshire, England, 1903.
WALLGATE, C.A., & CO. LTD.; 36 Southwark Bridge Rd., London. Manufacturer of parts for pianos and reed organs, 1921 through at least 1954.
WALLIS, J.; *Joseph Wallis & Son (Ltd.)* in 1903, 133-135 Euston Rd., London NW, England. Established in 1848. He was succeeded by his son James Wallis, who in turn was followed as head of the company by H.E.H. Standish. In 1915 George Wallis headed the business. Maker of Wallis' Patent Table Organ, harmoniums and American organs. In 1906 listed as making reed organ parts and reeds and in 1921 as a maker of pianos and players.
WALTER, see *Tenscher & Walter*.
WARD; England 1879; harmonium maker.

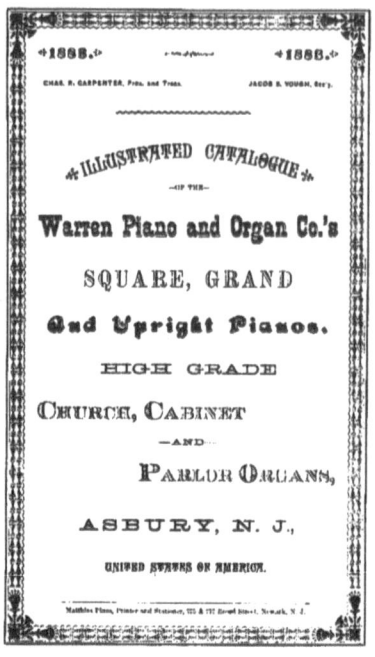

WARKHOLD, HANS; Weinbergsweg 5, Berlin, Germany, 1909, 1913; harmonium maker. Instrument repairman through 1930.

WARMHOLZ, CARL SALOMO; Eisleben, Germany. Made a combination piano-äolodikon in 1829.

WARREN ORGAN CO.; Washington, NJ; organized 1878 by *Alleger, Bowlby & Co.*, became *Warren Piano & Organ Co.* 1881, removed to Asbury, NJ July 7, 1883. Charles R. Carpenter, president and treasurer, Jacob S. Vough, secretary.

WARREN, S.R.; Montreal, Quebec; "makers of church, parlour, reed organs, seraphims, melodeons and pianofortes." Samuel Russell Warren previously worked with Thomas Appleton, a pipe organ builder in Boston. He also had a brief connection with Baillie-Hamilton and the Vocalion. Later relocated to Toronto in 1878 where he built pipe organs in partnership with his son Charles S. Warren as S.R. Warren & Son. Acquired by *D.W. Karn* in 1897.

WARREN, T.D.; 615 Washington St., Boston, MA 1852; melodeons.

WARREN, see *Clough & Warren.*

WATERLOO ORGAN CO.; Waterloo, NY. Successors to *Stilwell & Genung* and *Roth, Halloran & Miles*, operating as the *Waterloo Organ Co.* Acquired by Alexander C. Reed and Malcolm Love. The factory burned in 1881 and in 1882 they purchased the former I.L. Huff machine shops and foundry as a factory location, operating under the name of *Malcolm Love & Co.* In 1888 the business was incorporated as *Waterloo Organ Co., Inc.* In 1897 they built a new three-story factory on the site of the former William W. Wood mill; this building was destroyed by fire in 1928. The company went bankrupt in 1902, and was run briefly by the First National Bank of Waterloo until the business and plant were sold to the Vough Piano Co. in 1903; see *Malcolm Love & Co.* Alexander Reed was previously associated with the *Alexander Organ Co.* of Chicago.

WATERS, HORACE, & SON; 247 Broadway, New York, NY; 487 Broadway in 1864; factory corner Broome & East St., New York. A composer and publisher of hymns, Horace Waters began selling the Gilbert piano with the Coleman reed organ attachment in 1845 to help promote his hymns. Established a retail store in New York where he also sold organs made by others with the Waters stencil. He may have manufactured organs also. Later hired William B. Tremaine (qv) and his brother to sing his hymns and demonstrate the Gilbert piano. Incorporated 1886 as *Horace Waters & Co.* Horace Waters died in 1893, but the company continued in business at least through 1925. Awarded a third prize at Sydney, Australia in 1878. Serial numbers:

```
1856—20001    1865—27900    1877—36570
1858—22670    1870—31890    1880—38477
1860—24186    1875—34789
```

WATSON & BROTHER; 220-26 S. Tenth St., Mt. Vernon, IL. Fred P. and Harry Watson, wholesale and retail dealers in vehicles, farm implements, pianos, organs and sewing machines. Organs with this name were made by others with the Watson stencil.
WATSON, J.V., organ made by *W.W. Kimball*, identical to a model sold under the *Great Western* name. Refer to Kimball for serial numbers.
WEAVER, O.D., & CO.; 195-197 Wabash Avenue, Chicago, IL. Sold organs made by Kimball with the O.D. Weaver stencil. For serial numbers refer to *W.W. Kimball.* O.D. Weaver was manager of the *H.D. Bentley* Chicago office in 1894.
WEAVER ORGAN CO.; 304 W. Market St. in 1871; 332 W. Market St. in 1882; Walnut & Broad Streets, 1884-1916, York, PA. Established by J. Oliver Weaver in 1870. Also listed as *Weaver Organ & Piano Co.* as early as 1885. Officers in 1899: Milton B. Gibson, president; William S. Bond, secretary-treasurer. Factory built in 1882, enlarged in 1891.This building is still standing in 1996 with the Weaver sign faded but visible. Capacity 4,000 organs per year in 1902 and 5,000 per year in 1908. Made the York Cottage Organ. Discontinued reed organ production about 1916.

Serial numbers:

```
1890—7238     1896—19503    1906—49248
1893—14942    1898—24800    1911—63164
1894—15542    1900—30742
```

WEDLAKE, HENRY THOMAS; 8 Berkeley Road, near Chalk Farm Station, Regent's Park, London. Maker of church pipe organs and harmoniums from 1862 to about 1900. Previously worked for *Boosey & Co.*

Style M.

**MADE IN BLACK WALNUT OR SOLID OAK,
5 OR 6 OCTAVE.**

M No. 2.—Eleven Stops. Two full sets of 5 octave reeds each, treble and bass octave coupler. Vox Humana.

M No. 3.—Twelve Stops. Two full sets of reeds, octave coupler and an extra 3-5 sets of reeds. Vox Humana.

M No. 4.—Thirteen stops. Two full sets of reeds, octave coupler, an extra 3-5 sets of reeds and sub-bass. Vox Humana.

O. D. WEAVER & CO.

195-197 Wabash Avenue　　　　　　　CHICAGO, ILL.

The former Weaver Organ & Piano Co. factory in York, Pennsylvania. (1996 photo.)

WEIDENMÜLLER, ERHARD; Klingenthal, Germany 1961. Made the "Orchestrale", a five-rank reed organ with an electric suction unit, and the portable "Harmona-cabinet" and Choretta.

```
ERHARD WEIDENMÜLLER KG, KLINGENTHAL/SA.
       ELEKTRO-MUSIKINSTRUMENTE
```

WEIPERT, STIEGLITZ & GEN.; Obere Heusteigstr. 10, Stuttgart, Germany. Established 1870. Vinzens Weipert, Emil Stieglitz, Johannes Trefz and Richard Fischer, proprietors. Acquired by *Trefz & Feucht* about 1872.
WEISCHET, see *O. Lindholm*.
WEISER & NEUMANN; 37 passage Jouffroy, Paris. Made harmoniums, harmoniflutes and orchestrions, 1883.
WELLS, WILLIAM; Brookfield, VT. An Englishman, made organs and melodeons ca. 1859-61.
WELLSTEAD, H.; West Street, Wimborne, Dorset, England. Organ builder, piano and harmonium manufacturer, 1906.
WERDAUER HARMONIUMFABRIK MAX HORN, see *Horn, Max*.
WERDAUER MOBEL- UND HARMONIUMFABRIK, see *Emil Müller*.

WERLEIN, PHILIP P.; 605 Canal St., New Orleans, LA. Philip P. Werlein established a music dealership in Vicksburg, MS in 1842. In 1853 he moved his business to New Orleans, joining William Mayo at 5 Camp Street. Werlein soon bought out Mayo and continued in business until 1861 when he was closed down as a result of the Civil War. His son, Philip Werlein II, resumed business in 1865 at 80 Baronne St., moving to 135 Canal St. in 1878. From 1896 to 1905 the business operated at 614 Canal St., and in 1905 it was moved to its present location, 605 Canal St. Philip II also established a store at 1212 Market Street in San Francisco. The Pacific Queen organ was made by *Kimball* apparently for Werlein and sold out of the San Francisco store. Werlein was the original publisher of the popular song "Dixie." The company is still in business with Philip Werlein IV as president.

WERNER, HANS, Herrengasse 3, Graz, Austria-Hungary; established 1836.

WERNER, J.; Vorsetzen 27, Hamburg, Germany. Established 1877. Made a combination piano-harmonium.

WERNER, KARL; Privatstr. 29, Leipzig-Gohlis, Germany, 1915-30.

WEST, ELIJAH; West Farnham, Quebec 1860-75.

WEST LONDON PIANO & ORGAN CO., LISTER & SONS; 246 Harrow Rd., London; established 1878.

WEST, see *Ross & West*.

WESTERN COTTAGE ORGAN CO.; Mendota, IL; organized 1875 as successor to *Carpenter, Scott and Wise*; in 1887 also incorporated as *Mendota Cottage Organ and Piano Co.* and as the *Mendota Organ and Piano Co.*; relocated to Ottawa, IL in 1887; also listed as *Western Cottage Piano & Organ Co.* Officers in 1897: L.B. Merrifield, president; O.C. Merrifield, treasurer; A.H. Merrifield, secretary; L.W. Merrifield, superintendent. Officers in 1910: L.W. Merrifield, president; George R. Woods, vice-president and treasurer. The factory burned in 1918 and the company apparently went out of business. Serial numbers:

| 1883—23297 | 1886—28140 | 1891—42319 |
| 1885—27786 | 1890—39158 | |

Western Cottage Organ Co. styles 24 and 25.

WESTMINSTER organ, see *Hamamatsu Musical Instrument Mfg. Co. Ltd.*

WEVER, EDWIN, & SOHN; Gesundheitstr. 146, Wuppertal-Elberfeld, Germany. Established 1889, in business through 1929.

WHEATSTONE & CO.; London; Sir Charles Wheatstone, physicist and inventor of the Wheatstone bridge for accurate measurement of electrical resistance, invented the concertina in 1829, made a harmonium 1834 and a portable harmonium in 1851, had early patents on the telegraph and many inventions relating to musical reeds.

WHIPPLE & BOWE; Westville, CT. Makers of a melodeon with US Patent No. 13021 granted 5 June 1855.

WHITAKER & FRISBIE; Orange St. near Court St., New Haven, CT. Founded in 1847 by David Whitaker and William Frisbie. H.N. Goodman bought out Whitaker in 1852 and the firm was renamed *Goodman & Frisbie*, shown at Leavenworth Court, New Haven. Dr. Baldwin bought Frisbie's interest and the firm became *Goodman & Baldwin*. This firm was sold to John L. Treat and Nelson Linsley in 1856, becoming *Treat & Linsley* (qv). Also see *H.N. Goodman*.

WHITE, A.L., MANUFACTURING CO.; also *White Piano & Organ Co.*; 150-160 West Erie St. in 1903; 215 Englewood Ave. in 1906; 1900 W. Grand Ave., Chicago, IL in 1943; maker of folding organs as well as a few conventional models. Albert L. White worked for *Bridgeport, Farrand & Votey, Story & Clark, Williams,* and *M. Schulz Co.* before starting this company in 1900; made folding chaplain organs for the US Army during World War I. Officers in 1910: A.L. White, president; R.L. Lanyon, secretary; M.M. Snow, treasurer. Closed in 1946.

WHITE, HENRY KIRK; New London, CT, Nantucket, MA 1847-52, Washington, NJ 1853-61; Philadelphia, PA ca.1861-64; melodeon maker, later worked for *Estey* 1865-77. He was one of the founders of *Wilcox & White*.

WHITE, JAMES PAUL; Boston, MA. A piano technician, he experimented with pure tuning and in the 1880s designed the "Harmon," an enharmonic reed organ similar to Henry Poole's design with 53 tones per octave, which was built for him by A.O. Alden. A Harmon is still extant at the New England Conservatory of Music, Boston. This instrument has a large flat keyboard with diamond-shaped keys. Serial number: 1883—3.

WHITE, SON COMPANY; 149-151 Summer St., Boston, MA; 592 East First St., South Boston, MA; organ leather dealer, still in operation.

WHITE, THOMAS, & CO.; Hamilton, Ontario, 1863 until after 1869.

WHITE, see *Kirkman & White, Murch & White*.

WHITEFIELD, FRANK; Brighton, Sussex, England. Manufacturer of small portable reed organs.

WHITEHEAD, HENRY; 51 Coney Street, York, England. Organ and harmonium manufacturer, 1855-61. Whitehead left for Dublin in 1863.
WHITEHEAD, R.R., & BROS. LTD.; 10 Endell St., Longacre, London. Felts and cloth for organs and harmoniums, 1896.
WHITELOCK, WM.; Ridge View, Armley, Leeds, England. Piano, harmonium, American organ and pipe organ builder from 1879 at least through 1885. Also listed as *Whitelock & Sons, Ltd.*
WHITMAN, G.P.; Detroit, MI; melodeons.
WHITNEY, A.H., see *Whitney & Holmes*, also *J.W. Whitney.*
WHITNEY, CLARK J.; see *Farrand & Votey.*
WHITNEY & CO.; Detroit, MI 1866-67; see *Simmons, Clough & Co.*
WHITNEY, GEORGE B.; Bridgewater, MA 1861. Melodeon manufacturer.
WHITNEY & GREER. (No other information available.)
WHITNEY, H.A.; 96 Middle St., Portland, ME. Melodeon maker 1858-59.
WHITNEY, H.A.; 18 St. Joseph St., Montreal, Canada 1861. Reed organ manufacturer.
WHITNEY & HOLMES ORGAN CO.; Quincy, IL. Established 1868 by August H. Whitney and Delvine T. Holmes, located on the second floor of the Benneson Bldg. at 508-510 Main St. Relocated to 122-128 S. Fifth St. in the early 1880s, remaining until 1891 when the factory burned. Occupied 26-28 N. Third St. until 1900, then moved to 411 Hampshire. Incorporated 1870 with Gen. James D. Morgan as president. He was succeeded by Lorenzo Bull, then Charles Keyes and Robert W. Gardner. Holmes apparently left the company early. A.H. Whitney had previously been a principal in *Whitney & Currier* and in *A.H. Whitney Organ Co.* Whitney died in 1891, succeeded by his son Frank H. Whitney. Manufacturing was discontinued in 1906 and the business continued as a piano dealership. Serial number: 1890—25229.
WHITNEY & HOLT; Meadville, PA, 1865. See *Whitney & Raymond.*
WHITNEY, J.W.; son of *A.H. Whitney*, built reed organs in his own name. See *Whitney & Holmes.*
WHITNEY, JONAS; worked for his father Jonas P. from age 18, and with his brother Josiah D. 1853-65; after 1865 he maintained a small organ shop in Boston and was still in operation in 1906.
WHITNEY, JONAS PRESCOTT; Ashby, MA; Salem, MA, Fitchburg, MA. Established 1845; pipe organ builder, later built melodeons with his three sons Josiah D., Jonas and Andrew.
WHITNEY, JOSIAH DAVIS.; Springfield, Fitchburg and Worcester, MA; (1818-1902), son of Jonas P., started with his father at age 21; then formed a partnership in 1853 in Worcester with Rice and Robinson for making reeds. His brothers Jonas and Andrew entered the firm and at

ILLUSTRATED PRICE LIST.

UNITED STATES ORGANS

MANUFACTORY: WINDSOR AVENUE, NEAR EUCLID AVENUE STATION, NON CLEVELAND & PITTSBURGH R. R.

E. TOURJÉE, Agent, - BOSTON, MASS.

WHITNEY & RAYMOND
CLEVELAND, OHIO.

BROOKS & CO., STATIONERS & PRINTERS, CLEVELAND.

some point it was relocated to Fitchburg, MA. Andrew left the firm in 1855 to go into real estate. In 1865 Josiah sold the reed-making machinery he had invented to *Estey* and went to work for Estey in Brattleboro. The youngest brother Julius also worked for Estey. Josiah left Estey and formed *J.D. Whitney and Son* in Brattleboro in 1878 and began to make reeds again, using machinery he had invented in 1876. In 1887 his reed-making business was located in the Harmony Block House, 30 Western Avenue in Brattleboro. The business produced some 500,000 reeds per year, most of which were sold to *Wilcox & White*. Estey bought out this business in 1893 and J.D. Whitney retired. He died in Brattleboro in 1902.

WHITNEY, O.C., see *Whitney & Raymond.*
WHITNEY ORGAN CO.; Detroit, MI 1885; see *Clough & Warren.*
WHITNEY & RAYMOND; 120-122 Champlain St., Cleveland, OH 1873-88; 131 Windsor Ave. in 1888; *O.C. Whitney* began making melodeons in Conneautville, PA in 1856, moved to Meadville, PA in 1865 where he formed a partnership as *Whitney & Holt*, and then to Cleveland, OH in 1870 where he established the firm of *Whitney & Slayton*. Later F.L. Raymond acquired Slayton's interest and the firm was renamed Whitney & Raymond, and was operating under this name in 1885. A.H. Steadman was admitted and the name became *Whitney, Raymond & Co.* From 1889 to 1895 the firm became known as *F.L. Raymond*; manufactured the United States Organ. Serial number: 1871—4716.
WHITNEY & SLAYTON, see *Whitney & Raymond.*
WHITNEY, W.W., see *Loring & Blake.*
WHOLESALE PIANO & ORGAN MANUFACTURING CO.; Phoenix Works, Boleyn Rd., Dalston Junction, London. In 1900 shown at 2A Wiesbaden Road, Stoke, Newington, London. Working 1903, 1906. See *Ingleton & Co.*
WHOMES, E.; 240-242 Broadway, Bexleyheath, Kent, England 1914, 1930; made the Orgapian, a combination piano and reed organ for motion picture theaters, and a smaller model without the piano called the Cinema Reed Organ or Orchestra-ette. Principals: Edmund Whomes, E. de Gruchy Whomes, Walter S. Whomes. Later called *Whomes Ltd.*, which is still in operation as a retail store.
WICK, O. E., & SON; Humboldt Park, IL. Ole E. Wick and George C. Wick, reed organ makers. Made a desk organ, ca. 1868. Patents granted 1888, 1895, 1916.
WICK ORGAN CO.; 125 South Clinton St. in 1899; 629-635 North Wood St., Chicago, IL in 1902. Established 1886, capacity 300 organs per year in 1899 and 1,500 per year in 1902. Located on Northeast Henry Street in North St. Paul, MN by 1905, incorporated there in 1906 as the

P.S. Wick Co. by Peter S. Wick. Still there in 1913, and in 1925 is listed as a piano manufacturer. Made the "Wick" organ.

WIDER, ANDREAS; Guttenbergerstr. 58, Stuttgart, Germany, 1883. Awarded a silver medal at Frankfurt in 1881 for a player harmonium. Also received an honorable mention at Stuttgart in 1881.

WIECK, FRIEDRICH WILHELM; Lüttichaustr. 29 in 1871, Johannesplatz 5f in 1873, Dresden, Germany. Piano and physharmonika maker.

WIED, H.; Hottingen, Switzerland, 1883.

WIEDEL, JAKOB; Brigachstr. 2, Villingen, Germany. Established in 1866; Aug. Wiedel, proprietor in 1930; reed maker.

WIENINGER, GUSTAV, SEN.; Lindwurmstr. 93 and Tumbingerstr. 32, Munich, Germany; G. Wieninger jun. & Karl Wieninger, proprietors; components, 1903.

WIESBAUER, ANDREW; 187 E. 12th St., Erie, PA 1867, 9th & German St., 1885. Piano and reed organ manufacturer.

WIESNER, JOSEF; Ungererstr. 30, München, Germany; established 1870; klein-harmonium, concertina and harmonica maker. Working at least through 1930.

WIEST, ANTON; Josephstadt Langen Gasse No. 59, Vienna, Austria. Barrel harmonium, ca. 1860.

WIKSTROM OCH NORD ORGELFABRIK: Kristinehamn, Sweden, 1930.

WILCOX & WHITE ORGAN CO.; Meriden, CT 1877-96; name changed to *Wilcox & White Co.*, 1897; founded by Horace C. Wilcox, a silver-plate manufacturer, and Henry Kirk White, an experienced reed organ builder, with White's sons James H., Edward H. and Howard. E.H. White was factory superintendent and developed the Angelus player. The company went bankrupt in 1921. Its assets and name were acquired by Conway Musical Industries, a piano manufacturer, in 1922. See *White, Henry Kirk*. Serial numbers were assigned in consecutive order. Serial numbers: 1882—11028, 1891—44253.

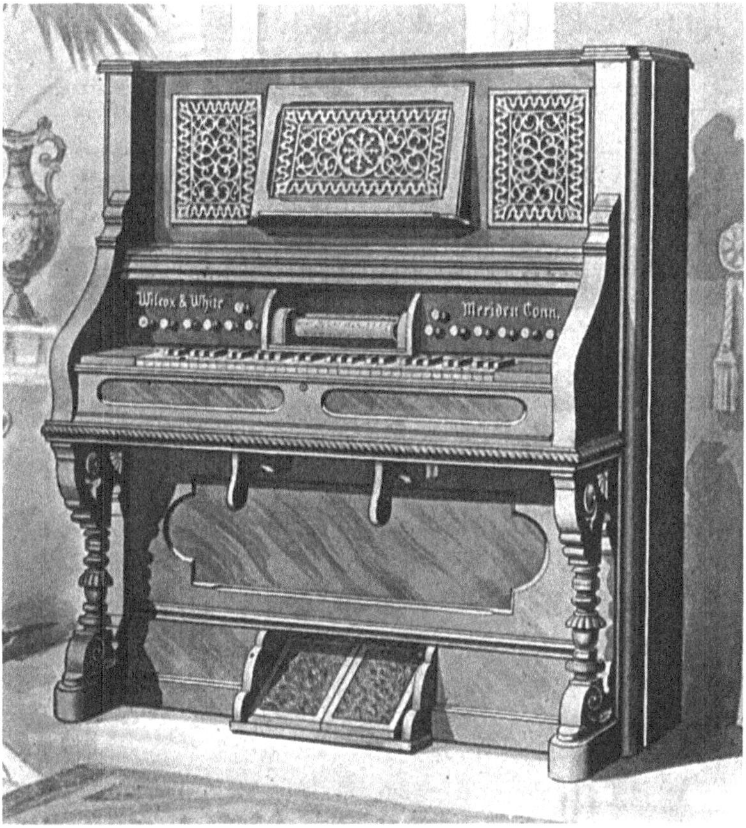

The Wilcox & White Symphony Style 210 player organ, about 1893.

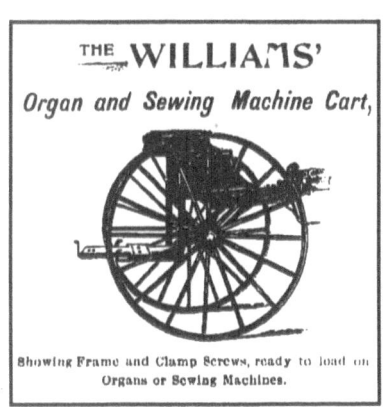

WILGREN, A.G.; Stockholm, Sweden 1871; harmoniums.
WILKE, JOHANN GOTTLIEB; Halle, Germany. Made a free-reed instrument in 1826.
WILLCOCKE, WILLIAM J.; 55 & 70 Barsbury Road, London, 1883.
WILLIAMS BROTHERS; DeSoto, MO. Maker of organs, wagons, buggies and carts. Made a special cart for delivery of organs and sewing machines.

267

WILLIAMS & EATON ORGAN CO.; Hill, NH; F.W. Eaton, proprietor; A.A. Williams, business agent 1877.

WILLIAMS, G.; 244 Caledonia Road, N. London. Factory located at Milton Yard, Cloudesley Rd., Barnsbury in 1897. In 1900 shown at 123 Parchmore Road, Thornton Heath as a portable harmonium maker.

WILLIAMS, HERBERT; 37 Shepperton Rd., New North Road, Islington, London. Manufacturer of American organs 1894 through at least 1900.

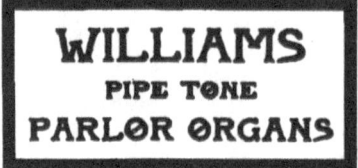

WILLIAMS ORGAN & PIANO CO.; 1427-1433 Carroll Ave., 1257 Fullerton Ave. in 1925, Chicago, IL; also located in Centerville, IA. Founded as *J.W. Williams* in 1855, then *J.W. Williams and Sons* in 1884, *Williams Organ & Piano Co.* in 1889. In 1899 the office was located at 57 Washington St. and the factory at 2622-2626 Shields Ave., Chicago. Officers in 1925: H.B. Williams, president; Carl S. Williams, VP; Bradley P. Williams, secretary. Capacity in 1899: 1,500 organs per year. Made the "Epworth" and "Williams" organs, sold through ministers, particularly Methodists. Active through 1934. Serial number: 1908—26056.

WILLIAMS, R.; Chicago, IL. (No other information available.)

WILLIAMS, R.S., & SONS; Queen St.; 143 Yonge St., Toronto, Ontario. Richard Sugden Williams was apprenticed to *William Townsend*, a melodeon maker in Toronto in the late 1840s and opened a repair shop in Hamilton or Kingston in 1849. Moved to Toronto in 1854 and begain making melodeons and other instruments. The *Toronto Melodeon Manufacturing Co.* and *The Canada Organ and Piano Co.* were established as subsidiaries in 1862 and 1873 respectively to manufacture reed organs, and the parent company remained as a retailer. The parent company was renamed *R.S. Williams & Son* in 1879 and later R.S. Williams & Sons. The factory was moved to Oshawa, Ontario in 1889 under the supervision of Robert Williams, one of the sons, who became president on the death of his father.

WILLIAMS, R.S. & W.H.; Toronto, Ontario, 1873. Probably the same as *R.S. Williams & Sons*.

WILLIAMS, V.R.; Canada. "I am a Canadian by birth and a melodeon maker by trade, and I work at it. V.R. Williams," inscription on an 1856 melodeon.

WILLIAMS, see *Foley & Williams, Nichols Williams Co.*

Style 622 — Williams Parlor Queen
List Price $150   Factory Price $75

The Williams Organ and Piano Company, Chicago

WILLING, WILLIAM; Erie, PA 1861. Professor of music, operated a music store on West State Street on the southwest corner of 8th St. for many years and manufactured pianofortes and music stools. Also made melodeons 1860-62.

WILLIS, J.; St. James's Street, London; 75 Lower Grosvenor Street in 1836. Musical instrument dealer, sold Willis's Seraphines, possibly made by others.

WILLIS PIANO & ORGAN CO.; Halifax, Nova Scotia, Canada, 1897 until at least 1932. Factory located in Stellarton, ware rooms and offices in Halifax. Listed in 1886 as James Willis & Co., a sewing machine dealer, in Stellarton.

WILSON & CO.; Sherbrooke, Quebec.

WIMMER, FRIEDRICH; Flemingstr. 9-11, Leipzig, Germany; formerly *Wimmer & Lewy*, established 1907, Friedrich Wimmer, proprietor; harmonium components.

WIND, see *Goulden, H. J.*

WINDSOR ORGANS; see *Montgomery, Ward & Co., Greenwood.*

WINFIELD reed organ, "a button-chord, wind blown reed organ with smart Bakelite beige and cream casing," costing £16.13s.6p, available in the 1950s from F.W. Woolworth & Co. in the U.K.

WING & SON; 202-204 East 12th St. in 1903; 9th Ave. corner of 13th & Hudson in 1907; 352-362 West 13th St. in 1925; all in New York. Piano and reed organ manufacturer, selling by mail order. Began making pianos in 1868 as *Doane, Wing & Cushing*, then became Wing & Son in 1870 with Luman B. Wing and his son Frank L. as partners. Luman died in 1873 and in 1905 Frank's son R. Delano Wing became a partner. Organ manufacture began about 1902. The firm was still in business in 1925 making pianos, player pianos, expression player pianos and phonographs. Serial number: 1902—74521.

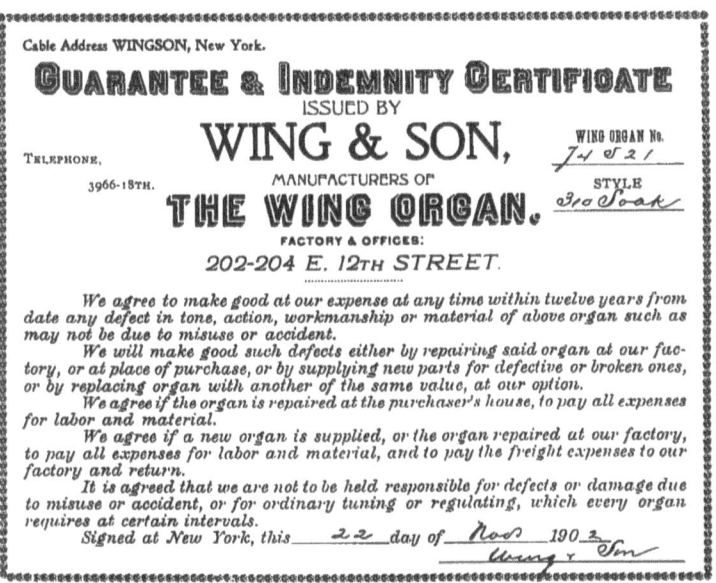

WINKLER, G.; Trenton, NJ, 1883.
WINTER, see *Cornish & Winter*.
WINTHER, CHRISTIAN; Frederiksborggade 36, Copenhagen, Denmark. Winther also established an organ factory in Norway in 1909 in association with Theodor Frobenius. Winther withdrew from the Norwegian company in 1917.
WISE, see *Carpenter, Scott & Wise*.
WISSMANN, ERNST; Hahnwaidstr. 9, Nürtinger Str. 17, Kircheim-Teck, Germany. Established in 1914 as a piano and harmonium dealer; began making harmoniums in 1925, closed in 1938. Made about 1,200 harmoniums.
WISSMANN & HEPPERLE, see *Teck-Harmoniumfabrik*.
WISSMANN, R.; Nurtinger Str. 17, Kircheim, Germany, 1940.
WIT, H. DE; Groningen, Netherlands. Piano dealer and harmonium maker, 1883.

WOERNER & KOLB; Rothebühlstr. 119 in 1863, Olgastr. 83 in 1864, Stuttgart, Germany. Harmonium maker 1862-64, G.F. Woerner and Heinrich Kolb, proprietors. Woerner had previously worked for *Ph. Trayser & Co.*

WOIZECHOWSKI, JOSEPH; Kouno (Kaunas), Lithuania, 1895, Elizabethstr., St. Petersburg, Russia, 1903.

WOLF, H. & H.; 2 rue St. Joseph and 1 rue St. Marc, Quimper, France, 1903, 1909.

WOLFENDEN, ROBERT S.; 82 Fortess Terr., Junction Rd., Kentish Town, London 1883.

WOLFINGER ORGAN CO.; Ann, corner of W. Randolph in 1880; see *Chicago Cottage Organ Co.*

WOLFRAM, HERMANN; Leipzig, Germany. Physharmonica maker, originally from Taucha. Came to Leipzig in 1848, later became a pipe organ maker.

WONDER ORGAN, see *C.G. Conn.*

Granville Wood

WOOD, GRANVILLE, & SON; Northville, MI; established 1876; Granville Wood previously worked for *S.D. & H.W. Smith*, then moved to Detroit, MI, starting *Wood & Simmons*, which later became *Simmons & Whitney*, where he became a junior partner in 1868; started manufacturing reed and pipe organs under his own name in 1876, associated with his son Will Wood in 1884; father and son later worked for *Farrand & Votey* where Granville was factory superintendent. He retired in 1900. Will continued as sales agent in Europe, then worked for Price & Teeple and later became head of the pipe organ department of Sherman Clay in San Francisco.

WOOD, LUCIUS A.; Worcester, MA. Active 1886-87.

WOOD, POWELL & CO.,; Guelph, Ontario 1883-84. (No other information available.)

WOOD, see *McLeod, Wood & Co.; Grover & Wood; Garvie & Wood.*

WOODBRIDGE BROS.; Chicago, IL. (No other information available.)

WOODBURY, see *Samuel H. Jones.*

WOODMAN, A.G. & B.M.; Salisbury, MA; seraphine manufacturers.

WOODRUFF, T.D.; Quincy, IL. (No other information available.)
WOODS, C.A.; Clinton, Ontario. (No other information available.)
WOODS, GEORGE C.; Pittsfield, NH. Making melodeons at 137½ Hanover St., Boston in 1853. Became a partner in *Jones, Carpenter & Woods*, Brattleboro, VT 1853, sold his interest in 1856 and returned to Boston. By 1862 he was a factory foreman at *Mason & Hamlin*; later founded *George Woods & Co.*, factory located at Cambridgeport, MA., office at 608 Washington, Boston in 1883, also at 423 Broome St., New York. In addition to conventional reed organs, he made a few barrel organs and a combination pipe and reed organ. Serial numbers: 1871—709/2823, 1873—19558, 1874—11056, 1875—26681.

George Woods Company,

608 WASHINGTON STREET, BOSTON, MASS.

MANUFACTURERS OF

PARLOR ORGANS AND UPRIGHT PIANOS.

WOODS, see *M.O. Nichols*.
WOODWARD, C.F. (No additional information available.)
WORCESTER, A.; New York, NY; lyre-legged melodeon.
WORCESTER ORGAN CO. (I); Worcester, MA. Established in 1872; shortly afterwards William B. Taber bought the business and in 1877 renamed it *Taber Organ Co.*
WORCESTER ORGAN CO. (II); 9 May St., Worcester, MA. Unrelated to the previous Worcester Organ Co., it was established in 1883 as a continuation of *E.P. Carpenter & Co.*. Decals on the instruments show the proprietors as H.W. Metcalf and J.P. Brown. By 1888 the proprietors were Theo. P. Brown and H.Y. Simpson, and Metcalf is no longer mentioned in published data, however the Metcalf and Brown decals continued to be used. Serial number: 1890—42522.
WORCESTER REED ORGAN WORKS, NEDERLANDSCHE ORGELFABRIEK, see *Nederlandsche Orgelfabriek Worcester*.
WORLD MANUFACTURING CO.; 122 Nassau St., New York; organettes.
WOTRUBA, JOSEF; Pocatek, Czechoslovakia, 1903.
WRIGHT, WILLIAM KING; Northampton, MA 1861. Melodeon maker.
WULSCHNER, EMIL; Indianapolis, IN, 1886. Sold organs made by others with the Wulschner stencil.

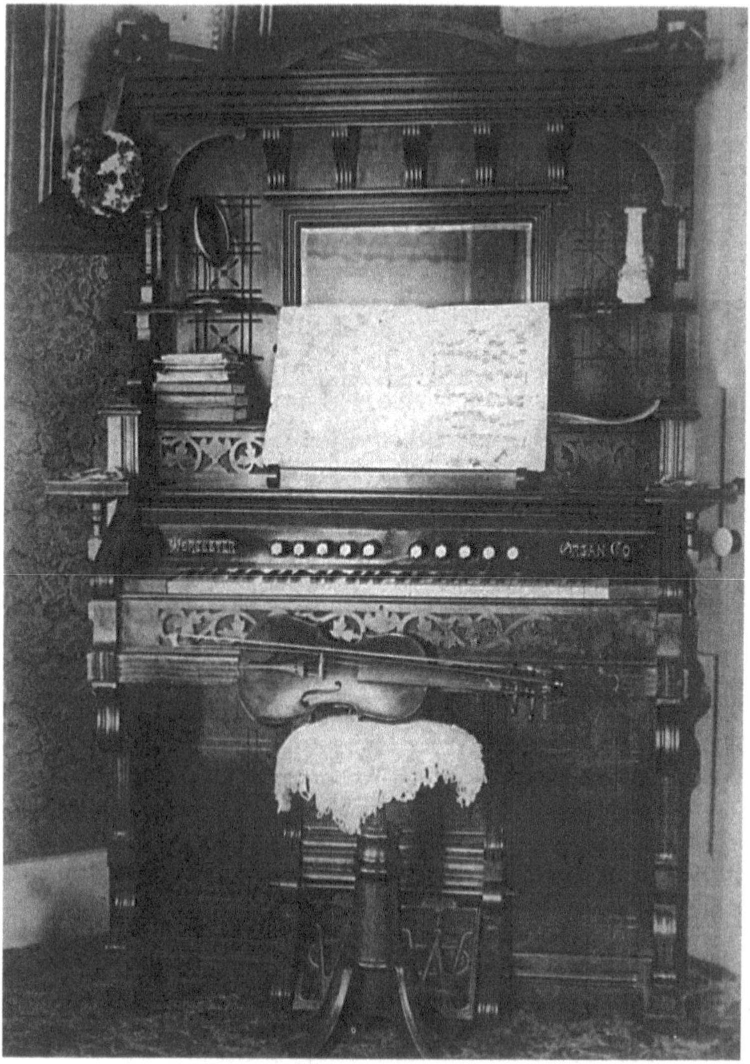

Worcester Organ Company, Worcester, Massachusets.

WÜNSCH, JOHANN DANIEL; Leipzig, Germany. Physharmonica maker.

WURLITZER, RUDOLPH, CO.; North Tonawanda, NY; purchased the rights to the semi-electronic Orgatron from *Everett Piano Co.* after World War II, improved the design and manufactured it. The Orgatron was never as popular with the public as its principal competitor, the Hammond Organ. See *Orgatron*. The following serial numbers include other instruments as well as reed organs:

1903—1910	1940—195000	1963—815000
1905—4500	1950—400000	1964—860000
1910—11600	1955—537000	1965—905000
1920—40000	1960—657000	1972—1000000
1930—112000	1961—715000	
1935—136000	1962—760000	

The Yamaha Style 3A organ, 1969.

Y

YAESU PIANO CO.; 1-9-8 Yaesu, Chuo, Tokyo 103, Japan. Sold the Sister organ from 1952 to 1972, made by *Shimada Gakki* (qv).

YAMAHA CORP.; P.O. Box 1, Hamamatsu, Japan. Torakusu Yamaha (1851-1916), assisted by Kisaburo Kawai, built his first reed organ in 1886, began manufacturing in 1887; organized as *Yamaha Hukin Seizo-sho* (Yamaha Organ Manufacturing Co.) 1888; then *Yamaha Hukin Seizo-sho Co. Ltd.* 1889; then *Yamaha Gakki Seizo-sho* (Yamaha Musical Instrument Manufacturing Co.) 1891; then incorporated as *Nippon Gakki Co. Ltd.* (qv), and finally renamed *Yamaha Corp.* in 1987, which continues in operation to the present. Presidents after Torakusu Yamaha: Chiyomaru Amano, 1917-27; Kaichi Kawakami, 1927-50; Genichi Kawakami, 1950-77; Hiroshi Kawashima, 1977-80; Gen-ichi Kawakami, 1980-83; Hiroshi Kawakami, 1983-1992; Seisuke Ueshima, 1992-present. In the early years, Yamaha organs were sold mainly by two dealers: Kyoeki-Shosha in eastern Japan and *S. Miki & Co.* in western Japan. Yamaha also made the Tiger brand organs, made at Yamaha's Tenryu factory and sold by *Zen-on*, and the Miki brand sold by Miki. Won second prize at the 3rd Domestic Industrial Exhibit in Tokyo, 1890. The Yamaha factory was taken over by the Army and Navy in 1942 to produce airplane propellers. It was destroyed by an earthquake in 1944 and again by bombing in 1945. See *Steigerman, Nishikawa, Kawai, Miki, Yamano*. Serial numbers:

```
1927—188232    1931—223622    1941—308857
1928—198331    1932—224891    1943—325682
1929—207656    1935—256070    1944—326441
1931—216516    1937—281318    1950—400000
```

YAMANO MUSIC; Ginza St., Tokyo. A music dealer, established by Matsumoto, which formerly sold reed organs made at the Yokohama factory of *Nippon Gakki (Yamaha)* with the Yamano stencil, ca. 1914.

YAMASHITA ORGAN FACTORY; 3-9 Kobaricho, Naka-ku, Nagoya, Japan in 1932, also shown at Hishiike, Gokiso, Naka-ku, Nagoya. Established by Kanzo Yamashita on February 25, 1932.

YARWOOD, see *Mudge & Yarwood*.

YAZAKI, TEINOSUKE; Takaoka, Gunma, Japan. Exhibited at the 3rd Domestic Industrial Exhibition, Tokyo, 1890.
YORK & SONS. (No other information available.)

Z

ZACHARIAS, P.; Inselstr. 31, Leipzig, Germany; established 1892, Hans Meyer & Alfred Zacharias, proprietors, 1930; harmonium components.
ZACHARIASSEN, A.; Nystadt, Finland; established 1869 by Dr. Alex G. Zachariassen and brothers. Shown in 1883 as an organ builder, in 1903 shown as church organ and harmonium maker. Awarded a silver medal at Moscow in 1882 for a pipe organ.
ZANFERLI, LUIGI; via S. Faustino, Brescia, Italy, 1909.
ZAVIER, X.; New York. (No other information available.)
ZEN-ON GAKUFU SHUPPAN-SHA CO. LTD.; 25 Higashi Gokencho, Shinjuku, Tokyo. Organ dealer and music publisher. Sold the *Yamaha organs*, including the Tiger brand, until 1960, then the *Shimada Gakki* organ from 1961 to the present. Also sold organs made by either Yamaha or Shimada with the Zen-on stencil.
ZIEGLER, PHILIPP; Steinsfurt b. Sinsheim, Germany. Organ and harmonium maker, established 1911; working at least through 1929.
ZIKA, WILHELM, LEOPOLD BREINBAUERS NACHF.; Trollerberg 40, Ottensheim, Austria. Established in 1834, still in business in 1930.
ZIMMERMANN, JULES HEINRICH; Querstrasse 26-28, factory at Sedanstr. 17, Leipzig, Germany; retailer and manufacturer of pianos, harmoniums and organettes. Established 1884, later became a part of *VEB Deutsche Piano-Union*. The following serial numbers may include both pianos and reed organs:

1884—1	1961—198000	1969—239000
1908—60000	1962—201000	1970—246000
1915—92000	1963—205000	1971—253000
1919—108000	1964—210000	1972—260600
1930—165000	1965—215000	1974—275800
1940—174000	1966—221000	1976—292500
1950—180000	1967—227000	
1960—195000	1968—233000	

ZIMMERMANN, PAUL, HARMONIUMFABRIK; Gräfenhainichen, Germany. Established 1898, closed 1932. Also listed as *Holzindustrie Paul Zimmermann* and as *Harmoniumfabrikation Gräfenhainichen*. Factory located in Radis.

ZIMMERMANN, RICHARD; Werdauer Str. 15, Gera-Zwötzen, Germany. Established 1922, closed 1934. Harmonium maker.

ZIMMERMAN, WILLIAM; 262 Catherine St., Detroit, MI 1867. Melodeon maker.

ŽUJA, BLASIUS; Zerotingasse 270, Uhersky Brod (Ungarisch-Brod), Czechoslovakia. Established in 1884, in business at least through 1930. Barrel organ and harmonium maker.

ZULEGER, A.; Königsplatz 6, Leipzig, Germany; maker of the Harmonola harmonium, 1930. Established in 1872 as an agent and distributor.

ZWAHLEN, LOUIS; New York, NY. Awarded a patent in 1832 for a "Seraphina or harmonicon organ."

Hollandsche Huiselijkheid

DOUBTFUL LISTINGS

The following names have appeared in various publications as reed organ manufacturers. Some of them may be legitimate manufacturers, but no supporting evidence has appeared at the time of this publication. Others are clearly music dealers and still others are makers of pipe organs or other instruments, repairmen, tuners, etc., and thus are excluded from the listing of reed organ manufacturers.

ADAMS, C.W.; 10 Linwood Ave., Providence, RI.
AEOLINE CO.
ANSON & CLARK; instrument formerly in the L.B. Green collection, "thought to be by Anson & Clark."
ANTON, P.G.; St. Louis, MO. Reed and pipe organ maker 1871-1874. St. Louis directories show him as a dealer.
ARNOLD, C.F.; Hasenbergerstr. 12, Stuttgart, Germany, 1883.
ARNOLD, HEINRICH; Rheinstr. 29, Darmstadt, Germany. Established 1830; piano and harmonium maker and dealer.
BARLON, G.A.; Trenton, NJ.
BERGER, ED.; Hallesche Str. 3 in 1903, Forstereistrasse 52 in 1909, Dresden, Germany. Listed as harmonium maker 1898-1905.
BERGSTROM, J.; Calif. Ave. between Virginia & Esmeralda Aves., San Francisco, CA.
BERNHARDT, GEBRÜDER; Gamback, Germany, 1903, 1930.
BRIELMAYER, A.; Stuttgart, Germany, 1890.
BURKHARDT, G.E.; Hamburg 5, Germany in 1885.
CASPER, FRANZ; Reinickendorferstrasse 37B, Berlin, Germany, 1903. Harmonium maker and tuner.
COTTAGE ORGAN CO.; Chicago IL. Probably *Chicago Cottage Organ Co.*
COURTING HARMONIUM, (no additional information available.)
CRESCENT, (no additional information available.)
DAVIS, WILLIAM J.; 7 W. Chippewa, Buffalo, NY., 1880, 1883. Probably a pipe organ builder.
DEESZE, JUL.; Saarbrucken and St. Johann, Germany. Piano and harmonium dealer, 1883.
DENT, E.J.; 64 Ashville Rd., Leyton, Leytonstone, London.
DICKEL & BAUM; Brückengasse, Rotenberg a. d. Fulda, Germany; dealer, founded 1928.
DIEKMANN, WILHELM; Baerwald-Str 60, Berlin in 1903, Kalkreuthstr. 14, Berlin in 1930. Also F. Dieckmann is shown at the same address, 1903-1909.

DIENST, E.; Leipzig-Gohlis, Germany. Agent for *Wilcox & White*, 1892.
DINSE, GEBRÜDER; Dresdener Str 12, Berlin. Established 1839, O. and P. Dinse, proprietors. Still in business in 1909.
DORMAN, R., & CO.; Nashville, TN.
EAST INDIA COMPANY; probably an exporter of small table harmoniums.
EFFNER, ROBERT; Blumenstr. 77, Berlin, 1885; Frau Pauline Effner & Rob. Effner jr., proprietors, 1903, 1913. Established in 1866.
EHRLICH, FRANZ ADAM; Neumarkt, Germany, 1930.
ENGLEBRECHT & THOMSON; Binghamton, NY.
FELGENMAKER, A.B., & CO.; Erie, PA.
FELSING, CONRAD W.; Berlin. Pipe organ and harmonium maker, 1883.
FULLER, LEVI K.; Knight organs.
GABLER & MULLER.
GENG JUN., ROBERT; St. Georgen, Blumenstr 14, Freiburg-im-Breisgau, Germany, 1940.
GLATZL, GEORG; Guttenburg, Germany, 1930.
GROB, J.M., & CO.; Eutritzsch, Germany. Founded by Johann Matthäus Grob. Later *Ludwig Hupfeld AG*.
HARE, JOHN; Newcastle upon Tyne. Bookseller, music and musical instrument dealer, 1863-1938.
HARNMONA CO.; Blenheim, MA.
HARTAFFEL; Pennsylvania. Organ and melodeon maker, est. 1753. Robert Hartaffel, Lancaster, PA, reportedly died in 1782, before melodeons were invented.
HAUCK, J.B.; Bruchsal, Germany.
HEPBURN, GEORGE; Pictou, NS, Canada. A miniature harmonium is attributed to him. Listed as an undertaker in Teare, *Directory of Pictou and New Glasgow for 1879-80*. Possibly a brother of *James Hepburn*, (qv).
HERTEL, F.; 1624 Fulton, St. Louis, MO.
HILLS, H.A.; St. Louis, MO. (Not listed in St. Louis Directory.)
HOLLENBERG, H.G.; Memphis, TN.
HOUSE, G.; 122 Clinton, Buffalo, NY.
IBACH, RICHARD, Barmen, Germany. Maker of church organs, pianos, harmoniums and American organs.
IBACH, RUDOLPH; Neuerweg 40, Barmen, Germany; piano manufacturer since 1794, made harmoniums and pianos as *Rudolf Ibach Sohn* at least through 1930.
JAPAN MUSICAL INSTRUMENT FACTORY. Possibly the same as *Nippon Gakki Seizo Sho*, one of the *Yamaha* names.

JENNINGS JR., R.; Detroit, MI.
KEROPHON, (no additional information available.)
KILGEN, G.; 641 Summit Ave., St. Louis, MO. Pipe organ maker.
KLAPROTH, FR.; Eichstr. 218, Hannover, Germany, 1930; estab. 1912.
KOCH, HUGO; Bad Säckingen, Germany, 1903; established 1900.
KOEPPEN, PAUL; Friedrichstr. 235, Berlin, Germany 1889. Publisher.
KRÖGER, J.P. HEINRICH; 20 Schulstr., Elmshorn, Germany, 1930. Piano and harmonium maker, established in 1890.
KYOEKI-SHOSHA; Japan. Organ dealer, sold *Yamaha organs*.
LAEMMERHIRT, EMIL; Berlin. Harmonium maker, 1896-1913.
LITURISTIC ORGANS, INC.; 121 W. High, Lima, OH. Dode M. Lamson, manager, 1931.
MAYER, J.; 127 Page, San Francisco, CA. Pipe organ maker.
MEINHARDT & KÖRNER; Gera, Germany, 1883.
MEINSCHENK, WALTER; Frauengasse 27, Altenburg, Germany, 1940. A retail dealer: organs with this name were made by others.
MOORE. J.D.; Worcester, MA. Probably a pipe organ maker.
NEWCASTLE Delaware organ factory, name unknown.
NORRIS, WILLIAM; bookkeeper for *R.S. Williams* until 1879 when he joined Lewis Soper to import and sell pianos.
ORGAN CO., THE; Meriden CT, 1881.
OTT, M.; Launtal 13, Giengen, Brenz, Germany, 1940.
PETERNELL GEBR.; Seligenstadt in 1883; Poststr. 47, Seligenthal, Germany 1903. Organ and harmonium maker.
PETERS, WEBB & CO.; Main Street, Louisville, KY, 1850. Music publisher and musical instrument dealer. Advertised as a builder of church and parlor organs. Henry J. Peters and Benedict J. Webb, owners. The organ builder is thought to be John Koenke (Konkey, Conkey), a pipe organ builder. The parlor organs may have been pipe organs as well.
PFEFFER, J.G., & SON; 1007 Marion, St. Louis, MO. Pipe organ maker.
REICH, H.; Weissenburgerstr. 29, Berlin, Germany, 1903.
REICHELT, C.F.; Klingenthal, Germany. Zither and harmonium maker, 1912.
REUSCH, L.; 16 Seelowerstr., Berlin, Germany, 1930.
RICHART, HEINRICH; Berlin, Germany, 1900. Established 1874.
RIECK, ERNST; Schuhagen 33, Greifswald, Germany, 1903; established 1892.
ROEHM, OTTO; Urbanstr. 33, Stuttgart, Germany, 1883.
RYDER, GEO. H.; 2058 Washington St., Boston, MA 1883; also shown at 1057 Washington St. Address in 1888 was Music Hall Bldg., and in 1900 it was Tremont Temple, Boston.

SAGE, (no additional information available.)
SARAPHONE, (no additional information available.)
SARDARFLUTE, (no additional information available.)
SCHERZER, A.; Solmsstr. 10, Berlin, Germany, 1909.
SCHINDLER, ANTON; Berlin-Nonnendamm, Germany, 1908.
SCHUSTER, C.; Brattleboro, VT.
S.D. ORGAN CO.; Brattleboro, VT. Probably ST (Estey).
SHAVER, G.S.; Erie, PA.
SHELLARD, B.; 1250 Montgomery, San Francisco, CA in 1883.
SIMON, CARL, MUSIKVERLAG; Markgrafenstr. 101, Berlin. Published most of Karg-Elert's harmonium music.
SPÄTH, GEBR.; Ennetach-Mengen, Germany; Franz Xaver Albert & Dr. Karl Späth, proprietors, 1930; established 1882. Also *Spaethe*.
STANDARD ORGAN CO. (USA).
STEVENS & GAYETTY; Cambridge, MA; later George Stevens & Co. Pipe organ builder.
SWISS.
VADI VALA, D.R.; Bombay, India. Repairman, 1949.
VOCALLIO.
VOTTELER, G.F.; 9 Jennings Ave., Cleveland, OH. Pipe organ builder.
WATEROUS & TAYLOR; Princetown, IL.
WETZEL & SOHN; 1 Haller Str., Hamburg, Germany, 1930.
WHEELDEN, LINCOLN J.; Bangor, ME. In 1869 shown as a partner with John S. Patten in Patten & Wheelden, music dealers, located in the J.C. White block on Main St. Patten retired about 1881 and Wheelden continued in business with George Silsby at 76 Main St. Silsby stayed only a few years and Wheelden continued at the same address until 1890 when he sold out to Andrew Matthews. Wheelden died in 1892. Advertisements and Wheelden's obituary make no mention of manufacturing reed organs, so it is supposed that he was strictly a dealer.
WHITE & DUNKLEY; (1889); Pedminster Parade, Bristol, England.
WOODSTOCK ORGAN FACTORY; Woodstock, Ontario. Pipe organ maker.
ZIMMERMAN, CHARLES; Carlsfield, Nr. Elbenstock-Zollverein, Germany. Exhibited harmonicas, accordions and concertinas at the London Exhibition of 1851.
ZIMMERMANN, LEON; Markenbildechen 32, Koblenz, Germany, 1903.
__NTING, E.; 34 Causeway St., Boston, MA. Reed organ, seraphine and melodeon maker.

GEOGRAPHICAL INDEX

AUSTRALIA

Adelaide   Rendall, W.C.
Annandale, NSW   Beale & Co.
Melbourne   Kilner, Frank
   Tuller, A.

AUSTRIA

Bozen
Deveeser
Gmund
Görz

Graz
Hotzendorf
Kraslice
Lemberg

Linz
Mährisch-Neustadt

Neusohl
Oberlaibach
Obertrattnach
Ottensheim

Raab
Salzburg

Trautenau
Triest
Vienna

Socin, Fidel
Pizenhoffer, Alois
Koller, Lukas
Potocnik, Felice
Potvenik, Pietro
Werner, Hans
Barton, Fr.
Heinl, Andr.
Haase, Rudolf
Sliwinski, Johann
Kranzer, Johann
Brauner, W.E.
Swoboda & Brauner
Kepszely, Johann
Lenarcic, Jos.
Steininger
Breinbauer, Leopold
Panhuber, Josef
Zika, Wilhelm
Hesse, Carl Jr.
Katholnig, Heinrich
Mertel, Hans
Singer, Peter
Kunz, Frz.
Bossi, Vicenzo
Albouy
Bauer, Matthäus
Deutschmann, Jakob
Erste Productiv
Friemel
Glaser, S.
Haeckl, Anton
Handwerck, Adolf
Hoffman & Czerny
Horbiger, Aloysius
Kauffmann, Johann
Klein, Joh.
Kotykiewicz, Teofil
Linard, Dr.

Vienna

BELGIUM

Andenna
Antwerp
Arlon
Audenarde
Averbode
Boitsfort
Brussels

Brussels

Neschuta, Josef
Okenfuss, Anton
Schatzel, Joseph
Schuster
Strauch, Josef
Strizik, Josef
Titz, Peter
Ullmann, Josef
Vanderburg
Wiest, Anton

Mossoux, Ad.
Verhaert, A.
Bungert, E.
Godefroid-Vossaert
Joris, Leo
De Volder Frères
Blangenois
Bodau
Boeckx, Theofile
Bons, Egide
Bous, Jules
Cloetens, Georges
Cnobloch-Bar, G.
De Lil, Albert
De Volder Frères
De Vos, Joseph
Duray, H.
Jamard
Kerkhoff, J.-E.
Koeller-Vandenakkr
Landrien, Alphonse
Loret, Joseph L.
Maver, Rob.
Mazet, Victor
Merklin & Schutze
Oor, J.
Riesenburger, P.
Rousseaux, W.C.
Sax, Adolphe
Schmidt, M.
Schyven, Pierre
Slootmaeckers

Smeetz, J.
Solari, Jean
Umbreit

Brussels	Verhasselt d'Outrel.	Halifax	Willis Piano
	Verhasselt, François	Melvern Square	Gates Organ
Courtrai	Anneessens, Oscar	Pictou	Hepburn, James
	Anneessens-Verann.	Stellarton	Willis Piano
Ghent	Gévaert, Charles L.	Truro	Gates Organ
	Gévaert, Vitus	Yarmouth	Chute, Hall & Co.
	Heyerick, Jos.		Chute, H.E. & Co.
Grammont	Anneessens		
	Bourguignon-B.	**ONTARIO**	
	Raygaert Frères	Aylmer	Rowe, J.T.
Halluin	Anneessens, Charles	Berlin (Kitchener)	Berlin Piano
Huy	Delhauteur, Joseph	Bowmanville	B'ville Organs
	Paquot, S.		Dominion Organ
Liege	Cohnen	Chatham	Smith & Scribner
	Gerome, L.	Clifford	Eben-Ezer Organ
	Renson, A.J.	Clinton	Clinton Organ Co.
Menin	Anneessens		Doherty, W., & Co.
Molenbeck	Gys, Pierre		Oakes Organ Co.
Namur	Balthasar-Florence		Sherlock-Manning
	Brachot, Joseph		Woods, C.A.
	Geyzen, Achille	Elora	Blatchford, G.
	Schuttê, H.	Galt	Blatchford, G.
	Simon, A.	Goderich	Goderich Organ Co.
Noduwez	Purnelle, H.-J.	Guelph	Bell, W.
Renaix	Joris, François		Bell & Wood
Ruisbroek	Boeckx, Theophile		Guelph Melodeon
	Joris, Joseph		Hardy, A.S., & Co.
Tournai	Delmotte, Theophile		Jackson, John
City unknown	Baron		James, T.
	Van Bever-Lacken		McLeod, Wood
			Wood, Powell
		Hamilton	Kilgour, J. & R.
BRAZIL			Thornton, James
			Townsend, William
Bento Gonçalves	Todeschini		White, Thomas
Novo Hamburgo	Bohn	Kingston	Mee, Charles
			Rappe & Co.
			Reyner, J.
		Kitchener (Berlin)	Hallman, J.C.
		London	Andrus Brothers
CANADA			Canada Organ Co.
			Sherlock-Manning
BRITISH COLUMBIA		Madoc	Conley Church
Vancouver	Vancouver Organ	Newmarket	Dales & Dalton
Victoria	Bagnall, John	North York	Stevenson, Frank
		Oshawa	Darley & Robinson
NEW BRUNSWICK			Oshawa Melodeon
Saint John New Dominion			Oshawa Organ Co.
		Owen Sound	Slown, J.
NOVA SCOTIA		Picton	Andrews, & Simcoe
Annapolis	Annapolis Organ		Malhoit & Co.
Bridgetown	Acadia Organ Co.	Toronto	Bancroft, Marshall
Halifax	Halifax Piano		Bell, Daniel
			Clarabella Organ

Toronto	Coleman & Sons	
	Compensating	
	Dalton, R.H.	
	Livingstone, J.A.	
	Mason & Risch	
	Nordheimer Organ	
	Ontario Organ Co.	
	Palmer	
	Toronto Melodeon	
	Toronto Organ Co.	
	Toronto Standard	
	Townsend, William	
	Williams, R.S.	
	Williams, R. & W.	
Uxbridge	Clay City Organ Co.	
	Uxbridge Cabinet	
Waterloo	Hallman, J.C.	
Whitby	Mudge & Yarwood	
Woodstock	Karn, D.W., Co.	
	Miller, John M.	
	Miller & Karn	
	Thomas Organ Co.	

QUEBEC

Brome	Smith, D.W. & C.D.
Huntingdon	Cornwall, G.W.
Montreal	Brown, Abner
	Pratte Piano Co.
	Warren, S.R.
	Whitney, H.A.
Sherbrooke	Wilson & Co.
West Farnham	West, Elijah

PROVINCE UNKNOWN

St. Johns	Peters Organ Co.
City unknown	Imperial Organ Co.
	Williams, V.R.

CHINA

Beijing	Hsinghai Piano Co.
Shanghai	Shanghai Organ
City unknown	Blessing
	Pearl River

CZECHOSLOVAKIA

Eger	Peter, Andreas
Gemer Sajavsky	Bertek, Johann
Georgswald	Förster, August
Graslitz	Meinl, Ernst
Hradec Kralové	Pajkr, Rudolf
Komotau	Glassl, Egyd
Königgratz	Lhota, Al. Hugo
	Petrof, Anton
Kutná Hora	Bartunek, Adolf
	Melzer, Josef
	Tuček, Johannes
	Tuček, W.
Moravský-Krumlov	Lídl & Velík
Neutitschein	Neusser, Johann
	Neusser, Karl
Olomouc	Maretka, Franz
Pardubice	Sturma, Josef
Petrovice	Mader, Josef
Pocatek	Wotruba, Josef
Policka	Čápek, Friedrich
Prague	Broz, Josef
	Heubesch, Wenzel
	Hummel, Franz
	Orchestra Spol Sro
	Řemek, Johann
	Tuček, W.
Prešov	Guna, Julius
Puste Zibridovice	Kolb, Franz, Söhne
Rájec	Fabianek, Franz
Rychnove	Polacek, Vaclav
Seestadtl	Loos, Josef
Tabor	Skopek, Vincenz
Tachov	Helfert, Anton
Tisnov	Mudroch, Jan.
Uhersky Brod	Žuja, Blasius
Uhirske Hradiste	Strmisko, Matth.
Unicov	Katzer, Franz
Volary	Bohm, Franz
Zakupy	Bergmann, Anton

DENMARK

Aalborg	Andresen, P., & Co.
Copenhagen	Allin, Otto B.
	Ericson, Franz
	Petersen & Steenstr.
	Winther, Christian
Fredensborg	Rechnagel, Leo
Hadersleben	Jacobsen, J.
Haslev	Haslevs

Haslev	Mølgaard-Jensen	Annecy	Bildé, Ch.
Holstebro	Kamstrup, K.	Asnieres	Pape, Chr.
Nykøbing	Hansen, F., & Son	Avallon	Chazelle, P.
Odense	Schóier, L.C.	Bagnolet	Mustel, Victor
Randers	Koefoeds, H.P.	Bar-le-Duc	Przyiemsky
Ringkøbing	Andresen, J.P.	Bordeaux	Cauderès, Jean-Jules
Thisted	Christensen, N.C.		Commaille, Auguste
Vejle	Berntsen, Anton		Durand & Cie.
City unknown	Ericson, Osc.	Charcey	Tremaux, Pierre
		Charlieu	Valla, Abbé
		Choisy-le-Roi	Jacques, R.
ESTONIA		Clichy	Mustel, Victor
		Dijon	Javelier, A.
Parnu	Saks, I.		Paris
Reval	Normann, Rudolph	Dinan	Larche, E.
	Olbrei, J.	Doubs	Bach
	Orntlich, Hans	Etrépagny	Richard, J.
Tallin	Olbrei, J.	Flers	Menard Fils
Tartu	Astron	Halluin	Beaucourt, H.-C.
		Ivry-sur-Seine	Alexqndre
		Jambes	Lemerciniere, Louis
		Les Andelys	Dumont & LeLievre
FINLAND		Lourdes	Petitqueux-Hillard
		Lyon	Beaucourt, H.-C.
Dorpat	Matto, M.		Favre, J.
Helsinki	Musiikki Fazerin		Michel-Merklin
Hirvensalmi	Lapuan Harmon.		Morel, E.
	Liukkonen, Eino		Ruche, J.
Jyväskylässaa	Halonen ja Kumpp	Magny-Cours	Martin, F.
Kangasala	Kangasalan	Malakoff	Collet, A.
Urkutehdas	Pulkkila, Veljekset	Marseille	Abeille, Léon
	Rautavuori Suomen		Mader, F.
Lapua	Aho & Niemi		Meritan & Cie.
	Hissa, Jaakko		Soubeiran, J.
	Källmann, A.	Mirecourt	Poirot Frères
	Perälä, K.W.		Thibouville-Lamy
	Saarimaa, Juho	Nancy	Musillon, E.
	Sillanpää, Elias	Nantes	Testé, J.A.
Nystadt	Zachariassen, A.	Nice	Martella, Florentin
Pännäinen	Andersen, Veljekset	Nogent-sur-Seine	Rodolphe, Alphonse
Sortavala	Mäkinen	Orbev	Henry, Justin
Tampere	Hedén, A.A.	Paris	Alexandre
	Pilvinen, Yrjö T.		Abbey Frères
Uukuniemi	Tiainen, A.J.		Abbey, J.
Vihdin-Nummela	Hedén ja Kumpp		Alexandre
	Nummelan		Bacclieri, G.
City unknown	Känsälä, Aleksi		Barrouin, F.
			Baudet, Florentin
			Bertheaux Frères
FRANCE			Bonnel, G.
			Bourlet
Agen	Magen		Boutevilin, L.
Angers	Pinault		Boutin, Louis
			Brown, A.

Paris	Bruni, Francesco	Paris	Mayer-Marix
	Busson, Constand		Merklin & Schutze
	Cavaillé-Coll		Moonen, L.
	Cesarini et Cie.		Morhange, A.
	Chabin, M.		Morhange, L.
	Changuion, A.		Müller, Théodore-A.
	Chaperon, A.		Mustel, Victor
	Chaperon, Noel		Nisard, Th.
	Chauffer		Ostrorog, Comte de
	Christophe &Etien.		Pasdeloupe
	Cottino & Tailleur		Périchon, A.
	Courtier		Picard
	Couty & Liné		Pregniard, M.
	Couty & Richard		Prosper & Coles
	Debain, Alexandre		Reisner, A.
	Dewingle		Richard, J.
	Ducasse et Oliveau		Rodolphe, Alphonse
	Elcke S.A.		Rousseau, Alex.
	Fourneaux, J.-B.N.		Rudolphe, H.
	Galante Vasseur		Salaün, Schwaab
	Garnier, Marcel		Stein, Emile
	Gasparini, Alex.		Stein & Sergeant
	Gavioli & Cie.		Stoltz, Eugène
	Gavioli, C., Fils		Tailleur, Pierre
	Gebhardt, J.		Thibouville-Lamy
	Gilbert		Tourneur, A.
	Grandjon, J.		Touzaa et Houpin
	Guesné, J.		Ullmann, Ch. & J.
	Henry & Cie.		Vallé
	Husson-Buthod		van Gruisen, N.L.
	Isoard		Vygen Jeune
	Jaulin, Julien		Weiser & Neumann
	Kannegiessert, G.	Quimper	Wolf, H. & H.
	Kasriel, Maurice	Rennes	Claus, F., Fils
	Kleinjasper, Charles	Rouen	Bernard
	Labrousse, J.		Klein, Alphonse
	Lacape, J.	Saintes	Gentis & Capuron
	LaMartine & Cie.	St. Etiénne	Dard-Janin
	Lamberf, Vve.		Reverchon & Merl.
	Lavaud, Vve. P.D.	St. Ouen	Debain
	LeComte, A.	Schiltigheim	Roethinger, E.A.
	LeFerme, Louis-C.	Sourdun	Martin de Provins
	Legris, Alexandre	Strasbourg	Grucker & Schott
	Leroux, Alex.		Roethinger, E.A.
	Lesieur, Aug.	Vanves	Meinvere, Vve.
	Leterme, C.	Verdun	Alibonssy, P.
	Limonaire Frères	Versailles	Abbey Frères
	Maillard & Cie.	Vesoul	Constr. d'Automates
	Maison Parfait Clav.	City unknown	Blondel, Alphonse
	Malleville		Boyer & Marty
	Marix, Leon		Chameroy, E.-A.
	Martin, Albert		De Gromard, A.Q.
	Martin, Ch.		Dubus, Fr.
	Maugé		Ducroquet, Pierre

City unknown	Dumont, L.	Berlin	Strauche, Carl H.
	Ferat et Game		Warkhold, Hans
	Godault	Bernau	Hermann, Heinrich
	Grenie, Gabriel-Jos.	Bochum	Thürmer, Ferdinand
	Gué roult	Böhlitz-Ehrenberg	Hupfeld, Ludwig
	Kelson, P. Ern.	Bonn	Klais, Johannes
	Lempereur		Kratochwil, Otto
	Piron	Borna	Heyl, G.
	Poinctes		Lindholm, O.
	Rousselot		Mannborg, Karl
	Simon		Schmidt, W.
		Brackwede	Beyer, L.M.
		Braunschweig	Sander, Gustav
GERMANY		Bremen	Gehlhar & Co.
			Schindle
Allenstein	Howe, M.H.	Breslau	Bowitz, C.A.
Altenburg	Pitzschler & Co.	Buttstedt	Schortmann
Augsburg	Müller, Sebastian	Cannstatt	Walcker, E.F.
Augustusburg	Graf, Hermann	Chemnitz	Graf, Hermann
Barmen	Bruning & Bongardt		Uhlig, C.F.
Bayreuth	Burger, Hermann	Cologne	Reiser, J.H.
Beitigheim	Steirer, Franz	Crailsheim	Sindel, Heinrich
Berlin	August & Co.		Schwarzkopf, Carl
	Berliner Harmonium	Creglingen	Schaefer, August
	Emmer, Wilhelm	Danzig	Heinrichsdorff, Otto
	Fratti & Co.	Döhren	Beckmann, Heinrich
	Germania Industrie	Dragsdorf-Zeitz	Frohlich, E.
	Grunow, Ad.	Dresden	Bollermann, D.L.
	Grunzweig & Schl.		Gräbner, W.
	Hofmann, G.		Jahn & Sohn
	Howe, Hermann		Jähnert, Julius
	Howe, M.H.		Kanneggiesser, E.
	Kalbe, J.F.		Kaps, Ernst
	Kercher, Friedrich		Kaufman, F.
	Kewitsch, Johannes		Kirscheisen, E.B.
	Krause, H.		Müller, J.T.
	Krause, Theodore		Rossberg, E.
	Lammbrecht, Wilh.		Sommer
	Lenk, E.		Ullrich & Philipp
	Menzenhauer Schm.		Wieck, F.W.
	Möllinger, Christian	Eisenach	Roth & Schönbrodt
	Neufeind, R.	Eisenberg	Horn, Max
	Neumann, E.	Eisleben	Warmholz, Carl S.
	Prinz, E.	Elberfeld	Kanpmann, A.W.
	Raith, Gustav		Mager, Siegrfried
	Reich, H.		Wever, Edwin
	Remler, W.	Erling	Beer, Joh. Gg.
	Richartz, Heinrich	Ertzgebirge	Löffler & Co.
	Schiedmayer, J	Esslingen	Schaeufele, Ferd.
	Schwechlen, G.	Feuchtwangen	Hollander, Georg
	Seydel, Franz Fred	Forst	Philipp, G.
	Seydler, Rudolph	Frankfurt/Oder	Baltzer, Adolph
	Straube, J.		Schulz, Gustav
		Freiburg	Raska, Ignatz

Freiburg	Voigt & Goll	Königshofen	Schlimbach, Martin
Friedrichrodo	Buschmann	Langensalza	Steinbrück, Fried.
Frohberg	Metzner, Richard	Leipzig	Bannicke, Max
Fulda	Maier, Aloys		Böhlitz-Ehrenberg
	Maier & Co.		Buff-Hedinger
Furth	Reich		Conrad Martin
Gera	Högner, Freyerr		Deutsch-Amerikan.
	Krumbholz, Paul		Dietz, Marie
	Liebmann, Armin		Ehrlich, Paul
	Liebmann, Ernst		Essig, Rudolf
	Schlunzig, Wilhelm		Euphonika Musikw.
	Spaethe, Wilhelm		Leipziger Musikw.
	Thuringia Piano		Fiedler, Gustav
	Wagner, P.J., & Co.		Frenzel, Fritz
	Zimmermann, Rich.		Friedrich & Schulze
Gorlitz	Eichler, Max		Geissler, Bruno
Göttingen	Hack		Grossmann & Leid.
	Hofbauer, Carl H.		Hardt, Walther
Gräfenheinichen	Zimmermann, Paul		Hartung, Robert
Gutwoehne	Feldner, C., & Co.		Hofberg, Magnus
Halle	Wilke, Johann G.		Horn, Max
Hamburg	Buschmann, G.A.		Hörügel, M.
	Grossmann, F.		Hug, Gebrüder
Hamburg	Kruse, L. Ed.		Hüller & Co.
	Ritz, Louis		Hüttner, Eduard
	Skala Harmonium		Köhler
	Wage, L.		Kössling, Johann G.
	Werner, J.		Kreutzbach, Julius
Hannover	Patschke, J.W.		Kronig, Franz
	Rissmann, C.C.		Kuper, Adolf
	Schake, H.D.		Leideritz
Hartha	Perl, Bernhard		Leipziger Musikw.
Heidelburg	Bettex, Friedrich		Leipziger Pianoforte
Heutingsheim	Albrecht		Leistner & Co.
Hindelang	Gerl, Dr. F.M.		Leonhardt & Co.
Holzkirchen	Sieber, Phil.		Leutke, Herbert
Ilshofen	Schwarzkopf, Carl		Merhaut, Alfred
Insterburg	Ippig, A.		Metzner, Richard
Jessnitz	Klotzsch, Wilhelm		Oettingen, A. von
Kirchheim	Bartz, R.		Oschatz, Paul
	Barz, Otto		Phönix Musikwerke
	Kaim & Sohn		Polyphon
	Schürer, Albert		Popper & Co.
	Teck-Harmonium		Rudert, G.
	Truchsess, Theodor		Schmidt & Co.
	Wissman, Ernst		Sprössel, W.
	Wissman, R.		Stiehler, Max
Kleinzschocher	Schirling, Johann A.		Stock, Karl
Klingenthal	Fiedler, Carl E.		Teuscher & Walter
	Weidenmüller, Erh.		Werner, Karl
Kommern	Richartz, Heinrich		Wimmer, Friedrich
Königsberg	Bendzko, F.		Wolfram, Hermann
Königshofen	Eschenbach, Bernd.		Wünsch, Johann D.
	Schlimbach, J-C		Zimmermann, J.H.

289

Leipzig	Zuleger, A.	Stargard	Breekow, C.
Lemgo	Klassmeyer, Friedr.	Steinpleis	Ehrler, Alfred
Lenne	Mues, F.A.	Steinsfurt	Zeigler, Philipp
Lich	Förster & Nikolaus	Stettin	Bötcher
	Straube, J., & Co.		Kaltschmidt, F.W.
Liebenwerda	Voigt, Arno	Stötteritz	Hartung, Robert
Linz	Kranzer, Johann	Stuttgart	Ahlborn & Steinb.
Lissa	Ratzke, Ferd.		Braendle, Friedrich
	Ratzke, Paul Jr.		Essig, Rudolf
Lobau	Förster, August		Greuling & Hinkel
Löwenberg	Titz, Johannes		Gschwind, J.G.
Ludwigsberg	Albrecht		Kahn, Leopold
	Harmoniumbau		Kärcher, Karl F.
	Renner, Wilhelm		Klein, Georg
	Sauter, Christian		Krause, Emil
	Walcker-Mayer, J.		Lämmle, Albrecht
Ludwigshafen	Steirer, Franz		Pross, Gschwind
Magdeburg	Schneider & Co.		Ramsperger, J.
Meissen	Thurmer, Ferd.		Reitheimer, C.
Metzingen	Schwarzkopf, Karl		Renner, Louis
Mindelheim	Schwarzbaur, Julian		Scheytt, C.G.
Münchhausen	Matschke, Traugott		Schiedmayer, J.&P.
Munich	Hechinger		Schiedmayer Söhne
	Schramm, J.		Steirer, Franz
	Wieninger, Gustav		Stuttgart Harm.
	Wiesner, Josef		Sulzer, Leopold
Münster	Walhorn, A.		Trayser, Philip J.
Neu Ulm	Voigt & Goll		Trefz & Feucht
Nieder-Ohmen	Schlosser, Ludwig		Truchsess, Theodor
Nürnberg	Schierks, Egon		Weipert, Stieglitz
	Strebel, Johannes		Wider, Andreas
Oberglogau	Hoffmann, Benedict		Woerner & Kolb
Öettingen	Kunkel, Wilhelm	Suhl	Sturm, Friedrich
	Steinmeyer, G.F.	Taucha	Wolfram, Hermann
Ohrdruff	Ratzmann, F.H.	Trossingen	Hohner, Matth.
	Schlimbach, J.C.		Schwarzkopf, Carl
Plauen	Vogel, J.C., & Sohn	Überlingen	Raffin, Joseph
Pretzsch	Köhler	Ulm	Hinkel, Ernst
Quakenbrük	Kleinert, Robert		Ruckh, Balthasar
Radis	Zimmermann, Paul	Unterwiesenthal	Schreyer, Müller
Regensburg	Renner, Joseph	Vlotho-Werendorf	Steinmann, G.
Reutlinger	Harm. Peter	Volksen	Katz, Heinrich
Römhild	Helbig, Johann J.	Walheim	Steirer, Franz
Ruckmarsdorf	Hörügel, M.	Werdau	Hermann, Albin
Rudolstadt	Butscher, Aug.		Horn, Max
	Dornheim, F.W.		Müller, Emil
Schlesien	Neis		Werdauer Mobel
Schorndorf	Bacher, Eugen	Wiehe	Beyer
	Fischer, Karl J.		Bongardt & Herf.
Schweinfurt	Voigt		Hildebrandt, Herm.
Seligenthal	Peternell Gebr	Wuppertal	Mager, Siegfried
Sondershausen	Moeller, Frz.	Wurzburg	Schlimbach, B.
	Moeller, Friedr.	Zeitz	Förster, Heinrich
Spaichingen	Sautter, Christian		Hölling & Spang.

Zeitz	Liebig, Gustav	Delhi	Lahore Music House
	Rinkowski, Alfred		Shivcharan Music
Zweigwerke	Schneider & Co.		Singh, Anand
Zwickau	Hanel	Gujranwala	Tansain Harmonium
	Horn, Max	Madras	Venkat & Co.
	Oschatz, Paul	Mysore	City Harmonium
Zwota	Tröger, Max		Swamy, C.S.N.
City unknown	Bärmig	Phagwara	Vishwakarma Music
	Choretta	Rājkot	Khimji, Mistri
	Kerophon	Tirunelveli	Achari Sons
City Unk.	Menzenhauer	City unknown	Neeremola
	Niedermayer		Surpeti
	Paul & Co.		
	Rigoletto		
	Schmid, G.		

IRELAND

Dublin	Bussell, H.
Kilkenny	Grinstead, W.F.

HUNGARY

Brünn	Káš, Adalbert
	Kolař, Bohumil
Budapest	Eder, Anton Julius
	Fittler, Sandor
	Mogyorossi Guala
	Országh, Alexander
	Országh, Sandor
	Pokorny, Josef
	Umlauf, Josef
	Végh, V. Károly
Kolin	Pospisil, Jos.
Pecs	Angster, Josef
Przemysl	Konieczny, Alojzy
Teplitz	Thiel & Tschiedel

ITALY

Acciano	Cristini, Giuseppe
Alessandria	Amelotti, Carlo
Ancarano	Jaglioli, Marco
Ancona	Farfisa
Arezzo	Chise, Giuseppe
Bitonto	Cuonzo, Vincenzo
Bolzaneto	Bressani, Giovanni
Bolzano Novarese	Socin, Fidel
Borgo de Valsugana	Galvan, Egidio
Borgosesia	Maiolo, Giovanni
Bratovecchio	Ghisci, Giuseppe
Brescia	Landi, Desiderio
	Porro, Diego
	Zanferli, Luigi
Brindisi	Macchitella, Terigi
Campli	Donzelli, Raffaele
	Piercecchi, Vinc.
Casale Monferrato	Mentasti, Paolo
Caselle Torinese	Corneglio, G.
	Miglia, Giuseppe
Castello	Tubi, Graziano
Cava de Tirreni	Venditi, Francesco
Centallo	Vittino, Fratelli
Diano S. Pietro	Tomati & Cia.
Florence	Conti, Enrico
Giuliano di Roma	Jorio, Fratelli
Lucca	Piatrasranta, Figli
Messina	Barbato, C.
Milan	Balbiani, Natale

INDIA

Amritsar	Singh, Baba Kishan
Baroda	Pandharpurkar Bros.
Bombay	Fernandez, P.J.
	Ram Singh, D.S
	Sardarflute
Calcutta	Biswas & Sons
	Eastern Harmonium
	Mohn Bros.
	Mundul & Co.
	Paul & Sons
	Reynold, J.
	Shaw, M.L.
Delhi	Bina Musical Stores
	Kailash Harmonium

Milan	Barbieri, Angelo	Matsuzaka	Nagao, Yoshizo
	Conti, Gio.	Nagoya	Brother Musical
	Maffei, Carlo		Miwa Organ Mfg.
	Mariani, Antonio		Sakai Gakki-Ten
	Ratti, Emilio		Yamashita Organ
	Schone & Bocchese	Naka-Izumi	Union
	Tagliabue, Giulio	Osaka	Ikeuchi Fukin
Mondolfo	Sora, Giovanni		Ishii, Harutaro
Monza	Alletti, Carlo		Maekawa Zenbei
Naples	Cioffi, Vincenzo		Miki, S.
	D'Avenia, Luigi		Okada, Yonezo
	Fummo, A.		Tsuji Piano
	Giuliano, Vittorio	Shiogama	Mizuma, Totoine
Padova	Malvestio, Dom.	Shizuoka	Shimada Gakki Co.
Potenza Picena	Comus, S.p.A.	Takaoka	Yazaki, Teinosuke
Quinzano d'Oglio	Sora, Don Cesare	Tatsuno	Tōyō Gakki Seizo
Rivoli	Aggio, L. & C.	Toda	Tombo Gakki
Rome	Lucilla & Cia.	Tokyo	Croda Organ
Sammarcello	Veneri, Nestori		Dobunkan
Sampierdarena	Pittaluga e Figli		Hiramatsu Gakki
San Giovanni	Benvenuti, Carlo		Jujiya Gakki-Ten
Seveso San Pietro	Radice e Figli		Kaiho, M.
Sissa	Pecchioni, Redento		Matsumoto Gakki
Talamona	Petrelli, Giovanni		Mihara, Chikasuke
Trento	Branz e Cia.		Nakajima, Y.
	Delmarco		Nihon Fukinsha
Turin	Aggio, Fratelli		Ono Gakki-Ten
	Berruti, Luigo		Sanseido
	Boca, G.		Shimazaki, K.
	Collino, Vittoria		Shinseisha
	Fab. Italiana Piano		Tanaka Fukin
	Mola, Cav. G.		Tokyo Fukinsha
	Restagno, Vicenzo		Tombo Gakki
	Rivoreda, G.		Tōyō-Sha Fukin
	Vegezzi-Bossi, C.		Yaesu Piano Co.
Vercelli	Merlo, Simone		Yamano Music
Viareggio	Tofanelli, Emanuele		Zen-On Gakufu
Vicenza	Bonato, Antonio	Yokohama	Nishikawa & Son
	Tealdo, Antonio	City unknown	Kaiho
Vicomoscano	Colla, Ernesto		Miki
City unknown	Catterini		Minami
			RCA Victor
			Saita, Mitsunori
			Toda, Kindō

JAPAN

Asakusa	Nakajima		
Hamamatsu	Kawai		
	Nippon Gakki Co.		
	Tsuchiya, Ichitaro	**KOREA**	
	Yamaha, Torakusu		
Kobe	Sato, T., & Co.	Anyang City	Hyundae Mus. Instr.
Matsuzaka	Murakami, Y.	Inchon	Samick Mus. Instr.

LATVIA

Liepaja	Bokums, Bräli
Marijampol	Macilius, Ant.

LITHUANIA

Kaunas	Woizechowski, Jos.

MADAGASCAR

Tananarive	Racelina, J.

NEPAL

Kathmandu	Nepal Musical Inst.

NETHERLANDS

Amersfoort	Worcester Pedalion Organ
	van den Burg, R.
Amsterdam	Goldschmeding
	van Raay, J.
Barneveld	Barnova
	Tusseling, H.J.
Delft	Hees & Co.
Dortrecht	Beversluis
Enschede	Steinmann & Vierd.
Gennep	van Kesteren, J.
Goes	Dekker, A.S.J.
Gorinchem	Sommer, W.
Gouda	American Organ Co.
Groningen	Nauta, Dirk
	Wit, H. de
Leiden	Bender, C.C.
Roermond	Franssen, Gebr.
Rotterdam	DeHeer, Johannes
	van der Tak
	Reyns, S.G.
Tiel	Beversluis, P.
Tilbourg	Kessels, M.J.H.
Vriezenveen	Borger, Herman
Woerden	Vermeulen
Zwolle	Ganzevoort

NORWAY

Å	Karlsaunet, Kristian
Asen	Tørkildsen
Bergen	Buchner, O.
	Kaland, Einar
	Knudsen, Jacob
	Petterson & Gjelles.
Christiania (Oslo)	Brantzeg, Paul C.
	Buchner, O.
	Cappelen, Jergen
	Hals, Brødrene
Drammen	Eriksen, L.
Fredrikstad	Jakobsen, Reidar
Gjøvik	Berntzen, Bernhard
Haramsøy	Vestre's
Hardanger	Sværen, Johannes P.
Harstad	Tømmeraas, Peder
Kvinnherad	Ness, Johannes L.
Levanger	Isachsen & Renbjør
Lofoten	Jakobsen, J. Th.
Ofoten	Larssen, Ole
Ringebu	Erichsen, P.
Snertingdal	Berntzen, Bernhard
	Norsk Orgel-Harm.
Torsken	Andreassen, Karl
Trondheim	Aagesen, N.O.
Vefsn	Skogsaas, Joh.
Volda	Haugen, Bernt M.
	Ulvestad & Haugen
Voss	Kvarme, Niels
Ytterøya	Gjermstad
City unknown	Eriksen, Amund
	Hals, Bremer Olsen
	Jensen, Claus
	Nilsen, August

PAKISTAN

Gujranwala	City Trading Co.
Nawad Shahad Sind	Permanand

POLAND

Katowice	Sotyga
Klodzko	Tuček, W.
Warsaw	Bruner, Fidelis
	Datyner & Szpecht
	Veit, Antoni

PORTUGAL

City unknown — Vaz de Carvalho

RUMANIA

Bucharest — Nagy, Josef

RUSSIA

Bendzin	Krzemiński, Josef
Kiev	Grossman
	Strobl, August
Moscow	Sitnikow, E.P.
Novgorod	Mitropolsky, D.A.
Odessa	Howeck
Pekrowka	Slesskin, J.W.
Perm	Jumanow, E.A.
St. Petersburg	Baranoff, J.S.
	Glavatch, V.J.
	Iljin, N.J.
	Schpikin, N.N.
	Stadlez, M.
	Woizechowski, J.
Wologda	Mamontow, A.P.

SPAIN

Albox	Fábrega, Alfredo
	Sanchez, Alfredo
Azpeitia	Loyeluxt
Barcelona	Alberdi
	Estadella, Cayetano
	Maristany, Romulo
	Raynard, S.A.
Bilbao	Dourte, Juan
Gracia-Barcelona	Bertrán, Miguel
Jaen	Lopez, Eusebio
Madrid	Casa, Aset
	Meig
	Orean y Cía.
	Rodriguez, Ricardo
Villanueva	Casillas, Jose
Vitoria	Cotrina

SWEDEN

Amal	Broberg & Co.
	Rålin, A.G.
Arvika	Östlind & Almquist
Bjerges	Cedergren, A.
Boden	Alm, N.O.
Eshof	Swenssons, A.
Gefle	Eriksson, E.
	Gefle Orgel Fabrik
Gothenburg	Östlind & Almquist
	Risberg, Johannes
Gullspang	Josefson, Adolf
Hessleholm	Benson, A.
Kage	Eriksson Karlskrona
	Liljerg, G.M.
Karlstad	Nyström, J.P.
Kristinehamn	Kristinehams Orgel.
	Nyström, C.G.
	Wikstrom och Nord
Landvetter	Ljungquist, S.
Lindköping	Herngren, C.A.
	Andersson, K.A.
Ljungby	Elfstrom, C.
Mellerud	Lindmark & Jons.
	Ryrfeldt, C.J.
Örebo	Lagerquist & Co.
	Sundqvist, Leon
Ostersund	Erikssons, J.
Råå	Norling, Aug.
Seffle	Berggreb & Bengz.
Sköfde	Johansson, P.A.
Stockholm	Åkerman & Lund
	Andersson, K.A.
	Lundholm, C.A.V.
	Rålin, A.G.
	Risberg, F.
	Skandinaviska
	Svensson, Alfred
	Wilgren, A.G.
Uddevalla	Jansson, A.
Vara	Lidén & Olsson

SWITZERLAND

Basel	Dethloff
Bern	Gallmann, G.
	Heller, J.H.
Geneva	Baker, Geo.
	Brémond, B.J.
	Du Commun-Girod

Geneva	Kimmerling	Cambridge	Bedwell
	Langdorf et Fils	Canterbury	Goulden, H.J.
	Nicole Frères	Cheltenham	Evans, Wardle
	Tschanun, B.		Pear, Thomas
	Tschanun Frères	Chesham	Patriot Excelsior
Hottingen	Wied, H.	Chesterfield	Lea & Son
Männedorf	Kuhn, Theodor		Slack, Edward
Oberhofen	Keller, Heinrich	Chipping Norton	Cotswald
	Otzinger, H.	Cirencester	Powell, H.
St. Croix	Bendon, Geo.	Crewe	Pioneer Organ Co.
Schaffhausen	Neef, G.	Derby	Blount, H.A.
Wilchingen	Kurz, Karl Friedrich		Grimes, Arthur
City unknown	Hug, Gebrüder	Durham	Lawson & Co.
		Eckington	Smith, Herbert H.
		Frome	Prosser, Henry J.
		Gloucester	Liddiatt, Thomas

UNITED KINGDOM

		Grimsby	London & Prov.
		Halifax	Pohlman & Son
ENGLAND		Huddersfield	Scholefield, J.F.
Barnsbury	Williams, G.	Kirton Lindsay	Clarke & Sons
Bath	Milsom & Son	Launceston	Hicks, H.
Battersea	Jones, F.	Leeds	Beeston Organ Wks.
Bedford	Hands, C.W., & Co.		Benton, Samuel
Bexleyheath	Whomes, E.		Dawes, William
Birmingham	Adams, Wm.		Mann, F.
	Daniels, Edward		Proctor, William
	Holt, John		Ramsden, Archibald
	Jacot, Michel		Reyner, Joseph
	Knight, John		Sawyer, J.W.
	Pell, John, & Co.		Smith & Whincup
	Pickens, Jas.		Waddington
	Riley, Joseph		Whitelock, Wm.
	Sames, Jacob	Lewes	Milham, Joseph
	Sames, William	Liscard	Clarry, W.W.
	Scotcher, C.	Liverpool	Davies, Wm. H.
Blackburn	Draper, Joseph M.		Hopley, Wm.
Boston	Enderby, Edw.		Lea, Wm.
Bradford	Walker, Samuel		Riley, Joseph
Brighton	Cramer, J.B.		Riley, W. Joseph
	Farrant, Henry		Rushworth & Dreap.
	Scott, J.	London	Ajello, Giuliano
	Whitefield, Frank		Allison, Arthur
Bristol	Baldwin, W.T.		Apollo Co., Ltd.
	Briffett, G.B.		Auto-Organ Co.
	Brunt, W.		Avill & Smart
	Cool, Isaac		Bacon, James
	Jones, John, & Co.		Bailey, Claudius R.
	Marsh, C.H.		Baker, G.F.
	Punter, John W.		Ball, Jacobus
Bromwich	Poulton		Barnes, W.H.
Burnley	Smith, A.		Barnett, Samuel
Bury Saint Edmunds	Gildersleeve, J		Bates, Theodore C.
Camborne	Skewes, H.		Bauer, Gilbert L.
			Baynton, J.

295

London

Beasant, Thomas
Bedford, Dan.
Bedford, F.
Bedford, Joseph
Bell & Co.
Bennetts & Bennetts
Blaker, A.
Bliss American
Bloe, C.
Bock, A.
Boosey & Ching
Bork, H.
Boyd Ltd.
Brastead, H. & R.
Bridges, John
Brooks, F.
Butcher, J.W.
Cadby, Charles
Camp, Geo.
Carloss, H.
Carroll, James Jos.
Cassini, H.T.
Chappell & Co.
Charlick, R.
Chartier, C.
Chiappa & Fersani
Claude, Ch.
Cobden Pianoforte
Cocks, Robert
Colclough & Scott
Collard & Moutrie
Collins Organ
Collinson, William
Cook, Richard
Cooper, James
Cottino, Joseph
Cox, Alfred J.
Crabb, Wm. R.
Cramer, J.B.
Craven & Co.
Crawford, F.
Croger, Richard
Croger, Thomas
Cullum, Charles
Curtis, Charles
Dale, Daniel
Dale, Samuel
D'Almaine, T.
Dawkins & Co.
Day & Myers
Derbayne & Co.
Dicks & Co.
Dodson, Wm.
Duffield, Wm .H.

London

Dunn & Nicholls
Eason, Alexander
Ebblewhite, J.H.
Fenton, Chas. E.
Fidler, J.
Foucher, G.
Godby, Williams
Graham, Walter
Graham, Wm.
Gratian, H.
Graves, Henry
Green, D.C.
Green, John
Green & Savage
Griffen, E.C.
Grover & Grover
Grover & Wood
Gunther & Horwood
Hargrave, J.W.
Harland, A.J.
Hattersley, Wm
Hepworth Organ
Hermann
Hill, William
Hillier, James
Holderness
Humphreys, A. & E.
Humphreys, C.
Humphreys, James
Imperial Organ
Isaac, F.W.
James, Henry
Jarret, R.W.
Jeffreys, G.W.
Jenkinson & Co.
Jennings, T.A.
Jones, George
Kelly, Charles
Kemmler, C., & Co.
Kemp, Robert A.
Kesner & Turner
Kirkman & White
Kitly & Co.
Knott, H., & Son
Laurent, Constant
Lawrence, F.
Layland, C., & Co.
Layton, Edward
Linstead, G.
Lister & Sons
London Pianoforte
Luff, George, & Son
Lyon, Louis George
Malcolm, John

London		London	
	Malkin, E.		Slater, Robert
	Marshall Bros.		Smith & Co.
	Marshall, J.H.		Smith, H.H.
	Mattika, E.H.		Smith, Hermann
	Maxfield, Alfred		Smith & Smith
	Mercik, E.L.		Smith, W.F.
	Mesnage, F.		Snell, E. & W.
	Metzler, George		Snell, Harry
	Minasi, C.		Snell, Robert
	Mojon, Manger		Sprague, William
	Montree, J. & R.		Stanley, Egerton
	Moore & Moore		Stather, Robert
	Morandi, Jos.		Stevens, F.C.
	Morton, A.		Stevens, R.F.
	Mott, Isaac		Stonefield
	Moutrie, G.		Storer, Joseph
	Moutrie, J.		Storey, Henry
	Moutrie, J. & R.		Stromenger, J.
	Munch		Tate, John
	Myers & Storer		Temlett, W.
	Nelson, Joseph		Tidder, W.H.
	Nicholls, Edward		Totterdell & Price
	Orchestrelle Co.		Tree, Chas. B.
	Pasquale & Co.		Trost, E.
	Payne, W.T.		Tucker, W.B.
	Peachey, George		Tyler Apparatus Co.
	Penso, Victor		Virot, Charles
	Pichler, Francis		Wallgate, C.A.
	Pilcher, W.		Wallis, J.
	Porter, Graham		Wedlake, Henry T.
	Powell, Francis		West London Piano
	Price, E.		Wheatstone & Co.
	Pridham, W.		Wholesale Piano
	Ramsden, Archibald		Willcocke, Wm. J.
	Rand, John		Williams, G.
	Reed, J.W.		Williams, Herbert
	Reeves & Co.		Willis, J.
	Roberts, Alfred G.		Wolfenden, Robt. S.
	Robertson & Co.	Manchester	Bogg, Wm.
	Robertson, W.J.		Challenger, G.
	Rolfe, William		Hale, C.E.
	Rudd, A.		Hargreaves, Wm.
	Rudolphe, Max		Higham, Thos.
	Rutt & Cowing		Howard, Samuel
	St. Mary's Organ		Locke & Son
	Sames, William		Manchester Piano
	Saunders		Melody Organ Co.
	Schaeffer, C.		Spence & Co.
	Seager, George		Spencer, Arthur J.
	Sebright, T.		Spencer Bros.
	Sewell & Sewell		Varetto, Peter
	Shaefer, C.		Venables & Co.
	Shipman, E.		Wagenhaus, Karl
	Shirley, G.		West London

Measham	Chancel Works	SCOTLAND	
	Proudman, J.D.	Clyde	Nichols, M.O.
Melton Mowbray	Valentine, Lorenzo	Edinburgh	McClure, Dr. A.R.
Newbury	Cary, Alphonse	Glasgow	Ballard, Geo.
Norfolk	Downs, A.R., & Co.		Brown, Colin
Northampton	Lumley, W.H.		Findlay, Alex
Northwich	Knott, J.C.		Gilmour, James
Norwich	Chilvers, W. & J.		Graham Organ Co.
Nottingham	Gregory, John		Hay, Sam.
Offenham	Jacot, Michel		Lindsay, Adam
Oldham	Travis, Wm.		Maver, Rob.
Penrith	Clark, William		Peterkin, J.A.
Pimlico	Hattersley, Wm.		Simpson, Jas.
Plumstead	Soper, W.		
Ramsbottom	Schofield, J.	WALES	
Ripley	Walker, T.W.	Cardiff	Heath, R. & E.
St. Thomas	Geake, H. & R.		Thompson & Shack.
Sheffield	Crokaert, Sebastien	City unknown	British Aeolus
	Hoyland, John		Brown & Sons
Sherborne	Grimes, T., & Co.		Cabinetto
Small Heath	Bentley, J.		
Southampton	Sims, H.C.		
	So. of England		
Stockport	Hardy, Chas.	**UNITED STATES**	
Stoke on Trent	Latham, P.		
Stratford	Luck, Walter V.	ALABAMA	
Taunton	Knight, W.H.	Birmingham	Seals
	Minns, J.E.		
Thornton Heath	Williams, G.	ARKANSAS	
Vauxhall	Hattersley, Wm.	Fort Smith	Bollinger, R.C.
Warrington	Greenwood	Little Rock	Hourk, O.K.
Wellington	Moore, W.H.		
Wexham	Crane & Sons	CALIFORNIA	
Wickham Market	Kent, Wm. Barker	Fresno	Neufeld, Dr. Vernon
Wimborne	Wellstead, H.	Kelseyville	Gunn, James A.
Wiveliscombe	Hancock, Wm.	Oakland	Clark & Co.
Wokingham	Allen, Wm. J.	San Francisco	Balch, H.M.
Worcester	Mead, A.C.		Kohler & Chase
York	Bell, Joseph		Werlein, Philip P.
	Duffill, Charles	Santa Monica	Artcraft Organ Co.
	Pexton, Bart.		
	Preston, Benjamin	CONNECTICUT	
	Richardson, Geo.	Ansonia	Fisk, C.W., & Co.
	Smith, William		Page, Potter & Co.
	Waddington & Sons		Pratt & Colburn
	Whitehead, Henry		Sommers & Colburn
City unknown	Brown & Sons	Birmingham	Birmingham Organ
	English Seraphone		Sterling Organ Co.
	Stercus	Bridgeport	Bridgeport Organ
	Trueman, Peter		Corwall & Patterson
	Ward		Gardner, William P.
	Winfield		Patterson, James T.
		Bristol	Potter, Herald J.

Derby	Pratt, J.J.	Chicago	Cook, David C.
	Sterling Organ Co.		Davie, Jackson &
Granby	Dibble, George H.		Davis, J.D.
	Jewett & Hillyer		Duff & Tate
	Jewett, Peter		Earhuff, John G.
Hartford	Harris, John		Faber, Homo
Manchester	Landfear, Mervin T.		Fowler
Meriden	Aeolian Co., The		Gulbransen Co.
	Vocalion Organ Co.		Hamilton Organ Co.
	Wilcox & White		Helmkamp, Anthony
New Haven	Cook, Geo., & Co.		Hillstrom & Breds'll
	Frisbie & Treat		Howland & Boman
	Gardner, W.P.		Kenwood
	Goodman & Bald'n		Kimball, W.W.
	Goodman & Frisbie		Lakeside Organ Co.
	Goodman, Horatio		Larson & Bowman
	New Haven Melod.		Lyon & Healy
	Shoninger, B.		Mathias Organ Co.
	Temple		Montgomery Ward
	Treat & Linsley		Moore Organ Co.
	Whitaker & Frisbie		Newman Brothers
New London	Smith, Nathan D.		Noble, Don, & Co.
	White, Henry Kirk		Oxford Mfg. Co.
Norwich	Vogel & Hughes		Payne, Geo., & Co.
	Walker		Preston, J.
Preston	Bull, Harry M.		Randall, R.H.
Westville	Whipple & Bowe		Reed & Son
Wolcotville	Dayton, Arvid		Reynolds Organ Co.
	Dayton, Jonah		Rodeheaver Co.
Woodbridge	Fisk & Randall		Schulz, Mathias W.
	Shoninger, B.		Sears, Roebuck
			Singer Organ Co.
GEORGIA			Smyth, John M.
Savannah	Ludden & Bates		Springfield Organ
			Story & Camp
ILLINOIS			Story & Clark
Bloomington	Andrus Brothers		Sweetland, E
Blue Island	Kiessling, N.		Thompson Organ
Chicago	Alexander Organ		Tryber & Sweetland
	Andrews, A.H.		Victor Piano
	Bauer, Julius		Weaver, O.D
	Bent, Geo. P.		White, A.L.
	Bentley, H.D.		Wick Organ Co.
	Bilhorn Brothers		Williams Organ
	Brainard's Sons		Williams, R.
	Bredshall Organ Co.		Wolfinger Organ
	Burdett Organ Co.		Woodbridge Bros.
	Cable Co., The	Danville	Miller and Son
	Camp & Co.	Elgin	Seybold Reed-Pipe
	Chicago Cabinet	Elmhurst	Rosche, Geo. F.
	Chicago Cottage	Freeport	Bentley, H.D.
	Chicago Music Co.		Burdett Organ Co.
	Clark & Rich		Cable, Hobart M.
	Columbian Organ		Swan, S.N.

299

Grand Crossing   Columbian Organ
Humboldt Park   Wick, O.E., & Son
Lockport   Evans, Wm., & Co.
Mendota   Carpenter Organ Co.
    Carpenter, Scott
    Co-operative Organ
    Mendota Cottage
    Mendota N'western
    Tewksbury, Carp'r
    Tewksbury, G.W.
    Western Cottage
Moline   Colseth, Peter
    Moline Cabinet
    Peterson, J., Co.
    Peterson, Thuli
Mount Vernon   Watson & Brother
Pekin   Hinners & Albertsen
    Hinners Reed Organ
    Schaefer, Fred
Peoria   Seybold Reed-Pipe
Quincy   Clark & Baughm
    Letton, R.E.
    Magnusson, Olof
    Quincy Organ Co.
    Whitney, A.H.
    Whitney & Currier
    Whitney & Holmes
    Whitney, J.W.
    Woodruff, T.D.
Springfield   Armbruster, R.H.

INDIANA
Chesterton   Hillstrom, C.O.
Elkhart   Conn, C.G.
Evansville   Crescent
    Decker Jr., Christian
Fort Wayne   Fort Wayne Organ
    Packard Organ Co.
Huntingburg   Thies, William
Indianapolis   Trayser Melodeons
    Wulschner, Emil
La Fontaine   Butler Music Co.
    Chute & Butler
Lebanon   Stevens, W.W.,
Marion   Chute & Butler
Muncie   Ketterman Organ
Peru   Chute & Butler
Richmond   Trayser, George

IOWA
Centerville   Williams Organ Co.

KANSAS
Leavenworth   Kansas Organ Co.

KENTUCKY
Louisville   Adler Organ Co.
    Atlas Piano Co.
    Beckwith Organ Co.
    Hill, R.S., Co.

MAINE
Augusta   Hovey & Bachelder
Biddeford   Andrews, W.F.
Foxcroft   Dyer & Hughes
    Hughes & Son
Limerick   Folsom, Simeon
Portland   Cheney, J.D.
    Hastings, William P.
    Small & Knight
    Whitney, H.A.
Stevens Plains   Cheney, J.D.
Union   Brown Bros.
    Morse Brothers

MARYLAND
Hagerstown   Möhler, M.P.

MASSACHUSSETTS
Ashby   Whitney, Jonas P.
Boston   American Automatic
    Bates Organ Mfg.
    Bay State Organ Co.
    Boston Organ Co.
    Bruce & Chard
    Chard, David
    Chard, Granville
    Clark, T.C.
    Ditson, Oliver, &
    Dyer & Hughes
    Gately Mfg. Co.
    Gerrish, Wm. H.
    Gilbert, T., & Co.
    Goodrich, Ebenezer
    Hildred Bros.
    Hunt, C.B.
    Hunt & Krause
    Hunting, W.S.
    James & Franklin
    Lucas, M., & Co.
    Mason & Hamlin
    Massachusetts
    Merrill Piano Mfg.
    New England Organ
    Nichols, M.O.
    Parks, James S.
    Peaseley, Aaron
    Ruck, Joseph

Boston	Schleicher	West Killingly	Kenyon, R.B.
	Smith American	West Townsend	Bruce & Haselton
	Smith, S.D. & H.W.		Haselton, D., & Co.
	Treat & Richardson	Worcester	Brown & Simpson
	Van Oeckelen, C.J.		Bushnell, O.P.
	Warren, T.D.		Carhart & Needham
	White, James Paul		Carpenter, E.P.
	Woods, George		Clarabella Organ
Bridgewater	Packard Bros.		Clark, Lewis C.
	Packard, Caleb H.		Farley, Pearson &
	Reynolds, Philip		Hamilton Vocalion
	Whitney, George B.		Hammond, A.H.
Cambridgeport	McTammany John		Jewett, N.B., & Co.
	Tower, Sylvester		Leland, S.R., & Co.
	Woods, George		Loring, Blake & Co.
Campello	Marston, A.B.		McTammany, John
	Packard, Isaac T.		Morse, Milton M.
Canton	Bazin, James A.		Munroe Organ-Reed
	Shepard, Luke J.		New York Church
Chelsea	Black, A.D.		Palace Organ Co.
Chicopee Falls	Taylor, V.N. & J.E		Pearson, John G.
Great Barrington	Morgan, William		Pearson & Loring
Fitchburg	Whitney, Jonas P.		Small, C.W.
Haverhill	Bradley, Isaac		Taber Organ Co.
	Nichols, Algeron P.		Taylor & Farley
Leominster	Allen & Jewett		Tournaphone Music
	Jewett & Carpenter		Wood, Lucius A.
	Jewett & Co.		Worcester Organ (I)
New Bedford	Globe Organ Co.		Worcester Org'n (II)
	Union Organ Mfg.		
Newburyport	Alley, Joseph	MICHIGAN	
	Bradley, Isaac	Adrian	Cordley, J.
North Adams	Steinart		Pruden & Cordley
	Stewart, C.A.		Smith, John R.
Northampton	Wright, William K.		Allmendinger
North Bridgeport	Ruck, Joseph	Ann Arbor	Ann Arbor Organ
North Bridgewater	Marston, A.B.		Arbor City
	Packard & Foss		Gaerttner, G.F.
Pittsfield	Cox & Pierce		Henderson Organs
	Pierce, William	Battle Creek	Compensating Pipe
	Tolliver, O.		Jefts, Greble & Co.
	Woods, George	Corunna	Sloan, J.E., & Son
Rockport	Manning Organ Co.	Detroit	Blakeman & Phillip
Roxbury	New England Organ		Blakeman, Wm. P.
	Stewart, Dr. A.		Chandler, G.S.
Salem	Manning & Nichols		Clough & Warren
	Whitney, Jonas P.		Couse, A.
Salisbury	Woodman, A.G.		Detroit Melodeon
Springfield	Alden, A.O.		Detroit Organ Co.
Taunton	Sweet, A.S.		Farrand & Votey
Townsend	Green, Oliver M.		Farrand Organ Co.
	Smith & Green		Grinnel Brothers
	Smith, Henry		Jennings Jr., R.
Westfield	Johnson, William A.		Ling & Borgman

Detroit	Ling & Chandler	NEW HAMPSHIRE	
	Ling, Conrad	Bristol	Eaton, C.W., &
	Simmons, A.A.	Boynton	Ingalls & Eaton
	Simmons & Blake.	Concord	Austin, Charles
	Simmons, Clough &		Austin, Charles E.
	Simmons & Whitn'y		Austin & Dearborn
	Van Dinter, L.		Ballou & Curtis
	Whitman, G.P.		Bartlett, Daniel B.
	Whitney & Co.		Bartlett, Josiah
	Whitney, Clark J.		Curtis, George H.
	Whitney Organ Co.		Dearborn, Andrew
	Zimmerman, Wm.		Dearborn & Bartlett
Grand Haven	Story & Clark		Dearborn, David M.
Grand Rapids	Empire Organ Co.		Dearborn, Severance
	Gardner, C.A.		Ingalls & Crocket
	Piggott, Burch		Liscom, Dearborn
	Piggott, George		Liscom, Levi
	Piggott, Sees		Mitchell, C.C.
Jackson	Kline, T.S.		Morrison & Courser
Kalamazoo	Cady & Phillips		Morse, Milton M.
	Blakeman & Gibbs		Parker & Secomb
	Blakeman & Phil.		Parker & Tracy
	Empire Organ Co.		Prescott, Abraham
	Phillips, Delos		Prescott & Brothers
	Simmons & Van D.r		Prescott, Joseph W.
	Star Organ		Rand, Jacob B.
Lansing	Capital City Organ		Secomb, Daniel F.
Lexington	Dickenson-Gould	Fisherville	Granite State Mfg.
	Gould & Sons		Rand, Jacob B.
Monroe	Knight, C.S.	Hill	Williams & Eaton
Northville	Wood, Granville	Keene	Foster & Felt
Ovid	Jenks, Nelson W.		Foster, J. & E.
Romeo	Nutting, Rufus	Meredith	Ladd, S.A.
South Haven	Everett Piano Co.		Robinson & Sons
		Nashua	Sawyer, T. & E.
MINNESOTA			Tobin & Co.
Minneapolis	Nichols, G.H.	Pittsfield	Woods, George C.
North St. Paul	Earhuff, J.G., & Co.	Winchester	Foster, Joseph
St. Paul	Beckwith		Foster & Thayer
	St. Paul Organ Co.		Jones, Samuel H.
	Wick, P.S., Co.		
		NEW JERSEY	
MISSOURI		Bloomfield	Bloomfield Organ
Desoto	Williams Brothers		Peloubet Columbian
Hamilton	Jordon, W.C.		Peloubet, L.C.
Kansas City	Harwood		Peloubet & Pelton
St. Louis	Darling, Joseph L.		Peloubet Standard
	Musical Products	Burlington	Chein & Co.
	Temple	Camden	Doughton & Sayre
			Monkhouse, S.I.
NEBRASKA		Frenchtown	Hummer, H.A.
Omaha	Collins	Jersey City	Otto, F.G., & Sons
	Schmoller & Muell.	Newark	Magnus Harmonica
		Phillipsburg	Shimer & Hulshizer

Pittstown	Stires, Wm.	New York	Bodge, Henry
Trenton	Hattersley Bros.		Brainard's Sons Co.
	Winkler, G.		Carhart & Needham
Washington	Alleger, B'by & P.		Columbia Organ Co.
	Alleger, Bowlby		Dorf, Ole
	Alleger & Sons		Ducker, M.
	Beatty Organ Co.		Elder, William
	Beatty & Plotts		Emenee Industries
	Beethoven Organ		Gally, Merritt
	Bowlby, Charles P.		Garvie & Wood
	Cornish & Co.		Ginocchio, A.
	Cornish, Winter		Groteau
	Dawes & Wyckoff		Grovesteen & Tr'ow
	Excelsior Organ Co.		Jardine, George
	Florey Bros.		Knauer, Christopher
	Gem Organ Co.		Marchal & Smith
	Hornbaker, Robert		Mechanical Org'ette
	Kennedy & Morse		Molinari, G., & Son
	Plotts Organs		Needham Piano
	Smith, John A.		Nunns & Clark
	Spangenberg, Daniel		Pain, Robert W.
	Star Parlor Organ		Pelton, Jeremiah M.
	Van Doren & Carter		Percival, J.
	Vrom & Kennedy		Schaffner, Jacob
	Warren Organ Co.		Sheib, W.B.
	White, Henry Kirk		Stevens, C.E.
Westminster	Bethlehem Organ		Truslow, Grovesteen
			Van Dyke, J.M.
NEW YORK			Van Minden, R.
Albany	Brooks, C.		Vocalion Organ Co.
Attica	Dodge & Lord		Waters, Horace
Auburn	Percival, J.		Wing & Son
Brooklyn	Brandrup, Claus		Worcester, A.
	Midmer, Reuben		World Mfg. Co.
Buffalo	Hintermeister United		Zavier, X.
	Kent Organ Co.		Zwahlen, Louis
	Prince & Bacon	North Tonawanda	Wurlitzer, Rudolph
	Prince & Co.	Rochester	Cook & Martin
Cherry Valley	Eldredge, O.H.		Mackie & Co.
	Fea, Alex, & Sons		Upton & Miller
	Swan, Amos L.	Sauquoit	Barnard & Prior
Churchville	Stone, P.	Syracuse	Allen, Thomas R.
Clayton	Brush, Alexander		Cabinet Organ Co.
Cortland	Arion		Cabinet Pipe Organ
Goshen	Bishop & Healey		Carpenter, U.S.
Greenpoint	Mechanical Org'ette		Chase, Austin C.
Ithaca	Autophone Co., The		Chase & Babcock
	Gem Roller Organ		Goodman, H.N.
	Ithaca Organ Co.		Karloff, J.C.
	Straub, Alois		Neal & Pratt
	Swiss		Nichols, M.O.
New York	Aeolian Co.		Phelps & Chase
	American Organ		Phelps & Goodman
	Berry & Thompson		Phelps, Henry R.

Syracuse	Spang, Xavier	Orville	Schantz Organ Co.
Utica	Andrews, Alvinza	Painesville	Bishop, E.M.
Waterloo	Genung, Seth J.	Pomeroy	Barckhoff, Carl
	Love, Malcolm	Ripley	Trayser, G.W.
	Roth, Holleran	Salem	Barckhoff, Carl
	Stilwell & Genung	Zanesville	Clay City Organ Co.
	Vough Piano Co.		
	Waterloo Organ Co.	PENNSYLVANIA	
Waterville	Andrews, Alvinza	Allentown	Fisher, H.M.
West Troy	Meneely & Co.		Scheffel & Stolpe
West Winfield	Dexter, F.N.	Aspinwall	Pittsburgh Organ
		Beaver Falls	Swoger, T.
NORTH CAROLINA		Easton	Bowlby's Sons
High Point	Gatewood Organ		Lawrence Organ
	High Point Organ		Lehr, H., & Co.
	Piedmont Mfg. Co.	Erie	Burdett Organ Co.
	Shipman Organ Co.		Smith, John A.
			Wiesbauer, A.
OHIO			Willing, William
Akron	Blodget & Horton	Greencastle	Möller, M.P.
	Horton & Rose	Harrisburg	McKillips, Alex
	Melo-pean Co.		Shoemaker, W.H.
	Rose, Ira	Hazleton	Kellmer, Peter
	Straub, Alois	Lancaster	Lancaster Organ
Cadiz	Scott, John M.		McKillips, Alex
Chillicothe	Prante, Joseph		Paull & Hamilton
Cincinnati	Baldwin, D.H.	Latrobe	Mendelssohn, Carl
	Champion Piano	Lebanon	Long, John H.
	Church, John		Miller Organ Co.
	Foley & Williams		Shepard, George S.
	Hemlock, F.M.	Meadville	Whitney & Holt
	Johnston, D.S., &	Mendelssohn	Barkhoff, Carl
	Murch & White	Mercer	Nelson Mfg. Co.
Cleveland	Bishop, Child & Co.	Mount Etna	Fieman, F.S.
	Child & Co.	North East	New Era Organ Co.
	Clark & Bishop		Reed, Joseph H.
	Cleveland Melodeon		Smith, John A.
	Cleveland Organ	Philadelphia	Bellack, Jas., &
	Dreher, B.		Belmont
	Jewett & Goodman		Harback Organina
	Kinnard, Dreher &		Hughes, A.P.
	Philpot-Camp Co.		Hughes & Hale
	Raymond, F.L.		MacNutt, A.
	Whitney & Raym'd		Morris, H. & M.
	Whitney & Slayton		White, Henry Kirk
Clyde	Clyde Mfg. Co.	Pittsburgh	Barckhoff, Carl
Coshocton	Boston Piano		Pittsburgh Organ
Dayton	Lorenz Supply Co.	Quakertown	Durner, Charles
Geneva	Ferris & Rand	Reading	Fisher, H.M.
Hudson	Nutting, Rufus		Kantner, Dr. Frank
Kidron	Schantz, Abraham J.		Reading Organ Co.
Marietta	Stevens & Klock	Scranton	Perry Organ Co.
Massillon	Edna Organ Co.	Souderton	Cope, M.L.
Norwalk	Chase, A.B.	Telford	Leidy, E.C.

Wilkes-Barre	Perry, J.R.
York	Julius & March
	Livingston
	Smith, J.C., Organ
	Weaver Organ Co.

RHODE ISLAND

Providence	Baker, Henry
	Baker & Randall

SOUTH DAKOTA

Lead	Wagoner & French

TENNESSEE

Athens	Southern Organ Co.
Chattanooga	Sterchi Bros.
Memphis	Hourk, O.K.
Nashville	French, Jesse
	Houck

TEXAS

Ft. Worth	Collins & Armstr'g
Galveston	Goggin, Thomas
Houston	England Organ
Slaton	Behlen, Stinson R.

VIRGINIA

Basic	Barkhoff, Carl
Churchville	Lutz, J.A.
Richmond	Spotless Co.
Staunton	Putnam, W.W.

VERMONT

Barre	Nichols Williams
Brattleboro	Brattleboro Melod.
	Brattleboro Organ
	Burditt & Carpenter
	Carpenter Co., The
	Carpenter, Edwin B.
	Carpenter, Jones
	Empire Organ Co.
	Estey & Green
	Estey, J., & Co.
	Hines, Isaac, & Co.
	Jones & Burditt
	Jones, Samuel H.
	Jones, Woodbury
	Minshall-Estey Inc.
	Stewart, C.W.
Brookfield	Wells, William
Burlington	Powers & Story
Chester	Sprague, D.L.

East Poultney	Merriam, E.N.
	Ross & West
North Montpelier	Nye, E.D. & G.G.
Poultney	Green, Rufus H.
West Halifax	Dutton & Plumb
West Townsend	Sprague, Derek L.
City unknown	Nichols, G.H.

WISCONSIN

Beloit	Van Matre, W.N.
Milwaukee	Abel & Sherman
	Foerster, Carl
	Loduca Brothers
	Meissner Co.
	Netzow, Charles F.
	Odenbrett, Abler
	Puetz, Peter J.
	Taylor, Charles
	Thiery Milwaukee
Prescott	Nicole, Geo. H.

STATE unknown

City unknown	Alvah
	Burlington
	Case, William &
	Daniell, William
	Everhart Organ
	Farley & Holmes
	Feuhr & Stemmer
	Forbes, E.E.
	Hardin Organs
	Haynes
	Hemstead, H.N.
	Kennedy Brothers
	Keystone Organ Co.
	Linderman
	Louisville
	Mansons, G.S.
	Masons, F.S.
	Matchless Organ
	New Western
	Oliver
	Pitman, William
	Presto
	Radareed
	Reynolds & Th'sn
	Ruck, Y.
	Salem Bros.
	Schram & Meandler
	Schutz, M.
	Semple, J.W.
	Sieber, J.P.
	Sloan & Co.
	Smith & Hamlin

State unknown	Taylor, A. Taylor, A. & G. Taylor, C.R. Taylor, James B. Taylor, P.H. Watson, J.V.	City unknown	Domingolle Drexler, C. Fitz Forward Huntington, W.D. Imperiale Kortenback Little Sonic

URUGUAY

Salto Oriental	Calame, Robert V.		Lotus Luchart Marion Marks Martinelli Meaner Micado Co. Millet

COUNTRY UNKNOWN

City unknown	Abbot & Smith Bardell Benham Berry Brothers Blake, John P. Burlington Cottage Gem Creswell & Ball Demeny		Pathé Piron Pritchard Ramsperger, F. Sonata Stein & Sergeant Virgil Whitney & Greer Woodward, C.F.

CONTRIBUTORS

A great many people have contributed information to this *Atlas*, helping to make it as complete and accurate as possible. When I first began collecting data I didn't make note of individual contributors, but later realized it would be useful as a way of tracing the sources of information. Thus, the list that follows is incomplete; my apologies to those not listed. Although they may not be specifically mentioned here, all contributors are appreciated and encouraged to send in additional information whenever they come across it. The names that follow, then, are some of the valued contributors to this work:

John J. Adams, England; Charles M. Ahlgrim, Stoughton, WI; Rey Akai, Japan; Jean Akers, Sonora, KY; Paul Amundson, Frost, MN; Chester Arthur, Remsen, NY; John Barrett, Mt. Dora, FL; Michael Barone, St. Paul, MN; Capt. Robert S. Bates, Gales Ferry, CT; David Bettinger, Waco, TX; Nicholas Beveridge, New Zealand; David Bonk, Poplar Bluff, MO; Stephen L. Bowman,, Emporia, VA; Dr. James M. Bratton, Denver, CO; Wayne Brown; D.L. Bullock, St. Louis, MO; Dr. E. Lee Chaney, Jr, Jacksonville, AL; Claremont College, Claremont, CA; Don Clark, Moravia, Iowa; Margaret P. Cloe, Stafford, VA; Floyd Cluff, Marion, IN; Norma R. Cole, St Paul, Alberta, Canada; Colorado State Hist. Soc., Trinidad, CO; Mrs. James W. Colvin, Ruston, LA; Lee Conklin Antique Organ Museum, Hanover, MI; Robert Cooper, Oklahoma City, OK; Joe Corkedale, Newburg, NY; Rev. Craig L. Cowing, Milford, ME; Harold E. Davis, Leslie, MI; William J. Dennison, Falls Church, VA; James Donovan, Miami, FL; Dr. Jules J. Duga, Bexley, OH; Ray Eberhard, Endicott, NY; Dr. Robert V. Edwards, Coral Gables, FL; Dr. John K. Estell, Berkey, OH; Bob Estes, Denton, TX; Douglas R. Eyman, Lancaster, PA; Gregory K. Filardo, Milwaukee, WI; C.P. Fisher, Framingham Centre, MA; Pam & Phil Fluke, England; Paul Foeller, Florissant, MO; Robert C. Frey, San Gabriel, CA; Claes O. Friberg, Denmark; Edward J. Gardyan, Melville, NY; Mary Gary, Dallas, TX (granddaughter of R.S. Hill); Robert Gault, Oregon; Russ Giacofei, Rochester, NY; Carl E. Gillespie, West Jacksonville, FL; Maurice B. Goodwin, Moseley, VA; Roger Graf-Engel, Switzerland; Grazier, Scott, Garrison, MT; Sam Gould, Dayton, OH; L.B. Green, Montgomery, AL; Bert W. Grimmius, Outlook, WA; Don & Laura Hager, New Britain, PA; R. Harper, Bluepoint, NY; Marvin Hart, Stillwater, MN; Keith W. Heiss, Nashville, MI; W.V. Henderson, England; Michael Hendron, Washington, DC; Larry J. Higdon, Ardmore, OK; Larry Hilliard, St. Paul, MN; Jos. E. Hopwood, Quantico, MD; Mary Hundery, Zumbrota, MN;

Edward Honeyman, Hedinger, ND; Edward F. Irwin, Florence, OR; David Kershaw, York, England; Sylvan K. Ketterman, Muncie, IN; Coleman E. Kimbrell, Florence, AL; Joyce Kirschner, DeLand, FL; Roger W. Kline, Roseville, MN; Herbert T. Kurz, Athens, TN; C.S. Lamberth, Dallas, TX; Nelson Lee, Norway; Theodore W. Leverett, Concord, NC; Jim Lewis, Pasadena, CA; Wesley Lewis, Los Angeles, CA; The Lightner Museum, St Augustine, FL; Rev. Robert Linnstaedt, Fort Worth, TX; Leonard T. Mann, Wheaton, IL; Archie Marchi, Newburgh, NY; Sherry Marlatte; Obert L. Maves, Racine, WI; Scott McIntyre, Austin, TX; Meredith Historical Society, Meredith, NH; Miles Musical Museum, Eureka Springs, AR; Charles Netzow, Milwaukee (grandson of Charles F. Netzow); George O. Nichols, Australia; Wim Olthoff, Netherlands; Hal O'Rourke, Lanexa, VA; Barbara Owen, Newburyport, MA; Charles Paris, Baltimore, MD; Lee Parks, Cary, NC; Lauren Peckham, Breesport, NY; Keith Petersen, New York, NY; Dr. E.A. Peterson, Lebanon, IN; Horton Presley, Dalton, GA; Albert R. Rice, Fiske Musical Instrument Museum, Claremont, CA; The Ringve Museum, Trondheim, Norway; Darryl Ricketts; Charles A. Robison, Sedalia, MO; Scott Robson, Nova Scotia Museum, Halifax, NS, Canada; Joop Rodenburg, Netherlands; Harlan Rollenhagen, Colorado Springs, CO; C.A. Rosenberger Jr, Ashland, NH; Dr. Roger Rowell, Madison, WI; Eric J. Ruff, Curator, Yarmouth County Museum, Yarmouth, Nova Scotia, Canada; Wallace C. Rust, Greece, NY; Arthur H. Sanders, The Musical Museum, Deansboro, NY; Craig Sarsony, Kemptown, MD; The Schantz Organ Co., Orrville, OH; Leonard W. Schaper, Berkeley Heights, NJ; Scott Schaut, Washington, DC; Gary R. Schmidt, Cambridge, Ont., Canada; Horace W. Sellers, East Woodstock, CT; Keith Senior, England; Alvin Florey Sloan, Washington, NJ (grandson of Alvin F. Florey); B. Jessup Small, Cherokee, OK; SMS-Musikmuseet, Stockholm, Sweden; Sylvia Steeves, Bedford, NH; Dennis M. Stephens, Fredericksburg, VA; Bill Stewart; Stiftelsen Musikkulturens framjande, Stockholm, Sweden; James W. Stocking, Athens, TN; H. Strengers, Netherlands; Liz Sullivan, Washington, DC ; Dept. of Arts, University of Tampere, Finland; James B. Tyler, San Francisco, CA; Jan Van der Leest, Truro, NS, Canada; Alan G. Vincent DDS, Modesto, CA; Douglas C. Warren, Detroit, MI; Warshaw Collection of Business Americana, The Smithsonian Institution, Washington, DC; Margaret West, Half Moon Bay, CA; Mrs W.A. White, Brandon, MS ; Frances & Felix Winsett, Florence, AL; Gerry Roebuck; Masahiro Yamamoto, Japan; Nancy Yao, Gilboa, NY; Robert J. Yates, Glenshaw, PA; Eugene W. Yeager, Lansdown, PA.

BIBLIOGRAPHY

Abbott, Frank D., & C.A. Daniell, eds. *International Music Trade Directory.* Chicago: The Presto Co., 1897-8.
Adrian (MI) City Directory, various years.
Ahrens, Christian, et al. *Das Harmonium in Deutschland.* Frankfurt am Main, Germany: Erwin Bochinsky, 1996.
Ala-Kõnni, Erki. "Perhonjokilaakson Suomalaispitajien Kansanmusiikki u 1800-luvulla," *Suomen Kansanmusiikki.* Finland, 1986.
All Nations Exhibition, Catalog of. London, 1851.
Atwater, Edward E. *History of the City of New Haven* (CT). New York: W.W. Munsell, 1882.
Ayars, Christine M. *Contributions to the Art of Music in America by the Music Industry of Boston 1640-1936.* 1937.
Barnes, William H. *The Contemporary American Organ.* New York: J.W. Fischer, 1956.
Barry, Harold A., et al. *Before Our Time.* Brattleboro, VT: Stephen Green Press, 1974.
Becker, John E., *A History of the Village of Waterloo* (NY).
Bent, George P. *Four Score and More.* Los Angeles: Geo. P. Bent Publishing Co., 1929.
Bloomfield and Montclair and Their Leading Business Men. Newark, NJ: Mercantile Publishing Co., 1891.
Bouvilliers, Dom Adelard. "The Harmonium, Its History, Its Literature." *The Caecilia* 60 (March 1934).
Bowers, Q. David. *Encyclopedia of Automatic Musical Instruments.* Vestal, NY: The Vestal Press, 1972.
Bradley, Van Allen. *Music for the Millions.* Chicago: Henry Regnery Co., 1957.
Branning, Penelope. "The Industries of Buffalo 1887." *North East Breeze,* 1979.
Bumstead's Directory of Wheaton City and DuPage Co. (IL), 1915-16.
Cabot, Mary R. *Annals of Brattleboro* 2. Brattleboro, VT: Stephen Green Press, 1922.
Cappelens Musikkleksikon, Oslo, Norway, 1979-80.
Caron's Louisville Directory, 1914.
Charuhas, Toni. *The Accordion,* New York: Accordion Music Publishing Co., 1955.
Clark, J.J. *Cleveland City Guide 1872-3.* Cleveland: Clark & Lawler, 1872.

Coleberd, Robert E. Jr. "The Hinners Organ Story." *The Tracker* (September 1960): 11.

Connors, Daniel J. *Deep River*. Stonington, CT: Pequot Press Inc., 1966.

Coward, Elizabeth Ruggles. *Bridgetown Nova Scotia, Its History to 1900*. Kentville, NS: Kentville Publishing Co., 1955.

Crandall, Richard L. "Peerless, America's First Coin Piano Maker." *MBSI Journal* XXXIII, no. 3: 16.

Cummings, C.H. *Leading Business Men of Worcester* (MA). Boston: Mercantile Publishing Co., 1889.

de Wit, Paul, & Oscar Laffert. *Internationales Hand und Addressbuch*. Leipzig: Paul de Wit, 1883.

de Wit, Paul. *Welt Addressbuch der Gesamten Musikinstrumenten Industrie*. Leipzig: Paul de Wit, 1903, 1929/30.

DeYoung, Gordon. *The Reed Organ Society Bulletin*. (Nov. 90): 30.

Diapason (periodical).

Directory of the Music Trade. New York: H.A. Rost, 1885, 1889.

Dolge, Alfred. *Pianos and Their Makers*. Covina, CA: Covina Publishing Co. 1911 reprint 1972 Dover, NY.

Draper, D. Murray. *W. D., The Story of Doherty & Sherlock-Manning*. Clinton, Ontario, 1986.

Dun, Wiman & Co. *The Mercantile Agency Reference Book*. Montreal: 1886-. (Later Dun & Bradstreet.)

Duncan, Dorothy. "The Bell Organ Co." *Canadian Collector* (March/April 1978).

DuPage County (IL) Directory, 1924-25.

Elmhurst, Lombard & Villa Park (IL) Directory, 1928-29.

Erie (NY) City Directory, 1859-62.

Exportación Alemana (periodical), Chamber of Foreign Commerce, German Democratic Republic, 1961.

Fitch, Howard M. "The Magnus Self-Player Organ." *Bulletin of the Musical Box Society International* (Winter 1980).

Fox, David H. *A Guide to North American Organbuilders*. Richmond, VA: The Organ Historical Society, 1991.

Freeport and Vicinity. Freeport, IL: W.H. Wagner & Sons, 1892.

Freund, John C. *The Piano and Organ Purchaser's Guide*. New York: The Music Trades Co., 1897-1925.

Friesen, Michael D. "The Davie, Jackson & Co. and Its Reed Pipe Organ." *The Reed Organ Society Bulletin* (November 1986).

General History of the Music Trades in America. New York: Bill & Bill, 1891.

Gernhardt, Klaus, et al. *Orgel-Instrumente Harmoniums*. Wiesbaden, Germany: Breitkopf & Hartel, 1984.

Goodrich, Henry A. "Church Organs—Some Early Builders in New England." *Choir & Choral Magazine*: 6, no. 5: 5.
Green, John. *Concise Instructions for Performance on the Royal Seraphine and Organ*, London, ca. 1833.
Groves Dictionary of Music, no. 6, American Supplement, 3d ed. [1927-28]. New York: Macmillan, 1938.
Harrison, Arthur P. *Journal of Mechanical Music* (Autumn 1989.)
Heritage of Granby 1786-1965, The. Granby, CT: The Salmon Brook Historical Society, 1967.
Herzog, Hans K. *Europe Piano Atlas*, 7th ed. Frankfurt am Main: Erwin Bochinsky, 1989.
Hill, Everett G. *A Modern History of New Haven*, 1. New York: S.J. Clarke Publishing Co., 1918.
Hinners, John L. "The Henry Ford of the Pipe Organ." *The Tracker* (Spring 1966): 4.
Hinners, John R. "Chronicle of the Hinners Organ Company." *The Tracker* (Dec. 1962): 1.
Hutchinson, Thomas. *American Musical Directory*. New York, 1861. Reprint 1980, DaCapo Press.
Independent Press (periodical) Bloomfield, NJ. (March 1961, 21 June 1962, 28 April 1983).
Industries of Worcester. Worcester, MA: The Davis Press, 1917.
International Exhibition, Record of. London, 1862.
Journal-Gazette, Ft Wayne, IN (21 November 1981).
Kalamazoo (MI) City Directory.
Kallmann, Helmut, et al. *Encyclopedia of Music in Canada*. Toronto: University of Toronto Press, 1951.
Kansanmusiikki (periodical). Finland.
Kasahara, Mitsuo ed. *Shasi* (History of the Yamaha Co.). Japan: Nippon Gakki Seizo (Yamaha), 1 July 1977.
Kingman, Bradford. *History of Brockton* (MA).
Kjeldsberg, Peter Andreas. *Piano i Norge*. Oslo: C. Huttfeldt Forlag, 1985.
Kolnes, Stein Johannes. *Norsk Orgelkultur*. Oslo: Det Norske Samlaget, 1987.
Korea Trade & Business. Seoul, Korea (October 1985).
Ladd, Warren. *The Ladd Family*. New Bedford, MA, 1890.
Landrum, Carl, *Quincy Herald Whig*, 26 October 1969.
Leading Business Men of Portland (ME) and Vicinity. Boston: Mercantile Publishing Co., 1887.
Lewis, Jim ed. *The Cremona*. Organ Historical Society, Southwest Chapter, Pasadena, CA.

Lindwall, Bill, et al. "J.P. Nystrom's Reform-Orgel." *Journal of the Music Box Society of Great Britain*: 8 (Spring 1977): 2.
Loop, A.I. "One Hundred Years of North East." *North East Breeze* (1934).
MacLaren, George E. *Antique Furniture by Nova Scotia Craftsmen*. Toronto: McGraw-Hill Ryerson, 1961, 1975.
McTammany, John. *Technical History of the Player*. Reprint Vestal Press, Vestal, NY.
Mendota Reporter (Mendota, IL).
Menestrel, Le (December 1919).
Michel, N.E. *Michel's Organ Atlas*. Pico Rivera, CA: N.E. Michel, 1969.
Michigan State Gazeteer and Business Directory.
Musical Courier (1880).
Monitor (Bridgetown, Nova Scotia), 11 July 1973.
Musical Instruments at the World's Columbian Exposition. Chicago: The Presto Co., 1895.
Musical Opinion and Musical Trade Review (London).
Morrow, Thomas J. *Hotel del Coronado*. Coronado, CA: Hotel del Coronado, 1984.
Mustel, Alphonse. *L'Orgue-Expressif ou Harmonium*. Paris: Mustel Pere & Fils Editeurs, 1903.
Nashua Historical Committee, The. *The Nashua Experience*. Nashua, NH: Phoenix Publishing, 1978.
Neal, John. *Account of the Great Conflagration in Portland* (ME), 1866.
Nugue, E., et al. *Practical Manual for the Piano and Harmonium Tuner*. Paris: Leon Pinet, 1913.
Oakland Trade Directory (Oakland, CA 1876-78).
Ochse, Orpha. *The History of the Organ in the U.S.* Bloomington: Indiana University Press, 1975.
Organ Grinders' News, British Organ Grinders' Association, Stoke Mandeville, England.
Organ Register (periodical), The Reed Organ Preservation Society of Australia.
Otavan Iso Musikkitietosanakirja, Part 2: Finland, 1977.
Ord-Hume, Arthur W.J.G. *Player-Piano*. New York: A.S. Barnes, 1970.
Ord-Hume, Arthur W.J.G. *Harmonium*. Vestal, NY: The Vestal Press, 1986.
Owen, Barbara. *The Organ in New England*. Raleigh, NC: Sunbury Press, 1979, and correspondence.
Presto Buyers' Guide. Chicago: The Presto Co., 1913.
Peck, Epaphroditus. *A History of Bristol, Connecticut*. Bristol, CT: The Lewis Street Bookshop, 1932.

Pierce, W.R. *Pierce Piano Atlas*, 10th ed. Albuquerque, NM: Larry E. Ashley, 1990.
Pierre, Constant. *Les Facteurs d'Instruments de Musique*. Paris, 1893. Minkoff Reprints Geneva, 1976.
Ramsey County (NH) Historical Society Magazine: (Spring 1972): 20.
Richards, James C. "Reed Organs in the Floyd C. Miles Collection of Musical Instruments." *The Diapason* (October 1972).
Reblitz, Arthur A. and Q. David Bowers. *Treasures of Mechanical Music*. Vestal NY: The Vestal Press, 1981.
Riemann Musik Leksikon, 12th ed. Mainz Schott, 1959-75.
Roehl, Harvey. *Vestal Press House Organ*. Vestal, NY: The Vestal Press.
Sawyer, John H. *History of Cherry Valley* (NY). 1898.
Schmitt, Elizabeth T. "Notes on Early Organbuilders in Ann Arbor." *The Tracker* 36 No. 3 (1992).
Scientific American (7 June 1879).
Sentinel (North St. Paul, MN) 25 September 1891.
Sisler, Carol U. *Enterprising Families—Ithaca, New York*. Ithaca, NY: Enterprise Publishing, 1986.
Skumner, Leslie. *The Organ*. London: MacDonald & Co., 1952.
Sohlmans Leksikon, 2nd revised ed. Stockholm, 1975-79.
Stedman's Directory of the City and Town of Norwich (CT) 1869-77.
Stephenson County (IL), History of, 1970.
Summers, T.J. *History of Marietta* (OH). Marietta, OH: The Leader Publishing Co., 1903.
Swan, Marshall W. *Town on Sandy Bay*. Sugar Hill, NH: Phoenix Pub Co., 1980.
Turcotte, Barbara Dixon. "Concord Musical Instrument Makers." *Historical New Hampshire* (Spring 1967).
Washburn, Charles G. *Manufacturing and Mechanical Industries of Worcester* (MA). Philadelphia: J.W. Lewis & Co., 1889.
Whiting, Robert B. *Estey Reed Organs on Parade*. Vestal, NY: Emprise Publishing Co., 1996.
Wirling, Eliot I. *Pipe Organs of New England*.
Yamaha Hyakunen-shi (Yamaha Centennial History). Japan: The Yamaha Corp., 1987.
Youth's Companion (27 May 1886): 208.

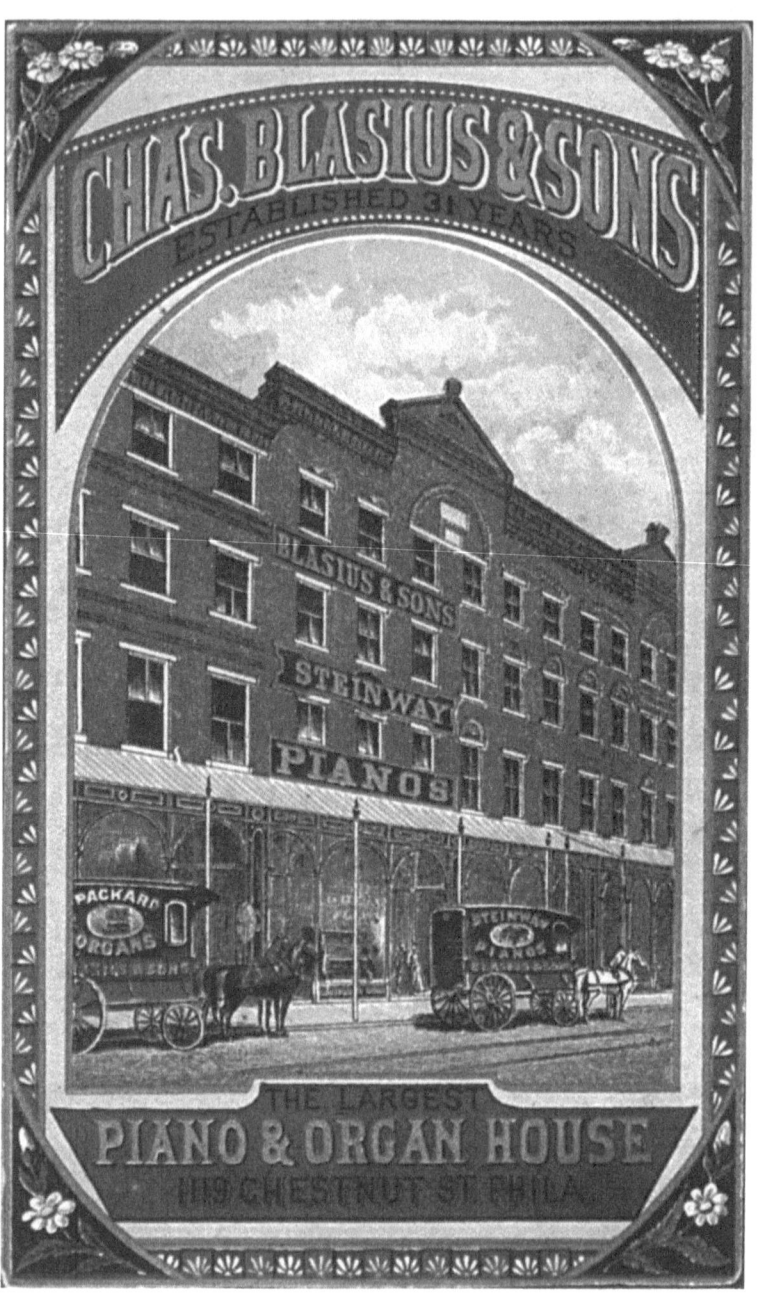

PHOTOGRAPHIC CREDITS

Page

3, 246: Thomas Hutchinson, *The American Musical Directory*, DaCapo Press, 1980.
7: Michigan Historical Collection, Bentley Historical. Library, University of Michigan.
8, 14, 156: Mike Perry.
18: Pam and Phil Fluke.
27, 92: P.A. Kjeldsberg, *Piano i Norge*, Huitfeldt Forlag, Oslo, 1985.
54: A. Scheer.
66, 89, 96, 115, 177, 178: Library of Congress.
70: Charles Robison.
71: Nebraska State Historical Society.
77, 272: George P. Bent, *Four Score & More*, Los Angeles, 1929.
79: Brattleboro P.H.O.T.O.S.
101, 259: Robert F. Gellerman.
104: Matth. Hohner.
109: Bamforth & Co.
111: Leif Renbjør.
126: Sylvan K. Ketterman.
133: *Exportación Alemana*, Berlin, June 1961.
134: Prof. E.L. Cheney, Jr.
161, 243: Yoshihito Namura.
165, 278: Wim Olthof.
173: Gary Stevenson.
194: Nicholas Beveridge.
202: Leonard Mann.
217: Shimada Gakki Co., Ltd.
274: Worcester Organ Co.